DANA CARPENDER

500 KETOGENIC RECIPES

Hundreds of Easy and
Delicious Recipes for
Losing Weight,
Improving Your Health,
and Staying in the
Ketogenic Zone

FAIR WINDS

Inspiring | Educating | Creating | Entertaining

Brimming with creative inspiration, how-to projects, and useful information to enrich your everyday life, Quarto Knows is a favorite destination for those pursuing their interests and passions. Visit our site and dig deeper with our books into your area of interest: Quarto Creates, Quarto Cooks, Quarto Homes, Quarto Lives, Quarto Drives, Quarto Explores, Quarto Gifts, or Quarto Kids.

First Published in 2018 by Fair Winds Press, an imprint of The Quarto Group, 100 Cummings Center, Suite 265-D, Beverly, MA 01915, USA.
T (978) 282-9590 F (978) 283-2742 QuartoKnows.com

Fair Winds Press titles are also available at discount for retail, wholesale, promotional, and bulk purchase. For details, contact the Special Sales Manager by email at specialsales@quarto.com or by mail at The Quarto Group, Attn: Special Sales Manager, 401 Second Avenue North, Suite 310, Minneapolis, MN 55401, USA.

22 21 20 19 18   1 2 3 4 5

ISBN: 978-1-59233-816-0

Library of Congress Cataloging-in-Publication Data is available

Design: Laura H. Couallier, Laura Herrmann Design
Cover Design: Laura H. Couallier, Laura Herrmann Design, with images from Shutterstock, Inc.
Page Layout: Laura H. Couallier, Laura Herrmann Design

The information in this book is for educational purposes only. It is not intended to replace the advice of a physician or medical practitioner. Please see your health-care provider before beginning any new health program.

Printed in China

SUSTAINABLE FORESTRY INITIATIVE
Certified Chain of Custody
Promoting Sustainable Forestry
www.sfiprogram.org
SFI-01268

SFI label applies to the text stock

To the memory of the late, great Robert C. Atkins, M.D. I only wish he had lived to see his work utterly vindicated—but by all reports, he never doubted the truth he could see in his patients.

And to Eric Westman, M.D., and Jacqueline Eberstein, R.N., the true carriers of his torch. I am proud to call them friends and colleagues.

CONTENTS

CHAPTER 1

Welcome to Keto—We've Been Here Longer Than You Thought

Well, well, well, look at where we are. How things can change! In 2010, a blog reader asked me why "the powers that be" couldn't just admit they'd been wrong, that a low-fat, high-carb diet didn't work—not for weight loss and not for health—while a low-carb, high-fat diet did. I quoted an old saw: "First they ignore you, then they ridicule you, then they fight you, then you win." Back then I added, "I'm pleased to report that we're way past the 'ignore' phase, moving from the 'ridicule' into the 'fight' stage. I hope to see 'win' in my lifetime."

I am pleased to announce that "win" appears to be here. Nobody is laughing at carbohydrate restriction anymore. More and more people are accepting that fat, far from being the enemy, is a very powerful ally indeed. Somewhere, Dr. Atkins is laughing. Let's be clear: Ketogenic diets are nothing new. When *Dr. Atkins' Diet Revolution* was first published in 1972, he had the nation peeing on ketone test strips and crowing about "turning purple!" I know: I was one of them, although at all of thirteen years old I was not ready for the concept of a permanent lifestyle change.

Indeed, many of us who have been eating a low-carbohydrate diet for a long time—I started in 1995—and have been in ketosis for years. There has, however, been a change in focus. People have long referred to *Dr. Atkins' Diet Revolution* and *New Diet Revolution* and other low-carbohydrate diets as "high-protein diets." But Dr. Atkins never recommended a high-protein diet. He did advocate eating all the animal products one wished, but from the beginning, he recommended fatty meats, seafood dipped in butter, rich sauces, and heavy cream in your coffee. He openly advocated a *ketogenic* diet.

Then came the dreadful years when Americans were urged to slash fat from their diets, replacing it with "healthy whole grains." We scraped the barest coating of butter or cream cheese on our bagels and felt virtuous using low-fat mayonnaise on our pasta salad. Everyone "knew" that it was fat that made you fat and sick. Which explains why, as more and more of us rediscovered low-carbohydrate diets after the abject failure of low-fat, high-carb diets, the "high-protein diet" moniker stuck: it was less scary, less controversial, than saying, "I'm eating a high-fat diet."

Huzzah! The day has come when we can openly proclaim, "I'm eating a low-carbohydrate, moderate-protein, high-fat diet. Why aren't you?" Or we can use the shorthand and just say, "I'm eating keto."

WHAT'S A KETONE?

Ketones, more properly referred to as *ketone bodies*, are a breakdown product of free fatty acids. When your body burns fat—instead of glucose—for fuel, ketones are created. These, in turn, serve as fuel for tissues that cannot use fat for fuel, most notably the brain.

When the Atkins Diet first hit in 1972, the presence of ketones was largely seen as proof that your body was, indeed, using fat as its primary fuel source. Recent research indicates that ketones are considerably more important than that.

NOT JUST WEIGHT LOSS

In a 2013 article appearing in the *European Journal of Clinical Nutrition,* researchers concluded (emphasis mine), "Recent work over the last decade or so has provided evidence of the therapeutic potential of ketogenic diets in many pathological conditions, such as diabetes, polycystic ovary syndrome, acne, neurological diseases, cancer and the amelioration of respiratory and cardio-vascular disease risk factors.

"The possibility that modifying food intake can be useful for reducing or eliminating pharmaceutical methods of treatment, which are often lifelong with significant side effects, calls for serious investigation."

Gee, you think?

It's generally accepted that low-carb, high-fat diets work for weight loss. Still, many have worried that weight loss came at the cost of general health, that fatty meat, butter, mayonnaise, and heavy cream were going to give us heart attacks or destroy our kidneys. From the beginning, I found it hard to believe that a diet that made me feel so much better—and resulted in great blood work—was actually a stealthy killer. So, it has been with growing delight and great satisfaction that I have watched the research into the benefits of a ketogenic diet burgeon. Long used for seizure control, ketogenic diets are showing promise for treating myriad health problems.

- A study published in 2011 in the scientific journal *PLOS ONE* looked at the effects of a ketogenic diet on diabetic nephropathy—the most common cause of kidney failure—in diabetic mice. The result? Two months on a ketogenic diet actually reversed kidney damage. Such reversal has hitherto been virtually unheard of.

- In August 2013, the *Clinical Journal of the American Society of Nephrology* published the results of a small human trial, again showing an improvement in kidney function in type 2 diabetics with nephropathy after twelve weeks on a ketogenic diet. I find this not only wonderful, but happily ironic, considering how many times I've been told that my diet will damage my kidneys.

- In 2012, in the journal *Nutrition*, Richard D. Feinman, M.D., and Eugene Fine, M.D., published groundbreaking work regarding the effectiveness of such diets in inhibiting cancer growth by reducing insulin signaling.

- In 2016, a study was published in *Frontiers in Molecular Neuroscience* regarding the effects of a ketogenic diet on glioblastoma, a particularly devastating kind of brain tumor. It states that a ketogenic diet does reduce tumor growth. This has been attributed to the fact that cancer cells are glucose dependent. The authors added, however, that "additional studies in vitro have indicated that increasing ketones such as ß-hydroxybutyrate (ßHB) in the absence of glucose reduction can also inhibit cell growth and potentiate the effects of chemotherapy and radiation." In other words, it's not simply that a ketogenic diet drastically reduces the supply of the glucose cancer needs to grow; ketones themselves appear to inhibit cancer growth even when glucose is provided.

- In 2006, the journal *Behavioral Pharmacology* published an article about the benefits of a ketogenic diet for a broad range of neurological illnesses. Ketogenic diets have long been used to treat epilepsy, but are now showing promise for treating Parkinson's disease and Alzheimer's as well. As I write this, I have on my desk the newly published book *The Alzheimer's Antidote*, by Amy Berger, MS, CNS, NTP, about the promise of ketogenic diets to prevent or treat dementia. Having watched my mother succumb to dementia, this is, for me, the most thrilling possibility.

- The same article in *Behavioral Pharmacology* also states that ketogenic diets are being explored for limiting inflammation in general. Because inflammation now appears to be the root of a great deal of illnesses, from heart disease to cancer, this is no small thing.

- In 2005, *Nutrition & Metabolism* published an article regarding a pilot study of a ketogenic diet for treatment of polycystic ovary syndrome (PCOS). The study found that the diet not only caused "significant" weight loss, but also improved hormone balance and lowered fasting insulin. I have been fortunate enough to speak with two top-flight reproductive endocrinologists, Michael Fox, M.D., of Jacksonville, Florida, and Gil Wilshire, M.D., of Columbia, Missouri. Both consider a very low carbohydrate diet an essential intervention for PCOS and one of the most powerful tools in their fertility practices.

- I am fortunate enough to number among my friends and business associates Eric Westman, M.D., the country's leading researcher into the use of ketogenic diets in the treatment of diabetes. More than 90 percent of Dr. Westman's type 2 diabetics wind up with normal—not controlled, but normal—blood sugar with no medication at all.

SO WHAT MAKES A DIET KETOGENIC?

It's a matter of macronutrient balance, sometimes referred to as "macros." What are *macronutrients*?

Well, *micronutrients* are nutrients you need in teeny doses, anywhere from a few micrograms to several milligrams—vitamins and minerals. Macronutrients, on the other hand, are the nutrients you consume in quantities measured in ounces or pounds (or kilos, if you're in the civilized world). There are three broad classifications of macronutrients: protein, fat, and carbohydrate. It is the balance of these three that will determine whether you are in ketosis or not. From the journal *Behavioral Pharmacology*: "The classic ketogenic diet is a high-fat diet developed in the 1920s to mimic the biochemical changes associated with periods of limited food availability. The diet is composed of 80 to 90 percent fat, with carbohydrate and protein constituting the remainder of the intake." This describes the ketogenic diet used to treat epilepsy and other neurological disorders, where the ketones are serving as medication.

If you're not eating a keto diet for medical purposes, you probably don't have to be that careful. How careful do you have to be? I'm afraid the answer is "It depends." Many people will go into ketosis if they drop below 50 grams of carbohydrate per day, while others have to go as low as 10 grams. Some people do well at 70 percent of their calories from fat, while others really do need to go as high as 90 percent. Some people can count "net" or "usable" carbs—that is, total carbs minus fiber—while others have to count total carbs—which is just another way of saying they have to be stricter about their carbohydrate intake.

Also, some of us have to pay attention to our protein intake. I'm one of them—my fasting blood sugar improved when I dropped from about 120 grams of protein per day down to 60 to 80 grams per day, increasing my fat intake to make up the difference. The liver can turn excess protein into sugar, a process called *gluconeogenesis*. Turns out my liver is really good at it. According to the college-level nutrition text on my shelf (*Understanding Nutrition*, 7th edition, by Eleanor Noss Whitney and Sharon Rady Rolfes), a minimum of 10 percent of calories should come from protein or about 50 grams of protein if you're eating 2,000 calories per day. A bit more is fine, but unless you're a bodybuilder, you're unlikely to need hundreds of grams of protein per day. (That's not 50 grams of meat, by the way; 1 ounce [28g] of meat contains about 7 grams of protein, while 1 egg contains about 6 grams of protein.)

WE'RE TALKING PERCENTAGE OF CALORIES, NOT VOLUME OR WEIGHT

It's important to understand that we're talking percentage of total calories, rather than percentage by weight or volume. For example, ¼ pound (115g) of green beans will have 31 calories, with 7 grams of carbohydrate, 2 grams of protein, and only a trace amount of fat. This translates to those beans getting 78 percent of their calories from carbohydrate and only 3 percent from fat. But because fats are very calorically dense, adding only ½ ounce (15g) of butter and ½ ounce (15g) of slivered almonds will create a dish with 216 calories, 75 percent of them from fat. Bring on the Green Beans Almandine!

Please note that in the example above, those green beans actually have 3 grams of fiber, a carbohydrate that some subtract from total carbs. Because my MasterCook software doesn't take this into account, the fat percentages in this book will not be calculated on net or usable carbs, but on total carbs. Why? Because I don't want to do that much math, that's why. However, if you'd like to do it yourself, here's how:

Assume that carbohydrate and protein have 4 calories per gram and fats have 9. This is only loosely true, but for our purposes it is near enough. So, we have 216 calories total, but we want to subtract out the 3 grams of fiber: $3 \times 4 = 12$, so we subtract 12 calories, for a total of 204. Our Green Beans Almandine contains 19 grams of fat and $19 \times 9 = 171$. To figure out what percentage of the adjusted calorie count that constitutes, divide 171 by 204. According to my trusty calculator, that gives us 84 percent of calories from fat.

All of the recipes in this book list the carb, fiber, and fat grams, so if you want to do this, you certainly may. Me, I just figure my fat percentage is a little higher than the software tells me and don't sweat it.

A CAUTION

We're not talking about simply adding fat to your existing diet. If you eat your usual 2,000 to 2,500 calories per day of a "balanced diet" and then add fat on top of it, you're going to gain weight. The increased fat is meant to replace other food, got it? Fat bombs and Bulletproof Coffee™ have grown hugely popular, but they only help if they're replacing carbs and protein you would otherwise be eating.

Also, if you're going keto because you're seriously overweight, quite a lot of the fat you'll be burning should be coming from your body's fat stores, rather than from food.

A BIG HONKING WARNING

A ketogenic diet is powerful medicine; it will bring down blood sugar and insulin levels overnight. If you are on medication for any of the health problems associated with metabolic syndrome and especially if you are on diabetes medication, you *must* be under a doctor's supervision. Your dosages are predicated on your current intake of carbohydrate. Stop eating carbs and they will quickly become overdoses, possibly disastrous overdoses. Getting off medication is a good thing, but it must be controlled and supervised. I recommend you check at www.healclinics.com for more information. (Full disclosure: HEAL Clinics Diabetes and Medical Weight Loss has been started by Dr. Westman. I am involved both as a diet and lifestyle advisor and as an investor.)

Another condition that resolves quickly is hypertension. If you're on blood pressure medication, you must be under medical supervision as you transition to a ketogenic diet. It is likely that your dosages will need to be reduced very quickly and quite possible you will end up not needing antihypertensive drugs at all. But the only way to know is to check! *Do not fly blind.*

HUNGER GONE

Do you know the hardest thing about writing a keto cookbook? I simply am not hungry. As I write this, it is a good seven hours since my last meal. I did have a handful of nuts a couple of hours ago. And I simply am not hungry. The food tastes amazing, but the urge to eat is dramatically suppressed.

If you have been plagued all your life by constant hunger, you are going to be flat-out dazzled. Once you're in ketosis, you may have to remind yourself to eat.

INTERMITTENT FASTING

Intermittent fasting, or IF, is just what it sounds like—the practice of fasting off and on. Many people, me among them, simply try to wait 14 to 16 hours between dinner and when we eat the next day. Others skip eating for a day or two a

week or eat on alternate days. I will not go into the benefits of intermittent fasting here; if you are interested, I recommend you read *The Complete Book of Fasting* by Jason Fung, M.D. I just want to make the point that if you would like to try intermittent fasting, it becomes vastly easier once you're thoroughly keto-adapted, if only because of the appetite-suppressant effect.

WAYS TO INCREASE FAT INTAKE

It's not essential that every dish be over 70 percent fat. You can combine dishes to get the percentages you're looking for. For instance, a piece of roasted chicken gets about 55 percent of its calories from fat. But pair it with a green salad with plenty of olive oil, and the percentage for your meal can easily go up to 75 percent.

Make use of naturally high-fat foods: nuts, bacon, avocados, olives, fatty cheeses, heavy and sour cream, and full-fat coconut milk all add flavor and texture to your meals along with the fat you seek. You'll find them used in abundance in these recipes.

Fat is a very concentrated source of nutrients; 2 tablespoons (28g) of butter or (28ml) oil will have 200 calories or more. They'll quell your hunger, but most of us want to eat more than that. Yet, you don't want to blow past either your carb limit or your protein requirement. How to get a full plate of food? Think water and fiber. Both water and fiber contribute no calories, no carbs, no protein, no nuthin', to your meal, yet they can expand your portions deliciously to satisfying proportions.

Low-carb vegetables are largely water and fiber and make a great fat-delivery system—

salads with plenty of olive oil or mayonnaise, vegetables with butter, celery stuffed with pâté or blue cheese dip. You get the picture: serve your vegetables with fat. Interestingly, this will greatly enhance your body's absorption of fat-soluble vitamins and antioxidants.

Think about it: 2 tablespoons (28g) of mayonnaise has 200 calories, 99 percent of them from fat. But while those 2 tablespoons (28g) of mayo will keep you full and energetic for quite a while, they're barely more than a mouthful. Add a cup (70g) of shredded cabbage, and suddenly you have a big ol' portion of coleslaw—while adding only 15 calories and 4 grams carbohydrate (2 of 'em fiber)—so just 2 grams net carbohydrate.

Likewise, broths are mostly water. (Homemade bone broth is mostly water, gelatin, calcium, and sheer magic.) One-half cup (120ml) coconut milk has 222 calories, 91 percent of them from fat, with just 3 grams of carb. But who drinks ½ cup (120ml) of coconut milk and feels like she's had a meal? Now, combine that coconut milk with 1 cup (235ml) of chicken broth, plus curry powder and a touch of garlic, and you've got a fabulous, warming soup.

Use sauces and dips to your advantage—you'll find plenty of them in this book. Sirloin steak gets 63 percent of its calories from fat. Add a couple of tablespoons (28g) of blue cheese steak butter, and that goes up to 74 percent. Two cups (110g) of lettuce have 20 calories, only 12 percent of them from fat. Add 2 tablespoons (28ml) of vinaigrette dressing, and that jumps to 160 calories, 85 percent of them from fat.

Choose fatty cuts of meat—pork shoulder or spare ribs, chicken and turkey dark meat with the skin on, beef rib eye, chuck, and brisket, 70/30 ground beef instead of the pricey 90/10 stuff, and of course everybody's favorite, bacon. If you're choosing a lower fat protein—fish, chicken breast, or the like—again, use a fatty sauce and add a salad or a vegetable with a fatty dressing on the side or have a high-fat, sugar-free dessert.

Your meals will be very nutrient dense and high in calories. This is okay; if you pay attention to your hunger, you will very quickly learn to eat to satiety, rather than eating just because the food is there. I have long since reached the point where I eat only two meals per day, with a snack if I'm peckish in between. If you're used to the constant, driving hunger of a low-fat diet based on grains, this will seem incredible, even impossible. Don't force it. Just shift your macronutrient balance and pay attention to your hunger.

ON TAKING CONTROL

Celebrity chef Emeril LaGasse likes to say, regarding various seasonings, "You want more? Put in more. You want a little less? Use less. Hey, we're just cooking; it's not rocket science." Words to live by. I love cilantro: it tastes like the very essence of fresh and green to me. But, if you're one of those people to whom cilantro tastes like soap, leave it out, for goodness' sake. I've been known to get up in the morning and eat a jalapeño jack omelet with salsa and extra habanero sauce; I love breathing fire. You don't? Cut back on the hot sauce. You think I'm a big wussy? Add more. As my idol Peg Bracken said, it's all a matter of deciding who's in charge here: you or the food.

REGARDING MICROWAVE OVENS

I use my microwave all the time, not just for reheating leftovers, but also for cooking, especially for steaming vegetables. I know of no simpler or more satisfactory method, and my Tupperware microwave steamer is out of the cabinet more often than in it. Furthermore, I have seen some fairly convincing arguments for microwave steaming of vegetables retaining more nutrients than most other cooking methods. I also often cook bacon in the microwave; I haunted the local Goodwill until I found a circular microwave bacon tray that would go around on my microwave's turntable.

However, I suspect that at least some of you will be appalled that I would even consider using a microwave. There is a faction that considers them, and all food cooked in them, to be horribly dangerous. I'm not going to argue the point here. Just take it as read that anything I cook in my microwave, you are welcome to cook on your stove top.

CHAPTER 2

Some Ingredients to Know

WHICH FATS DO I USE?

When you're deliberately eating a high-fat diet, it is vital that you pay attention to the quality of those fats. Unfortunately, officialdom has misinformed us about "healthy fats" for a good thirty years now. We were told to drastically limit "artery-clogging saturated fats" and substitute unsaturated vegetable oils. This led to the current disastrous imbalance of unsaturated fatty acids in the American diet; the optimal 1:1 ratio of omega-3 and omega-6 fatty acids has been skewed to an average of 15:1. You think sugar intake has increased? According to the *American Journal of Clinical Nutrition*, "The estimated per capita consumption of soybean oil increased by more than 1000-fold from 1909 to 1999." The result is a harvest of all kinds of inflammatory illnesses, including cardiovascular disease, cancer, and autoimmune illnesses.

The demonizing of traditional animal fats was to a great degree driven by the burgeoning vegetable oil industry. Are you old enough to remember ads crowing about how polyunsaturated this or that vegetable oil was? Have you noticed that those ads have passed quietly from our midst? Margarine ads have been radically reduced as well. You know why? Because it turns out that swapping in highly processed vegetable oils for traditional animal fats, such as butter, lard, tallow, and chicken fat, is terrible for you, increasing the risk of everything from heart disease to cancer. Oops. I trust you know, too, that substituting trans-fat-rich hydrogenated vegetable shortening for naturally saturated fats has turned out to be a disaster. In this book, we return to more traditional fats. These are the fats I use most in this book:

Butter

I don't need to tell you that butter tastes wonderful, but perhaps you need to be told that it is healthful as well. We'll start with the fact that butter is a good source of vitamin A—true, preformed vitamin A, rather than the "provitamin A" you get from plant sources. It's also a source of vitamin E, a powerful antioxidant, and vitamin K, essential for calcium absorption, creating strong bones and teeth. This is especially true if the butter is from grass-fed cows. Butter is also a source of selenium and iodine, the main constituents of thyroid hormone.

What about saturated fat? Butter is rich in saturated fats, it's true—about 60 percent of the fatty acids in butter are saturated. Interestingly, quite a lot of that is in the form of *lauric acid.* More than any other fat tested, lauric acid raises HDL cholesterol, which is thought to lower heart disease risk. There is some feeling that lauric acid has other benefits, ranging from antimicrobial and antifungal activity to stimulating the thyroid gland, thus raising metabolism.

Then, there's *conjugated linoleic acid* (CLA), a naturally occurring trans fat that is not only harmless but even beneficial. When CLA was first identified in the 1980s, it was shown to help prevent and even treat cancer; there were gleeful headlines about how Velveeta was a cancer cure. Exaggerated, of course, but the benefits of CLA are real. Further testing of CLA has repeatedly demonstrated an effect on body composition, reducing fat, especially belly fat, and increasing muscle mass.

Grass-fed raw butter is higher in nutrients than the standard grocery store stuff and worth the extra money. I know people who buy the popular Kerrygold grassfed butter a dozen bars at a time. Living, as I do, in the Midwest, there are many local small farms producing butter of excellent quality. Check health food stores and farmers' markets or look online for local small dairies. That said, standard grocery store butter is still a healthful fat.

Ghee

Also called clarified butter, ghee is butter that has had all the milk solids removed, leaving only the fats. This makes ghee less likely to spoil than butter—useful in warm climates like India—and less likely to burn. Because the milk solids have been removed, ghee is well tolerated by many people who are lactose intolerant; I know many people who avoid dairy products except for ghee. Ghee is available in jars in stores that carry a selection of Indian foods and ingredients. Once opened, it should be refrigerated. You can make your own ghee quite easily: Melt butter over very low heat. Let the light-colored solids sink to the bottom, pour off the liquid butterfat, and discard the solids. Like butter, ghee is most nutritious if it comes from grass-fed cows. I have not specifically called for ghee in this book, but feel free to use it in place of regular butter if you are lactose intolerant.

Lard

Yes, I said lard. Until Americans were sold a bill of goods about vegetable oils and hydrogenated shortening, lard was the most-used fat in the

American diet, not only for frying and sautéing, but also as shortening in baked goods. My grandma used it in pie crust. It is lard that Crisco and other hydrogenated shortenings supplanted in American cooking. Lard was also spread on bread, just like butter, and still is in much of the world.

Yet, lard has been so defamed that it has become symbolic of "artery-clogging saturated fat," though, ironically, it has slightly more unsaturated than saturated fat—about 57 percent. Most of that unsaturated fat in lard is in the form of monounsaturates, the same sort of fat that is considered healthful when found in olive oil. Unfortunately, most of the lard in grocery stores cannot be considered a good fat. Not only does it come from animals raised on the cheapest, nastiest feed, but also much of it is hydrogenated, specifically because lard is unsaturated enough to be soft at room temperature.

Seek out a local small farm that produces pasture-raised pork and buy a bucket of unprocessed lard. This is glorious stuff, bland yet rich, wonderful for all kinds of sautéing, basting, and even baking. It's worth the money—at this writing, I pay about $15 for a 4-pound (1.8kg) bucket of lard from locally raised pastured pigs. Because lard is rich in monounsaturates, it will go rancid eventually. Scoop out enough for a week or so, put it in a clean jar, and freeze the rest.

BONUS: Because pigs, like us, create vitamin D in their skin when exposed to sunlight, and that vitamin D is stored in their fat, this means that lard from pasture-raised pigs is one of the few naturally rich food sources of vitamin D. (The vitamin D in milk has been added.)

Bacon Grease

Lard with a salty, smoky, amazing flavor, bacon grease is pure culinary gold. If you shell out the money for good, small-farm bacon from pastured hogs, then throw out the grease, I will personally come to your house and dope-slap you. Around here, we keep the stuff from cheap grocery store bacon, too. I pour it into an old salsa jar, keep it by the stove, and use it for all sorts of things, from frying eggs to roasting vegetables. I'd refrigerate it, but I use it up too fast for it to go bad.

Olive Oil

It's hard to get a handle on olive oil. The common wisdom is that it's the healthiest possible fat, but the paleo faction disputes that, especially if used for cooking, rather than in uncooked applications like salad dressings. I'm of the opinion that olive oil has been around long enough to be considered pretty safe, and the flavor is essential to Mediterranean and Middle Eastern cuisines, of which I am seriously fond. I use it for salad dressing and in cooking where the flavor is essential to the dish.

Coconut Oil

Coconut oil is a favorite of the keto world and with good reason: coconut oil is very healthful stuff. Coconut oil is very saturated, far more so than lard, beef fat, or butter. It turns out that this is a good thing. Saturated fats barely oxidize, you see, eliminating the risk of rancid fats. Even at room temperature, coconut oil will keep as long as a year.

Coconut oil raises your HDL cholesterol levels (the good stuff), increases immunity, improves insulin sensitivity, and stimulates the thyroid gland. Most of the saturated fat in coconut oil is in the form of *medium-chain triglycerides* (MCT), a fat that can be used directly by the muscles for fuel—it's true energy food. MCT is also highly ketogenic. And it is high in lauric acid, with all its benefits. Coconut oil is solid below 76°F (24°C), making it inappropriate for salad dressings. But it makes it a terrific substitute for hydrogenated shortenings (Crisco and the like) in baking. It's great for all sorts of cooking applications, too.

I find two kinds of coconut oil in my local stores: some are labeled "extra-virgin coconut oil," while the rest are simply labeled "coconut oil." Extra-virgin is nutritionally superior, but has a mild but distinct coconut fragrance and flavor. Depending on the recipe and your taste, this may or may not work for you. The stuff labeled "coconut oil" has been refined and is bland. While it is not as nutritionally pristine as the extra-virgin stuff, plain old coconut oil is still a healthful fat. In my area, extra-virgin coconut oil is found in health food stores, while the refined stuff is found in the international aisle—it's a staple of Indian cooking—and our local international/health food grocery store, Sahara Mart. (Unpaid plug and shout-out: I love Sahara Mart.) Costco also now carries it in big buckets. I mean, it is Costco.

Medium-Chain Triglyceride (MCT) Oil

Derived from coconut oil, MCT oil has been popular with athletes for a while because it can be burned directly by the muscles, offering a quick burst of energy without the crash that sugar would bring. It is also used for people who need concentrated nutrition; it can be particularly useful in cancer patients, for instance. Also, because MCTs are highly ketogenic, the oil is a great choice for keto dieters. Because it is concentrated, MCT oil is even more ketogenic than coconut oil. Unlike coconut oil, MCT oil is liquid at room temperature, making it useful for salad dressings and the like. It has become my oil of choice for making mayonnaise.

A word to the wise: I just bought a whole gallon (3.8L)—two half-gallon (1.9L) jugs—of MCT oil for under $50 through Amazon.com. In the meanwhile, my pharmacy has a 1-liter (1 quart) bottle of the stuff behind the counter with a price tag of $91. Shop around.

OTHER FATS TO CONSIDER

I haven't used these in the recipes in this book, but other traditional fats include the following:

Chicken Fat

Also known as *schmaltz*, rendered chicken fat is a staple of Jewish cuisine. Whether you can find it in local stores may depend upon whether you live where there is a substantial Jewish population. Good specialty butchers should have this, too. Properly rendered, chicken fat is a bland, neutral fat that can be used in a wide variety of foods—my mother claimed her mother used it as shortening in brownies! Again, the quality of chicken fat will depend on how the chicken was raised. No hormones, antibiotics, or soy feed will make for more healthful schmaltz.

Duck Fat

If you roast a duck, do not, I say DO NOT, throw away the fat. Use it for sautéing and roasting vegetables. It's amazing. And ducks have a lot of fat!

Tallow

Remember how good McDonald's fries were when you were a kid? You know why? They were fried in tallow, also known as beef fat. In the 1980s, the OMG-Saturated-Fat-Is-Eeeevul Squad bullied them into switching to vegetable oil, which not only made the fries less tasty, but filled them with trans fats, too. Especially if you can get fat from grass-fed beef, it's an excellent cooking fat. Indeed, make it a rule never to discard fat from properly raised meat.

On the Interchangeability of Fats

If I call for coconut oil for sautéing, and you want to use lard, or chicken fat, or tallow, go ahead, okay? I won't care, and your recipe will come out fine.

REGARDING VEGETABLE OILS

There are other vegetable oils I'd be willing to use—macadamia nut oil, for one, or walnut oil if a recipe specified it. Avocado oil is good, too. Still, in general, I prefer the fats I've listed; most vegetable oils in quantity have to be considered experimental in the human diet. Here's my rough rule of thumb: If I can figure out how they got the oil out of the source, I'm probably willing to use it, at least in limited quantity. If you rub a piece of coconut or walnut meat or an avocado on a piece of paper, you'll get a grease spot. Heck, you can practically squeeze the oil out of olives right there in your kitchen.

Can you figure out how you'd get oil out of a soybean? An ear of corn? I've never found those things to be oily, have you? I'm not even sure what a safflower is. As for "canola," it's a hybrid of a plant that has the unfortunate name "rape." Rapeseed oil has historically been used as varnish, but has been considered too toxic for human consumption because of a constituent called *erucic acid.* It was also bitter and unpleasant tasting. Canola is the trade name of a low-erucic-acid hybrid of rapeseed initially bred for use in animal feed and then eventually marketed for human consumption. I've heard some dire stories about canola, but like so much weblore, they strike me as questionable. What is not in question is that canola oil is novel in the human diet and has been highly processed. I don't use it. The most important thing is to stay away from excessive polyunsaturated oils. They are highly inflammatory.

SWEETENERS

The Sweetener Wars are the bane of my professional existence. No matter which sweetener I use in a recipe, someone will object. A recipe uses Splenda? How can I use that evil artificial sweetener? Don't I know it's poison?! Can't I use stevia? The recipe calls for stevia? Oh, dear, that stuff is nasty, so bitter. And expensive! Why can't I use Splenda? Why don't I use xylitol? And so on.

I have, therefore, used the sweeteners I felt best suited each particular recipe, but offer this rundown for those of you who wish to make substitutions.

Granular Sucralose (Splenda and Knockoffs)

Confession: I still like Splenda. I remain unconvinced that, in the modest quantities in which I historically have used it, sucralose is hideously dangerous. I think it tastes good and find it easy to use. However, I do not write recipes for me, I write them for you. So many of you have let me know that you no longer use sucralose that I don't generally use it for developing recipes for publication anymore. Still, some of you use it, so I'm including it in this list.

The granular stuff is bulked with maltodextrin, a carbohydrate. Why does it say 0 carbs on the package? Federal labeling law allows manufacturers to round down anything under 0.5 gram per serving. Accordingly, I count 0.5 gram of carb per teaspoon, 24 grams per cup (24g). The little yellow packets have less maltodextrin, so fewer carbs, but for more than a teaspoon or two of sugar's worth of sweetening, the packets are a pain. *Do not use SPLENDA "Sugar Blend" or "Brown Sugar Blend."* As the names suggest, they contain sugar.

Liquid Sucralose

If you're unafraid of sucralose, the liquid has the advantage of containing no carby fillers. I like EZ Sweetz brand, available through Amazon.com or Netrition.com. It's great stuff. You can get teeny bottles that fit nicely in a purse or pocket, if you'd like to keep it on hand for coffee. You need to know the sweetness equivalency of your liquid sucralose. The EZ Sweetz I have on hand is 1 drop = 2 teaspoons sugar, but it comes in more than one concentration. Read the label! They offer free samples at www.ez-sweetz.com/free-sample.

Liquid Stevia

While I found the old-school highly concentrated powdered stevia difficult to use, the liquid stevia extracts in dropper bottles are far easier and taste far better. Furthermore, they come in a broad array of flavors. The ones I keep on hand and have used in this book are the following:

- Plain—that is, it's just sweet. I've been using NOW brand plain liquid stevia. This is great when you want a touch of sweetness in a recipe, without any other overtones.

- English toffee—I use this constantly. Why? Because the flavor bears a similarity to brown sugar.

- Vanilla—The uses for a sweetener with a vanilla flavor added should be obvious! I do often add vanilla extract as well. I also often combine vanilla stevia with English toffee or other flavors.

- Chocolate—Again, the uses here are obvious, from cocoa to cookies.

- Lemon drop—This is not only good in lemon-flavored recipes, but it is great in all sorts of recipes with a fruit flavor and a natural in iced tea.

- Valencia orange—Again, this is great for lending a fruit flavor in all sorts of recipes.

I can buy all of these flavors and more at Sahara Mart, my beloved local health/international /gourmet grocery. If your health food store doesn't carry these, they can very likely order them for you; most health food stores are awesome about special orders. Ask them about NOW and Sweet-Leaf brands.

If you're not blessed with a great local health food store, you can order these from Amazon.com, like everything else on the planet.

It's essential to have an idea of how many drops of a given brand of stevia are roughly equal to a teaspoon of sugar in sweetness. These recipes assume liquid stevia of a sweetness where 6 drops = 1 teaspoon sugar. Both SweetLeaf and NOW brands are about this strength. I use ¼ teaspoon stevia to replace ¼ cup (50g) sugar and ½ teaspoon stevia to replace ½ cup (100g) sugar. If your liquid stevia is considerably more or less sweet than this, you will need to adjust the quantities. Look at the manufacturer's website for equivalencies. Again, this applies only to the liquid extracts! If you put that much of the concentrated white stevia powder in a recipe, the result is likely to be inedible. EZ Sweetz makes a good liquid stevia, but it is stronger than I've been using: 2 drops = 1 teaspoon sugar.

Monk Fruit

At this writing, I have just received a liquid monk fruit sweetener from Natural Mate, the same company that makes EZ Sweetz, but have not had time to try it. If you dislike stevia and distrust sucralose, you can use monk fruit extract in place of liquid stevia. You will, however, need to know the conversion factor. For the Natural Mate liquid monk fruit extract, the conversion factor is 2 drops = 1 teaspoon sugar. That means that 6 drops = 1 tablespoon (13g), and theoretically, 24 drops would equal ¼ cup (50g) sugar in sweetness. However, I repeat, I have not tried it.

To use liquid monk fruit in place of flavored stevia extracts, you will need an extract or flavoring such as those found in the baking aisle. Vanilla, lemon, and orange extracts are easy to find; most grocery stores should have them. Chocolate extract is a little harder to come by; I get mine, once again, at Sahara Mart. Unsurprisingly, you can get it through Amazon; they also carry English toffee extract. I'm afraid I cannot give you exact measurements, but liquid monk fruit plus anywhere from a few drops to a teaspoon or so of the desired extract should give you a similar result to those I get from flavored stevia extracts.

Natural Mate sells a liquid stevia/monk fruit combination: 2 drops = 4 teaspoons (16g) sugar. I have this, and like it just fine.

Erythritol

Of all the sugar alcohols, aka polyols, erythritol has the least blood sugar impact—indeed, officially zero blood sugar impact—because it is neither digested nor absorbed, simply passed through. By contrast, you absorb roughly half of maltitol, the sugar alcohol most used in commercial sugar-free sweets, so it cannot be completely discounted. Also, unlike maltitol, which is notorious for its embarrassing and even uncomfortable gastric effect, erythritol causes virtually no gut upset. These two qualities have made erythritol a real comer in the burgeoning sugar-free sweetener market; it has been one of the sweeteners I reach for most often for a few years now. It is also the only sugar alcohol or polyol deemed acceptable by Eric Westman, M.D., and Jacqueline Eberstein, R.N., who, between them, know everything worth knowing about ketogenic diets. (Full disclosure: I work with Eric and Jackie with HEAL Clinics and HEALCare. I also consider them both good friends.)

So, why hasn't erythritol supplanted maltitol in commercial sweets? It's harder to work with. Maltitol behaves remarkably like sugar in cooking; you can get all the textures of sugar—gooey caramels, silky sauces, crunchy brittles. Erythritol melts in warm mixtures, but has a tendency to recrystallize as it cools, making the final results grainy. Most confounding, erythritol has the peculiar property of being *endothermic*—when it hits the moisture in your mouth, it quite literally absorbs energy, creating a cooling sensation. This works well in ice cream, but can be a little disconcerting in a cookie. One more hitch: Erythritol is not quite as sweet as sugar, about 70 percent.

All of this explains why I usually combine erythritol with liquid stevia extracts. Indeed, the industry does as well; Truvia is a combination of erythritol and stevia. (Why didn't I use Truvia in these recipes? I'm just not crazy about the flavor of the stuff; I find it bitter.) Of the erythritol products I have used, my favorite by far is one called Swerve*, a combination of erythritol and oligosaccharides, a sweet-tasting fiber. Swerve measures like sugar, and because of the oligosaccharides, it browns. Swerve comes both in a granular version and a powdered "confectioner's" version. Because of the potential for graininess with erythritol, I generally prefer powdered Swerve, though I keep both versions on hand. The main drawback of Swerve is the price; the stuff is not cheap. Because I don't use a ton of sweeteners when I'm not working on a book, this is not a major issue for me, but it may be for you.

I buy Swerve at my health food store, but you may not find it locally. Again, you should be able to special order the stuff through your local health food store, and again, you can order it through Amazon.com and Netrition.com. Plain erythritol, though not cheap, is less expensive than Swerve —I pay about $12 per pound (455g) for Swerve and have seen erythritol as cheap as $7 per pound (455g).

*No, I do not get a kickback from Swerve. Not even a free bag. I just think the stuff is really good.

Erythritol and Monk Fruit Blends

Geez, the sweeteners are multiplying so fast it's hard to keep up! I was more than halfway through developing recipes for this book when William Davis, M.D.—the Wheat Belly and Undoctored guy—sent me a new sweetener to try, called Virtue. Virtue is a blend of erythritol and monk fruit. I like it a lot and have used it in a few of these recipes. The label on Virtue gives its sweetness equivalency as ¼ teaspoon = 1 teaspoon sugar. I disagree; I find it to be closer to ⅓ teaspoon Virtue = 1 teaspoon sugar. Or, to state it another way, I find Virtue to be about three times as sweet as sugar, not four times. Figure 1 teaspoon Virtue = 1 tablespoon (13g) sugar.

Similarly, the nice folks who make EZ Sweetz liquid sucralose have just released an erythritol—monk fruit blend in their Natural Mate line. The label gives the sweetness equivalence as 1 teaspoon = 2 teaspoons sugar, or twice as sweet as sugar.

Because I have long been pairing erythritol with the much more concentrated stevia, and because these blends do not, to my palate, have the bitterness of Truvia, I find them real comers in the sugar-free sweetener wars. I expect to use them more and more often.

Sugar-Free Coffee Flavoring Syrups

DaVinci, Monin, and Torani all put out sugar-free syrups in a wide variety of flavors. Because they are all artificially sweetened, which so many people find objectionable, I have used them in only a few recipes where I didn't think I could get the flavor or texture I wanted any other way. That said, if you've got a frappuccino monkey on your back, these syrups are a far better choice than the sugared varieties. A grande (medium) Starbucks Mocha Frappuccino contains a whopping 54 grams of sugar.

Why Not Xylitol?

I've been asked why I don't use xylitol instead of erythritol. Some people prefer xylitol, and it does have the big advantage of actually remineralizing tooth enamel. However, xylitol is partially absorbed in the gut, rather than passed through, and therefore is not zero carb. It also has the much-dreaded polyol laxative effect. And it shares the cooling effect of erythritol, so no advantage there.

However, the big reason I don't use xylitol is that it is profoundly toxic to dogs, and I have three. If one of them stole a cookie and died, I would never forgive myself. If you do use xylitol, be very careful to keep it away from your canine pals.

About Maltitol

I have historically used some maltitol-based sweeteners, particularly sugar-free imitation honey. However, I have not done so in this book. Why? Because you absorb roughly half of maltitol, and therefore, it cannot be entirely discounted from carb intake. On a keto diet, where we need to keep carb intake very low, maltitol is problematic.

OTHER INGREDIENTS

Salt

In *The Art and Science of Low Carbohydrate Living*, researchers Stephen Phinney, M.D., Ph.D., and Jeff Volek, Ph.D., R.D., state that people who cut out concentrated carbohydrates often find themselves weak and tired, not from lack of carbs, but from lack of sodium.

I, myself, have learned I need extra salt, and I have occasionally become uncomfortably sodium deficient. If you feel weak, light-headed, achy, and especially headachy, get more salt. This goes double if you go to bed without a headache, but wake up with one. Again, salt is an essential nutrient, so don't shun it. The advice to eat a low-salt diet makes about as much sense as the advice to eat a low-fat diet.

However, grocery store salt is refined to eliminate all minerals except for sodium and chlorine, often with iodine added as well. (The iodine is beneficial; it's the other additives and the lack of trace minerals I object to.) Other stuff is added, largely to keep the salt from caking in damp weather. One popular brand of table salt includes sodium silicoaluminate, dextrose, potassium iodide, and sodium bicarbonate. Yep, dextrose, as in sugar. Yuck.

Sea salt, on the other hand, contains a wide variety of trace minerals. It shouldn't contain any noxious additives, either. There's just one problem: our seas and oceans are sadly polluted. There is, however, a way around this: mined sea salt. All around the world, there are deposits of salt that are remnants of ancient seas. This salt was deposited long before mankind was around, much less had a chance to dump chemicals in the oceans. This is the finest and most nutritious —and most paleo—salt you can use.

I use a brand called "Real Salt" that is mined in Utah, while friends of mine favor salt from deposits in the Himalayas. (And how long ago did an ocean have to dry up to have left salt in the Himalayas?!) Any salt from ancient deposits should be fine, as long as nothing is added. Your ancient seabed salt will not be pure white. Real Salt brand is pale pink, as is a lot of Himalayan salt. Pure white salt is suspect.

Good salt is more expensive than table salt; at this writing, Real Salt runs about $10 per pound (455g). I pay it gladly because I consider good salt a very important part of my nutritional plan, and I have been using it for many years.

Be aware that unadulterated salt will clump in damp weather. The only solution I have is the old tradition of the salt dish, in place of the salt shaker—just put a small dish of salt on the table, pinch up a bit, and sprinkle as needed.

Because you're not using iodized salt (which is highly refined and is missing important trace minerals), make sure you're getting iodine elsewhere. If you eat a lot of seafood—freshwater fish doesn't count—that may be enough. Seaweed is also an excellent source of iodine, if you're fond of it. I take a few drops of Lugol's solution, a combination of iodine and potassium iodide, in my tea every morning.

Eggs

You will find a few recipes in this book calling for raw eggs. This runs directly counter to the food safety information we've had drummed into our heads for the past couple of decades. According to the Centers for Disease Control, only one out of every 20,000 uncracked, properly refrigerated eggs is actually contaminated. As one woman with degrees in public health and food science put it, "The risk is less than the risk of breaking your leg on any given trip down the stairs." And that's with factory-farmed eggs. I consider small farm eggs— and the eggs from my backyard—even safer.

It's not that there's no risk in eating raw eggs; there's a risk to everything. But, I'm increasingly convinced that people worry about the wrong things. They get panicky about raw eggs while consuming Coca-Cola, Lucky Charms, and Wonder Bread. For what it's worth, I've never gotten sick from a raw egg. But your risks are your own to take.

If you're really unhappy about raw eggs, you can pasteurize them. You'll need a digital thermometer or one of the new electronic induction burners. Put the eggs in a saucepan and cover them with water. Quickly bring the water to 140°F (60°C). Hold them at that temperature—and no hotter—for 3 minutes. Then, immediately pour off the hot water and flush the eggs with several changes of cold water. Use the eggs right away or store them in the refrigerator until needed.

Guar and Xanthan

What the heck are these? They're finely milled soluble fibers, and they're hugely useful in low-carb cuisine. These are what you use in place of flour, cornstarch, or arrowroot for thickening sauces or soups. What do they taste like? Nothing at all; they couldn't be blander if they tried. In fact, you've been eating them all along —the processed food industry uses guar and xanthan all the time. These are far more powerful thickeners than flour, cornstarch, or arrowroot, however, so do not try a one-for-one substitution. The results could be used to surface roads. Instead, fill an old salt or spice shaker with whichever you have on hand—I marginally prefer xanthan—and keep it by the stove. When you have a sauce or soup you need to thicken, start whisking first, then *lightly* sprinkle the thickener over the surface as you whisk. Do *not* spoon in some guar or xanthan and then start whisking. You'll get lumps.

Go slowly; it's easy to put in more and impossible to remove too much. Keep in mind that these continue to thicken a bit on standing, so quit when your dish is a little less thick than you want it to be. Unlike starchy thickeners, these do not need

to cook to thicken or to get rid of a raw taste, so they can also be used in cold applications like smoothies. Both of these thickeners will keep pretty much forever as long as they're dry. These have another use: they lend structure to nut- or seed-meal-based baked goods. In the Baked Goods chapter, I've used small quantities of these repeatedly to improve the texture of the finished product. Again, these are health food store items, and again, all of them can be ordered online, too. What can't, these days?

Shirataki Noodles and Miracle Rice

Most "low-carb" noodles are nothing I'll eat. There is one widely distributed brand, made with the same ingredients as standard pasta, that I doubt is anywhere near as low carb as its label claims. The only noodles I eat are shirataki, and they are a staple in my kitchen. Shirataki are traditional Japanese noodles made from the fiber glucomannan, derived from *konjac* or *konyaku*, a root vegetable. (This is often translated as "yam," but konjac is a completely different plant.) Being made almost entirely of fiber, shirataki are very low in both carbohydrate and calories. Shirataki come in two basic varieties: traditional and tofu. Traditional shirataki are made entirely of glucomannan fiber. They're translucent and kind of gelatinous, really quite different from the wheat-based noodles we grew up on. I only like traditional shirataki in Asian recipes—sesame noodles, Asian soups, and the like. Tofu shirataki, as the name suggests, have a little bit of tofu added to the glucomannan. This makes them white and gives them a more tender texture than traditional shirataki. They're not identical to "regular" pasta, but they're closer, and I like them in all sorts of things, from fettuccini Alfredo to tuna casserole. Both traditional and tofu shirataki come in a variety of widths and shapes. If you are concerned about soy, be aware that my best calculations suggest there is roughly 2 teaspoons of tofu in a packet of tofu shirataki.

A new addition to my kitchen is Miracle Rice —traditional shirataki in small spheres, about the size of short-grain rice. I really like Miracle Rice, often ordering it by the carton, and have used it in several recipes in this book. If you don't like it, you may substitute Cauli-Rice (page 107), but it will add a few grams of carbohydrate to your finished dish.

Preparing shirataki: Unlike the pasta and rice you're used to, shirataki come prehydrated in a pouch of liquid. To use them, snip open the pouch and dump them into a strainer in the sink. You'll notice the liquid smells fishy. Do not panic. Rinse your noodles well and put them in a microwaveable bowl. Nuke them on high for 2 minutes and drain them again. Nuke them for *another* 2 minutes and drain them one more time. This renders them quite bland and also cooks out extra liquid that would otherwise dilute any sauce you put on them. Long noodles are considered good luck in Japan, but I find shirataki a bit too long. I snip across them a few times with my kitchen shears. All of this microwaving and draining and snipping takes less time than boiling water for standard pasta. You now have hot noodles or "rice!" Add sauce, stir them into soup, or do whatever you like to do with noodles and rice.

I find shirataki especially useful when I want to increase my fat percentage for the day. Because the shirataki themselves have almost no carbs or calories, they don't "dilute" the fat you add to them. A bowl of shirataki with a fatty sauce, or just with butter and Parmesan, makes a satisfying meal. I can get shirataki both at my local health food stores and at Asian markets. If you can't find them locally, you can order them online, but be aware: they do not tolerate freezing; they disintegrate into mush. This means you may not want to order them in the dead of winter. On the other hand, they keep for months in the fridge, so if you decide you like them, go ahead and stock up.

Coconut

It's worth shopping around for your coconut. Around here, one of the health food stores carries shredded coconut only in 12-ounce (340g) packets for something like $5. The other one sells coconut in the bulk section, where I can scoop it out of a bin for a big $3 per pound (455g). Coconut keeps well—because the fat in it is so saturated, it doesn't go rancid—but it does lose water. You may find your batter or dough a little dry. Buying only as much as you'll use up in a month or so and buying from a store with a brisk turnover should take care of that. Do be sure to buy plain shredded coconut, not the sweetened "angel flake" stuff!

Canned Coconut Milk

Full of MCT-rich coconut oil, coconut milk is a wildly versatile ingredient, useful in everything from coffee drinks to curries. It is especially useful for those of you who are avoiding dairy.

While coconut milk has its own flavor, it gives a similar creamy texture to all kinds of recipes. It also can be cultured to create "Cocoyo"—a yogurt substitute—and coconut sour cream; see instructions on page 259. The thick, canned coconut milk should be available in the international aisle of your big grocery store with the Thai or Indian ingredients, at health food stores, and at Asian markets. I was pleased to find recently that Kroger, the nation's biggest grocery chain, now carries a house brand of coconut milk. I find coconut milk in both 14 fluid ounce (390ml) and 13.5 fluid ounce (380ml) cans. Trust me, ½ ounce (15ml) of coconut milk one way or the other is not going to spoil your dish. Don't sweat it. Do I need to tell you to buy full-fat coconut milk, not light?

Pourable Coconut Milk

Pourable coconut milk is a new addition to my kitchen. Though it is thinner than the canned stuff, the macros are the same. I like Silk brand pourable coconut milk, which is stocked with the cow's milk, soy milk, almond milk, etc., in all my local grocery stores. Be sure to buy the unsweetened variety.

Flaxseed Meal

This is pretty easy to get; all my local grocery stores have it in the baking aisle. I use Bob's Red Mill brand golden flaxseed meal; I like it, and it's easy to find.

Vanilla Whey Protein Powder

A few of these recipes call for vanilla whey protein powder. I've used several brands over the years and never had one not work. Designer Whey protein is perhaps most widely available; GNC stores carry it. Recently, I've been using Vitacost.com's house brand because the price is right, and it's fine.

Unflavored or Natural Whey Protein Powder

This is my protein powder of choice for non-sweet recipes. Again, I'm currently using one I got through Vitacost.com, but I've never noticed a big difference among protein powders.

Generally, these protein powders are sold in canisters that hold a pound (455g) or more. As long as you keep them lidded and in a dry place, they should keep for a long, long time.

Bouillon Concentrate

I use bouillon concentrate as a seasoning all the time. You can use bouillon granules or liquid, but my preferred form is Better Than Bouillon paste: it actually contains some of the protein source listed on the label, is gluten-free, and I think the flavor is superior to granules or cubes. I keep beef and chicken Better Than Bouillon pastes on hand. If you're eating paleo, or just "clean," there's a simple substitute for bouillon concentrate: reduced stock. The easiest way I know to make this is to put good strong chicken or beef stock in your slow cooker, on low, with the lid off, and let it cook down until it's syrupy. Store this in a lidded jar in the freezer and use just like you would bouillon concentrate—which is, after all, what it is. How salty homemade reduced stock will be depends on the saltiness of the stock you start with.

Because I generally suggest you salt "to taste," this shouldn't change things.

Creole Seasoning

I've been known to make my own, but generally I use Tony Chachere's "More Spice" blend. It's widely available. Use a milder version if you're not as devoted to hot food as I am.

Vege-Sal

One of my favorite seasonings, Vege-Sal is a blend of salt and powdered vegetables. It's subtle, but I think it improves many savory dishes, and you'll see that I often have specified "salt or Vege-Sal." Vege-Sal is made by Modern Products and has recently had their popular "Spike" name added to the title, so it's "Spike Vege-Sal." If your health food store doesn't have it, they can order it for you, or you can order it online. Or just use salt. If you're going to try Vege-Sal, be aware that along with coming in a shaker, it also comes in 10- or 20-ounce (280 or 560g) boxes. If you decide you like it, this is considerably cheaper than buying a shaker every time you need Vege-Sal!

Onions, Scallions, Garlic, and Shallots

All of these members of the allium family are somewhat carby as vegetables go, but they're so flavorful and versatile that it's impossible to imagine cooking without them. I just watch the quantities. When a recipe simply calls for an "onion," I'm talking about the common yellow onions you can buy in a net sack at any grocery store in America. Those are your all-purpose cooking onions. If you swap in a sweet onion, like a Vidalia or a red onion, you'll get a considerably milder flavor than I was going for. On the other hand, those red onions, along with Vidalias and lovable little scallions, are mild and sweet, perfect for use in salads and other recipes where you'll eat them raw. Again, swap in those yellow cooking onions, and you'll get a harsher flavor.

I buy fresh garlic two or three heads at a time; I couldn't keep house without it. Be aware that a garlic "clove" is one of those little segments that makes up the larger head of garlic. Use a whole head of garlic where I've called for a clove, and—well, your dish may be strong, but you won't have to worry about vampires.

I've grown quite fond of shallots, which occupy a botanical niche between onions and garlic. Look for them in with the onions and garlic at your grocery store—they're bigger than garlic, usually smaller than onions, more teardrop shaped than round, and generally red. Most shallots are made up of two segments inside a papery skin. When I call for "a shallot," I'm talking about one of those segments, not both.

FYI: Refrigerated onions won't make you cry. Try it.

Hot Sauces

I am a bona fide chile-head and have an extensive collection of hot sauces, but there are only a few I have called for repeatedly in this book:

- **Tabasco**—The familiar original, this is a Louisiana-style hot sauce. Frank's or Louisiana brand will do fine as substitutes.

- **Frank's**—Another Louisiana-style hot sauce, Frank's is the canonical hot sauce used in the original Buffalo wings. As far as I'm concerned, that's enough reason to keep it on hand, but again, Tabasco or Louisiana will do.

- **Chipotle**—Tabasco Chipotle is good, so are Louisiana and Melinda brands. I reach for this stuff all the time.

- **Sriracha**—This stuff is taking over the world. From a specialty ingredient a decade ago, it's now everywhere. Much of sriracha contains some sugar, but you'd be hard-pressed to consume enough to move your blood sugar.

Harissa

My new culinary love is harissa, a North African condiment of hot peppers and spices. Often harissa contains junk, but I have discovered both Mina brand—in paste form—and Frontier brand, a powder—which are free of objectionable ingredients. Harissa is not blow-the-top-of-your-head-off hot, just pleasantly spicy. I can get both Mina and Frontier brand harissa at my local health food stores, but if you can't find it locally, like everything else, it is available online.

Soy Sauce

A word of warning for those of you who avoid gluten: most soy sauce has wheat in it. I use San-J brand gluten-free soy sauce, which is widely available. If you're avoiding all soy, coconut aminos are remarkably similar to soy sauce; look for them in health food stores or buy them online.

Nonstick Cooking Spray

You will notice that I frequently call for coating pots and pans with cooking spray. Just FYI, I use LouAna brand, which is made with coconut oil. I can get it at my local grocery stores.

Lily's Chocolate Chips

As far as I know, the only chocolate chips currently on the market that not only have no sugar added but also have no maltitol, are Lily's, which are sweetened with erythritol and stevia. This gives them a slightly different texture from the chocolate chips we grew up with, but I have found them easy to work with and certainly quite delicious. I order them from my local health food store a case at a time, but no doubt you can find them online as well.

CHAPTER 3

Snacks, Finger Foods, and Party Munchies

The truth is, once you're in ketosis, your urge to snack will drop dramatically. You simply won't be anywhere near as hungry as you once were. Also, there simply are no very low-carb/moderate-protein/high-fat foods that you can eat endlessly and mindlessly—think a giant bucket of popcorn at the movies—without making yourself sick.

However, there are times when finger foods are called for! And that's at parties, of course. There are few better party survival strategies than to take along some stealth health food—wings, stuffed eggs, seasoned nuts—all snacks that will please the crowd while giving you something to eat other than potato chips and pizza.

There's another great reason for all these recipes: because your hunger will be so much less, there will be times when you're not interested in a whole meal. These tasty nibbles are so nutritious they're perfectly good substitutes for a meal now and then. How about on family movie night or game night? Or on a day when everyone is going to be working on some major project together? Just put out a few of these and figure they're a fine alternative to a sit-down meal.

½ cup (112g) butter

¼ cup (60ml) Worcestershire sauce

2½ cups (360g) raw, shelled sunflower seeds

2½ cups (348g) raw, shelled pumpkin seeds (aka pepitas)

1 cup (145g) almonds

1 cup (100g) walnuts

1 cup (100g) pecans

1 cup (140g) raw cashew pieces

2 ounces (55g) pork rinds, broken up into almond-size pieces (about 2 cups)

1 tablespoon (12g) seasoned salt

1½ teaspoons garlic powder

1 teaspoon onion powder

YIELD: 12 cups (1.2kg), 48 servings — Per serving: (¼ cup, or 25g): 178 calories; 16g fat (81% calories from fat); 8g protein; 5g carbohydrate; 2g dietary fiber; 3g net carbohydrate.

SNACK CRACK

You want crunchy, salty, and flavorful? You got it. This amazing recipe makes a lot!

Preheat the oven to 250°F (120°C, or gas mark ½). While it's heating, put the butter in a huge roasting pan and slide it in to melt.

When the butter is melted, stir the Worcestershire into it. Now, add all the seeds and nuts and the pork rinds. Stir until everything is evenly coated with the butter mixture.

In a small dish, stir together the seasoned salt, garlic powder, and onion powder. Now, sprinkle this mixture evenly over the nut and seed mixture, a teaspoon at a time, stirring each addition in before adding more. Spread everything evenly in the pan. Toast the mixture in the oven for 2 hours, stirring every 30 minutes or so.

Store in a snap-top container. If you're not having a party, you might want to divide this into a few smaller containers and freeze the extra, so it doesn't go bad on you. That would be a darned shame.

¼ cup (55g) butter

3½ ounces (100g) pork rinds

½ teaspoon Amaretti sweet corn flavoring

Salt to taste

YIELD: 5 servings — Per serving: 189 calories; 15g fat (73.9% calories from fat); 12g protein; trace carbohydrate; 0g dietary fiber; trace net carbohydrate.

BUTTERED "POPCORN"

Okay, it's not exactly like popcorn, but it's a darned good snack. You can order the sweet corn flavoring from Amazon.com.

Preheat the oven to 325°F (170°C, or gas mark 3). Put the butter in a large roasting pan and slide it into the heating oven to melt.

Meanwhile, poke a hole in your bag of pork rinds to let the air out and bash it a bit. You're breaking them up into roughly popcorn-size bits—it's easier to coat them with the butter that way.

When the butter is melted, stir the sweet corn flavoring into it. Add the pork rinds to the pan and stir until they're all evenly coated. Spread them out evenly, put them in the oven, and set the timer for 5 minutes.

When the timer beeps, stir and turn the pork rinds. Put them back in the oven for another 5 minutes, and they're done. Season with salt to taste. Store in an airtight container.

3½ ounces (100g) pork rinds

3 tablespoons (45ml) olive oil

2 tablespoons (8g) nutritional yeast flakes

1 teaspoon red pepper flakes

1 teaspoon salt

YIELD: 6 servings — Per serving: 164 calories; 12g fat (66.0% calories from fat); 13g protein; 2g carbohydrate; 1g dietary fiber; 1g net carbohydrate.

3½ ounces (100g) pork rinds

3 tablespoons (45ml) MCT oil

6 tablespoons (36g) **Nacho Cheese Powder (page 247), divided**

YIELD: 6 servings — Per serving: 190 calories; 14g fat (65.5% calories from fat); 14g protein; 3g carbohydrate; 1g dietary fiber; 2g net carbohydrate.

EVERYTHING OLD IS NOOCH AGAIN RINDS

When I was a baby health food freak in the 1970s, nutritional yeast was widely touted as the most super of superfoods, a powerhouse of protein and vitamins. Unfortunately, people insisted on mixing it in juices or smoothies, where it tasted awful. It fell out of favor, partly because yeast-laced orange juice is revolting and partly because people wrongly believed it caused yeast infections. (Nutritional yeast is dead; it won't grow inside you.)

However, I learned back then that nutritional yeast is great used in savory foods, adding body and umami, not to mention vitamins. And sure enough, there is a revival in popularity of nutritional yeast used in savory foods. It even has a trendy new nickname: nooch. Get some! It has tons of uses. Yes, it has a few carbs, but the vast majority of them are fiber.

Preheat the oven to 350°F (180°C, or gas mark 4).

Poke a hole in your bag of rinds and bash 'em up a bit into smaller pieces.

Put the olive oil in a shallow roasting pan and dump in the rinds. Stir and turn them until they're evenly coated. Stick 'em in the oven and set the timer for 5 minutes.

Meanwhile, combine the nutritional yeast flakes, red pepper flakes, and salt in either a spice grinder or a mortar and pestle. Grind them together until the nooch is finely powdered.

The timer beeped! Pull out your pan. Sprinkle half of the yeast mixture over the rinds, stirring as you do so. Put them back in the oven and bake for another 5 minutes.

When the rinds are done, sprinkle and stir in the rest of the yeast mixture. Store in an airtight container.

NACHO CHEESE PORK RINDS

This is for all you Nacho Cheese Doritos fans out there, and I know your name is Legion. These will fill the crunchy-cheese-snack void nicely.

Preheat the oven to 350°F (180°C, or gas mark 4).

Poke a hole in the bag of pork rinds and break them up a bit.

Put the MCT oil in a 9 × 13-inch (23 × 33cm) pan and slosh it around. Dump in the rinds, and stir and turn them, coating them as evenly as possible. Put them in to bake, setting the timer for 4 minutes.

When the timer beeps, sprinkle 3 tablespoons (18g) of the Nacho Cheese Powder over them, 1 tablespoon (6g) at a time, stirring each in well before adding the next. You're trying to coat the rinds as evenly as possible.

Bake the rinds for another 4 minutes. Then, repeat the sprinkling and stirring with the remaining 3 tablespoons (18g) of Nacho Cheese Powder.

Store in an airtight container. Hide from the family.

2 tablespoons (28g) butter

1 tablespoon (15ml) MCT oil

3½ ounces (100g) pork rinds

1 teaspoon paprika

1 teaspoon garlic powder

1 teaspoon salt

1 teaspoon pepper

2 teaspoons hot sauce
(I used Frank's.)

YIELD: 5 servings — Per serving: 177 calories; 14g fat (69.6% calories from fat); 12g protein; 1g carbohydrate; trace dietary fiber; 1g net carbohydrate.

SPICY PORK RINDS

People think of pork rinds as being very fatty, but the truth is that most of the fat has been cooked out in the frying process—they have more protein than fat. Adding butter and MCT oil brings them closer to our desired macros. It improves the flavor and texture, too!

Preheat the oven to 350°F (180°C, or gas mark 4). Put the butter and MCT oil in a 9 × 13-inch (23 × 33cm) roasting pan and slide it in to the oven, so the butter melts while you're prepping the rest.

Poke a hole in your bag of pork rinds to let the air out. Now, squeeze or punch it to break the rinds up a bit; you want pieces in the 1-inch (2.5cm) range.

In a small dish, stir together the paprika, garlic powder, salt, and pepper.

By now, your butter is melted! Pull the pan out of the oven. Add the hot sauce and stir it into the butter and oil and then add the pork rinds. Stir, turning everything over frequently, coating the pieces as evenly as you can.

Now sprinkle in the spices, about one-fourth of the mixture at a time, stirring each addition in before adding the next. Again, you're trying to coat all the pieces evenly.

Roast for 5 minutes and then stir again, turning everything over. Roast for another 3 to 4 minutes.

If you don't devour these while they're warm—try making these on family movie night!—store them in an airtight container and consume within a few days.

2 tablespoons (28g) butter

1 tablespoon (15ml) MCT oil

3½ ounces (100g) pork rinds

1 teaspoon dried dill weed

¾ teaspoon garlic powder

½ teaspoon salt

⅓ cup grated (33g) Parmesan cheese

YIELD: 6 servings — Per serving: 166 calories; 13g fat (69.2% calories from fat); 12g protein; 1g carbohydrate; trace dietary fiber; 1g net carbohydrate.

PARMESAN-DILL PORK RINDS

This is another seasoning originally invented for popcorn that takes beautifully to pork rinds. It's sure to please. Do make sure your dried dill has been recently purchased. That stuff you bought a year ago has no oomph left.

Preheat the oven on to 350°F (180°C, or gas mark 4). Put the butter and MCT oil in a 9 × 13-inch (23 × 33cm) pan and put it in the oven while it heats.

Poke a hole in the bag of pork rinds to let the air out and then pound or squeeze them. You're breaking them up into pieces a little bigger than popcorn (only flatter).

Measure the dill, garlic powder, and salt into a small cup and stir them together.

When the butter is melted, pull the pan out of the oven. Stir the butter and oil together and then add the pork rinds. Stir and turn them over until they're evenly coated and all the butter mixture has been absorbed from the bottom of the pan.

Now, sprinkle on the seasoning mixture in three additions, stirring after each to help distribute it evenly. Put the pan back in the oven and set the timer for 4 minutes.

When the timer beeps, pull out the pan again. Sprinkle in the Parmesan in two or three additions, stirring to distribute it evenly. Bake for another 4 minutes. Let cool and store in an airtight container.

7 ounces (200g) pork rinds (This was 2 bags of Aldi's house brand.)

⅓ cup (80ml) MCT oil

1 teaspoon ground cumin

1 teaspoon ground ginger

1 teaspoon salt

½ teaspoon pepper

½ teaspoon cayenne

½ teaspoon ground allspice

¼ teaspoon smoked paprika

¼ teaspoon ground cloves

YIELD: 12 servings — Per serving: 146 calories; 11g fat (70.7% calories from fat); 10g protein; trace carbohydrate; trace dietary fiber.

MOROCCAN-SPICED PORK RINDS

I saw a recipe for Moroccan-spiced oyster crackers and thought, "Hmm. Pork rinds aren't traditionally Moroccan, but neither are oyster crackers. I'll give it a shot." I'm glad I did; these are fantastic—one of the most impressive recipes in this book.

Preheat the oven to 350°F (180°C, or gas mark 4).

Poke a hole in each bag of pork rinds and then smash them a bit with your fists—you're looking for pieces a little bigger than popcorn.

Pour the MCT oil into a huge roasting pan and then dump in the broken-up pork rinds. Stir until they're all equally coated with the oil.

Measure all the seasonings into a small bowl and stir until they're evenly blended. Now, use a spoon to sprinkle the spices over the rinds a bit at a time—sprinkle a little, stir, sprinkle a little more, stir. You want all your pork rinds to get acquainted with the seasonings.

Bake for 7 minutes and then stir. Bake for another 7 minutes, stir again, and give them another 3 or 4 minutes. Pull them out and let them cool a bit before transferring to a resealable plastic bag for storage.

½ cup (50g) grated Parmesan cheese

YIELD: 8 servings — Per serving: 23 calories; 2g fat (60.0% calories from fat); 2g protein; trace carbohydrate; 0g dietary fiber; trace net carbohydrate.

NOTE: If you need to grate your own Parmesan, the easiest way I know is to run it through the shredding blade of your food processor and then swap that out for the S-blade and pulse until it's finely grated.

PARMESAN CRISPS

These are becoming ubiquitous in grocery stores and even Costco. Still, they're fresher this way. Do use Parmesan with no additives, even if it means you have to grate your own. The cellulose in most packaged grated Parmesan doesn't work here.

Preheat the oven to 400°F (200°C, or gas mark 6). Line a baking sheet with parchment paper.

Put tablespoonfuls of Parmesan on the parchment, patting each little heap down a little and spacing them at least ½ inch (1.3cm) apart. Bake for 4 to 5 minutes.

These are also wonderful made in the microwave: coat a microwaveable plate or pie plate with cooking spray, arrange your little piles of Parmesan, and nuke on high for about 1 minute to 75 seconds, depending on the power of your microwave. It's a different texture, but I actually prefer it to the baked; it has the same great flavor.

---

1 slice of American cheese—the deluxe stuff

YIELD: 1 serving — Per serving: 424 calories; 35g fat (74.8% calories from fat); 25g protein; 2g carbohydrate; 0g dietary fiber; 2g net carbohydrate.

CHEESE CRACKERS

It's shocking how much like a cracker this is. Really, try it.

Coat a microwaveable plate with nonstick cooking spray and lay the cheese on it. Microwave for 1 minute to 75 seconds. Let it cool a minute or so, peel it off the plate, and eat. If you'd like more cracker-size portions, cut the cheese into quarters before you nuke it.

1 egg white

2 tablespoons (28ml) vanilla extract

¼ teaspoon liquid stevia, English toffee

1 dash of water–just a few drops

⅓ cup (64g) erythritol

2 tablespoons (16g) cocoa powder

1 teaspoon ground cinnamon

½ teaspoon cayenne

½ teaspoon salt

3 cups (300g) pecan halves

YIELD: 3 cups (300g), 14 servings — Per serving: 163 calories; 16g fat (82.4% calories from fat); 2g protein; 5g carbohydrate; 2g dietary fiber; 3g net carbohydrate.

COCOA-SPICE PECANS

Wow! Sweet, spicy, chocolaty, crunchy—what's not to love? Your serving here is a scant ¼ cup (28g), though, so no devouring them all at once.

Preheat the oven to 275°F (140°C, or gas mark 1). Line a jelly-roll pan or large, shallow roasting pan with parchment paper.

In a mixing bowl, whisk together the egg white, vanilla, liquid stevia, and water until frothy. In a small bowl, mix together the erythritol, cocoa, cinnamon, cayenne, and salt. Stir until evenly blended.

Dump your pecans into the egg white mixture and stir until they're all evenly coated.

Sprinkle about one-fourth of the cocoa-spice mixture over the pecans, and stir until it's evenly distributed. Repeat another three times until all the mixture is worked in and all the pecans are evenly coated.

Spread the pecans on the prepared baking pan. Bake for 30 minutes, stirring every 10 minutes. Cool and store in a snap-top container, preferably somewhere out of sight.

1 egg white

1 teaspoon water

¼ teaspoon liquid stevia, vanilla

3 cups (300g) pecan halves

¼ cup (48g) erythritol

½ teaspoon ground cinnamon

½ teaspoon salt

YIELD: 3 cups (300g), 12 servings — Per serving: 181 calories; 18g fat (84.7% calories from fat); 2g protein; 5g carbohydrate; 2g dietary fiber; 3g net carbohydrate.

CINNAMON-GLAZED PECANS

Mildly sweet, a little salty, nicely crispy—these are irresistible.
Take note: I made several batches of glazed pecans trying this idea out, and the friend who was helping (read: tasting) liked this mildly sweet version better than the sweeter Maple-Glazed Pecans (recipe follows).

Preheat the oven to 250°F (120°C, or gas mark ½). If you don't have a nonstick 9 × 13-inch (23 × 33cm) pan, line one with nonstick foil.

Put the egg white in a deep, narrow bowl with the water and liquid stevia. Whisk until frothy. Add the pecan halves and use a spoon to stir until they're all evenly coated with the egg white mixture.

In a small bowl, stir together the erythritol, cinnamon, and salt. Sprinkle this mixture, 1 tablespoon (12g) at a time, over the pecans, stirring each addition in well before adding the next.

Spread the pecans in your prepared pan and put them in the oven. Bake for 1 hour, stirring every 15 minutes.

Let cool before storing in an airtight container—for as long as you can keep them around!

1 egg white

1 teaspoon water

¼ teaspoon maple extract (I use Boyajian, purchased through Amazon.com.)

¼ teaspoon liquid stevia, English toffee

3 cups (300g) pecans

½ cup (96g) erythritol

½ teaspoon ground cinnamon

½ teaspoon salt

YIELD: 3 cups (330g), 12 servings — Per serving: 182 calories; 18g fat (84.7% calories from fat); 2g protein; 5g carbohydrate; 2g dietary fiber; 3g net carbohydrate.

3 cups (300g) walnuts

¼ cup (60ml) olive oil

2 tablespoons (3g) finely minced fresh rosemary

1 tablespoon (12g) erythritol

2 teaspoons salt

1 teaspoon pepper

YIELD: 12 servings — Per serving: 230 calories; 22g fat (81.2% calories from fat); 8g protein; 4g carbohydrate; 2g dietary fiber; 2g net carbohydrate.

2 cups (200g) walnuts

2 tablespoons (28ml) MCT oil or (28g) coconut oil

3 tablespoons (36g) erythritol

1 teaspoon salt

1 teaspoon ground cumin

½ teaspoon ground coriander

⅛ teaspoon cayenne

MAPLE-GLAZED PECANS

These are more heavily glazed, and therefore sweeter—of course—than the Cinnamon-Glazed Pecans. Pass a dish of these around after a company dinner and call it dessert.

Preheat the oven to 250°F (120°C, or gas mark ½).

In a deep bowl, whisk the egg white with the water, maple extract, and liquid stevia until frothy. Add the pecans and stir until they're evenly coated with the egg white mixture.

Stir together the erythritol, cinnamon, and salt. Sprinkle this mixture over the pecans, 1 tablespoon (12g) at a time, making sure each addition is evenly distributed before adding more.

When all the erythritol is worked in, spread the pecans in a 9 × 13-inch (23 × 33cm) baking pan. Bake for 1 hour, stirring every 15 minutes. Let cool and break up any clumps before storing in an airtight container.

ROSEMARY WALNUTS

Serve these at your next party and watch your reputation as a host or hostess soar. Or, hide them in the back of the cupboard and eat them all yourself; it's up to you.

Preheat the oven to 350°F (180°C, or gas mark 4).

Spread the walnuts in a 9 × 13-inch (23 × 33cm) baking pan.

Combine the olive oil and rosemary in a small bowl. Let it sit for 10 minutes for the flavor to infuse the oil.

While that's happening, stir together the erythritol, salt, and pepper.

Pour the olive oil and rosemary over the walnuts and stir until they're all evenly coated. Stir in the erythritol mixture in three additions, sprinkling each over the nuts and stirring it in well before adding more. Spread the nuts evenly in the pan.

Roast for 20 minutes, stirring two or three times. Let cool and store in an airtight container.

SPICED WALNUTS

These are slightly sweet, slightly spicy, entirely enchanting. Feel free to up the cayenne if you like or leave it out altogether, though there is only a hint of heat here.

Preheat the oven to 250°F (120°C, or gas mark ½). If you like, line a 9 × 13-inch (23 × 33cm) baking pan with nonstick foil. (My pans are nonstick.)

Put the walnuts and the oil in the pan—if you're using coconut oil, melt it first by putting it in the pan and sliding it into the oven for a few minutes. Either way, stir until the walnuts are evenly coated with the oil.

SPICED WALNUTS *(continued)*

YIELD: 2 cups (240g), 8 servings — Per serving: 221 calories; 21g fat (80.5% calories from fat); 8g protein; 4g carbohydrate; 2g dietary fiber; 2g net carbohydrate.

Measure everything else into a small dish and stir together. Now, sprinkle this mixture over the walnuts, just a little at a time, stirring well between each addition.

When all the spice mixture is in and your nuts are evenly coated, spread them evenly in the pan and put them in to roast. Set the timer for 12 minutes.

When the timer beeps, pull your walnuts out, stirring and turning them over, and then spread them out again. Put them in for another 12 minutes. Do this twice more—the stirring and turning and spreading out—for a total of 48 minutes baking time. (This is not crucial, an extra minute or two is not a big deal.)

Let the nuts cool in the pan before transferring to an airtight container for storage.

WICKED WINGS

1½ cups (150g) grated Parmesan cheese–the cheap stuff in the green shaker

3 tablespoons (15g) dried parsley

1½ tablespoons (5g) dried oregano

1 tablespoon (7g) paprika

1 teaspoon salt (optional)

¾ teaspoon pepper

4 pounds (1.8kg) chicken wings, cut up

½ cup (112g) butter, melted, or more if needed

YIELD: 50 servings— Per serving: 72 calories; 6g fat (72.1% calories from fat); 5g protein; trace carbohydrate; trace dietary fiber; 0g net carbohydrate.

This is my most-pirated recipe—I've seen it all over the Internet. But then, I pirated it from my mom, and I think she got it from someone else long about 1965. So hey, pass on the love. I've increased the cheese mixture here because I've occasionally heard from people who ran out before they coated all their wings.

Preheat the oven to 350°F (180°C, or gas mark 4). Line a couple of roasting pans with foil. Do not skip the foil, or you'll be faced with a two-fisted job getting the pans clean.

In a large bowl, mix together the parmesan, parsley, oregano, paprika, salt (if using), and pepper.

Now, make an assembly line: Dip each wing piece in the melted butter, then the seasoned parmesan, and then lay it in the foil-lined pan.

Bake for an hour. Serve to clamorous applause. Kick yourself for not making a double batch.

SOY AND GARLIC WINGS

20 chicken wings

¼ cup (60ml) soy sauce

2 cloves of garlic, crushed

1½ tablespoons (23g) Virtue or Natural Mate sweetener

1 teaspoon sriracha (optional)

YIELD: 20 servings — Per serving: 56 calories; 4g fat (59.3% calories from fat); 5g protein; trace carbohydrate; trace dietary fiber; 0g net carbohydrate.

Sticky and tasty, these wings will liven up any gathering or just please the family on movie night. Don't forget the napkins!

Preheat the oven to 350°F (180°C, or gas mark 4).

Arrange your wings in a nonreactive baking pan—Pyrex is good, so is the new ceramic nonstick, which is what I used.

Mix together the soy sauce, garlic, Virtue, and sriracha (if using). Pour over the wings and turn them over so that they're all coated on both sides. Put 'em in the oven and set the timer for 15 minutes.

When the timer beeps, use tongs to turn the wings over, dipping them in the sauce as you go. Bake for another 15 minutes and repeat until your wings are cooked through—mine were done in 45 minutes, but they were pretty small. If you've got big, meaty wings, they may take an extra 15 minutes.

1½ pounds (680g) chicken wings, cut up

2 tablespoons (28ml) extra-virgin olive oil

1 teaspoon granulated garlic

2 teaspoons salt or Vege-Sal

2 teaspoons Italian seasoning

¼ cup (60ml) balsamic vinegar, divided

⅔ cup (160ml) Caesar Dressing (page 101)

YIELD: 6 servings — Per serving: 236 calories; 22g fat (83.9% calories from fat); 6g protein; 3g carbohydrate; trace dietary fiber; 3g net carbohydrate.

BALSAMIC-GLAZED WINGS WITH CAESAR DRESSING

A little sweet, a little tangy, these wings are simple and good. The Caesar dressing is just the right foil.

Preheat the oven to 350°F (180°C, or gas mark 4).

Put the wings in a mixing bowl. Pour in the olive oil and toss until they're evenly coated.

In a small dish, mix together the granulated garlic, salt, and Italian seasoning. Sprinkle over the wings, a teaspoon at a time, tossing after each addition, until the wings are evenly seasoned.

Arrange the wings in a roasting pan. Roast for 30 minutes or until crunchy, basting once or twice with the fat in the pan.

Baste the wings with the balsamic vinegar—the first basting will use up about half of it. Roast for another 10 minutes and then baste with the rest of the balsamic vinegar. Give them another 5 to 10 minutes. Serve with Caesar Dressing for dipping.

4 pounds (1.8kg) chicken wings, cut up (sometimes labeled "party wings")

½ cup (112g) butter

½ cup (120ml) hot sauce, such as Frank's, Louisiana, or Tabasco

YIELD: 28 servings— Per serving: 107 calories; 9g fat (75% calories from fat); 6g protein; trace carbohydrate; trace dietary fiber; 0g net carbohydrate.

BUFFALO WINGS

Restaurant Buffalo wings are commonly floured, or even breaded, before being fried in dubious oil. It is so unnecessary! Once you realize how easy these are, you'll make them all the time. You can doctor this up if you want to—add a little cayenne if you like breathing fire or a crushed clove of garlic if you're crazy about it. But the original hot-sauce-and-butter combo is deservedly adored. Don't forget the blue cheese dressing and celery.

Depending on the season, you can grill your wings or you can roast them at 375°F (190°C, or gas mark 5) for about 45 minutes; either way, get them good and crisp.

Meanwhile, melt the butter and stir in the hot sauce.

When the wings are crisp and done, put them in a big mixing bowl. Pour on the sauce, and use tongs to toss until they're all coated. That's it. Set them out with a stack of napkins and plates for the bones.

3 pounds (1.4kg) chicken wings, cut up

¼ cup (60g) chili-garlic sauce or sriracha

¼ cup (60g) no-sugar-added ketchup

3 tablespoons (45g) tahini

1 teaspoon rice vinegar

1 teaspoon soy sauce

1 clove of garlic, crushed

1 teaspoon grated fresh ginger

1 teaspoon dark sesame oil

YIELD: 6 servings — Per serving: 101 calories; 11g fat (64.3% calories from fat); 14g protein; 4g carbohydrate; 1g dietary fiber; 3g net carbohydrate.

HOT AND CREAMY WINGS

The combination of chili-garlic sauce, no-sugar-added ketchup, and tahini makes this sauce hot, a little sweet, and creamy. You'll need lots of napkins. Better yet, put a roll of paper towels on the table!

Preheat the oven to 350°F (180°C, or gas mark 4).

Arrange your wings on a couple of broiler racks or on racks in roasting pans. Roast them until crisp, a good 50 minutes.

In the meanwhile, simply put everything else through your food processor or blender. Dump the mixture into a big mixing bowl.

When the wings are done, use tongs to transfer them to the bowl of sauce and toss them until coated. That's it!

Chicken skin–however much you've got

Salt or other seasonings

CHICKEN CHIPS

This is a ringer, brought in from *500 Low-Carb Recipes*. I invented it because of all my recipes that called for skinning the chicken before cooking. It's hugely popular; every time I mention Chicken Chips online, people demand the recipe. Despite all the hand wringing over fat, skin is very nutritious stuff, full of gelatin. I buy extra chicken skin to make these with! If you have a local specialty butcher or poultry processor, ask them if they can save chicken skin for you. I buy 10 pounds (4.6kg) at a time and freeze it in baggies, each with just enough for a batch.

Preheat the oven to 350°F (180°C, or gas mark 4).

While that's happening, spread your chicken skin flat on a broiler rack. Include any lumps of fat you might have pulled off the chicken, too. Now, bake for 15 minutes or so, until it's brown and crunchy. Sprinkle it with the seasoning of your choice or just eat them plain.

I have not been able to find nutrition stats for plain chicken skin, but here's the important part: It's zero carbs. You can save the fat that renders off the skin for cooking, too.

2 cloves of garlic

2 scallions, trimmed and cut in a few shorter sections

½ teaspoon Old Bay Seasoning

8 ounces (225g) cream cheese, softened

¼ cup (60g) mayonnaise

1 teaspoon lemon juice

1 teaspoon Worcestershire sauce

6 ounces (170g) crab (Canned is fine.)

Salt to taste

YIELD: 6 servings — Per serving: 226 calories; 21g fat (82.5% calories from fat); 8g protein; 2g carbohydrate; trace dietary fiber; 2g net carbohydrate.

CRAB DIP

Do not, for the love of all that is nutritious, use fake crab in this dip. The stuff almost always has added carbs, often quite a lot of added carbs. If you can't afford crab, you could try tuna or just make a different recipe.

With the S-blade in place in your food processor, add the garlic, scallions, and Old Bay. Pulse until the garlic and scallions are chopped medium fine.

Add the cream cheese, mayonnaise, lemon juice, and Worcestershire and process, scraping down the sides once or twice, until it's evenly blended. Dump in the crab and pulse just enough to mix it in—you want there to still be recognizable bits of crab in the mixture. Add a pinch or two of salt if you think it needs it.

Serve this with celery, cucumbers, and/or green peppers for dipping or use it as an extremely luxurious omelet filling. Hey, you could even stuff mushrooms with it!

5 ounces (140g) canned tuna in olive oil

4 ounces (115g) cream cheese, softened

3 tablespoons (42g) mayonnaise

2 tablespoons (28ml) Cognac

2 hard-boiled eggs, peeled and chunked

3 tablespoons (23g) shelled pistachios

¼ teaspoon pepper

YIELD: 5 servings — Per serving: 267 calories; 22g fat (75.7% calories from fat); 14g protein; 2g carbohydrate; 1g dietary fiber; 1g net carbohydrate.

UPSCALE TUNA DIP

It's the Cognac and pistachios that lift this above the ordinary. If you can't or don't want to use Cognac, there is brandy flavoring available, but not having used it, I can't swear it will work here. But it's worth trying, I'd think.

Put the tuna in your food processor, undrained. Add the cream cheese, mayonnaise, and Cognac. Process until smooth. Add the eggs, pistachios, and pepper and pulse to chop, but leave recognizable bits for texture.

Serve with celery sticks, pepper strips, and cucumber rounds for dipping.

12 ounces (340g) cream cheese, at room temperature

1 tablespoon (6g) Italian seasoning

3 cloves of garlic

⅔ cup (168g) pizza sauce

1 cup (115g) shredded mozzarella cheese

½ cup (40g) shredded Parmesan cheese

2 tablespoons (28ml) olive oil

PIZZA DIP

Holy cow. Just . . . wow. This is amazing. But do be careful about your pizza sauce—most have added sugar. I like Pastorelli's best, if you can get it. Read the labels!

Preheat the oven to 350°F (180°C, or gas mark 4). Coat an 8 × 8-inch (20 × 20cm) baking pan with cooking spray.

With the S-blade in place in your food processor, add the cream cheese, Italian seasoning, and garlic. Process until the garlic is fully pulverized, about 3 minutes.

Spread the cream cheese mixture evenly in the prepared pan. Spread the pizza sauce over that, then the mozzarella, and finally the Parmesan. Drizzle the olive oil over the whole thing, as evenly as possible.

Bake for 25 to 30 minutes. Serve hot with Pepperoni Chips (page 48).

YIELD: 6 servings — Per serving: 348 calories; 32g fat (80.5% calories from fat); 11g protein; 6g carbohydrate; trace dietary fiber; 6g net carbohydrate.

BEAN DIP

I know many of you no longer eat soy. But I specifically had requests for dairy-free dips in this book, and bean dip is popular stuff. Do use black soybeans; they're lower carb than the white ones. My local grocery stores carry them, but if yours don't, try the health food store or, of course, online. Warmed through and topped with melted cheese, this would make a great side dish.

13 ounces (365g) canned black soybeans

2 cloves of garlic

1 chipotle chile canned in adobo, plus 2 tablespoons (28ml) of the sauce

2 tablespoons (28ml) lime juice

¼ cup (60ml) melted bacon grease

½ teaspoon salt

3 tablespoons (3g) minced cilantro (optional)

Lightly drain the soybeans and put them in your food processor. Add the garlic, chipotle and sauce, lime juice, bacon grease, and salt and process until everything is ground to a smooth paste, scraping down the sides of the processor as needed.

Add the minced cilantro, if using, and pulse to mix it in. Done! Serve with veggies and pork rinds and tortilla chips for the carbivores.

YIELD: 1 cup (225g), 5 servings — Per serving: 167 calories; 14g fat (72.1% calories from fat); 7g protein; 6g carbohydrate; 4g dietary fiber; 2g net carbohydrate.

RICOTTA HERB DIP

Our tester, Tere, suggests you try mixing this with shredded chicken to make chicken salad. Sounds good to me!

15 ounces (425g) full-fat ricotta cheese

¼ cup (10g) fresh basil

2 tablespoons (28ml) white balsamic vinegar

2 tablespoons (8g) fresh oregano

2 scallions, roots and any limp greens trimmed, and cut into a few chunks

¾ teaspoon salt

1 teaspoon pepper

2 tablespoons (28ml) olive oil

½ cup (68g) pine nuts

¾ cup (60g) shredded Parmesan cheese

Put everything but the shredded Parmesan and pine nuts in your food processor with the S-blade in place. Pulse until the herbs and scallions are finely chopped.

Stir the pine nuts in a dry skillet over medium-low heat until they're golden. Add to the dip and pulse just one or two times to coarsely chop the pine nuts while mixing them in. Don't overprocess!

Turn the dip out into a bowl and stir in the Parmesan.

Serve with celery sticks, cucumber slices, and green pepper strips for dipping. If you have carbivores around, pita chips would be good with this.

YIELD: 2½ cups (560g), 10 servings — Per serving: 164 calories; 13g fat (71.6% calories from fat); 9g protein; 3g carbohydrate; 1g dietary fiber; 2g net carbohydrate.

NOTE: A little of this spread on sliced deli turkey and rolled up would be good, too.

TUNA TAPANADE

6 ounces (170g) canned tuna in olive oil, lightly drained

¼ cup (25g) pitted black olives

¼ cup (25g) pitted green olives

2 anchovy fillets

2 tablespoons (17g) capers, drained and rinsed

1 tablespoon (15ml) lemon juice

1 teaspoon Dijon mustard

½ teaspoon dried basil

1 pinch of pepper

1 clove of garlic, chopped

2 tablespoons (28ml) olive oil

2 tablespoons (28g) mayonnaise

2 tablespoons (20g) diced red onion

Serve this as a dip with vegetables or stuff into celery or cherry tomatoes for a killer hors d'oeuvre. It also makes an awesome omelet filling, especially with some feta thrown in.

Just add everything to your food processor and pulse until the olives are chopped, but not puréed—you want a slightly rough texture.

YIELD: 6 servings — Per serving: 149 calories; 12g fat (72.3% calories from fat); 9g protein; 2g carbohydrate; 1g dietary fiber; 1g net carbohydrate.

CHILE EGG ROLL-UPS

3 scallions

2 teaspoons minced hot red pepper, about 1 small red chile, such as a Thai bird pepper, or to taste

½ of a clove of garlic

3 eggs

5 tablespoons (75ml) soy sauce, divided

2 tablespoons (2g) minced cilantro (optional)

1 drop of liquid stevia, plain

¼ teaspoon salt

¼ teaspoon pepper

1½ tablespoons (23ml) MCT oil

¼ cup (60ml) soy sauce

2 teaspoons lime juice

¼ teaspoon sriracha (optional)

This turns scrambled eggs into an appetizer—one that isn't deviled eggs. It still has its share of heat, though. Feel free to reduce the pepper if you like or even cheat with sriracha.

Remove just the root and any limp greens from the scallions and cut them into a few chunks each. Put them in your food processor with the S-blade in place. Remove and discard the seeds and ribs from the pepper, mince to measure, and put that in, too. Immediately wash your hands thoroughly with soap and water! Then crush in the garlic.

Run the food processor until the scallions and pepper are finely chopped. Now, add the eggs, 1 tablespoon (15ml) of the soy sauce, cilantro (if using), liquid stevia, salt, and pepper. Run just 20 seconds or so to mix everything up.

Put a large nonstick skillet—or a large skillet coated with nonstick cooking spray —over medium-high heat. Add the MCT oil and swirl it to coat the bottom of the pan. When the pan is good and hot, pour in the egg mixture. Again, swirl the pan and lift up the sides as they cook to let the raw egg flow under, as you would for an omelet. Turn the heat down to low, cover the pan, and give it 1 to 2 minutes.

When the eggs are just done and the bottom is turning golden, slide the eggs out onto a plate—flat, like a pancake. Let the eggs cool for a few minutes.

YIELD: 2 servings — Per serving: 224 calories; 17g fat (67.2% calories from fat); 11g protein; 7g carbohydrate; 1g dietary fiber; 6g net carbohydrate.

CHILE EGG ROLL-UPS *(continued)*

Meanwhile, make your dipping sauce by mixing together the remaining 4 tablespoons (60ml) of soy sauce, lime juice, and sriracha (if using).

When the eggs are cool enough to handle, roll them up jelly-roll fashion. Slice into ½-inch (1.3cm) lengths—on the diagonal is prettier than straight across—and serve with the dipping sauce. Eat with your fingers!

MID-CENTURY MUSHROOMS

This recipe started with an old cookbook I inherited from my mom— one of the spiral-bound kind, compiled and sold as a fundraiser. There was a dip recipe I found fascinating, but I didn't want to "serve hot with crackers." Then it hit me: mushrooms! Do buy average-sized mushrooms. I chose boxes with big ones, only to discover that on the really big mushrooms some of the filling "slumped" and wound up on the bottom of the pan, while all of the average-sized mushrooms looked like a picture in a magazine. They all tasted fantastic.

Preheat the oven to 350°F (180°C, or gas mark 4).

First, put the pecans in your food processor with the S-blade in place. Pulse to chop them medium fine. Transfer them to a bowl and put the processor bowl and S-blade back on the processor base.

Open your jar of beef slices. They will come out in a roll. Do not bother to separate them. Just lay the roll of beef on your cutting board and slice across it at ½-inch (1.3cm) intervals. Then, slice the other way, making ½-inch (1.3cm) bits. Put 'em in your food processor. Add the onion and pepper. Crush in your garlic clove, too. Pulse until everything is finely chopped. Cut your cream cheese into 5 or 6 smaller chunks and put them in the food processor along with the sour cream. Run until everything is evenly blended.

Now for the mushrooms: remove the stems and the little "skirt" over the gills, leaving a nice big surface for stuffing. Save the stems for an omelet or to top a hamburger!

Put the melted butter in a 9 × 11-inch (23 × 28cm) roasting pan. Grab your processor bowl full of yummy stuffing and your bowl of chopped pecans. Stuff each mushroom with the chipped beef–cream cheese mixture, using a spoon to pack it in and round the top. As each is filled, turn it over and dip the top in the pecans. I had no trouble with filling dropping out, but if the first one does, pack the next one more firmly. As each mushroom is filled and topped with pecans, arrange in the pan, rolling the bottom slightly in the melted butter.

Bake for 20 minutes and serve hot.

¾ cup (75g) pecans

4 ounces (115g) dried beef slices (aka chipped beef; you can buy it in 4-ounce [115g] jars)

¼ of a small onion, cut into chunks

¼ of a green pepper, cut into chunks

1 clove of garlic

12 ounces (340g) cream cheese, at room temperature

2 tablespoons (30g) sour cream

1 pound (455g) mushrooms (average size; don't buy the super-huge ones)

3 tablespoons (45ml) melted butter

YIELD: 20 servings —
Per serving: 121 calories; 11g fat (79.4% calories from fat); 4g protein; 3g carbohydrate; 1g dietary fiber; 2g net carbohydrate.

NOTE: It's embarrassing how long I can take to figure things out. I've been coming up with stuffed mushroom recipes for fifteen years now, and it was only with this recipe that it hit me: leftover stuffed mushrooms, chopped up, make a fantastic omelet filling.

2 pounds (910g) cremini mushrooms

¾ cup (165g) butter, divided

3 cloves of garlic

6½ ounces (185g) no-sugar-added canned clams (check the label), minced, juice reserved

¾ cup (60g) Pork Rind Crumbs (page 63)

⅓ cup (20g) minced parsley

¾ teaspoon salt or Vege-Sal

¼ teaspoon pepper

YIELD: About 30 servings
— Per serving: 60 calories; 5g fat (73.0% calories from fat); 3g protein; 2g carbohydrate; trace dietary fiber; 2g net carbohydrate.

CLAM-STUFFED MUSHROOMS

Recipe tester Virginia says, "This is a great idea for an impressive appetizer." She also recommends that if you have any mushrooms left over, you slice them up and sauté them in the drippings the next day for an omelet filling. Who could argue with that?

Preheat the oven to 350°F (180°C, or gas mark 4).

Remove the stems from the mushrooms and reserve. Use the tip of a spoon to scrape the "skirt" from over the gills of the mushrooms, widening the opening. Discard the bits you scrape out. Finely chop the mushroom stems.

Put a large, heavy skillet over medium heat. Melt ½ cup (112g) of the butter and sauté the garlic in it for a minute or two. Turn off the heat and roll the mushroom caps in the garlic butter, coating them, arranging them in a baking pan as you go.

Melt the remaining ¼ cup (55g) of butter in the skillet. Throw the chopped mushroom stems in the skillet and sauté for 4 to 5 minutes. Drain the juice from the clams into the skillet and stir the mushroom stems in the clam juice and garlic butter until softened.

When the liquid has evaporated from the skillet, stir in the clams, Pork Rind Crumbs, parsley, salt, and pepper, combining well. Stuff the mixture into the mushroom caps.

Bake for 20 minutes. Then, turn on the broiler and run the mushrooms under it for just 3 to 4 minutes to brown. Serve hot.

8 ounces (225g) mushrooms

¼ cup (55g) butter

1 large shallot, minced

½ cup (60g) chopped walnuts

½ cup (40g) Pork Rind Crumbs (page 63)

½ teaspoon thyme

¼ teaspoon pepper

Salt to taste

YIELD: About 12 servings
— Per serving: 89 calories; 8g fat (76.6% calories from fat); 4g protein; 2g carbohydrate; 1g dietary fiber; 1g net carbohydrate.

WALNUT-STUFFED MUSHROOMS

Our tester, Angele, says, "If these were at a party, I'd probably sit next to the tray. The filling tasted like it had meat in it, and it could easily pass itself off as a keto Thanksgiving stuffing." She also says that she had about ⅓ cup (80g) leftover stuffing, and wished she's had more mushrooms. I hesitated to rewrite the recipe because I didn't want to make you buy another box of mushrooms and only use a few of them. But you can feel free to do so if you like. Just plan on another mushroom dish within a few days.

Preheat the oven to 350°F (180°C, or gas mark 4). Coat an 8 × 8-inch (20 × 20cm) baking dish with nonstick cooking spray.

Remove the stems from the mushrooms and set aside. Use the tip of a spoon to scrape away the little "skirt" over the gills, making a larger opening for the stuffing. Chop the mushrooms stems.

Put a large, heavy skillet over medium-high heat and melt the butter. Throw in the shallot first and let it sauté for 1 to 2 minutes. Add the walnuts and chopped mushroom stems and sauté for another 3 to 4 minutes.

Stir in the Pork Rind Crumbs, thyme, and pepper. Taste and see if you think it needs a little salt. Stuff the mixture into your mushroom caps and arrange them in the baking dish.

Bake for 20 minutes. Serve hot.

SEAFOOD-STUFFED MUSHROOMS

This is called "Seafood-Stuffed Mushrooms" rather than "Crab-Stuffed Mushrooms" because, as our recipe tester Julie pointed out, you can substitute 1 pound (455g) of lobster meat for the crab—I mean, should you be feeling particularly flush or really want to impress somebody.

½ cup (112g) butter, divided

1 tablespoon (8g) minced celery

1 tablespoon (10g) minced onion

1 tablespoon (9g) minced jalapeño

1 tablespoon (4g) minced parsley

½ teaspoon salt

2 dashes of pepper

½ cup (120ml) seafood stock (I used Kitchen Basics.)

6 drops of liquid stevia, plain

¾ cup (60g) Pork Rind Crumbs (page 63)

1 cup (142g) lump crabmeat

1 egg, beaten

1 pound (455g) mushrooms

8 ounces (225g) shredded Monterey Jack cheese

Paprika, for garnish

YIELD: 24 servings —
Per serving: 82 calories;
7g fat (75.9% calories from fat);
4g protein; 1g carbohydrate; trace
dietary fiber; 1g net carbohydrate.

NOTE: Do not use fake seafood! It almost always has added carbs, often a lot of added carbs.

Preheat the oven to 375°F (190°C, or gas mark 5).

In a large saucepan over medium-low heat, melt 4 tablespoons (55g) of the butter. Add the celery, onion, jalapeño, and parsley. (Don't forget to wash your hands well after handling that jalapeño!) Sauté for 2 to 3 minutes. Stir in the salt and pepper. Add the seafood stock and liquid stevia and bring to a simmer. Decrease the heat to low and let it simmer gently for 5 minutes. Stir in the Pork Rind Crumbs and remove from the heat.

Mix the crabmeat with the egg, flaking up the crab as you stir. Then, stir the crab-egg mixture into the pork rind mixture.

Remove the stems from the mushrooms, saving them to sauté to top a steak or fill an omelet.

Melt the remaining 4 tablespoons (55g) of butter and brush the mushroom caps with it. Stuff each with 2 to 3 teaspoons (10 to 15g) of the crab mixture. Top each with a big pinch of shredded cheese and a light dusting of paprika.

Bake for 15 minutes or until the cheese is touched with gold. Serve hot.

1½ pounds (680g) mushrooms, wiped clean

2 tablespoons (28g) butter

½ of a large or 1 small onion, chopped

4 cloves of garlic, crushed

10 ounces (280g) frozen chopped spinach, thawed

4 ounces (115g) cream cheese

¼ teaspoon pepper

½ teaspoon salt or Vege-Sal

1½ teaspoons Worcestershire sauce

¼ cup (25g) grated Parmesan cheese

YIELD: 40 servings
— Per serving: 24 calories; 2g fat (62.7% calories from fat); 1g protein; 1g carbohydrate; trace dietary fiber; 1g net carbohydrate.

SPINACH-STUFFED MUSHROOMS

This is a classic crowd-pleaser. I've never brought a single one home from a party.

Preheat the oven to 350°F (180°C, or gas mark 4).

Wipe the mushrooms clean and remove the stems. Set the caps aside and chop the stems fairly fine.

In a large, heavy skillet over medium-low heat, melt the butter. Add the chopped stems and the onion. Sauté until the mushroom bits are changing color and the onion is soft and translucent. Add the garlic, stir it up, and sauté for another couple of minutes.

While that's happening, dump your thawed spinach into a strainer and press all the water out of it that you can. Now, stir it into the mushroom-onion mixture. Next, stir in the cream cheese. When it's melted, add the pepper, salt, and Worcestershire.

Stuff the spinach mixture into the mushroom caps. Arrange the stuffed caps in a baking pan as you go. When they're all stuffed, sprinkle the Parmesan cheese over them, doing your best to distribute it evenly.

Bake for 20 minutes. Serve warm.

1 pound (455g) mushrooms

12 ounces (340g) canned tuna in olive oil, lightly drained

1 cup (120g) shredded smoked Gouda cheese

4 tablespoons (25g) grated Parmesan cheese

6 tablespoons (84g) mayonnaise

2 scallions, finely minced

Paprika, for garnish

YIELD: 30 servings
— Per serving: 63 calories; 5g fat (64.7% calories from fat); 5g protein; 1g carbohydrate; trace dietary fiber; 1g net carbohydrate.

TWO-CHEESE TUNA-STUFFED MUSHROOMS

These may be my favorite stuffed mushrooms ever. But then, I have always loved canned tuna. It's such an odd thing to be passionate about, isn't it? Do pop for the good stuff in olive oil. When you're eating a high-fat diet, the quality of the fat matters.

Preheat the oven to 350°F (180°C, or gas mark 4). Coat an 11 × 13-inch (28 × 33cm) roasting pan with cooking spray.

Remove the stems from your mushrooms, reserving them to sauté for steak or omelets. Use the tip of a spoon to scrape the "skirt" from over the gills, leaving more space for filling.

In a bowl, combine the tuna, Gouda, Parmesan, mayonnaise, and scallion, mixing well. Stuff the mixture into the mushrooms, arranging them in the pan as you go. Sprinkle lightly with paprika.

Bake for 25 to 30 minutes. Serve hot.

½ cup (50g) walnuts

4 ounces (115g) cream cheese, softened

¼ cup (60g) sour cream

¼ cup (30g) blue cheese, divided

12 celery ribs (Use the tender center ribs.)

YIELD: 6 servings — Per serving: 179 calories; 16g fat (76.4% calories from fat); 6g protein; 5g carbohydrate; 2g dietary fiber; 3g net carbohydrate.

BLUE CHEESE–WALNUT CELERY STICKS

I'd go with a mild blue cheese for this, like Gorgonzola or Dana Blue, rather than something really strong, like Stilton. My tester Rebecca offers the useful advice that if you buy your walnuts chopped, you can skip the food processor and mix the filling in a bowl.

Preheat the oven on to 350°F (180°C, or gas mark 4). Spread your walnuts in a shallow baking dish. Put in the oven and set the timer for 7 minutes. You just want them to smell toasty.

With the S-blade in place in your food processor, add the cream cheese and sour cream and process until they're well combined. Add half of the blue cheese and pulse a couple of times.

By now, the walnuts are smelling toasty. Put them in the food processor and pulse until they're chopped to a medium consistency. Add the rest of the blue cheese and pulse just once or twice—you want to maintain chunks of blue cheese and walnut.

Stuff the mixture into the celery—cutting the ribs into whatever lengths you find appealing—and they're done.

6 hard-boiled eggs

5 or 6 saffron threads

1 teaspoon hot water

⅓ cup (75g) mayonnaise

2 ounces (55g) chèvre cheese

1 tablespoon (15g) harissa

½ teaspoon salt

¼ teaspoon cayenne

1 tablespoon (1g) minced cilantro

YIELD: 12 servings — Per serving: 90 calories; 8g fat (81.5% calories from fat); 4g protein; 1g carbohydrate; trace dietary fiber; 1g net carbohydrate.

EGGS IN TUNISIA

Harissa is a Tunisian spice mix using hot peppers and herbs. Locally, I can buy it both in powder and paste form—I used powder in this recipe. Mine was from an organic spice company called Frontier and not terribly hot, hence the cayenne. You'll want to taste your yolk mixture after you've added the harissa and salt before you decide whether you want cayenne.

Halve your eggs, turning the yolks out into a mixing bowl and arranging the whites on a platter.

Put the saffron threads in a small bowl or cup, stir them with the hot water, and leave them to sit for a few minutes.

Use a fork to mash your yolks as finely as you can. Add the steeped saffron, mayonnaise, chèvre, harissa, and salt and stir with a spoon, using the back of it to smash any lumps of yolk against the side of the bowl.

Now taste: Is the degree of heat to your liking? If not, add the cayenne. Heck, add more cayenne if you want to, who am I to judge? Stir in the cilantro and then stuff the yolk mixture into the whites.

12 hard-boiled eggs

3 tablespoons (42g) mayonnaise

1 tablespoon (15g) sour cream

1 tablespoon (4g) minced parsley, plus more for garnish (optional)

1 tablespoon (4g) minced fresh tarragon, plus more for garnish (optional)

1 scallion, including the crisp part of the green, cut into 1-inch (2.5cm) lengths

1 tablespoon (15ml) lemon juice

2 teaspoons Dijon mustard

1 anchovy fillet

1 clove of garlic, crushed

1 avocado, good and ripe

Salt and pepper to taste

YIELD: 24 servings —
Per serving: 67 calories; 6g fat (73.3% calories from fat); 3g protein; 1g carbohydrate; trace dietary fiber; 1g net carbohydrate.

GODDESS EGGS!

Care to hatch out a goddess or two? No, no, they're eggs based on Green Goddess Dressing. And you make a full dozen because otherwise you'd be left with half an avocado. Our tester Rebecca says that these are a little trouble to make because you need to have both a ripe avocado and fresh tarragon in the house at the same time. She adds, however, that her furnace guy was there when she had these in the house, and it turns out he's a serious foodie. She said he kept going on and on about these—"Said it was right up there with Oysters Rockefeller for the pizzazz coming out of nowhere." So, it's worth acquiring an avocado and some tarragon, especially if you're having a party.

Peel your eggs and halve them, turning the yolks out into a mixing bowl and arranging the whites on a platter.

With the S-blade in place in your food processor, add the mayonnaise, sour cream, parsley, tarragon, scallion, lemon juice, Dijon mustard, anchovy, and garlic. Process until the anchovy vanishes and the herbs are finely chopped.

Halve the avocado, remove the pit, and spoon half of the flesh into the food processor. Process again until it's blended in and the mixture is creamy.

Turning to those yolks, grab a fork and mash them quite well. Now, add the mixture from the food processor and continue mixing and mashing until it's all creamy and well blended. Spoon in the rest of the avocado in smallish spoonfuls. Mash and stir until it's blended in, but you still have some nice hunks of avocado.

Stuff your egg whites with this fantastic stuff! You'll really have to overstuff 'em because there will be plenty of yolk mixture. Pile it high.

Garnish with more herbs if you like and serve immediately.

---

6 hard-boiled eggs

3 tablespoons (42g) mayonnaise

2 tablespoons (30g) sriracha mustard

1 teaspoon fish sauce

2 teaspoons minced cilantro

YIELD: 12 servings —
Per serving: 66 calories; 6g fat (77.8% calories from fat); 3g protein; trace carbohydrate; trace dietary fiber; 0g net carbohydrate.

SRIRACHA MUSTARD EGGS

I love mustard and I love sriracha, so when I saw sriracha mustard at the grocery store, I had to have it. Once I had it, these eggs were simply a matter of time.

Halve the eggs, turning the yolks out into a mixing bowl and arranging the whites on a platter.

Using a fork, mash the yolks as fine as you can. Add the mayonnaise, sriracha mustard, and fish sauce and stir with a spoon, using the back of it to smash any chunks of yolk against the side of the bowl.

At this point, you can stir in the cilantro before stuffing the yolks into the whites —I did. Or, you can stuff the yolk mixture into the whites and then sprinkle the cilantro on top. It's your choice.

6 hard-boiled eggs

3 tablespoons (42g) mayonnaise

3 tablespoons (24g) green olive spread

1 teaspoon red wine vinegar

1 tablespoon (4g) minced parsley

¼ teaspoon salt or Vege-Sal

YIELD: 12 servings —
Per serving: 64 calories;
6g fat (77.9% calories from fat);
3g protein; 1g carbohydrate; trace
dietary fiber; 1g net carbohydrate.

¼ cup (25g) walnuts

6 hard-boiled eggs

2 ounces (55g) cooked ham, in a few small chunks

1 scallion, including the crisp green part, cut into a few pieces

¼ cup (60g) mayonnaise

1½ tablespoons (23g) Dijon mustard

2 teaspoons red wine vinegar

1 teaspoon hot sauce (Tabasco, Frank's, or Louisiana), or to taste

Salt and pepper to taste

2 tablespoons (8g) finely minced parsley (optional)

YIELD: 12 servings —
Per serving: 98 calories;
9g fat (76.8% calories from fat);
5g protein; 1g carbohydrate; trace
dietary fiber; 1g net carbohydrate.

GREEN OLIVE EGGS

If you're a stuffed egg fan, browse the condiments selection at your grocery and health food stores. You'll find all sorts of ideas! I found a lovely green olive spread—olives, olive oil, coriander, lemon juice, basil, and garlic—at my grocery store and used it to make these.

Halve your eggs, turning the yolks out into a mixing bowl and arranging the whites on a platter.

Use a fork to mash your yolks fine. Then, add the mayonnaise and stir with a spoon, using the back of it to smash lumps of yolk against the side of the bowl. When your yolks are getting smooth, stir in the green olive spread, red wine vinegar, parsley, and salt.

Stuff the yolk mixture into the whites.

HAM AND WALNUT STUFFED EGGS

I know, I know—no one ever gets tired of classic deviled eggs. But sometimes you want to take something a little different to the potluck, or you want a variety to choose from at your party. Or, as seems to happen to me at least once a year, you have an excess of both eggs and ham at the same time.

Preheat the oven to 350°F (180°C, or gas mark 4). Spread your walnuts on a shallow baking sheet and stick 'em in. Set a timer for 7 minutes—they're likely to be toasted before the oven is all the way up to temperature.

Peel your eggs. Halve them, turning the yolks out into a mixing bowl and arranging the whites on a platter. Do a preliminary mashing of the yolks with a fork.

When your walnuts smell toasty, put them in your food processor with the ham and scallion. Pulse until it's all ground medium-fine.

Add the mayonnaise, Dijon mustard, red wine vinegar, and hot sauce to the yolks and mash and stir until they're smooth and creamy.

Transfer the ham-and-walnut mixture from the food processor to the mixing bowl and work it into the yolks until it's all evenly blended. Season with salt and pepper to taste.

Stuff the yolk mixture into the whites. Because you've added ham and walnuts, you'll have enough to stuff them generously, so pile the filling high. If you want to make 'em look spiffy, sprinkle a little parsley on each one, but it's not essential. They'll vanish regardless.

6 slices (1 ounce, or 28g each) of deli ham

6 tablespoons (84g) mayonnaise

4 tablespoons (60g) brown mustard

6 tablespoons (43g) shredded Colby Jack cheese

2 dill pickle spears (or sugar-free bread-and-butter pickles)

YIELD: 6 servings — Per serving: 161 calories; 16g fat (81.4% calories from fat); 6g protein; 2g carbohydrate; trace dietary fiber; 2g net carbohydrate.

HAM ROLLS

Quick and easy to make, these are a terrific snack. The counts on this assume your ham runs 1 ounce (28g) per slice.

Lay a slice of ham on a cutting board or plate. Spread with mayonnaise, then mustard. Sprinkle the cheese evenly over that.

Slice each of your pickle spears lengthwise into 3 pieces. Lay one at the end of your now-bedecked ham slice and roll the ham and cheese up around the pickle. Repeat with the rest of your ingredients.

Store in a snap-top container, ready to pull out when hunger strikes.

NOTE: If you'd like to make these fancy enough for a party, simply slice each roll into 1-inch (2.5cm) lengths and lay the little pink-white-yellow-and-green pin-wheels on a lettuce-lined plate.

6 slices of salami

¼ cup (60g) sour cream

2 teaspoons pesto

Salt to taste

YIELD: 3 servings — Per serving: 173 calories; 15g fat (77.6% calories from fat); 8g protein; 2g carbohydrate; trace dietary fiber; 2g net carbohydrate.

SALAMI CHIPS WITH PESTO CREAM

I knew that pepperoni makes great chips, so why not salami? And why not their very own topping? It's quick, easy, and unusual.

Preheat the oven to 350°F (180°C, or gas mark 4). Line a cookie sheet with parchment paper.

Lay the slices of salami on the parchment. Bake for 10 to 12 minutes. It will not be quite crisp when it comes out—it will become crisper as it cools.

In the meanwhile, stir the sour cream and pesto together, adding salt to taste. Spread each salami chip with the pesto cream and serve.

6 ounces (170g) pepperoni slices

YIELD: 1 serving — Per serving: 845 calories; 75g fat (80.7% calories from fat); 36g protein; 5g carbohydrate; 0g dietary fiber; 5g net carbohydrate.

PEPPERONI CHIPS

I usually make pepperoni chips in the microwave—just lay 14 slices (1 ounce, or 28g) on a microwaveable plate and nuke for 60 to 75 seconds. But, you can do a whole lot more in your regular oven. So, if you're making them for the family or a party, do this.

Preheat the oven to 375°F (190°C, or gas mark 5). Line a baking sheet with parchment paper.

Lay the pepperoni slices on the parchment.

Bake for 10 minutes. Blot with paper toweling and then give them another 2 to 4 minutes until very crisp.

These are great served with whipped cream cheese, but for something really spectacular, use them to scoop the Pizza Dip (page 38).

MEATBALLS

3½ ounces (100g) pork rinds (There are bags just this size.)

2 teaspoons salt or Vege-Sal

1 teaspoon baking powder

¼ teaspoon pepper

¼ teaspoon allspice

2 cloves of garlic, crushed

2 eggs

½ cup (120ml) cream

2 pounds (910g) ground beef, divided

SAUCE

1 cup (240g) no-sugar-added ketchup

3 tablespoons (45ml) balsamic vinegar

4 teaspoons (20ml) Worcestershire sauce

½ of a shallot, minced

1 clove of garlic, crushed

¾ teaspoon liquid stevia, English toffee

¼ teaspoon pepper

¼ cup (48g) erythritol

¼ teaspoon molasses

YIELD: 80 servings —
Per serving: 49 calories;
4g fat (72.9% calories from fat);
3g protein; trace carbohydrate;
trace dietary fiber; 0g net
carbohydrate.

COCKTAIL MEATBALLS

The unusual preparation method makes for a fantastic texture to these meatballs, while the sauce lends a sweet-and-sour snap. A slow cooker full of these will please a party crowd. This is a huge batch! If you'd like to halve it, use ¾ cup (60g) pork rind crumbs.

Preheat the oven to 350°F (180°C, or gas mark 4). Coat 2 broiler racks with nonstick cooking spray.

To make the meatballs, with the S-blade in place in your food processor, dump the pork rinds in and process until they're crumbs. Add the salt, baking powder, pepper, and allspice and pulse to mix them in. With the motor running, add the garlic, then the eggs, and then the cream. You will quickly have a gloppy mess. Do not panic.

Set aside half of the ground beef. With the remaining beef, take the lid off the processor and add about one-third of it. Put the lid back on and process to work it in. Repeat twice, with the remaining two-thirds of beef. The mixture in the food processor will now be quite thick and sticky. Spoon/scrape it into a mixing bowl.

Wash your hands and then run them under cold water—this minimizes the meat sticking to your hands. Add the ground beef you set aside, and use your hands to smoosh it quite thoroughly into the processed mixture.

Despite the cold water, your hands will be a gloppy mess. Wash them. Now grab your prepared broiler racks and a bowl of cold water—this is for dunking your hands in.

Form the meat mixture into 1-inch (2.5cm) balls, dunking your hands in the water after every 2 or 3 meatballs. Arrange them on the broiler racks as you go.

Bake for 20 minutes.

To make the sauce, combine all the sauce ingredients in a nonreactive saucepan (stainless steel or ceramic nonstick are good). Bring to a simmer and cook for 10 minutes. Pour over the meatballs to serve. I put 'em in my slow cooker to keep them warm, but a chafing dish will do fine, too.

2 pounds (910g) ground turkey

½ of a medium onion

1 clove of garlic

1½ ounces (42g) pork rinds

¼ cup (28g) bacon bits

2 chipotle chiles canned in adobo plus 1 tablespoon (15ml) sauce

8 ounces (225g) finely shredded Mexican 4-cheese blend

2 eggs

1 teaspoon ground dried rosemary

1 teaspoon salt

½ teaspoon pepper

YIELD: Makes about 40 meatballs – Per serving: 49 calories; 3g fat (52.1% calories from fat); 5g protein; trace carbohydrate; trace dietary fiber; 0g net carbohydrate.

ALBONDIGAS DE GUATELOTE, QUESO, TOCINO, Y CHIPOTLE

That's "Turkey, Cheese, Bacon, and Chipotle Meatballs," for those of you who didn't take Spanish. And boy, are they tasty. You can serve these as is—they stand on their own—or dip them in queso or Crema Caliente (page 253) for extra fat.

Preheat the oven to 350°F (180°C, or gas mark 4). Coat your broiler rack with nonstick cooking spray.

Put your ground turkey in a big mixing bowl.

Cut your onion into a few chunks and throw it into the food processor along with the garlic. Pulse until they're finely chopped. Now, add the pork rinds, bacon bits, and chipotles to the processor and run until the pork rinds have been ground into crumbs. Add this mixture to the turkey, using a rubber scraper to get all of it out.

Add the adobo sauce, cheese, eggs, rosemary, salt, and pepper. Use clean hands to smoosh it all together very thoroughly, turning everything over several times to make sure there are no pockets of cheese that haven't been worked in.

Form into balls about 1½ inches (3.8cm) in diameter and arrange on the broiler rack.

Bake for 25 minutes or until cooked through.

4 ounces (115g) cream cheese, softened

2 scallions

1 tablespoon (4g) minced fresh dill

1 tablespoon (4g) minced fresh parsley

1 teaspoon prepared horseradish

8 ounces (225g) smoked salmon, any bones removed

¼ cup (60ml) heavy cream

¼ teaspoon hot sauce (Tabasco, Frank's, or Louisiana)

Salt and pepper to taste

YIELD: 6 servings – Per serving: 147 calories; 12g fat (72.9% calories from fat); 9g protein; 1g carbohydrate; trace dietary fiber; 1g net carbohydrate.

SMOKED SALMON MOUSSE

This can be served as a dip, as suggested—that's obviously the easiest route. But if you're feeling fancy, spoon the mousse into a pastry bag with a star tip and pipe it prettily onto the cucumber rounds and into the celery sticks. Me, I'd probably only do that for a pretty special occasion.

This could not be easier! Simply put everything but the salt and pepper in your food processor and process until it's smooth and creamy. Add salt and pepper to taste and process again for just a moment or two to mix it in. Scoop it into a pretty bowl and chill for a few hours to let the flavors blend.

Serve with celery and cucumbers for dipping.

8 ounces (225g) whipped cream cheese

2 tablespoons (30g) sour cream

2 scallions, finely minced

1 tablespoon (4g) minced parsley

2 ounces (55g) red caviar

12 ounces (340g) smoked salmon lox, thinly sliced

YIELD: 6 servings – Per serving: 228 calories; 18g fat (69.8% calories from fat); 15g protein; 3g carbohydrate; trace dietary fiber; 3g net carbohydrate.

12 ounces (340g) Jarred jalapeño peppers, sliced

¾ teaspoon liquid stevia, plain, or liquid monk fruit, or liquid sucralose to equal ¾ cup (150g) sugar in sweetness

Pork rinds

Whipped cream cheese

YIELD: Varies – Per serving: 92 calories; 3g fat (26.8% calories from fat); 3g protein; 16g carbohydrate; 9g dietary fiber; 7g net carbohydrate.

SMOKED SALMON ROLLS

I know you're not going to buy caviar every day, but this was just too impressive to pass up. If you're planning a get-together with people you really need to impress, look no further. Our tester, Rebecca, says that black caviar will serve as well and is less expensive than red caviar. She also says that leftovers, should you have any, are great chopped up and used as a spread or an omelet filling.

In a mixing bowl, work the cream cheese, sour cream, minced scallion, and parsley together until well blended. Gently fold in the caviar, trying not to break the eggs.

Spread the mixture on slices of salmon and then roll each up and cut into 1½-inch (3.8cm) lengths. Arrange the pretty pinwheels on a lettuce-lined plate and bear them forth, feeling smug.

HERBERT D. FOCKEN'S SWEETENED JALAPEÑO BITES, UPDATED

Herbert D. Focken sent in this idea for *500 More Low-Carb Recipes*, and I've been in love with it ever since. But I thought it time to create a version with today's more popular sweeteners.

This could not be simpler! Open your jar of jalapeños. Add the sweetener. Put the lid back on tightly and shake it up. Stick it in the fridge for a few days.

When snack time rolls around, grab your sweetened jalapeños, a bag of pork rinds, and a tub of whipped cream cheese. Spread cream cheese on a pork rind. Put a few slices of jalapeño on it. Stuff it in your face. Repeat.

NOTE: It was impossible to analyze per slice or per serving. The entire jar of jalapeños will have 16 grams of carbohydrate, 9 of those fiber, for a net carbohydrate count of 7 grams for the whole darned jar. Pork rinds are carb free, though a little high in protein and low in fat for our purposes. The whipped cream cheese has our needed fat. So make these. Eat these. They will make you happy.

CHAPTER 4

Baked Goods & Other Grain Substitutes

Hmm. I just got asked why I'd posted a picture on Facebook of toast made from one of the bread recipes in this chapter. The questioner likened it to vegetarians eating Tofurky. That's a fair point. But this is another: vegetarians do eat Tofurky. Not all the time and not for every meal, but for many, knowing they can have a holiday meal with a food that evokes the feasts of their childhood is a comforting thing.

I get requests for bread recipes. People want them, along with waffles, pancakes, and the like. I don't make low-carb baked goods often, though I enjoy them when I do. But as I have long asserted, I don't write recipes for me, I write them for you. I have enjoyed all of these, and I very much hope you will enjoy them, too.

4 cups (384g) almond meal

2 cups (454g) plain whey protein powder

½ cup (56g) flaxseed meal

5 tablespoons (70g) baking powder

1 tablespoon (20g) salt

½ cup (112g) refined coconut oil

YIELD: 7 cups (1,575g), 28 servings – Per serving: 108 calories; 10g fat (42.8% calories from fat); 21g protein; 9g carbohydrate; 2g dietary fiber; 7g net carbohydrate.

2 cups (450g) Bake Mix (above)

½ cup (120ml) pourable unsweetened coconut milk

YIELD: 12 servings – Per serving: 132 calories; 7g fat (43.5% calories from fat); 14g protein; 6g carbohydrate; 1g dietary fiber; 5g net carbohydrate.

2 cups (460g) Bake Mix (above)

1⅓ cups (315ml) pourable unsweetened coconut milk

1 egg

YIELD: 12 waffles – Per serving: 143 calories; 8g fat (45% calories from fat); 15g protein; 6g carbohydrate; 1g dietary fiber; 5g net carbohydrate.

BAKE MIX

Okay, this is too low fat to be ketogenic on its own. But you know what you're going to do with pancakes, waffles, and biscuits, don't you? You're going to slather them with butter, that's what! Refrigerate this if you don't think you'll use it up fairly quickly. The nut meal can go rancid, though the coconut oil shouldn't.

Put all the dry ingredients in your food processor and pulse until everything is evenly distributed. Add the coconut oil. Pulse until it's cut in; you'll want to scrape down the sides of the processor a couple of times.

Store in a snap-top container in a cool place. Use like Bisquick.

BIFFINS

Aka biscuits made in a muffin tin—the dough from the bake mix was too soft to roll out and flattened when made into drop biscuits. But made in a muffin tin, they're glorious!

Preheat the oven to 425°F (220°C, or gas mark 7). Coat a muffin tin well with nonstick cooking spray. (My muffin tin is nonstick, and I still used spray.)

In a bowl, whisk the Bake Mix and coconut milk together. Divide the batter among the muffin cups—I used my cookie scoop, and it was just the perfect size, one scoop per biffin. My scoop holds 2 tablespoons (28g).

Bake for 8 minutes. Serve hot with plenty of butter. Or turn them into Biscuits and Gravy!

WAFFLES

These are so light and crisp! Serve with butter and cinnamon-erythritol, or with Maple Butter (page 251), or Coffee Butter (page 250). They're the perfect weekend breakfast.

Plug in your waffle iron first—you want it hot when your batter is ready.

Combine everything in a mixing bowl and whisk it up.

Bake according to the instructions that come with your waffle iron.

1½ cups (338g) Bake Mix
(page 53)

2 tablespoons (24g) Natural
Mate or Virtue sweetener

2 tablespoons (6g) instant
coffee crystals

¾ cup (173g) sour cream

½ cup (120ml) pourable
unsweetened coconut milk

2 tablespoons (31g) full-fat
ricotta cheese

5 tablespoons (75ml) melted
butter

¼ teaspoon liquid stevia,
English toffee

YIELD: 12 waffles – Per serving:
177 calories; 13g (64.1% calories
from fat); 11g protein;
5g carbohydrate; 1g dietary fiber;
4g net carbohydrate.

COFFEE WAFFLES

These are super-tasty, whether with Coffee Butter (page 250), Maple Butter (page 251), or whipped cream. Two tablespoons (6g) of instant coffee is the equivalent of 6 cups (1.4L) of coffee, so these do pack a punch. Feel free to use decaf instant if you prefer.

Plug in your waffle iron so it will be hot when you need it.

In a mixing bowl, preferably one with a pouring lip, combine the Bake Mix, Natural Mate, and instant coffee. Stir them together.

In a separate bowl, combine the sour cream, coconut milk, ricotta, butter, and stevia and whisk it all together.

Pour the wet ingredients into the dry ingredients and whisk just enough that you're sure you have no pockets of dry stuff left.

Bake according to the instructions that come with your waffle iron. My waffle iron makes average-sized rectangular waffles, and my count is based on that.

1½ cups (338g) Bake Mix
(page 53)

1 cup (235ml) pourable
unsweetened coconut milk

6 tablespoons (85g) butter

YIELD: 9 pancakes –
Per serving: 209 calories;
15g fat (62% calories from fat);
14g protein; 6g carbohydrate;
1g dietary fiber; 5g net
carbohydrate.

PANCAKES!

These pancakes remind me of the whole-grain cornmeal pancakes I ate back in my low-fat, high-carb days—yummy and filling! Make a batch over the weekend, and you can warm them up in your toaster oven on busy mornings. (You can warm them up in your microwave, but they won't be crisp around the edges.)

This is a straightforward procedure: Combine the Bake Mix and coconut milk in a mixing bowl, preferably one with a pouring lip, and whisk until the lumps are gone. Let the batter sit for 5 minutes, during which time it will thicken a bit.

While the batter is thickening, put your large, heavy skillet or a griddle over medium heat. You want it good and hot before you add the batter.

My biggest skillet will fit three 4-inch (10cm) pancakes. I melted 2 tablespoons (28g) of butter in the skillet and then poured in the batter. Fry 'em just like the pancakes you're used to.

As you can see, the fat count is still a little low on these, so serve them with more butter and perhaps a sprinkle of erythritol and cinnamon. Or serve with Maple Butter (page 251).

1 cup (250g) full-fat ricotta cheese

2 tablespoons (14g) coconut flour

1 tablespoon (7g) flaxseed meal

1 tablespoon (12g) erythritol

3/4 teaspoon baking powder

½ teaspoon salt

5 eggs

¼ teaspoon xanthan gum

12 drops of liquid stevia, English toffee

¼ cup (56g) coconut oil

YIELD: 16 servings –
Per serving: 89 calories;
7g fat (73% calories from fat);
4g protein; 2g carbohydrate;
1g dietary fiber; 1g net carbohydrate.

BIRTHDAY RICOTTA PANCAKES

Feel free to make these on your UnBirthday!

First, put a big skillet or griddle over medium heat; you want it ready when your batter is prepared.

Measure everything but the coconut oil into your blender and run until you have a smooth batter.

Drip a drop or two of water onto your skillet or griddle; when it skitters around, it's hot enough. Melt 1 tablespoon (14g) or so of the coconut oil on it, sloshing it around to coat the whole thing.

Now, pour the batter out of the blender, into roughly 3-inch (7.5cm) rounds; these are tender and will be easier to turn if you don't make them too big. Fry like any pancakes. Make sure they're quite done on the bottom before turning; look for the top surface to have little holes where bubbles have burst and not filled in and to be starting to look a little dry. Flip and cook the other side. Repeat with the remaining oil and batter.

Butter and serve with low-sugar preserves or sugar-free pancake syrup.

---

2 ounces (55g) pork rinds (There are bags that hold just this amount.)

3 eggs

¼ cup (60ml) heavy cream

½ teaspoon baking powder

3 tablespoons (36g) erythritol

¼ teaspoon liquid stevia, French vanilla or English toffee

½ teaspoon ground cinnamon

1½ tablespoons (21g) coconut oil, for frying, or more as needed

---

YIELD: 8 pancakes –
Per serving: 111 calories;
9g fat (74% calories from fat);
7g protein; 1g carbohydrate; trace dietary fiber; 1g net carbohydrate.

PORK RIND PANCAKES

It sounds crazy, I know, but these are remarkably good. If you didn't know they were made from pork rinds, you would never guess. No fair serving them to unsuspecting vegetarians! The brand of pork rinds matters here. You want a brand that's quite fluffy, rather than super crunchy, and you want them to not be too heavily salted.

Dump your pork rinds in the food processor with the S-blade in place and process until they're reduced to fine crumbs.

In a mixing bowl, whisk together the eggs, cream, baking powder, erythritol, liquid stevia, and cinnamon. Now, add the pork rind crumbs and whisk them in. Let the batter sit for 10 minutes or so. During this time it will "gloppify"—thicken up and become gloppy. That's okay!

While you're waiting for the gloppification to occur, put your skillet or griddle over medium-high heat. You'll want it hot for frying your pancakes.

Back to your gloppy batter. Thin it with water if you like—this depends on how thick a pancake you want. Then, fry like any other pancake batter, using the coconut oil as needed. I scoop my batter with a cookie scoop—like an ice cream scoop, only smaller—so they all come out the same size.

Serve with butter and a sprinkle of cinnamon and erythritol or Maple Butter (page 251).

⅓ cup (32g) almond meal

1 teaspoon salt

½ teaspoon guar or xanthan gum

¾ cup (175ml) pourable unsweetened coconut milk

2 tablespoons (28ml) melted butter

3 eggs

YIELD: 6 servings – Per serving: 103 calories; 8g fat (68% calories from fat); 6g protein; 3g carbohydrate; 0g dietary fiber; 3g net carbohydrate.

1 cup (96g) almond meal

1 cup (228g) vanilla whey protein powder

2 tablespoons (24g) erythritol

1 teaspoon xanthan gum

1 tablespoon (14g) baking powder

1 teaspoon salt

¾ cup (195g) natural peanut butter

1 cup (235ml) pourable unsweetened coconut milk

1 egg

¼ teaspoon liquid stevia, English toffee

YIELD: 20 servings – Per serving: 132 calories; 7g fat (44.5% calories from fat); 14g protein; 5g carbohydrate; 1g dietary fiber; 4g net carbohydrate.

POPOVERS

I actually got only five popovers out of this recipe, but I have an actual popover pan, and the cups are larger than muffin cups. Unless you've got a really big muffin tin, you should get six.

Preheat the oven to 450°F (230°C, or gas mark 8). Coat a 6-cup muffin tin with nonstick cooking spray.

In a bowl, combine the almond meal, salt, and guar, stirring them together.

In a mixing bowl, preferably one with a pouring lip, combine the coconut milk, butter, and eggs. Whisk together well.

Do not proceed unless you're sure your oven is up to temperature! When it is, whisk the almond meal mixture into the coconut milk mixture. The batter should be about the thickness of heavy cream. Pour into the prepared muffin tin.

Bake for 20 minutes at 450°F (230°C, or gas mark 8). Then, without opening the oven, turn the heat down to 350°F (180°C, or gas mark 4) and let them bake for another 25 minutes.

Serve hot, with plenty of butter!

PEANUT BUTTER BREAD

Wow. I found a recipe for Peanut Butter Bread in *The Boston Cooking School Cook Book*, originally published in 1896. Intrigued, I decarbed it. It worked out even better than I hoped—mildly sweet, distinctly peanutty, with a lovely texture. You have to try this!

The loaf rises steeply in the center, tapering at the ends. This means the slices are of varying sizes, making exact per-slice statistics impossible. Still, you can count on this being quite low carb—and with added butter, fitting our macros.

Preheat the oven to 350°F (180°C, or gas mark 4). Generously coat a loaf pan with nonstick cooking spray.

In your food processor with the S-blade in place, add the almond meal, vanilla whey protein, erythritol, xanthan, baking powder, and salt. Pulse 15 to 20 times, making sure everything is evenly mixed. Add the peanut butter. Pulse 5 to 6 times and then run the processor for a minute or two, scraping down the sides at least once. Turn off the processor.

In a cup with a spout, combine the coconut milk, egg, and liquid stevia and use a fork or whisk until well blended.

With the food processor running, pour in the coconut milk mixture through the feed tube. When it's all in, scrape down the sides of the processor and process for another 30 seconds or so.

Scrape the batter into the prepared loaf pan, smoothing the top. Bake for 1 hour. Cool in the pan for 5 minutes before turning out onto a rack to cool.

Serve warm or toasted, slathered with butter!

1 cup (96g) almond meal
(Bob's Red Mill super-fine)

1 cup (228g) vanilla whey
protein powder, divided

4 teaspoons (18g) baking
powder

1 teaspoon guar or xanthan
gum

½ teaspoon salt

¼ cup (48g) erythritol

1 cup (145g) fresh blueberries

1 cup (235ml) pourable
unsweetened coconut milk

3 tablespoons (42ml) melted
butter

2 eggs

⅛ teaspoon (36 drops) liquid
stevia

1 teaspoon vanilla extract

1 teaspoon lemon zest

YIELD: 18 servings –
Per serving: 111 calories;
5g fat (37% calories from fat);
13g protein; 5g carbohydrate;
1g dietary fiber; 4g net
carbohydrate.

BLUEBERRY MUFFINS

Our tester, Christina Robertson, says, "These muffins are full of
blueberries. I like them that way, but my husband said they looked like
bruised muffins because of all the purple at the bottom—that didn't stop
him from eating them, though."

I realize this is an odd number of muffins; that's just the way it worked
out. You can vary this by using different flavors of liquid stevia—try lemon
drop, vanilla, or English toffee flavors.

Preheat the oven to 400°F (200°C, or gas mark 6). Line 18 muffin tins with
paper liners.

In a mixing bowl, combine the almond meal, ¾ cup (171g) of the vanilla whey,
baking powder, guar, salt, and erythritol. Stir together well, breaking up any clumped
bits of baking powder, until everything is evenly combined.

In a separate bowl, toss the blueberries with the remaining ¼ cup (57g) of vanilla
whey to coat.

In a bowl with a pouring lip or a large Pyrex measuring cup, combine the coconut
milk, melted butter, eggs, liquid stevia, vanilla, and lemon zest. Whisk together well.

Add the liquid ingredients to the dry ingredients all at once and whisk just until
everything is dampened and you are sure there are no big pockets of dry stuff left
at the bottom of the bowl. Do not try to beat out every lump—overmixing yields an
inferior muffin. Quickly stir in the berries.

Divide the batter among the muffin cups—an ice cream scoop is useful for
keeping them even sizes.

Bake for 18 minutes or until a toothpick inserted into the center of a muffin
brings out only a few moist crumbs. Serve hot, with butter!

⅓ cup (32g) almond meal

½ cup (114g) vanilla whey protein powder

1 tablespoon (14g) dried egg white powder

½ teaspoon guar or xanthan gum

¼ teaspoon salt

1 teaspoon baking powder

½ teaspoon ground cinnamon

½ teaspoon ground nutmeg

½ cup (123g) canned pumpkin

1 egg

2 tablespoons (28ml) melted butter

¼ teaspoon orange extract

⅓ cup (80ml) pourable unsweetened coconut milk

¼ teaspoon liquid stevia, English Toffee

½ cup (55g) chopped pecans

YIELD: 12 servings –
Per serving: 118 calories;
7g fat (52.9% calories from fat);
10g protein; 4g carbohydrate;
1g dietary fiber; 3g net
carbohydrate.

58

PUMPKIN MUFFINS

These make a great quick breakfast, especially if you are weary of eggs. Speaking of eggs: that egg white powder improves the texture of nut-based baked goods. You may find it in the baking aisle of your grocery store, but if not, as always when shopping for the odd item, the Internet is your friend. And that leftover pumpkin? Freeze it in an ice cube tray and then pop it out and store in a resealable plastic bag in the freezer. Voilà! You'll have just the amount you need next time. My ice cube trays hold about 2 tablespoons (28g) per cube.

Preheat the oven to 400°F (200°C, or gas mark 6). Spray a 12-cup muffin tin with nonstick cooking spray, or, if you prefer, line it with paper muffin cups.

In a mixing bowl, combine all your dry ingredients. Stir them together to evenly distribute ingredients.

In another bowl, combine the canned pumpkin, egg, melted butter, orange extract, coconut milk, and liquid stevia and whisk together. Make sure your oven is up to temperature before you take the next step!

Pour the wet ingredients into the dry ingredients and with a few swift strokes, combine them. Stir just enough to make sure there are no big pockets of dry stuff; a few lumps are fine. Stir in the pecans quickly and spoon into the prepared muffin tin. Bake for 20 minutes; remove the muffins from the pan to a wire rack to cool.

1½ cups (218g) raw sunflower seeds

½ cup (50g) grated Parmesan cheese

½ teaspoon salt

¼ teaspoon baking powder

2 tablespoons (28ml) water

YIELD: 12 servings –
Per serving: 118 calories;
10g fat (71.3% calories from fat);
5g protein; 4g carbohydrate;
2g dietary fiber; 2g net
carbohydrate.

SUNFLOWER QUICHE CRUST

You can cut a few carbs by making crustless quiches, but I like the texture and flavor contrast a crust offers. This one is low carb and highly nutritious.

Preheat the oven to 350°F (180°C, or gas mark 4). Coat a 10-inch (25cm) pie plate with nonstick cooking spray. (I also have a 9½-inch [24cm] deep-dish pie plate, which works fine.)

Put everything but the water in your food processor. Process until it's the consistency of a fine meal. With the food processor still running, drizzle in the water. When you have a soft dough, turn off the machine.

Turn the dough out into the pie plate. Use clean hands to press it firmly into an even layer across the bottom and up the sides—you may need to nip a little off here and move it over there to get it even. End at the top edge of the plate; don't try to build up a crimped edge like you might with a wheat flour pie crust.

Bake for 15 to 17 minutes until very lightly gold. Fill and bake again.

ALMOND-SUNFLOWER QUICHE CRUST

Here's another good and crunchy quiche crust. You'll want to use this with a nearly carb-free filling, though. How about Quiche Lorraine?

1 cup (145g) raw sunflower seeds

1½ cups (144g) almond meal

¼ cup (56g) coconut oil

½ cup (50g) grated Parmesan cheese

½ teaspoon salt

1 tablespoon (15ml) water

YIELD: 12 servings –
Per serving: 193 calories; 15g fat (64.3% calories from fat); 11g protein; 7g carbohydrate; 1g dietary fiber; 6g net carbohydrate.

Preheat the oven to 350°F (180°C, or gas mark 4). Coat a 10-inch (25cm) pie plate with nonstick cooking spray.

Put the sunflower seeds in your food processor and process until they're a fine meal. Add everything but the water and pulse until it's all well blended. Then, with the processor running, add the water. The dough should form a cohesive glob.

Turn off the processor and turn the dough out into the prepared pie plate. Use clean hands to pat it out evenly, all over the bottom and up the sides of the pie plate.

Bake for 12 minutes or until starting to get a touch of gold. Pull it out and let it cool while you prepare your quiche filling.

WALNUT BREAD

A recipe in an English cookbook called for "walnut bread," obviously assuming it was something one could buy. Well, I can't here, and even if I could, it would be full of things I won't eat. So, I made this. It's dense and flavorful and wonderful toasted and slathered with butter or cream cheese or both. For something elegant, toast, spread with chèvre (goat cheese), and then run it under the broiler until it melts.

1½ cups (150g) walnuts, divided

3 cups (240g) shredded coconut

2 teaspoons erythritol

1½ teaspoons baking soda

1 teaspoon guar or xanthan gum

¾ teaspoon salt

½ cup (56g) flaxseed meal

6 drops of liquid stevia, English Toffee

4 eggs

½ cup (120ml) water

1 tablespoon (15ml) cider vinegar

YIELD: 20 servings –
Per serving: 140 calories; 12g fat (71% calories from fat); 5g protein; 5g carbohydrate; 3g dietary fiber; 2g net carbohydrate.

Preheat the oven to 350°F (180°C, or gas mark 4). Line a loaf pan with nonstick foil.

Spread the walnuts on a shallow baking tray, put them in the oven, and set the timer for 6 minutes.

Meanwhile, put the coconut, erythritol, baking soda, guar, and salt in your food processor and start it running. Scrape down the sides every few minutes.

When the timer beeps, pull the walnuts out of the oven, and add 1 cup (100g) of them to the mixture in the food processor and then run it again. You want to keep running the food processor until the mixture has the texture of a nut butter.

When the coconut-walnut mixture reaches a nut butter consistency, add the flaxseed meal and run the processor, scraping down the sides once or twice, until it's well blended.

Add the liquid stevia, then the eggs, one by one, blending each in thoroughly before adding another. Don't forget to scrape down the sides when needed.

In a glass measuring cup, combine the water and cider vinegar. With the food processor running, pour this through the feed tube in three additions, letting each get worked in before adding more. Scrape down the sides if needed.

Once the water and vinegar are in, you need to work quickly. Add the remaining ½ cup (50g) of walnuts and pulse a few times to chop them in; you want there to be chunks of walnut in your finished bread. Scrape the dough into your prepared loaf pan, distributing it evenly, and smooth the top.

Bake for 75 minutes until it's pulled away from the sides of the pan and sounds hollow when you thump it with a finger. Turn out onto a rack to cool.

4 cups (320g) shredded coconut

¾ cup (84g) flaxseed meal

1 tablespoon (14g) xanthan or guar gum

1 teaspoon erythritol (not essential, but I think it improves the flavor)

1½ teaspoons baking soda

½ teaspoon salt

½ cup (120ml) water

2 tablespoons (28ml) cider vinegar

4 eggs

YIELD: 20 servings –
Per serving: 111 calories; 9g fat (69.9% calories from fat); 4g protein; 5g carbohydrate; 4g dietary fiber; 1g net carbohydrate.

COCONUT FLAX BREAD

This bread is grain-free, gluten-free, and delicious! Buttered toast is a staple again in my house. My thanks to Andrew DiMino of carbsmart.com for allowing me to use this recipe from *The Fat Fast Cookbook*.

Preheat the oven to 350°F (180°C, or gas mark 4). Grease a loaf pan (standard, not super-huge; the opening on mine is 8½ × 4½ inches [21.6 × 11.4cm]). Now, line it with nonstick aluminum foil or parchment paper.

In your food processor with the S-blade in place, combine the coconut, flaxseed meal, xanthan, erythritol, baking soda, and salt. Run the processor until everything is ground to a fine meal. Scrape down the sides and run the processor some more.

While that's happening, in a glass measuring cup, combine the water and the cider vinegar. Have this standing by the food processor.

While the food processor is running, add the eggs, one at a time, through the feed tube. Finally, pour the water and vinegar mixture in through the feed tube. Process for just another 30 seconds or so.

Pour or scrape the batter into the prepared loaf pan. Bake for 1 hour and 15 minutes. Turn out onto a wire rack to cool.

This slices beautifully and can be sliced thick or thin. I get about 20 slices per loaf, so that's what I calculated on.

2 cups (160g) shredded coconut

½ cup (48g) almond meal

½ cup (114g) vanilla whey protein powder

½ cup (56g) flaxseed meal

1 tablespoon (9g) xanthan or (10g) guar gum

6 drops of liquid stevia, English Toffee

1½ teaspoons baking soda

½ teaspoon salt

½ cup (120ml) water

2 tablespoons (28ml) cider vinegar

4 eggs

YIELD: 20 servings –
Per serving: 105 calories; 7g fat (53.1% calories from fat); 8g protein; 5g carbohydrate; 3g dietary fiber; 2g net carbohydrate.

COCONUT ALMOND FLAX BREAD

A good recipe deserves a variation! This is a riff on the Coconut Flax Bread I invented for *The Fat Fast Cookbook* and which has also appeared in *200 Low-Carb, High-Fat Recipes* and *The Low-Carb Diabetes Solution Cookbook*. It's great toasted and also makes a mean grilled cheese sandwich.

Preheat the oven to 350°F (180°C, or gas mark 4). Grease a loaf pan (standard, not super-huge; the opening on mine is 8½ × 4½ inches [21.6 × 11.4cm]). Now, line it with nonstick aluminum foil or parchment paper.

In your food processor with the S-blade in place, combine the coconut, almond meal, vanilla whey protein, flaxseed meal, xanthan, liquid stevia, baking soda, and salt. Run the processor until everything is ground to a fine meal. Scrape down the sides and run the processor some more.

While that's happening, in a glass measuring cup, combine the water and the cider vinegar. Have this standing by the food processor.

With the food processor running, add the eggs, one at a time, through the feed tube. Finally, pour the water and vinegar mixture in through the feed tube. Run just another 30 seconds or so.

Pour or scrape the batter into the prepared loaf pan. Bake for 1 hour and 15 minutes. Turn out onto a wire rack to cool.

This slices beautifully and can be sliced thick or thin. I get about 20 slices per loaf, so that's what I calculated on.

12 ounces (340g) cream cheese, at room temperature

¼ cup (55g) butter

¼ cup (60ml) MCT oil

4 eggs

3 drops of liquid stevia, plain

¼ cup (60ml) heavy cream

1⅔ cups (380g) plain whey protein powder

2½ teaspoons (12g) baking powder

1 teaspoon guar or xanthan gum

½ teaspoon salt

½ teaspoon baking soda

¼ teaspoon cream of tartar

YIELD: 20 servings –
Per serving: 201 calories; 14g fat (62.3% calories from fat); 17g protein; 2g carbohydrate; trace dietary fiber; 2g net carbohydrate.

SOUL BREAD

This recipe, originated by someone who goes by the moniker "Soul's Song," has made the rounds of the online low-carb community. I've changed it only a little—using MCT oil instead of olive oil and increasing the baking soda just a tad. It's remarkably, well, bread-like.

Preheat the oven to 325°F (170°C, or gas mark 3). Coat a 9 × 5-inch (23 × 13cm) loaf pan with nonstick cooking spray or line with nonstick foil (my preference).

Put the cream cheese and butter in a microwaveable bowl and nuke for 1 minute on high.

Add the MCT oil to the cream cheese and butter and use your electric mixer to beat them until well blended, scraping down the sides of the bowl as needed.

Now, beat in the eggs, one at a time, incorporating one thoroughly before adding the next.

Beat in the liquid stevia and heavy cream.

Combine all the dry ingredients in another bowl. Stir them together until everything is evenly distributed. Using a spoon rather than your mixer, stir the dry ingredients into the cream cheese mixture, adding about ⅓ cup (85g) at a time and stirring each addition in before adding more.

Pour or scrape the batter into the prepared loaf pan. Bake for 45 minutes or until golden brown. Turn out onto a wire rack to cool.

Store in a plastic bag in the refrigerator. Or, if you're not likely to eat it up quickly, slice it all, wrap it in a plastic bag, and freeze. You can remove and thaw just a slice or two at a time.

¼ loaf of bread (see headnote)

6 tablespoons (85g) butter

YIELD: 12 strips – Per serving: 135 calories; 12g fat (76.4% calories from fat); 7g protein; 1g carbohydrate; trace dietary fiber; 1g net carbohydrate.

BUTTER TOASTIES

Here's yet another idea poached from an old-time cookbook, written before fat phobia (and obesity and diabetes epidemic). Of course, they used standard bread. They also baked the strips of bread in the butter, turning them often, but doing them in a skillet seemed easier. Also, it was 90 degrees out, and I didn't want to turn the oven on. If you let these cool completely, then stash them in a resealable bag in the fridge, they'll warm up nicely in your skillet, oven, or toaster oven. You can use Soul Bread (above), Whole-Grain Soul Bread (page 62), Coconut Flax Bread (page 60), or Coconut Almond Flax Bread (page 60). Take your pick.

Cut the bread into 4 thick slices, 1 to 1¼ inches (2.5 to 4cm) thick. Cut each slice into 3 nice, chunky strips.

Melt the butter in a large, heavy skillet over medium heat. Fry the strips of bread until they're toasty brown all over and soaked in butter.

12 ounces (340g) cream cheese, at room temperature

¼ cup (55g) butter

¼ cup (60ml) MCT oil

4 eggs

⅛ teaspoon (36 drops) liquid stevia, English toffee

¼ cup (60ml) heavy cream

1 cup (228g) plain whey protein powder

⅓ cup (40g) oat bran

⅓ cup (37g) flaxseed meal

1 tablespoon (14g) baking powder

1 teaspoon guar or xanthan gum

½ teaspoon salt

¾ teaspoon baking soda

½ teaspoon cream of tartar

YIELD: 20 servings –
Per serving: 194 calories; 15g fat (67.6% calories from fat); 12g protein; 4g carbohydrate; 2g dietary fiber; 2g net carbohydrate.

½ cup (120ml) olive oil

2 cloves of garlic

⅛ of a loaf of Whole-Grain Soul Bread (above)

YIELD: 5 servings – Per serving: 290 calories; 29g fat (88.4% calories from fat); 6g protein; 2g carbohydrate; 1g dietary fiber; 1g net carbohydrate.

WHOLE-GRAIN SOUL BREAD

Long before I went low carb, I became a health food freak. I have long preferred whole-grain bread to white. The addition of oat bran and flaxseed meal brings a whole-grain flavor and texture.

Oats are not a gluten grain, but are sometimes processed in the same facilities as gluten grains and can be contaminated. I don't worry about it, but if you're seriously sensitive, look for oat bran marked "gluten-free."

Preheat the oven to 325°F (170°C, or gas mark 3). Coat a 9 × 5-inch (23 × 13cm) loaf pan with nonstick cooking spray or line with nonstick foil (my preference).

Put the cream cheese and butter in a microwaveable bowl and nuke for 1 minute on high.

Add the MCT oil to the cream cheese and butter and use your electric mixer to beat them until well blended, scraping down the sides of the bowl as needed. Now, beat in the eggs, one at a time, incorporating one thoroughly before adding the next. Beat in the liquid stevia and heavy cream.

Combine all the dry ingredients in another bowl. Stir them together until everything is evenly distributed. Using a spoon rather than your mixer, stir the dry ingredients into the cream cheese mixture, adding about ⅓ cup (85g) at a time and stirring each addition in before adding more.

Pour or scrape the batter into the prepared loaf pan. Bake for 1 hour or until golden brown. Turn out onto a wire rack to cool.

Store in a plastic bag in the refrigerator. Or, if you're not likely to eat it up quickly, slice it all, wrap it in a plastic bag, and freeze. You can remove and thaw just a slice or two at a time.

GARLIC CROUTONS

Do you miss croutons? You can make them! Really, it's quite simple. You can use these on salad or in soups, of course. They're also good just by themselves, as a snack.

Warm the olive oil in a large, heavy skillet over the lowest heat. Cut the garlic along the longest, widest dimension, exposing as much of the inside as possible. Put these cut-side down in the oil and let them sit for 5 to 10 minutes—you're infusing the oil with garlic.

Meanwhile, slice your bread about ½ inch (1.3cm) thick and cut each slice into cubes.

Remove the cut garlic from the oil. Turn the heat up to medium-low and add the bread cubes. Fry until they're a nice crisp brown all over. Don't walk away! It's a quick jump from brown to overdone.

Let them cool completely before storing in an airtight container in the refrigerator. Refresh in a warm oven before using.

2 eggs

½ cup (120ml) heavy cream

24 drops of liquid stevia, vanilla

1 pinch of salt

6 slices of Soul Bread (page 61)

4 tablespoons (55g) butter

YIELD: 6 servings – Per serving: 382 calories; 32g fat (74.7% calories from fat); 21g protein; 3g carbohydrate; 1g dietary fiber; 2g net carbohydrate.

FRENCH TOAST

If you prefer, you can make this with Whole-Grain Soul Bread (page 62), Coconut Flax Bread (page 60), or Coconut Almond Flax Bread (page 60). It's all good!

In a shallow, rimmed dish (a pie plate is great), combine the eggs, heavy cream, liquid stevia, and salt. Use a fork to blend until evenly mixed.

Dip both sides of your bread slices in the egg mixture. Let them sit for 30 seconds or so on each side to let them absorb the eggs and cream.

Put a large, heavy skillet or a griddle over medium-low heat. Melt 2 tablespoons (28g) of the butter. Remove the bread slices from the egg mixture and start them frying in the butter. Unless your skillet is bigger than mine, you'll need to cook in a couple of batches. Add the rest of the butter before the second batch.

Serve with more butter and erythritol/monk fruit or erythritol/stevia blend mixed with cinnamon.

If you're a die-hard fan of maple syrup on French Toast, add ½ teaspoon maple flavoring to the egg mixture and serve with Maple Butter (page 251).

3½ ounces (100g) plain pork rinds

YIELD: 10 servings, 1¼ cups (100g) – Per serving: 54 calories; 3g fat (53.5% calories from fat); 6g protein; 0g carbohydrate; 0g dietary fiber; 0g net carbohydrate.

PORK RIND CRUMBS

I admit this isn't a baked good, but I didn't know where else to put it. This is based on the size of the bags of pork rinds I buy at Aldi because that's what I buy. But whatever brand you buy, plain pork rinds should be carb-free.

Dump the pork rinds into your food processor. Process until they are crumbs. Store in a tightly covered container in the refrigerator. That is all.

---

1 recipe Pork Rind Crumbs (above)

¾ teaspoon dried parsley

½ teaspoon granulated garlic

½ teaspoon onion powder

¼ teaspoon oregano

YIELD: 10 servings, 1¼ cups (100g) – Per serving: 55 calories; 3g fat (52.4% calories from fat); 6g protein; trace carbohydrate; trace dietary fiber; 0g net carbohydrate.

ITALIAN CRUMBS

If you've been using Italian-seasoned bread crumbs in meatballs or to bread things, try these! They're good in meatloaf, too.

Just add the seasonings as you're processing your bag of pork rinds. Store in an airtight container in the fridge, if you're keeping them longer than a week or two.

½ cup (73g) raw sunflower seeds

1 cup (80g) shredded coconut

1 cup (96g) almond meal

1 cup (112g) golden flaxseed meal

1 cup (228g) vanilla whey protein powder

¾ teaspoon salt

YIELD: 4½ cups (1kg), 12 servings – Per serving: 270 calories; 15g fat (47% calories from fat); 25g protein; 13g carbohydrate; 8g dietary fiber; 5g net carbohydrate.

¾ cup (72g) almond meal

¾ cup (84g) flaxseed meal

6 tablespoons (86g) vanilla whey protein powder

6 tablespoons (30g) dried unsweetened coconut, finely shredded

6 tablespoons (96g) almond butter

6 pinches of salt

2 cups (475ml) boiling water

1½ cups (355ml) heavy cream

YIELD: 6 servings – Per serving: 580 calories; 47g fat (67.7% calories from fat); 29g protein; 21g carbohydrate; 12g dietary fiber; 9g net carbohydrate.

HOT CEREAL

This recipe from *The Insulin Resistance Solution* is only for those of you who are counting net carbs rather than total grams. If that's you, our tester, Rebecca, called this "a nice, simple option" for those cold winter mornings. This is low in fat for our purposes, so I'm trusting you to add heavy cream or coconut milk, plus a sprinkle of the sweetener of your choice, maybe even a dusting of cinnamon or a few drops of maple flavoring.

Preheat the oven to 325°F (170°C, or gas mark 3).

Use your food processor to chop your sunflower seeds a bit; you want them about the size of a grain of rice or a little smaller.

Spread the sunflower seeds, coconut, and almond meal on a rimmed baking sheet. Toast for 8 to 10 minutes or until just getting golden.

Dump this mixture into a big bowl and add the flaxseed meal, vanilla whey protein, and salt. Stir everything together well and then transfer to a snap-top container and store in the fridge.

To serve, put about ⅓ cup (77g) of your cereal in a bowl and stir in ½ cup (120ml) boiling water. Put a saucer on top of the bowl to hold in the heat and let it sit for 2 to 3 minutes.

Thin with a little more water to get the texture you prefer and then eat like any hot cereal.

ALMOND-COCONUT HOT CEREAL

Clearly, this recipe is only for those who are counting net rather than total carbs. If you're one of 'em, this is a comforting breakfast on a snowy morning—or an equally appealing late-night snack.

You don't need to have all of the almond butter or cream on hand when you put together the nut meal mixture. I just needed to include them this way to analyze the numbers.

In a bowl, combine the almond meal, flaxseed meal, vanilla whey protein, and coconut. Store in a snap-top container in the refrigerator.

When you want hot cereal, put ⅓ cup (80g) of this mixture in a bowl, along with 1 tablespoon (16g) of almond butter. Add a pinch of salt and ⅓ cup (80ml) of boiling water and then cover the bowl and let it sit for 2 to 3 minutes.

Add ¼ cup (60ml) of heavy cream or coconut milk and the sweetener of your choice.

3½ ounces (100g) pork rinds

2 cups (230g) shredded mozzarella cheese

¼ cup (20g) shredded Parmesan cheese

1 clove of garlic, crushed

½ teaspoon salt

½ teaspoon baking powder

8 ounces (225g) cream cheese, softened

4 eggs

YIELD: 16 servings –
Per serving: 151 calories; 12g fat (71% calories from fat); 10g protein; 1g carbohydrate; trace dietary fiber; 1g net carbohydrate.

PIZZA CRUST

You can have pizza! Just top this with pizza sauce, cheese, and your favorite toppings (I'm a pepperoni girl myself) and run it back into the oven for 15 to 17 minutes or until golden and bubbly. You can use this right away, but I think chilling it makes it easier to handle and improves the texture a little.

Read the labels to find pizza sauce with no added sugar or corn syrup. I like Pastorelli brand, but Ragú makes one (read the labels; they make two pizza sauces—one with sugar, one without) and Muir Glen brand is available in health food stores.

If you're going to use your pizza dough right away, preheat your oven to 425°F (220°C, or gas mark 7) and line 2 cookie sheets with parchment paper.

Put the pork rinds in your food processor and grind them into fine crumbs. Transfer to a bowl and reserve.

Now, put the mozzarella and Parmesan in your food processor, along with the garlic, salt, and baking powder, and process until the cheese is finely ground. Add the cream cheese and process for 20 seconds or so. Now, add the eggs, one at a time, working each one in well before adding the next.

At this point, you will have a soft and sticky mass of dough. If you want to use it right away, divide the ball in two. Place one on a parchment-lined cookie sheet. Coat your clean hands with nonstick spray or oil and pat or press the dough out quite thin until you have a circle between 10 and 12 inches (25 and 30cm) in diameter. Repeat with the second ball of dough.

If you make your dough in advance, make your dough balls, put them in a snap-top container or plastic bag, and refrigerate for several hours. I actually left mine in the fridge for 48 hours. Unsurprisingly, the refrigerated dough will be stiffer and less sticky than it was straight out of the food processor. I found I could roll it out with my rolling pin, directly on the parchment paper. Again, you're going for 10 to 12 inches (25 to 30cm) in diameter.

Bake your crusts for 20 minutes until golden. At this point, top and bake them just as you would any prepared pizza crust.

1½ cups (218g) raw sunflower seeds, shelled

1 cup (80g) shredded Parmesan cheese (no additives)

¼ teaspoon baking powder

1 teaspoon guar or xanthan gum

½ teaspoon salt, plus more for sprinkling

¼ teaspoon granulated garlic (optional)

1 egg white

1 tablespoon (15ml) water

YIELD: 72 crackers –
Per serving: 22 calories;
2g fat (69.5% calories from fat);
1g protein; 1g carbohydrate; trace
dietary fiber; 1g net carbohydrate.

SUNFLOWER PARMESAN CRACKERS

I realize that making your own crackers sounds like a lot of work, but these are addictive and worth every single second of your time. They're crunchy, crackery, and loaded with flavor. But remember that each one has 1 gram of carbohydrate and govern yourself accordingly.

Preheat the oven to 350°F (180°C, or gas mark 4).

Put the sunflower seeds, Parmesan, baking powder, guar, salt, and garlic (if using) in your food processor and process until the sunflower seeds are a fine meal. With the motor running, add the egg white and water through the feed tube. Keep it running, stopping and scraping down the sides, until you have an evenly mixed soft dough.

Line 3 cookie sheets with parchment paper. (If you don't have three, you'll bake 'em in batches.) DO NOT SKIP THE PARCHMENT. YOU WILL REGRET IT. Divide the dough into 3 balls.

Put one of the balls on a parchment-lined cookie sheet and put another piece of parchment over it. Roll it out as thin as you can get it without holes—you may need to nip off a bit of dough from one place and patch it in at another to get it as even as possible.

Remove the top layer of parchment and use a thin, straight-bladed knife to score the dough into squares or diamonds. Pressing the knife straight down into the dough works better than drawing it along in a slicing motion. I make mine about the size of Wheat Thins, so that's what the analysis is based on.

Repeat with the rest of the dough on the other cookie sheets. Sprinkle all your crackers lightly with salt. Bake for about 15 minutes or until golden. You may want to turn the cookie sheets end to end or even swap shelves to bake them evenly. Let cool, break apart, and store in a snap-top container.

12 ounces (340g) bacon

7 ounces (200g) fontina cheese

1½ cups (218g) raw sunflower seeds

¼ teaspoon baking powder

½ teaspoon xanthan gum

½ teaspoon pepper

1 egg white

Salt, for sprinkling

YIELD: 86 servings–
Per serving: 46 calories
4g fat (78.3% calories from fat);
2g protein; 1g carbohydrate; trace
dietary fiber; 1g net carbohydrate.

BACON CHEESE CRACKERS

Yes. Bacon. Cheese. Crackers. You're welcome.

Preheat the oven to 350°F (180°C, or gas mark 4).

Start cooking your bacon by your preferred method. I microwave mine. However you cook it, you want it crisp.

Run the fontina through the shredding disk of your food processor. Transfer to a bowl and swap out the disk for the S-blade.

Put the sunflower seeds, baking powder, xanthan, and pepper in the food processor and process until you have a fine meal. If your bacon isn't crisp yet, just turn off the processor and wait until it is. (You could separate the egg now if you like.)

When the bacon is crisp, turn the processor back on. Break the bacon into 3- to 4-inch (7.5 to 10cm) lengths and feed them into the processor while it's running. When the bacon is all worked in, the cheese goes in, about one-third at a time.

BACON CHEESE CRACKERS *(continued)*

When the cheese is worked in, add the egg white. Let the processor run until you have a clump of dough.

Line a cookie sheet with baking parchment. DO NOT SKIP THE PARCHMENT. REALLY. Divide the dough into 3 portions. Shape one into a rough ball and put it in the middle of the parchment. Cover with a second sheet of parchment. Now, roll the dough out into as thin and even a sheet as you can. (You can buy silicone rolling pin rings at housewares stores or online, which makes this much easier. I use the thinnest of my set of rings for making crackers.) Peel off the top layer of parchment.

Using a thin, straight-bladed knife, score the dough into squares, triangles, or diamonds. You'll find it far easier to place the whole edge of the blade along the line you want to cut and press down rather than to draw the blade along in a slicing motion. I make my crackers a little larger than Wheat Thins. Sprinkle lightly with salt.

Bake for 17 to 18 minutes or until browned. These crackers are better a little overdone than a little underdone, so if you're not sure, err on the side of another minute or two. Repeat with each of the remaining balls of dough.

Store in a snap-top container for the roughly 36 hours it will take for these to evaporate. They have a way of disappearing.

SKILLET "CORNBREAD"

1½ cups (203g) hazelnuts

2 ounces (55g) pork rinds

½ cup (114g) vanilla whey protein powder

½ teaspoon baking soda

2 teaspoons baking powder

2 teaspoons salt

½ cup (115g) sour cream

2 cups (475ml) pourable unsweetened coconut milk

4 eggs, beaten

¼ cup (60ml) melted butter

1 teaspoon corn flavoring

1 tablespoon (14g) butter

YIELD: 12 servings –
Per serving: 320 calories; 27g fat (75% calories from fat); 15g protein; 5g carbohydrate; 1g dietary fiber; 4g net carbohydrate.

The corn flavoring is not essential, but it does lend verisimilitude. I got mine (Amaretti brand) through Amazon.com. If you prefer, you can use plain whey protein instead of vanilla whey. I like the little touch of sweetness.

Preheat the oven to 425°F (220°C, or gas mark 7). Put a cast-iron skillet in the oven to heat at the same time.

Use your food processor to grind the hazelnuts and pork rinds into a cornmeal texture.

In a mixing bowl, combine the hazelnut meal, pork rind crumbs, vanilla whey protein powder, baking soda, baking powder, and salt. Mix these dry ingredients together until everything is evenly distributed.

In another bowl, combine the sour cream, coconut milk, eggs, melted butter, and corn flavoring. Whisk to blend. Do not add to the dry ingredients yet!

When the oven and the skillet are up to temperature, pour the sour cream and egg mixture into the dry ingredients and whisk until everything is wet.

CAREFULLY remove that smoking-hot skillet from the oven. Spray it with nonstick cooking spray and throw the 1 tablespoon (14g) butter in the bottom, quickly sloshing it around the bottom of the skillet. Pour in your batter and put the skillet back in the oven. Bake for 20 to 25 minutes or until a toothpick inserted into the center comes out clean. Let cool for at least 10 minutes before serving with butter and/or low-sugar preserves.

CHAPTER 5

Eggs

This chapter will make it obvious that this book was written in the spring when our chickens—at this writing, we have roughly thirty—were laying up a storm. There's lots and lots of egg recipes!

You may not have chickens, but eggs should still be a staple of your ketogenic diet. They're delicious, highly nutritious, quick to cook, and cheaper than most forms of meat. And, as this chapter amply demonstrates, endlessly variable.

I urge you to stop thinking of eggs as breakfast food and turn to them any time you want a quick and easy meal. And if you throw away the yolks and make egg white omelets, I will personally come to your house and dope-slap you. You've clearly missed the point. The yolks are where all the vitamins and antioxidants are.

Before we get started with the recipes, I'd like to mention a simple idea: fried eggs on leftovers for breakfast. I've done so many versions of this—fried eggs over meatloaf, fried eggs over cauli-rice "risotto," fried eggs over sautéed vegetables. They liven up all sorts of leftovers and turn them into a whole new dish. Try it!

DANA'S EASY OMELET METHOD

If I had to choose just one skill to teach people trying to improve their diet, it would be how to make an omelet. First, have your filling ready. If you're using vegetables, you'll want to sauté them first. If you're making an omelet to use up leftovers—a great idea, by the way—warm them in the microwave and have them standing by.

The pan matters. For omelets, I recommend an 8- to 9-inch (20 to 23cm) nonstick skillet with sloping sides. Even if you've been nervous about Teflon or Silverstone, do take a look at the new ceramic nonstick pans. They're wonderful. Put your skillet over medium-high heat. While the skillet's heating, grab your eggs— two is the perfect number for this size pan, but one or three will work—crack them into a bowl, and beat them with a fork.

The pan is hot enough when a drop of water thrown in sizzles right away. Add a little fat and slosh it around to cover the bottom. Now, pour in the eggs, all at once. They should sizzle and immediately start to set. When the bottom layer of egg is set around the edges—this should happen quite quickly—lift the edge using a spatula or fork and tip the pan to let the raw egg flow underneath. Do this all around the edges until there's not enough raw egg to run.

Now, turn your burner to the lowest heat if you have a gas stove. If you have an electric stove, you'll have need to have a "warm" burner standing by because electric elements don't cool off fast enough for this job. Put your filling on one half of the omelet, cover it, and let it sit over very low heat for a minute or two, no more. Peek and see if the raw, shiny egg is gone from the top surface. (Although you can serve it that way if you like; that's how the French prefer their omelets.)

When your omelet is done, slip a spatula under the half without the filling and fold it over. Then, lift the whole thing onto a plate. This makes a single-serving omelet. I think it's a lot easier to make several individual omelets than to make one big one, and omelets are so quick to make that it's not that big a deal. That way, you can customize your omelets to each individual's taste. If you're making more than two or three omelets, just keep them warm in your oven, set to its very lowest heat.

3 tablespoons (45ml) MCT oil, divided

1 clove of garlic, crushed

2 scallions, including the crisp green part, minced

4 ounces (115g) ground pork

½ of a medium tomato, finely diced

1 tablespoon (15ml) fish sauce (nam pla or nuoc cham)

1 tablespoon (1g) minced cilantro, plus extra for garnish (optional)

4 eggs

sriracha (optional)

YIELD: 2 servings – Per serving: 485 calories; 42g fat (77.3% calories from fat); 22g protein; 6g carbohydrate; 1g dietary fiber; 5g net carbohydrate.

5 tablespoons (70g) butter, divided

1 tablespoon (10g) minced shallot

1 clove of garlic, crushed

2 tablespoons (28ml) dry vermouth

1 can (6.5 ounces, or 185g) of chopped clams, no sugar added

1 tablespoon (11g) minced roasted red pepper

2 ounces (55g) cream cheese, cut into small chunks

6 eggs

YIELD: 3 servings – Per serving: 473 calories; 36g fat (69.8% calories from fat); 28g protein; 6g carbohydrate; trace dietary fiber; 6g net carbohydrate.

VAGUELY THAI-ISH OMELETS

If you made up a double batch of this pork omelet filling, you could have quick, super-tasty breakfasts four days in a row! How's that for a thought? Recipe tester Rebecca says that this is very simple and tastes wonderful. She adds that without cheese it falls apart a bit as you eat it. She tried it with a sprinkle of mozzarella and said it tasted good and held things together, but it's not very Thai.

Put your omelet-making skillet over medium heat. Add 1 tablespoon (15ml) of the MCT oil and sauté the garlic and scallions for just a couple of minutes. Add the pork and stir and crumble until all the pink is gone, about 5 minutes. Stir in the tomato, fish sauce, and cilantro, if using. Let cook just another minute or so. Transfer the pork mixture to a plate and wipe out the pan.

Make your omelets according to Dana's Easy Omelet Method (see page 69), using 2 eggs for each and cooking each in 1 tablespoon (15ml) MCT oil. Fill each with half of the pork mixture.

Serve with sriracha for those who like to breathe fire at breakfast and a sprinkling of extra cilantro if you desire.

CLAMLETS

Recipe tester Rebecca says, "My husband said, 'Wow. That's a fancy restaurant sort of thing.' And I was pleasantly surprised. I thought it would be a bit strange eating clams for breakfast, but with the vermouth and the cream cheese, it made the omelet really nice and slightly sweet." She rates this a 10, and adds, "I just now have to remember to stay stocked on cans of clams as well as vermouth, cans of roasted shallots, and red peppers. I already always have eggs and cream cheese in the house."

Put a medium-sized skillet over medium-low heat. Melt 2 tablespoons (28g) of the butter and add the shallot and garlic. Sauté for 2 to 3 minutes until starting to soften. Add the vermouth and clams, including the juice. Let the whole thing simmer until the liquid has reduced by half. Add the roasted red pepper and the cream cheese. Stir until the cream cheese is melted in.

I trust the rest is obvious: Make your omelets according to Dana's Easy Omelet Method (see page 69) using the clam mixture for the filling, 2 eggs per omelet, and the remaining 3 tablespoons (42g) of butter for frying.

¾ cup (175ml) heavy cream

2 cans (3.75 ounces, or 105g) of sardines in olive oil

1 tablespoon (15g) Dijon mustard

1 tablespoon (15ml) Worcestershire sauce

⅛ teaspoon pepper

1 pinch of nutmeg

2 tablespoons (10g) shredded Parmesan cheese

1 tablespoon (9g) capers, drained

6 eggs

3 tablespoons (42g) butter

YIELD: 3 servings – Per serving: 477 calories; 44g fat (83.3% calories from fat); 16g protein; 4g carbohydrate; trace dietary fiber; 4g net carbohydrate.

---

1 tablespoon (14g) butter

2 eggs, whisked

2 slices of Swiss cheese

1 ounce (28g) sliced deli turkey

2 slices of American cheese

1 ounce (28g) sliced deli ham

1 tablespoon (20g) no-sugar-added raspberry preserves

YIELD: 2 servings – Per serving: 701 calories; 56g fat (71.6% calories from fat); 43g protein; 6g carbohydrate; trace dietary fiber; 6g net carbohydrate

---

NOTE: Polaner Sugar-Free with Fiber Preserves are the lowest carb I know of, but I can't always find them in my grocery store. There's a recipe for no-sugar Raspberry Preserves on page 246.

SARDINE OMELETS WITH SARDINE-CAPER CREAM SAUCE

Sardines have many advantages: They're inexpensive, easy to find, and keep on the pantry shelf. They're also a great source of both calcium and omega-3 fatty acids. And unlike big fish—think albacore and swordfish—they're unlikely to be significantly contaminated with mercury. If you're a fish-o-phile, they're a great thing to work into your menu plan. Just make sure they're canned in olive oil, not soy oil!

Make your sauce first: Put a medium-size saucepan over medium-low heat. Start the cream warming while you open and drain one of the cans of sardines. Put half of them in the cream and use a fork to mash them in. Stir in the Dijon mustard, Worcestershire, pepper, and nutmeg. Bring to a simmer. Whisk in the Parmesan and capers. Let it simmer for 2 to 3 minutes and then turn off the heat.

The rest is a piece of cake! Make your omelets according to Dana's Easy Omelet Method (see page 69) using 2 eggs per omelet, cooking each in 1 tablespoon (14g) of the butter, and filling each with half a can of sardines. Divide the sauce among them.

MONTE CRISTO OMELET

In one of Todd Wilbur's *Top Secret Recipes* books there was a recipe for Bennigan's Monte Cristo Sandwich—a ham, turkey, and cheese sandwich dipped in an eggy batter, French toasted, and served with raspberry preserves. I was intrigued by the sweet-and-salty combo. So, I turned it into an omelet, and it was great! But this is a huge omelet; you'll want to split it.

This is just slightly different from the usual Dana's Easy Omelet Method (see page 69): Melt the butter, pour in the eggs, and do the lifting-the-edges-while-tipping-the-skillet routine. But leave the heat turned up as you layer in your filling in this order: Swiss cheese, turkey, American cheese, then ham.

Now, turn the heat down, but only to medium-low, not the lowest heat, and cover the skillet. The point is to get a nice golden brown on the outside of the omelet to get some of the French-toasty flavor of the original. Cook until the cheese is just melted and then fold, cut in half, and divide between 2 plates. You can either spread 1½ teaspoons of the preserves on each serving or put it on the plate for dipping.

2 eggs

1 tablespoon (15ml) olive oil or MCT oil

2 ounces (55g) chèvre (goat cheese)

¼ cup (8g) fresh baby spinach (bagged)

½ of an avocado, sliced

YIELD: 1 serving – Per serving: 670 calories; 58g fat (76.3% calories from fat); 30g protein; 10g carbohydrate; 3g dietary fiber; 7g net carbohydrate.

4 ounces (115g) smoked salmon

2 tablespoons (28g) butter, divided

6 tablespoons (90ml) heavy cream, divided

4 eggs, separated

3 tablespoons (22g) shredded sharp cheddar cheese

Salt and pepper

YIELD: 2 servings – Per serving: 496 calories; 43g fat (77.8% calories from fat); 25g protein; 2g carbohydrate; 0g dietary fiber; 2g net carbohydrate.

SPINACH, AVOCADO, AND GOAT CHEESE OMELET

This is one mighty upscale omelet. If you have weekend company you want to impress—say, your new in-laws—consider these for breakfast. I used plain chèvre for these, but you could use an herbed variety if you prefer.

This is so simple! Make your omelet according to Dana's Easy Omelet Method (see page 69), whisking the eggs, cooking it in the olive oil, and layering with the goat cheese first—spoon it in little chunks rather than trying to spread it—then the spinach and the avocado on top of that.

PUFFY SMOKED SALMON OMELET

This isn't like the omelets made by Dana's Easy Omelet Method (see page 69). It's more complicated, and you won't fold it. But what a great weekend brunch! Recipe tester Julie says, "If I have friends staying the weekend, and they are fans of smoked salmon, I would definitely whip this baby out in order to impress!"

Remove any skin or bones from the smoked salmon and then flake it up with a fork.

Grab a medium-size saucepan—nonstick is best, but if you don't have one, give whatever saucepan you have a shot of nonstick cooking spray. Put it over medium-low heat and melt 1 tablespoon (14g) of the butter. Stir in 2 tablespoons (28ml) of the cream and the flaked salmon, and remove from the heat.

This is when you'll need those eggs separated. Keep in mind that the tiniest pinhead speck of yolk will keep the whites from whipping. Do yourself a favor and separate them into a custard cup before dumping the whites in a deep, narrow, scrupulously clean mixing bowl and the yolks into another bowl. If you get yolk in one white, you can set it aside to make scrambled eggs tomorrow.

Put 2 tablespoons (28ml) of the cream in the bowl with the yolks. Whisk them together well and then stir into the fish mixture. Now, reuse that bowl to whisk together the cheese with the remaining 2 tablespoons (28ml) of cream.

We're getting toward the finish line. Remember those egg whites? Use a clean whisk or an electric mixer to beat the egg whites until stiff. Remember, any little bit of yolk (or grease, for that matter) will keep your whites from whipping. Use a rubber scraper to fold them into the fish mixture.

Put a 9-inch (23cm) nonstick skillet with sloping sides (you know, an omelet pan) over medium-high heat. When it's hot enough that a drop of water hisses, melt the remaining 1 tablespoon (14g) of butter, swirling it around the bottom to coat. Pour in the egg and fish mixture and turn the heat down to medium. With this omelet, you don't want to do the lifting-the-sides-and-tilting-the-pan routine. Just let it sit.

Meanwhile, turn on your broiler and put the oven rack in the top position.

When the bottom of the omelet is set and starting to brown, spread the cheese mixture over the top. Slide it under the broiler and let it broil for 2 to 4 minutes until bubbling and turning golden.

Wearing oven mitts, cover the skillet with a plate and turn upside down to remove the omelet from the pan and then cut in half and plate.

TUNA-AVOCADO OMELETS

The only problem with this recipe is that you really need to serve four people because that avocado ain't gonna keep. So, make these for a quick weeknight supper or Sunday brunch.

In my house, omelets are pretty much an eat-'em-as-they're-done proposition. But if you'd like the family to all sit down at the same time, just set your oven to its lowest temperature and transfer your omelets to a heatproof pan or platter as they're done—my Corelle will withstand the 170°F (77°C) that is my oven's lowest temperature. Stash them in the oven until all four are done, and everyone can sit down together.

5 ounces (140g) canned tuna in olive oil

1 ripe avocado

3 tablespoons (45g) pesto

2 tablespoons (28g) mayonnaise

8 eggs

4 tablespoons (60ml) MCT oil

4 ounces (115g) sliced cheddar cheese, in 4 slices (1 ounce, or 28g each)

YIELD: 4 servings – Per serving: 623 calories; 54g fat (76.4% calories from fat); 31g protein; 6g carbohydrate; 1g dietary fiber; 5g net carbohydrate.

Put the tuna in a mixing bowl. Whack your avocado in half, remove the pit, and use a spoon to scoop the flesh out into the mixing bowl. Add the pesto and mayonnaise. Mix it up with a fork, mashing it a bit, but leaving plenty of modest-size hunks of avocado.

Make your omelet according to Dana's Easy Omelet Method (see page 69) using 2 eggs and 1 tablespoon (15ml) of the MCT oil at a time and layering in the cheese first, then the tuna mixture.

CHEESE BALL OMELET

I got the idea for this omelet from a cheese ball recipe I saw. It looked good, but stated the cheese ball should be served with crackers—ha! It makes a great omelet filling.

2 eggs

1 tablespoon (14g) butter

2 tablespoons (25g) whipped cream cheese

2 tablespoons (16g) crumbled blue cheese

1 tablespoon (6g) chopped canned olives

1 scallion, thinly sliced

1 tablespoon (6g) chopped roasted almonds, smoked flavor

YIELD: 1 serving – Per serving: 439 calories; 39g fat (78.7% calories from fat); 18g protein; 6g carbohydrate; 2g dietary fiber; 4g net carbohydrate.

Make your omelet according to Dana's Easy Omelet Method (see page 69), cooking the whisked eggs in the butter. Layer in the ingredients in the order shown, though if you'd like a fancier presentation, you can save the almonds to sprinkle on top after the omelet is folded and plated.

8 eggs

¼ cup (55g) butter

½ cup (40g) shredded
Parmesan cheese

**1 recipe Creamed Spinach and
Mushrooms (page 120)**

YIELD: 4 servings
Per serving: 463 calories;
40g fat (77.7% calories from fat);
20 g protein; 6g carbohydrate; 2g
dietary fiber; 4g net carbohydrate.

SPINACH-MUSHROOM OMELETS

You don't have to make the Creamed Spinach and Mushrooms specifically to make omelets; this is a great way to use up any leftovers. Or, you could make the Creamed Spinach and Mushrooms over the weekend, stash it in the fridge, and have it ready for making omelets later in the week. If you do this, remember to warm your Creamed Spinach and Mushrooms in the microwave before adding them to the omelet.

Make your omelets according to Dana's Easy Omelet Method (see page 69) using 2 eggs per omelet, cooking each in 1 tablespoon (14g) of the butter, and filling each first with 2 tablespoons (10g) of shredded Parmesan, then one-fourth of the Creamed Spinach and Mushrooms.

¼ cup (55g) butter

**8 ounces (225g) sliced
mushrooms**

¼ cup (40g) finely diced onion

**1 chipotle chile canned
in adobo, minced, plus
2 teaspoons adobo sauce**

6 eggs

YIELD: 3 servings – Per serving:
291 calories; 24g fat (74.3%
calories from fat); 13g protein;
6g carbohydrate; 1g dietary fiber;
5g net carbohydrate.

HUEVOS REVUELTOS CON HONGOS Y CHIPOTLES (Scrambled Eggs with Mushrooms and Chipotles)

I was going to make rather plebeian eggs scrambled with mushrooms, onions, and green pepper, only to discover I didn't have the pepper I thought I did. My eye lit on the container of chipotles, and a new, more exciting recipe was born. These are great as is, but to gild the lily, you could sprinkle ½ cup (58g) of shredded Mexican blend cheese over the finished eggs, turn off the heat, and cover the skillet for a minute to let the cheese melt. Sliced avocado is the perfect accompaniment to these eggs!

Give your large, heavy skillet a shot of nonstick cooking spray and put it over medium heat. Melt the butter and then add the mushrooms and onion. Use the edge of your spatula to break up the mushrooms further as they cook.

When the onion is translucent and the mushrooms are softening (about 5 minutes), add the minced chipotle and the adobo sauce and then quickly wash your hands! Now stir the whole thing up and let it cook for another 3 to 4 minutes.

Scramble up the eggs and then pour over the mushrooms and scramble until set.

**4 slices of Mexican-Spiced
Crunchy Avocados (page 112)**

4 eggs

YIELD: 4 servings – Per serving:
562 calories; 49g fat (78.3%
calories from fat); 26g protein;
4g carbohydrate; 1g dietary fiber;
3g net carbohydrate.

EGGS IN AN AVOCADO FRAME

As soon as I'd made the Mexican-Spiced Crunchy Avocados (page 112), I knew I had to make them into eggs in a frame. You'll think that one slice with one egg isn't enough for a serving, but unless you're a linebacker or have a shrew's metabolism, it will be.

Make your Mexican-Spiced Crunchy Avocados from the 2 center slices of 2 avocados, saving the rest to put in a salad later. (Coat the cut surfaces with lime

EGGS IN AN AVOCADO FRAME *(continued)*

juice, put them in a resealable plastic bag, seal most of the way, suck out the rest of the air before sealing, and then refrigerate. It should be good for a day or so.) You want the slices with the big holes in the centers; those are where the eggs are going.

When you've flipped your avocado slices, break an egg into the hole in the center of each avocado slice. Reduce the heat to medium-low, cover the skillet, and let cook until the eggs are done to your liking, maybe 5 minutes. You can try flipping them, but I find it hard not to break the yolks. Serve these with more of the Tajin Clasico seasoning or hot sauce, if you like.

1 recipe Eggs in an Avocado Frame (above)

½ cup (58g) shredded Mexican blend cheese

4 tablespoons (65g) salsa

YIELD: 4 servings – Per serving: 566 calories; 49g fat (77.6% calories from fat); 26g protein; 5g carbohydrate; 2g dietary fiber; 3g net carbohydrate.

HUEVOS DE HUERTA DE AGUACATE

With huevos rancheros in mind, I came up with this. Do not fool yourself into thinking you really need two slices of avocado and two eggs—not if you want to eat again this week. It's very filling.

Make your Eggs in an Avocado Frame according to instructions. Uncover after 2 minutes and put 2 tablespoons (14g) of shredded cheese on each. Then, re-cover until the eggs are done to your liking and the cheese is melted. Plate and top with salsa.

1 chicken sriracha sausage (¼ pound, or 115g)

1 scallion

2 tablespoons (28ml) MCT oil, divided

4 eggs

1 clove of garlic, crushed

2 teaspoons fish sauce

1 tablespoon (1g) minced cilantro (optional)

sriracha (optional)

YIELD: 2 servings – Per serving: 373 calories; 29g fat (70.6% calories from fat); 21g protein; 6g carbohydrate; trace dietary fiber; 6g net carbohydrate.

CHICKEN SRIRACHA SAUSAGE SCRAMBLE

Kroger makes these in the meat department, and because they're the biggest grocery chain in the country, I figured many of you could find them. This is a great breakfast—or an easy supper—for anyone Asian-food-minded.

Slice your sausage into "pennies" about ¼ inch (6mm) thick. Slice the scallion, including the crisp part of the green shoot.

If you've got a 10-inch (25cm) nonstick skillet, grab it. If you don't, coat your large skillet with nonstick cooking spray. Put it over medium-low heat, add 1 tablespoon (15ml) of the MCT oil, and start the sausage slices browning.

In the meanwhile, break your eggs into a bowl and add the garlic and fish sauce. Scramble 'em up.

Flip your sausage slices! As the second side browns, add the scallion. When the sausage slices are browned, add the remaining 1 tablespoon (15ml) of oil and pour in the egg mixture. Scramble until set.

Top each serving with cilantro, if desired, and pass a bottle of sriracha at the table.

1 tablespoon (14g) butter

1 scallion, thinly sliced

3 eggs

1 tablespoon (15ml) dry white wine

1½ teaspoons roe or caviar

2 ounces (55g) chèvre

YIELD: 1 serving – Per serving: 475 calories; 37g fat (72.1% calories from fat); 29g protein; 3g carbohydrate; trace dietary fiber; 3g net carbohydrate.

MILLION DOLLAR SCRAMBLE

Okay, it doesn't really cost a million dollars. But what with roe or caviar, wine, and chèvre, it's about as luxurious as scrambled eggs can get.

Put a medium-size skillet over medium-low heat—if it's not nonstick, give it a shot of cooking spray first. Melt the butter and add the scallion. Let it sauté for 2 to 3 minutes while you break the eggs into a bowl and scramble them up with the wine and roe.

Turn the heat up to medium. Pour the eggs into the skillet and scramble until half-set. Add the chèvre, spooned into the pan in small chunks, and scramble until set.

---

3 eggs

2 tablespoons (19g) crumbled feta cheese

5 olives, sliced

½ teaspoon salt using McCormick Mediterranean Sea Salt Grinder

2 tablespoons (28ml) olive oil

YIELD: 1 serving – Per serving: 510 calories; 46g fat (82.0% calories from fat); 19g protein; 4g carbohydrate; 1g dietary fiber; 3g net carbohydrate.

FETA-OLIVE SCRAMBLE

It was breakfast time, and I had eggs, feta, and olives on hand. It seemed obvious to me. And turned out to be good stuff! As for that McCormick Mediterranean Sea Salt Grinder, I bought it on a whim, and it has turned out to have myriad uses.

Break your eggs into a bowl, add the feta, sliced olives (I used green ones because they were at hand, but kalamatas would be great here, too), and the seasoning from the grinder. Mix it up with a fork.

Put your skillet over medium heat and let it get hot before you pour in the olive oil. Add the egg mixture and scramble until set.

---

2 eggs

1 scallion, minced

2 ounces (55g) smoked salmon, coarsely chopped

1½ tablespoons (21g) butter

YIELD: 2 servings – Per serving: 177 calories; 14g fat (72.8% calories from fat); 11g protein; 1g carbohydrate; trace dietary fiber; 1g net carbohydrate.

SMOKED SALMON SCRAMBLE

While this is delicious as is, you could add a dollop of sour cream. Don't think of it as gilding the lily. Think of it as increasing your fat percentage.

Break the eggs into a bowl and beat with a fork. Stir in the scallion and salmon.

Put a large skillet, nonstick or coated with cooking spray, over medium-high heat. Let it get hot and then melt the butter, sloshing it around to coat the pan. Pour in the egg mixture and scramble until set. Done!

2 tablespoons (28ml) extra-virgin olive oil

2 tablespoons (20g) diced red onion

2 tablespoons (15g) chopped walnuts

2 tablespoons (8g) minced parsley

1 tablespoon (9g) capers

3 eggs

½ teaspoon turmeric

YIELD: 1 serving – Per serving: 545 calories; 49g fat (80.3% calories from fat); 21g protein; 6g carbohydrate; 2g dietary fiber; 4g net carbohydrate.

SIRT-AINLY TASTY SCRAMBLE

There's been a lot of talk about "SIRTfoods" lately—foods that cause the body to secrete healthful substances called sirtuins. The "SIRTfood Diet" is too high carb for me, but I saw no reason not to work the keto-friendly SIRTfoods into recipes when possible. So, I grabbed every SIRTfood in the house that I thought might go well with eggs, and this was the result. It was surprisingly tasty, worth eating for flavor alone, whether it has magical health-enhancing properties or not.

If you don't have a medium-size nonstick skillet, give yours a shot of nonstick cooking spray. Put it over medium-low heat. Add the olive oil, then the red onion and walnuts. Sauté for 4 to 5 minutes. Add the parsley and capers and sauté for another 3 to 4 minutes.

In a bowl, mix the eggs with the turmeric. This can be harder than you might think—mine wanted to clump up on me. In the future, I'll run them through the blender for a moment. Pour into the skillet and scramble until set.

8 eggs

¼ cup (60ml) heavy cream

2 teaspoons Dijon or spicy brown mustard

¾ teaspoon salt, divided

¼ teaspoon pepper

8 ounces (225g) skinless salmon fillet

1 shallot

2 ounces (55g) arugula

3 tablespoons (45ml) olive oil, divided

1 cup (100g) ripe olives, sliced

4 ounces (115g) shredded Monterey Jack cheese

YIELD: 4 servings – Per serving: 489 calories; 39g fat (71.4% calories from fat); 30g protein; 5g carbohydrate; 1g dietary fiber; 4g net carbohydrate.

OLIVE SALMON SCRAMBLE

Here's yet another egg recipe that would serve for breakfast, lunch, or supper. I adapted this from a recipe I got from the California Olive Board, so it seems only right that you use California ripe olives.

In a mixing bowl, preferably with a pouring lip, whisk together the eggs, cream, mustard, ½ teaspoon of the salt, and the pepper.

Cube your salmon, maybe ¾-inch (2cm) bits. While you've got the knife in your hand, mince your shallot. Pinch the stems off your arugula, too.

If you don't have a large nonstick skillet, coat yours with nonstick cooking spray and put it over medium heat. When it's hot, add half the olive oil. Throw in the salmon and sauté until the cubes are done through, about 3 to 4 minutes. Scoop 'em out and reserve on a plate.

Add the remaining half of the oil to the skillet and throw in the shallot. Sauté it for just a minute and then pour in the egg mixture. Scramble until three-fourths set, maybe 3 minutes.

Add the salmon, arugula, and olive and scramble another minute until set. Remove from the heat. Sprinkle the cheese over the top, cover the skillet, and let the cheese melt for a minute before serving.

3 eggs

2 egg yolks

¼ cup (60ml) heavy cream

2 anchovy fillets

¼ teaspoon pepper

1 tablespoon (14g) butter

Paprika, for garnish

YIELD: 2 servings – Per serving: 320 calories; 29g fat (81.3% calories from fat); 13g protein; 2g carbohydrate; trace dietary fiber; 2g net carbohydrate.

2 packages (8 ounces, or 225g each) of Miracle Rice

6 slices of bacon

6 scallions

¾ cup (47g) fresh snow pea pods

4¾ cups (143g) fresh baby spinach

4 eggs

1 tablespoon (15ml) MCT oil

1 teaspoon soy sauce

Salt and pepper to taste

1 tablespoon (13g) bacon grease (optional)

YIELD: 4 servings – Per serving: 203 calories; 16g fat (68.7% calories from fat); 10g protein; 6g carbohydrate; 3g dietary fiber; 3g net carbohydrate.

ANCHOVY EGGS

Extra yolks and heavy cream make these eggs extra tender, while anchovies add their hit of umami. A slice of buttered Coconut Almond Flax Bread (page 60), toasted and buttered, would be nice with this.

Why add pepper but not salt? It toughens the eggs a bit, and one of the charms of this scramble is the extraordinary tenderness from the extra yolks and cream. Sprinkle on salt to taste at the table.

If you prefer, you can put the eggs, yolks, cream, and anchovies through your blender, pulverizing the anchovies entirely. This makes for more umami in every bite, but no little nuggets of anchovy intensity in your scramble.

In a mixing bowl, combine the eggs, egg yolks, and cream. Mince the anchovies and add them to the mixing bowl, along with the pepper. Scramble everything together well with a fork.

Put a 10-inch (25cm) skillet, preferably nonstick, over medium heat and add the butter. Swirl it around the pan as it melts. As soon as it's melted and the pan is hot, pour in the egg mixture and scramble until set.

Sprinkle each serving with a little paprika after plating.

BACON-VEGGIE FRIED "RICE" AND EGGS

This started with a recipe I saw in *Good Housekeeping* magazine that had more than 40 grams of carbohydrate per serving! It took a few tweaks to make it keto-friendly, but boy, was it worth it. I immediately resolved to create variations.

First, drain and rinse the Miracle Rice and start cooking the water out of it according to the instructions on page 23.

Put your large, heavy skillet over medium-low heat. Use kitchen shears to snip the bacon into it.

While your bacon bits are cooking, slice the scallions, including the crisp part of the green shoot. Pinch off the ends of your snow peas, pulling off any strings, and cut them into ½-inch (1.3cm) lengths. Don't forget to stir your bacon!

When the bacon is crisp, use a slotted spatula or spoon to transfer it to a plate. Add the scallions, snow peas, and spinach to the bacon grease in the skillet. Sauté, stirring often, for 3 to 4 minutes or until the spinach is limp. Stir in the Miracle Rice, MCT oil, and soy sauce and salt and pepper to taste. Let the whole thing simmer for another 4 to 5 minutes and then stir in the bacon bits.

Now, you have a choice: If you are going to serve 4 people (or 2 really hungry ones) right then, use the back of a spoon to make four equidistant hollows in the top of the "rice" mixture. Carefully break an egg into each. Cover the skillet and let the eggs cook for 3 to 4 minutes—the whites should be set, but the yolks still runny.

(Unless you hate runny yolks; I won't argue with you.)

If you're not going to eat up all of your Bacon-Veggie Fried "Rice" and Eggs at once, it's easier to fry your eggs (in bacon grease), one per customer, and place them on top of each serving.

2 packages (8 ounces, or 225g each) of Miracle Rice

8 slices of bacon

6 eggs, divided

¾ cup (47g) fresh snow pea pods

6 scallions

3 tablespoons (45ml) dark sesame oil

3 tablespoons (45ml) soy sauce

2 tablespoons (30ml) sriracha (optional)

1 ripe avocado

YIELD: 4 servings – Per serving: 365 calories; 31g fat (73.1% calories from fat); 15g protein; 11g carbohydrate; 4g dietary fiber; 7g net carbohydrate.

BACON AND EGG FRIED "RICE"

See what it says in the previous recipe about creating variations? This is the first one I came up with. You're not likely to make this for a weekday breakfast, but how about a quick supper? If your family is fond of Chinese takeout, this can be on the table faster than the delivery guy can get there!

Prepare the Miracle Rice according to the instructions on page 23.

Meanwhile, grab your biggest skillet, put it over medium heat, and use your kitchen shears to snip the bacon into it.

While the bacon is cooking, scramble up 2 of the eggs in a small bowl. Coat a medium-size skillet with cooking spray, put it over medium-high heat, and when it's hot, pour in the eggs. You want to cook them into a sheet, so lift the edges and tip the pan as described in Dana's Easy Omelet Method (page 69). When there's not enough raw egg to run, flip the whole sheet over for a few seconds to cook the other side—don't worry if it tears a bit, you're going to cut it up anyway. Remove the sheet of egg to a plate. Go stir your bacon!

Pinch the ends off the snow peas, pulling off any strings. Snip them into ½-inch (1.3cm) pieces. Slice the scallions, including the crisp part of the green shoot.

By now, your bacon should be crisp. Use a slotted spoon to remove it to a plate. Crank up the heat under the large skillet to medium-high and throw in the snow peas and scallions. Stir-fry for just 2 to 3 minutes. Stir in the Miracle Rice, sesame oil, soy sauce, and sriracha (if using). Turn the heat to low.

Roll your sheet of eggs into a cylinder and use your kitchen shears to snip across it at ½-inch (1.3cm) intervals, making strips. Cut the strips into 1-inch (2.5cm) lengths and stir them into the Miracle Rice along with the bacon bits.

Use the back of a spoon to make 4 equidistant hollows in the "rice" mixture and break an egg into each. Cover the skillet and let the eggs cook for 4 to 5 minutes.

Meanwhile, halve, pit, peel, and slice your avocado.

Check your eggs—you want the whites set, but the yolks still a bit runny. When they're there, dish it up. Divide the avocado slices among the portions and pass extra soy sauce and sriracha, if desired!

4 tablespoons (55g) butter

8 eggs

½ teaspoon salt or Vege-Sal

¼ teaspoon pepper

¼ teaspoon paprika

¼ teaspoon hot sauce, or to taste (I use Frank's brand.)

¾ cup (86g) shredded Colby cheese

¾ cup (86g) shredded Monterey Jack cheese

1 cup (112g) packaged real bacon bits

YIELD: 6 servings – Per serving: 335 calories; 26g fat (69.4% calories from fat); 21g protein; 5g carbohydrate; 2g dietary fiber; 3g net carbohydrate.

8 ounces (225g) bulk sausage

1 tablespoon (13g) bacon grease

½ of a green bell pepper, diced

½ of a small onion, diced

1 tablespoon (15ml) Worcestershire sauce

4 eggs

½ cup (58g) shredded Colby Jack cheese

YIELD: 4 servings – Per serving: 344 calories; 31g fat (80.8% calories from fat); 12g protein; 4g carbohydrate; 1g dietary fiber; 3g net carbohydrate.

CHEESE AND BACON FRITTATA

This is super-easy if you have packaged bacon bits in the house—I use Oscar Mayer brand. They're made from real bacon, of course. This frittata is a glorious thing of animal fat and cholesterol—keto health foods.

Put a 10-inch (25cm) skillet, preferably nonstick, over medium heat. (If you don't have a nonstick skillet, give it a good shot of cooking spray.) Add the butter and let it melt.

Meanwhile, whisk together the eggs, salt, pepper, paprika, and hot sauce. When the butter is melted, pour this into the skillet and glory in how the butter rises up to envelope the eggs. Turn the heat to low and cover the skillet.

If you're not using preshredded cheese, that's your next job. Uncover the eggs and sprinkle the cheese evenly over them. Re-cover the skillet.

I'm assuming you are, indeed, using packaged real bacon bits. Spread them on a microwaveable plate and nuke them on high for 90 seconds or so. This helps them crisp up.

Once again, uncover the skillet. Sprinkle the bacon evenly over the frittata.

Now, give the pan a little shake. How set is the center? You want it mostly set, but the very center still a little shaky.

With the oven rack in the top position, turn on the broiler. Uncover the frittata and slide it under the broiler, setting a timer for 2 minutes. That's it! Let it cool for a minute or two on the stove top and then cut into wedges.

If you don't eat it all right away, this warms up beautifully, making it an ideal thing to cook over the weekend to provide quick breakfasts all week long.

SUNDAY SUPER-BREAKFAST

I really did make this on a Sunday—Easter Sunday, actually—from stuff I just happened to have on hand. It was marvelous and seriously filling. You don't have to use Colby Jack cheese. Cheddar would be fine or a Mexican blend. Use what you have.

Put your large, heavy skillet over medium heat and start browning and crumbling the sausage. When there's only a little pink left to the sausage, add the bacon grease, throw in the vegetables, and add the Worcestershire. Sauté everything until the sausage is completely done, the onion is translucent, and the pepper tender-crisp—about 5 to 6 minutes.

Spread the sausage mixture evenly in the bottom of the skillet. Break in the eggs, being careful not to break the yolks. Turn the heat to low.

Sprinkle the cheese over the whole thing and then cover the skillet. Let it cook for 5 to 6 minutes and then check—you want the whites set but the yolks still runny. Re-cover and give it a minute or two more if needed.

Use a big spoon to scoop each egg out with all the sausage and veggies beneath it.

3 tablespoons (42g) butter

1 clove of garlic, crushed

1 box (10 ounces, or 285g) of frozen chopped spinach, thawed

½ cup (40g) shredded Parmesan cheese, divided

6 tablespoons (90ml) heavy cream, divided

Salt and pepper

4 eggs

YIELD: 2 servings – Per serving: 540 calories; 47g fat (76.2% calories from fat); 24g protein; 9g carbohydrate; 4g dietary fiber; 5g net carbohydrate.

SHIRRED EGGS FLORENTINE

Can you tell I wrote this book in the spring, when our hens were laying like mad? Do use good, fresh eggs for this; they'll stand up nicely and lend a fine appearance to the dish.

Preheat the oven to 350°F (180°C, or gas mark 4). Coat 2 gratin dishes with nonstick cooking spray.

In a medium-size skillet, melt the butter over low heat and then add the garlic. Let it cook gently while you wring out your spinach. (I literally take the box of thawed spinach and twist it, as if wringing out a cloth—over the sink, of course.) Add the well-drained spinach to the skillet and stir the butter and garlic into it. Let the mixture get hot through, just a few minutes. Stir in ¼ cup (20g) of the Parmesan and ¼ cup (60ml) of the cream, stirring until the cheese melts. Season with salt and pepper to taste.

Divide the spinach mixture between the 2 gratin dishes, spreading it evenly from end to end. Now, make 2 hollows in the spinach mixture in each dish and break an egg into each. (The hollows just serve to keep your yolks prettily centered.)

Spoon the remaining 2 tablespoons (28ml) of cream over each dish, 1 tablespoon (15ml) each, and sprinkle each with the remaining 2 tablespoons (10g) of Parmesan.

Bake for 13 to 15 minutes.

1 package (8 ounces, or 225g) of Miracle Rice

3 tablespoons (17g) sliced almonds

1½ teaspoons butter

2 eggs

1 scallion

3 tablespoons (45ml) Soy and Mustard Dressing (page 100)

½ of an avocado, divided

YIELD: 2 servings – Per serving: 290 calories; 26g fat (74.9% calories from fat); 10g protein; 9g carbohydrate; 3g dietary fiber; 6g net carbohydrate.

EGG AND AVOCADO BREAKFAST BOWL

This idea started percolating when I saw a recipe for a quinoa breakfast bowl. Quinoa was out, of course, but Miracle Rice seemed a natural. There were other ingredients I didn't have, so I just improvised.

This is the result. You can eat this as one HUGE serving if you like, but don't count on eating much for the rest of the day. You can also, of course, eat this for lunch or supper. I invented it around noontime.

Prepare the Miracle Rice according to the instructions on page 23. Put a small saucepan of water over high heat, preparing to boil the eggs.

While the water is heating, put a small skillet over low heat and start sautéing the almonds in the butter. Keep an eye on them! You want them golden, not scorched.

Is your water boiling? Gently put in your eggs and set a timer for 7 minutes. (Time will vary a little with the size and freshness of your eggs and whether they're at room temperature or fresh out of the fridge.) Turn the heat down so the water's just simmering.

Slice your scallion thin, including the crisp part of the green shoot.

Okay, the Miracle Rice is ready. Put it in a salad or mixing bowl and add the almonds, scallion, and Soy and Mustard Dressing. Stir to coat everything. Pile into 2 bowls.

When the eggs are done, scoop each out of its shell and into the bowls. Slice the avocado, or, even easier, spoon it out of the shell, distributing it between the 2 bowls. Done!

8 ounces (225g) bulk pork sausage, mild or hot

¼ cup (40g) diced onion

½ cup (75g) diced green bell pepper

1 prepared Quiche Crust (page 58 or 59)

¾ cup (83g) shredded Swiss cheese

¾ cup (86g) shredded cheddar cheese

6 eggs

1 cup (235ml) heavy cream

½ teaspoon salt or Vege-Sal

¼ teaspoon pepper

YIELD: 8 servings – Per serving: 534 calories; 47g fat (77.7% calories from fat); 22g protein; 8g carbohydrate; 3g dietary fiber; 5g net carbohydrate.

SAUSAGE QUICHE

Of course you've had sausage and eggs for breakfast, but have you had them for supper? This quiche is a great make-ahead dish for brunches or just for busy mornings—you can warm a slice in the microwave in a jiffy.

Preheat the oven to 350°F (180°C, or gas mark 4).

Put your large, heavy skillet over medium heat and start browning and crumbling the sausage. As some fat cooks out of the sausage, add the onion and green pepper. Sauté until all the pink is gone from the sausage.

Mix together the two shredded cheeses and then layer half on the bottom of the Quiche Crust. Top with the sausage-vegetable mixture.

Whisk the eggs, cream, salt, and pepper together in a bowl until very well blended. Pour this over the sausage mixture. Top with the remaining cheese.

Bake for 40 to 45 minutes or until the center is set.

1½ cups (173g) plus 2 tablespoons (14g) shredded cheddar cheese, divided

1 prepared Quiche Crust (page 58 or 59)

8 ounces (225g) ground chuck

4 ounces (115g) sliced mushrooms

½ of a small onion, diced

1½ teaspoons salt or Vege-Sal, divided

5 eggs

⅓ cup (75g) mayonnaise

¾ cup (175ml) heavy cream

2 teaspoons prepared horseradish

½ teaspoon pepper

YIELD: 8 servings – Per serving: 535 calories; 47g fat (77.2% calories from fat); 23g protein; 8g carbohydrate; 3g dietary fiber; 5g net carbohydrate.

CHEESEBURGER QUICHE

You've heard of "fusion cuisine"? This is it: the all-American cheeseburger meets the oh-so-French quiche. The whole family will love it, and you don't need a thing with it except a tossed green salad.

Preheat the oven to 350°F (180°C, or gas mark 4).

Spread 1½ cups (173g) of the cheese in the bottom of the Quiche Crust. It's nice to do this first, while the crust is still hot—it helps to seal it against moisture from the filling and to keep it crisp.

Put your large, heavy skillet over medium heat and begin to brown and crumble the ground chuck. As some fat cooks out of it, add the mushrooms and onion. Use the edge of your spatula to break the mushrooms up further as they cook—you want them coarsely chopped. Sprinkle in ½ teaspoon of the salt as this cooks. When all the pink is gone from the meat, spread this mixture over the cheese in the quiche crust.

Whisk together the eggs, mayonnaise, cream, horseradish, the remaining 1 teaspoon of salt, and the pepper. Pour over the ground beef mixture. Sprinkle the remaining 2 tablespoons (14g) of cheese over the top to make it look pretty.

Bake for 45 minutes or until the center is set.

CRABMEAT QUICHE

Recipe tester Rebecca says, "Perfect texture, full of crab, just the right amount of herbs, and the cream/egg mixture cooked up and held everything together very well."

1 prepared Quiche Crust (page 58 or 59)

1½ cups (177g) crabmeat, fresh or canned

3 tablespoons (23g) diced celery—pale inner stalk, finely minced, including the leaves

1 shallot, minced

2 tablespoons (8g) minced parsley

2 tablespoons (28ml) dry sherry

6 eggs

1 cup (235ml) heavy cream

¼ teaspoon ground nutmeg

½ teaspoon salt

¼ teaspoon pepper

I'm assuming you already have your Quiche Crust made, although you can do the next step first and have breathing room to get around to the crust.

In a nonreactive mixing bowl (stainless steel, glass, or enamel), combine the crabmeat, celery, shallot, parsley, and sherry. Stir together well. Now, refrigerate this mixture for an hour or so to allow the flavors to blend. (This is not 100 percent essential, but will enhance the flavor.)

Preheat your oven to 350°F (180°C, or gas mark 4).

In a large bowl, whisk together the eggs, cream, nutmeg, salt, and pepper.

Spread the crabmeat mixture evenly in the crust and then pour the egg mixture over it.

Bake for 45 to 50 minutes or until just set.

YIELD: 8 servings – Per serving: 357 calories; 30g fat (72.9% calories from fat); 18g protein; 7g carbohydrate; 3g dietary fiber; 4g net carbohydrate.

FONTINA, BACON, AND MUSHROOM QUICHE

I mentioned in the notes for the Porcini, Portobello, and Button Mushrooms in Cream that as soon as I created it, I started coming up with ways to use it—and started making triple batches to freeze. This is one clear illustration of why!

1 prepared Quiche Crust (page 58 or 59)

7 ounces (200g) fontina cheese, shredded

½ cup (56g) bacon bits

⅓ recipe Porcini, Portobello, and Button Mushrooms in Cream (page 241)

6 eggs

1 cup (235ml) heavy cream

1 teaspoon salt

½ teaspoon pepper

Preheat the oven to 350°F (180°C, or gas mark 4).

Cover the bottom of your Quiche Crust with the shredded fontina. Cover that with the bacon bits.

In a medium-size mixing bowl, whisk together the Porcini, Portobello, and Button Mushrooms in Cream, the eggs, heavy cream, salt, and pepper. When it's well blended, pour over the cheese and bacon.

Bake for 40 minutes or until set in the center and golden.

YIELD: 8 servings – Per serving: 487 calories; 41g fat (74.4% calories from fat); 22g protein; 10g carbohydrate; 4g dietary fiber; 6g net carbohydrate.

2 tablespoons (28ml) olive oil

2 tablespoons (28g) butter

½ of a medium onion, chopped

2 cloves of garlic, crushed

1 teaspoon cumin

1 teaspoon sweet paprika

1 teaspoon smoked hot paprika

¼ teaspoon cayenne

10 ounces (280g) canned tomatoes with green chiles, undrained

Salt and pepper

¼ cup (16g) parsley

6 eggs

1 cup (150g) crumbled feta cheese

YIELD: 3 servings – Per serving: 444 calories; 37g fat (73.3% calories from fat); 20g protein; 10g carbohydrate; 1g dietary fiber; 9g net carbohydrate.

SHAKSHUKA WITH FETA

Hailing from the Middle East, shakshuka consists of eggs poached in a spicy, bright-flavored sauce. It will be a hit at any meal—and it's a great choice if you have vegetarians to feed.

Put your large, heavy skillet over medium heat. Add the olive oil and butter and swirl them together as the butter melts. Add the onion and sauté for 4 to 5 minutes, just until it starts to soften. Add the garlic, cumin, both paprikas, and the cayenne. Sauté for another minute or two and then add the canned tomatoes with green chiles. Let this sauce simmer for a couple of minutes to blend the flavors and then season with salt and pepper to taste. Stir in the parsley.

Now, carefully break in the eggs—you really don't want any yolks to break. Place 5 around the edge of the skillet, equidistant, and the sixth in the center. Sprinkle the feta over the whole thing. Cover the skillet and turn the heat down to medium-low.

Let it cook for 5 minutes and then check for doneness. You want the egg whites set but the yolks still runny. Re-cover and give it another couple of minutes if needed.

To serve, use a big spoon to scoop up each egg with the sauce around it.

3 tablespoons (42g) butter

8 ounces (225g) sliced mushrooms

1 bunch of scallions, thinly sliced

6 eggs

1 cup (225g) cottage cheese, creamed (small or large curd)

⅓ cup (33g) grated Parmesan cheese

2 tablespoons (28ml) dry vermouth or dry white wine (optional)

1 teaspoon salt or Vege-Sal

¼ teaspoon pepper

1 cup (110g) shredded Swiss cheese, divided

YIELD: 3 servings – Per serving: 260 calories; 18g fat (64.8% calories from fat); 18g protein; 5g carbohydrate; 1g dietary fiber; 4g net carbohydrate.

CHEESE AND MUSHROOM EGG BAKE

This is great for serving a weekend crowd. It's also great for stashing in the fridge for quick breakfasts and suppers for a few days—it reheats beautifully.

Our tester, Rebecca, tells us her husband says the vermouth makes this more a brunch or supper dish than a breakfast dish. She also says it's great with shallots in place of the scallions, so use whichever you have on hand.

Preheat the oven to 350°F (180°C, or gas mark 4). Coat an 8 × 8-inch (20 × 20cm) baking dish with nonstick cooking spray.

Give your large, heavy skillet a shot of nonstick cooking spray. Put it over medium heat, melt the butter, and add the mushrooms. Sauté until the mushrooms soften and turn dark. Add the scallions and sauté for another 1 to 2 minutes.

In a medium-size mixing bowl, whisk together the eggs, cottage cheese, Parmesan, vermouth (if using), salt, and pepper. Pour half of the egg mixture into the prepared baking dish. Spread the mushroom mixture over that and then sprinkle half the Swiss cheese over it. Pour in the rest of the eggs.

Bake for 30 minutes. Top with the remaining Swiss cheese and bake for another 15 minutes or until cheese is turning golden.

SUN-DRIED TOMATO AND CHEESE FRITTATA

1/4 cup (60ml) olive oil

1/2 of a small onion, minced

1/3 cup (37g) sun-dried tomatoes, oil-packed, slivered

1 1/2 teaspoons Italian seasoning

1 clove of garlic, crushed

6 eggs

1 tablespoon (15ml) oil from the sun-dried tomato jar

1/4 cup (30g) shredded mozzarella cheese, divided

1/4 cup (25g) Asiago cheese, divided

1/4 cup (20g) shredded Parmesan cheese, divided

1/2 teaspoon salt

1/4 teaspoon pepper

YIELD: 4 servings – Per serving: 344 calories; 30g fat (77.7% calories from fat); 14g protein; 5g carbohydrate; 1g dietary fiber; 4g net carbohydrate.

This is a nice breakfast for a family that is—to steal a phrase from my idol, Peg Bracken—pizza-prone or otherwise Italy oriented. It makes for a good quick supper, too. Add bagged salad and crusty bread for any carbivores and you can have dinner on the table in 20 minutes or less!

Grab your large, heavy-bottomed skillet. If it's not nonstick, give it a squirt of cooking spray. Put it over medium-low heat. Add the olive oil and sauté the onion gently for 5 minutes until translucent. Add the tomatoes, Italian seasoning, and garlic. Let it cook, stirring, for another 2 to 3 minutes.

Break the eggs into a mixing bowl. Whisk in the oil, half of the cheeses, and the salt and pepper.

Turn up the heat under the skillet to medium and distribute the tomato and onion evenly across the bottom. When a drop of water hisses when it hits the pan, give the egg mixture one more stir and then pour it in. Adjust the heat back to medium-low and let the whole thing cook for 5 to 6 minutes.

Meanwhile, turn on your broiler. Put the rack in the top position.

When the edges of the frittata are set, but the center's still a little shaky, sprinkle the remaining cheeses over the top. Slide it under the broiler for 2 to 3 minutes or until the cheese is melted and starting to turn golden. Cut into wedges to serve.

TURKEY-ASPARAGUS BRUNCH BAKE

1 pound (455g) asparagus

1/2 red bell pepper, diced

1 medium onion, diced

2 cups (280g) diced turkey

1 cup (110g) shredded Swiss cheese, divided

6 eggs

1 cup (225g) cottage cheese, creamed (large or small curd)

1/3 cup (33g) grated Parmesan cheese

1 teaspoon Italian seasoning

1 teaspoon salt

1/2 teaspoon pepper

YIELD: 6 servings – Per serving: 286 calories; 16g fat (49.9% calories from fat); 29g protein; 7g carbohydrate; 1g dietary fiber; 6g net carbohydrate.

Are you having houseguests Thanksgiving weekend? Feed everyone breakfast at the same time! Double this if you've got a big crowd. You really don't need anything but coffee or tea with this, but put out toast for the carbivores if you must.

Preheat the oven to 350°F (180°C, or gas mark 4). Coat a 2-quart (2L) casserole dish with nonstick cooking spray.

Snap the ends off the asparagus where it wants to break naturally, then cut it into 1-inch (2.5cm) pieces. Put them in a microwaveable bowl or microwave steamer. Add a tablespoon or two (15 to 28ml) of water, cover, and microwave for just 3 minutes. Uncover immediately! You only want to parcook it. Drain and put in the prepared casserole dish. Add the pepper, onion, turkey, and half of the Swiss cheese. Stir everything up so it's all evenly distributed.

In a medium-size mixing bowl, whisk together the eggs, cottage cheese, Parmesan, Italian seasoning, salt, and pepper. Pour this mixture over all the stuff in the casserole dish. Again, mess it around a bit with a spoon so the egg mixture gets down through all the other stuff.

Bake for 40 minutes and then sprinkle with the remaining Swiss cheese. Give it another 10 to 12 minutes until the cheese is touched with gold.

CHAPTER 6

Side Salads

Here is where the world turns upside down. For how long have you been told that salad is the dieter's best friend? It's so ingrained that there's a whole trope of "woman laughing eating salad"—no, really, Google it. It's a thing; you'll find endless photos of just that, illustrating how happy and healthy salad will make you feel.

Yet on a keto diet, salads are among your carb foods and must be appraised accordingly. Dr. Atkins limited folks on Induction to 2 cups (110g) of salad per day. Depending upon your metabolism and your reasons for eating keto, you may need to do the same.

But there are salads and then there are salads. As I developed these recipes, I ran the numbers on some very tasty salads whose macros just didn't make the cut. On the other hand, a salad of very low-carb vegetables with plenty of dressing made with healthful fats can balance the numbers of a lower fat dish such as fish or poultry.

Speaking of dressings: please, please make your own. I don't believe I have ever seen a packaged salad dressing that did not include objectionable fats. Most are laden with soy oil. When you're centering your diet on healthful fats, this simply will not do. And salad dressing is so quick and easy to make and so much better than the store-bought stuff, that you'll wonder why you ever bought a bottle of dressing. The dressings are at the end of this chapter. Make them and stash them in the fridge for the evening when you come home tired, cranky, and hungry. Then, pour them on some bagged salad, pile it next to the rotisserie chicken you picked up at the grocery store, and be the person laughing, eating salad.

CUCUMBER SALAD

2 pounds (910g) cucumbers (2 medium-size)

¼ cup (40g) finely diced red onion

¼ cup (60ml) cider vinegar

¼ cup (60ml) MCT oil

1 clove of garlic, minced

12 drops of liquid stevia, plain

½ teaspoon salt

¼ teaspoon pepper

2 tablespoons (8g) minced fresh dill or 2 teaspoons dried

This was billed as the World's Best Cucumber Salad, but from our perspective, it had a couple of flaws: it called for honey, and it contained no oil. I fixed that! Is it the World's Best? I dunno; I've loved a lot of cucumber salads in my day. But, it's darned good.

Slice the cucumbers in half lengthwise and then slice thin. You can peel 'em first if you like, but I don't. I like the color and texture contrast. Put them in a nonreactive mixing bowl—stainless steel, glass, or plastic will do. Add the onion.

Put the cider vinegar, MCT oil, garlic, liquid stevia, salt, and pepper in a jar, seal it, and shake hard. Pour this over the vegetables and stir to coat. Add the dill and stir it in, too. (If you're using dried, you may as well just put it in the jar with the other dressing ingredients.) Refrigerate for several hours before serving and then stir again right before you dish it out.

YIELD: 6 servings – Per serving: 104 calories; 9g fat (76.2% calories from fat); 1g protein; 5g carbohydrate; 1g dietary fiber; 4g net carbohydrate.

SQUASH AND "RICE" SALAD

½ of a head of cauliflower

1 small zucchini

1 small summer squash

4 scallions

⅓ cup (80ml) extra-virgin olive oil, divided

1 clove of garlic, crushed

¼ cup (16g) minced parsley

2 tablespoons (8g) minced fresh dill

2 tablespoons (28ml) white wine vinegar

Salt and pepper

4 ounces (115g) chèvre (goat cheese)

If your grocery store carries pre-riced cauliflower, feel free to use it! A half a head of cauliflower yields roughly 5 cups (600g) of Cauli-Rice.

Using the directions for Cauli-Rice on page 107, prepare your cauliflower.

Trim the ends from your squashes and cut them into ½-inch (1.3cm) dice. Slice your scallions about ¼ inch (6mm) thick, including the crisp part of the green shoot.

Put your large, heavy skillet over medium-high heat. When it's hot, add ¼ cup (60ml) of the olive oil and throw in the squash. Sauté it for 1 to 2 minutes and then add the scallions and the garlic. Sauté for another 2 to 3 minutes. Remove from the heat and let cool.

By now your Cauli-Rice is done microwaving—pull it out and let it cool, too. Indeed, you can sauté the zucchini and microwave the cauliflower in advance, stash them both in the fridge, and then pull them out at suppertime and assemble your salad quickly.

Put your cooled Cauli-Rice in a salad or mixing bowl. Add the squash, including all of the olive oil left in the pan. Add the parsley, dill, the remaining 4 teaspoons (20ml) of olive oil, and the white wine vinegar. Toss until everything is evenly mixed. Season with salt and pepper to taste.

Use the tip of a spoon to spoon out bits of goat cheese, about 1 teaspoon each. Stir gently into the salad and you're done.

YIELD: 6 servings – Per serving: 220 calories; 19g fat (74.8% calories from fat); 8g protein; 7g carbohydrate; 3g dietary fiber; 4g net carbohydrate.

1 medium cucumber

1 large tomato, good and ripe

1 avocado

⅓ cup (53g) finely diced red onion

¼ cup (4g) minced cilantro

¼ cup (60ml) extra-virgin olive oil

3 tablespoons (45ml) lime juice

1 teaspoon salt

¼ teaspoon pepper

2 dashes of hot sauce (optional)

YIELD: 6 servings – Per serving: 150 calories; 14g fat (80.7% calories from fat); 1g protein; 6g carbohydrate; 2g dietary fiber; 4g net carbohydrate.

½ cup (60g) chopped walnuts

½ of a medium cucumber, diced

2 celery ribs, thinly sliced

¼ cup (38g) diced red bell pepper

¼ cup (38g) diced green bell pepper

1 large tomato

3 scallions, including the crisp green part, thinly sliced

¾ cup (180g) mayonnaise

Salt and pepper to taste

6 lettuce leaves

YIELD: 6 servings – Per serving: 277 calories; 29g fat (89% calories from fat); 3g protein; 5g carbohydrate; 2g dietary fiber; 3g net carbohydrate.

TOMATO, CUCUMBER, AND AVOCADO SALAD

This is a salad to be saved for August and September, when the farmers' markets and roadside stands are flooded with gorgeous ripe tomatoes and cucumbers. It would be perfect alongside a grilled steak, but don't even try it with second-rate produce. Our tester Sheryl says, "Very easy to prepare, tastes awesome. I'd give it a 10. I will make this again. I just hope I don't eat the whole thing in one sitting. A definite YUM!" This is not a salad to make ahead of time. Freshness is of the essence. It's best to start dicing when the steak goes on the grill.

This couldn't be much easier: Dice the cucumber, tomato, and avocado—you can peel your cuke if you want, but I wouldn't unless it was coated with wax—and put 'em in a bowl. Throw in the onion and cilantro.

Put the olive oil, lime juice, salt, pepper, and hot sauce, if using, in a clean jar. Seal it tightly and shake like mad for 15 seconds or so. Pour this over your salad, stir gently to coat, and serve it forth.

WAYBACK SALAD

I just love old cookbooks—the ones written before fat phobia. The inspiration for this was a cookbook first published in 1896, though the next edition was positively recent: the 1965 edition of *The Fannie Farmer Cookbook*. Funny, isn't it, how Grandma and Grandpa didn't get fat? Our tester, Wendy, rated this a 10, adding, "I loved this salad. It's easy and it tastes great. It would be a great side salad for summer."

Preheat the oven to 350°F (180°C, or gas mark 4). Spread the chopped walnuts in a shallow baking dish and give them 7 to 8 minutes to toast a bit.

Add the cucumber, celery, green pepper, and red pepper to a salad bowl. Cut the tomato in half along the equator. Gently squeeze out the seeds and then dice the rest and add to the salad.

When the walnuts come out of the oven, let them cool for a few minutes and then add to the salad. Add the mayonnaise and stir to coat. Season with salt and pepper to taste. Serve in scoops on lettuce-lined plates.

1 large cucumber

¼ of a large red onion

⅓ cup (33g) pitted kalamata olives

½ cup (75g) crumbled feta cheese

2 tablespoons (8g) minced fresh dill

¼ cup (60ml) extra-virgin olive oil

2 tablespoons (28ml) lemon juice

¼ teaspoon pepper

Salt to taste

YIELD: 4 servings – Per serving: 237 calories; 23g fat (85.0% calories from fat); 3g protein; 6g carbohydrate; 1g dietary fiber; 5g net carbohydrate.

MEDITERRANEAN CUCUMBER SALAD

I'm thinking this would be just the thing with grilled lamb—or Greek chicken!

Peel your cucumber if you prefer; I like them skin-on. Quarter it lengthwise and then cut crosswise into ¼-inch (6mm) slices. Put in a nonreactive bowl (stainless steel, glass, or even plastic).

Slice the onion paper thin and add it to the cucumbers. Coarsely chop the olives and add them to the salad, along with the feta. Sprinkle in the minced dill. Gently stir everything together.

In a clean jar, combine the olive oil, lemon juice, and pepper. Seal tightly and shake it hard. Pour over the salad and stir to coat.

If you're serving the salad immediately, season with salt to taste. If you make it ahead, refrigerate unsalted and salt just before serving.

---

1 pound (455g) frozen green beans or haricot vert

2 tablespoons (28ml) extra-virgin olive oil

2 tablespoons (28ml) MCT oil

2 tablespoons (28ml) white wine vinegar

2 tablespoons (28ml) lemon juice

1 clove of garlic, crushed

1 tablespoon (1g) minced cilantro

1 tablespoon (4g) minced parsley

12 drops of liquid stevia, plain

½ teaspoon sriracha

4 ounces (115g) roasted, salted macadamia nuts

YIELD: 6 servings – Per serving: 241 calories; 23g fat (80.9% calories from fat); 3g protein; 9g carbohydrate; 4g dietary fiber; 5g net carbohydrate.

GREEN BEAN SALAD
WITH MACADAMIA NUTS

Made with thawed frozen green beans, this salad is super-simple, yet surprisingly elegant. Consider this the summer-night equivalent of Green Beans Almondine. Recipe tester Rebecca says that if you don't like cilantro, this will be just as delicious with 2 tablespoons (8g) of parsley instead.

Thaw your green beans: you may as well just take them out of the freezer in the morning and leave them in the fridge to thaw until suppertime. Drain them well and put them in a mixing bowl.

Combine the olive oil, MCT oil, white wine vinegar, lemon juice, garlic, cilantro, parsley, liquid stevia, and sriracha in a clean jar, seal tightly, and shake hard for 15 to 20 seconds. Then pour the dressing over the green beans and toss until they're all coated.

Leave the green beans to get acquainted with the dressing while you coarsely chop the macadamia nuts.

Give your green beans another stir and then arrange them prettily on a platter. Sprinkle the chopped macadamia nuts evenly over the green beans and serve.

NOTE: My local grocery store carries frozen green beans labeled "haricot vert." They are thinner and more delicate than the regular green beans, and preferable for this salad. But if your grocery store doesn't carry these, you can use regular frozen green beans, preferably whole. Or, for that matter, you can use fresh green beans, topped and tailed and steamed for just 5 minutes or so in the microwave. This will bring them to about the texture of the frozen beans, thawed.

For a change—and a more colorful salad—try making this with half green beans and half wax beans, which are similar to green beans, only yellow. My local grocery store carries the two frozen together.

¼ cup (34g) hazelnuts

1 tablespoon (15ml) cider vinegar

3 tablespoons (45ml) light olive oil

1 tablespoon (15ml) walnut oil

6 pale inner celery ribs

3 radishes

¼ cup (15g) chopped parsley

Salt and pepper to taste

YIELD: 4 servings – Per serving: 187 calories; 19g fat (88.1% calories from fat); 2g protein; 4g carbohydrate; 2g dietary fiber; 2g net carbohydrate.

CELERY AND RADISH SALAD

Originally appearing in *500 Paleo Recipes*, this salad fit our macros too well to not be included. For this you want pale, tender, inner celery ribs, but not the little teeny ones in the heart—just not the big, strong-flavored outer ribs.

Preheat the oven to 350°F (180°C, or gas mark 4). Spread your hazelnuts on a baking sheet, put 'em in the oven, and set your timer for 8 minutes.

Meanwhile, mix together the cider vinegar and oils in a jar. Reserve.

Slice your celery very thinly and put it in a salad bowl. Slice up any unwilted leaves and add them, too. Slice your radishes as thinly as possible and add them to the celery. Add the parsley, too.

Somewhere in here the timer will beep. Pull out your hazelnuts and let them cool for a few minutes. When you can handle them, rub them between your palms to flake off most of the brown skin. (Don't panic if a little clings. It's no big deal.) Chop them and add them to the salad.

Pour on the dressing and toss well. Season with salt and pepper to taste. You can serve this immediately or make it in advance and stash it in the fridge—it'll hold overnight, no problem. Indeed, it may improve on standing.

14 ounces (390g) coleslaw mix

¾ cup (75g) thinly sliced celery

¾ cup (180g) mayonnaise

2 tablespoons (28ml) cider vinegar

6 drops of liquid stevia, plain

¼ teaspoon salt or Vege-Sal

¼ teaspoon celery seed

⅛ teaspoon pepper

¾ cup (90g) crumbled blue cheese (Go with a mild one.)

YIELD: 6 servings – Per serving: 260 calories; 28g fat (92.3% calories from fat); 4g protein; 1g carbohydrate; trace dietary fiber; 3g net carbohydrate.

BLUE CHEESE SLAW

This upgraded coleslaw would be right at home next to a juicy hunk of grilled steak or as a bed for a smoking-hot bratwurst. It's likely to make you popular at the neighborhood cookout. Angele, our tester, proclaimed this "Really, really good!"

Follow your basic coleslaw procedure: put the coleslaw mix and celery in a big mixing bowl.

Combine the mayonnaise, cider vinegar, liquid stevia, salt, celery seed, and pepper in a bowl and stir to blend. Pour over the veggies and toss until everything is evenly coated. Add the blue cheese and toss to incorporate. Chill for a few hours before serving.

½ of a head of cabbage

¼ cup (40g) finely minced red onion

1 recipe Classic Coleslaw Dressing (page 103)

YIELD: 5 servings – Per serving: 234 calories; 24g fat (85.2% calories from fat); 2g protein; 7g carbohydrate; 2g dietary fiber; 5g net carbohydrate.

CLASSIC COLESLAW

I never tire of coleslaw. To me, it is the perfect side dish with roasted chicken, ribs, pork steaks, pulled pork, and all sorts of things. It's cheap and easy, too!

This is super-simple: Shred the cabbage and add it, along with the onion, to a big mixing bowl. Add the Classic Coleslaw Dressing and stir to coat. It's great served right away or refrigerated overnight.

½ cup (60g) walnuts

5 ounces (140g) baby spinach

2½ ounces (70g) mixed bagged salad including radicchio

1 scallion, including the crisp green part, thinly sliced

2 tablespoons (28ml) MCT oil

2 tablespoons (28ml) extra-virgin olive oil

2 tablespoons (28ml) sherry vinegar

1 teaspoon Dijon mustard

¼ teaspoon salt

⅛ teaspoon pepper

1 ripe avocado

4 ounces (115g) crumbled Gorgonzola cheese

YIELD: 4 servings – Per serving: 413 calories; 38g fat (79.8% calories from fat); 12g protein; 9g carbohydrate; 5g dietary fiber; 4g net carbohydrate.

AVOCADO, GORGONZOLA, AND WALNUT SALAD

This salad is filled with all sorts of yummy, fatty things! Our tester Rebecca says, "We all could easily imagine getting this salad as a first course in one of our favorite expensive restaurants." This serves four as a side salad, but consider splitting it two ways as a nice lunch. It's also great to serve with a less-fatty main course, such as fish.

Preheat the oven to 350°F (180°C, or gas mark 4). Spread the walnuts in a shallow baking dish, slide 'em in, and set your timer for 6 minutes.

Put your spinach, greens, and scallion in a big salad bowl.

Combine the oils, sherry vinegar, Dijon mustard, salt, and pepper in a clean old jar, seal tightly, and shake hard.

When the timer beeps, pull your walnuts out of the oven. Let them cool for a couple of minutes.

Meanwhile, halve your avocado, remove the pit, peel, and slice. Coarsely chop the walnuts.

Give the dressing a shake, pour it over the greens, and toss until everything is evenly coated. Artfully top the salad with the walnuts, avocado, and Gorgonzola. Done!

NOTE: Fresh Express brand has a 50/50 salad that is just about perfect for this. If your grocery store carries it, 8 ounces (225g) will be about perfect in place of both the spinach and the mixed greens.

2 cups (270g) hazelnuts

3 celery hearts (I can buy packages of 3 organic celery hearts at my grocery store.)

1½ cups (120g) shredded Parmesan, (150g) Romano, or a blend

⅔ cup (160ml) Lemon Vinaigrette (page 99)

Parsley leaves, for garnish (optional)

YIELD: 8 servings – Per serving: 339 calories; 32g fat (81.0% calories from fat); 10g protein; 7g carbohydrate; 2g dietary fiber; 5g net carbohydrate.

CELERY HAZELNUT SALAD

Our tester Rebecca said she expected this to be "weird," but that she found it very tasty. However, she also cautions that this makes a lot of salad. I would point out that there's no law against cutting the recipe down a bit! How about ⅔ cup (90g) hazelnuts, 1 celery heart, ½ cup (45g) shredded Parmesan, and dressing to taste? Just sayin'. Rebecca also mentions that Trader Joe's carries bags of toasted hazelnuts with the brown skin already removed.

Preheat the oven to 350°F (180°C, or gas mark 4). Spread the hazelnuts in a shallow roasting pan. Roast for about 12 minutes. Let them cool a little while you deal with the celery.

Trim any brown bits from the ends of your celery hearts and then slice across them at ¼-inch (6mm) intervals, including the leaves. Put in a salad bowl.

Your hazelnuts should now be cool enough to handle. Roll them between or under your palms to flake off the brown skin—don't obsess, it's not essential to get every single fleck. Chop the nuts coarsely and add to the celery. Add the shredded Parmesan and the Lemon Vinaigrette and stir it all up.

If you want to be spiffy, garnish each serving with a few parsley leaves and an extra sprinkle of shredded cheese.

1 pound (455g) asparagus

1 tablespoon (15ml) olive oil

Salt and pepper to taste

⅛ of a large red onion or ¼ of a small one, sliced paper-thin

1 cup (100g) pitted olives

¼ cup (60ml) vinaigrette of your choice

2 tablespoons (10g) shredded Parmesan cheese

YIELD: 4 servings – Per serving: 165 calories; 16g fat (80.9% calories from fat); 3g protein; 6g carbohydrate; 2g dietary fiber; 4g net carbohydrate.

ASPARAGUS OLIVE SALAD

This recipe is great for an electric contact grill or a stove-top grill pan. If you're going to grill it on the barbecue, do yourself a favor and get a small-holed grill rack, or you'll be losing asparagus through the grill and cursing, which is no way to start a nice dinner. Our tester Christina says, "This would be an excellent side to steak. It makes a nice presentation and would be worthy of serving to guests."

Whatever sort of grill you're using, start it heating. You want medium-high heat.

Snap the bottoms off the asparagus where they want to break naturally. Toss the spears with the olive oil and season with salt and pepper. Grill the asparagus 5 to 7 minutes until it has some brown spots.

When it's done, lay it in a shallow pan because asparagus spears don't fit in bowls very well. Add the onion and olives. Pour on the vinaigrette and toss until everything is coated. Plate and top each serving with a sprinkle of Parmesan.

1 pound (455g) asparagus

¼ cup (34g) hazelnuts

6 ounces (170g) mixed greens

¼ cup (60ml) extra-virgin olive oil

2 tablespoons (28ml) white balsamic vinegar

1 teaspoon Dijon mustard

¼ teaspoon salt

Salt and pepper to taste

⅛ teaspoon pepper

3 ounces (85g) soft and creamy goat cheese

YIELD: 4 servings – Per serving: 298 calories; 27g fat (77.6% calories from fat); 10g protein; 7g carbohydrate; 3g dietary fiber; 4g net carbohydrate.

NOTE: I used bagged salad mixes for this; mixed greens with butter lettuce is a good combo.

ASPARAGUS SALAD WITH GOAT CHEESE AND HAZELNUTS

This would be a perfect salad for a spring party—Easter dinner, a baby shower, or the like. Or, just because it's asparagus season! We must make our celebrations as we find them.

Preheat the oven to 350°F (180°C, or gas mark 4).

Snap the ends off of the asparagus where the spears want to break naturally. Lay the spears on your cutting board and cut into 1-inch (2.5cm) lengths. Put your asparagus in a microwaveable casserole dish with a lid or a microwave steamer, add a couple of tablespoons (28ml) of water, and nuke for 4 minutes on high.

The oven's hot! Spread your hazelnuts in a shallow baking dish, put them in the oven, and set the timer for 6 minutes.

Pile your greens into a salad bowl.

The asparagus is done! Pull it out of the microwave and uncover to let the steam out and stop the cooking.

Pull out your hazelnuts and let them cool a little, too.

Put the olive oil, white balsamic vinegar, Dijon mustard, salt, and pepper in a clean jar. Seal tightly and shake hard.

Okay, the asparagus has cooled a little. Add it to the greens.

When you can handle the hazelnuts, roll them between your palms to flake off most of the brown skin. Chop them coarsely.

Give the dressing another quick shake. Pour it over the greens and asparagus and toss. Pile this onto 4 salad plates. Top each serving with one-fourth of the hazelnuts.

Use the tip of a spoon to distribute dabs of the goat cheese over each salad—you can just dig it out of the plastic wrapper. Done!

2 medium cucumbers

1 medium tomato

½ cup (56g) bacon bits

⅓ cup (75g) mayonnaise

½ of a clove of garlic, crushed

Salt and pepper

YIELD: 6 servings – Per serving: 141 calories; 13g fat (73.6% calories from fat); 4g protein; 6g carbohydrate; 2g dietary fiber; 4g net carbohydrate.

CUCUMBER TOMATO SALAD

Ah, real bacon bits in packages—how you have changed my life! You can, of course, cook and crumble bacon to go in your salad, instead. Me, I buy real bacon bits in huge bags at Costco.

Slice your cukes in half lengthwise and use a spoon to scrape out the seeds. You can peel them, too, if you like, but I like the touch of dark green in my salad. Cut them lengthwise again, into quarters, and then slice crosswise ¼ inch (6mm) thick. Put 'em in a salad bowl or mixing bowl.

Dice your tomato fairly fine and add it to the cucumbers. Throw in the bacon bits, as well.

Stir together the mayonnaise and garlic and then stir into the salad. Season with salt and pepper to taste and you're done.

⅓ cup (33g) walnuts

1 cucumber

1 cup (230g) sour cream

2 cloves of garlic, crushed

½ teaspoon salt or Vege-Sal

2 tablespoons (8g) minced fresh dill

YIELD: 5 servings – Per serving: 159 calories; 14g fat (78.3% calories from fat); 4g protein; 5g carbohydrate; 1g dietary fiber; 4g net carbohydrate.

CUCUMBER WALNUT SALAD

Cool and creamy, this would be great on a summer night with just about anything grilled. The 78 percent fat content will help balance out a lower fat protein, such as chicken.

Preheat the oven to 350°F (180°C, or gas mark 4). Spread the walnuts in a shallow baking tray, put 'em in the oven, and set the timer for 7 minutes.

Halve the cuke lengthwise and then slice each half lengthwise into ¼-inch (6mm) slices. Now, slice across them, also ¼ inch (6mm) apart. Put all your little cucumber bits in a nonreactive bowl (stainless steel, glass, or plastic).

Mix together the sour cream, garlic, salt, and dill in a small bowl.

The timer beeped! Pull out the walnuts and let them cool for a minute or two.

Meanwhile, stir the sour cream mixture into the cucumbers.

Chop the walnuts and stir them in. Chill for a few hours before serving.

---

1 recipe Rebecca Says Make This Dressing! (page 102)

1 pound (455g) sliced mushrooms (Buy 'em that way!)

½ cup (40g) shredded (not grated) Parmesan cheese

YIELD: 6 servings – Per serving: 209 calories; 20g fat (82.8% calories from fat); 4g protein; 5g carbohydrate; 1g dietary fiber; 4g net carbohydrate.

MUSHROOM SALAD

Recipe tester Rebecca rates this recipe a 10 and says, "This is the easiest recipe I've made for you yet. And it was wonderful. The dressing is so thick and tangy, and I would put it in a dressing section so people know they can use it for other things. I think it would be delicious with any other kind of vegetable, too." However, she warns this salad does not keep well, so you should plan to eat it all up.

We're going to assume you've already make your dressing, since Rebecca says you should.

Just before serving, put the mushrooms in a salad bowl. Give the dressing another good shake, pour it on, and toss. Plate and top each serving with a generous 1⅓ tablespoons (8g) of shredded Parmesan.

2 medium tomatoes,
good and ripe

½ of a medium cucumber

4 scallions

¼ cup (25g) sliced
pimento-stuffed olives

2 tablespoons (17g) capers,
drained

1 recipe Paprika-Cumin
Vinaigrette (page 100)

1 bunch of watercress

5 ounces (140g) mixed greens

YIELD: 6 servings – Per serving:
138 calories; 13g fat (79.6%
calories from fat); 2g protein;
6g carbohydrate; 2g dietary fiber;
4g net carbohydrate.

GREEN SALAD WITH OLIVES AND CAPERS

This is a flavorsome combination of tomatoes, cucumber, scallions, and olives, served on greens. How unusual! How enticing!

Halve your tomatoes through the equator and squeeze each half gently to remove the seeds (or just stick in the tip of a spoon or your finger and flick 'em out). Cut into ¼-inch (6mm) dice and put in a salad bowl or nonreactive mixing bowl (stainless steel, glass, or plastic).

Cut your half-cucumber in half again lengthwise and scoop out the seeds. Cut it, too, into ¼-inch (6mm) dice. Let them go howdy with the tomato dice.

Slice the scallions, including the crisp part of the green shoot, and add them to the mix along with the olives. (If you want to cheat, you can buy jars of "salad olives"—presliced pimento-stuffed olives. Most of the pimentos will have fallen out, but they'll mix up fine in the salad.) Add the capers.

Pour the Paprika-Cumin Vinaigrette over the whole thing and stir to coat. Break the watercress into sprigs and stir it in gently. Make 6 beds of the baby greens and spoon the dressed mixture onto them.

2 tablespoons (28g) butter

¼ cup (30g) chopped pecans

2 cups (94g) romaine lettuce

1 cup (40g) radicchio

1 cup (55g) Boston lettuce

1 cup (50g) curly endive

1 cup (50g) frisée

½ cup (120ml) Raspberry
Vinaigrette (page 98)

¼ of a small red onion, sliced
paper-thin

¼ cup (30g) crumbled
blue cheese

4 slices of bacon, cooked until
crisp and crumbled

YIELD: 4 servings – Per serving:
287 calories; 29g fat (87.7%
calories from fat); 4g protein;
6g carbohydrate; 2g dietary fiber;
4g net carbohydrate.

BAYSIDE SALAD

Appearing first in *500 Low-Carb Recipes*, this is my knockoff of a fantastic salad I had at the Bayside Grill down on the Gulf Coast. You can play with the combination of greens, but just make sure some of them are bitter.

In a small skillet over medium-low heat, melt the butter and sauté the pecans until they smell toasty, about 5 minutes. Remove from the heat.

In a big salad bowl, combine all the leafy stuff. Pour on the vinaigrette and toss-toss-toss until every leaf is coated. Pile the lettuce onto 4 salad plates. Top each with the thin-sliced red onion and then a tablespoon each of the (8g) blue cheese, (7g) crumbled bacon, and those (8g) pecans you toasted. Serve immediately!

1 head of cauliflower, about 2 pounds (910g)

1 cup (120g) diced celery

½ cup (80g) diced red onion

⅓ cup (53g) chopped sugar-free bread-and-butter pickles

1¼ cups (285g) mayonnaise

2 teaspoons celery seed

2 teaspoons cider vinegar

2 teaspoons yellow mustard

1½ teaspoons salt

12 drops of liquid stevia, plain

½ cup (56g) bacon bits

2 hard-boiled eggs

YIELD: 12 servings – Per serving: 214 calories; 22g fat (84.2% calories from fat); 4g protein; 5g carbohydrate; 2g dietary fiber; 3g net carbohydrate.

CREAMY UNPOTATO SALAD

The potato salad recipe I adapted this from had dozens of 5-star reviews, and it really is quite wonderful as an UnPotato Salad. If your local grocery store doesn't carry sugar-free bread-and-butter pickles, tell them to get with it, already!

Trim the leaves and the very bottom of the stem from the cauliflower and cut the rest into ½-inch (1.3cm) pieces. Put them in a microwaveable casserole dish or a microwave steamer, add a couple tablespoons (28ml) of water, cover, and microwave on high until tender but not mushy, about 9 to 10 minutes.

Meanwhile, combine the celery, onion, and pickles in a large, nonreactive mixing bowl (stainless steel, glass, or plastic).

In a smaller bowl, combine the mayonnaise, celery seed, cider vinegar, mustard, salt, and liquid stevia. Stir it all together; this is your dressing.

When the microwave beeps, pull out the cauliflower and uncover immediately to stop the cooking. Drain and let cool to the point where it won't cook the other vegetables.

Drain the cauliflower very well and add it to the mixing bowl. Pour on the dressing and stir to coat.

I use packaged real bacon bits. I refresh them by spreading them on a plate and microwaving on high for about 45 seconds. Add to the salad.

Peel and chop the eggs. Stir in gently, so as to preserve some nice hunks of yolk. Chill for several hours before serving.

½ of a head of cauliflower

1 cup (120g) diced celery (pale inner ribs)

⅓ cup (53g) finely diced red onion

2 teaspoons salt

⅓ cup (80ml) vinaigrette (pages 98 to 100 or your favorite recipe)

½ cup (115g) mayonnaise

3 hard-boiled eggs

YIELD: 6 servings – Per serving: 251 calories; 25g fat (86.2% calories from fat); 5g protein; 5g carbohydrate; 2g dietary fiber; 3g net carbohydrate.

OLD-SCHOOL UNPOTATO SALAD

Okay, there's no such thing as an old-school unpotato salad. But this is an adaptation of a seventy-year-old potato salad recipe. I had never used vinaigrette in an unpotato salad recipe before, nor marinated the vegetables. I will again!

Trim the leaves and the very bottom of the stem from the cauliflower. Cut it into ½-inch (1.3cm) chunks, put 'em in a microwaveable casserole dish or microwave steamer, add a few tablespoons (45ml) of water, cover, and nuke on high for 8 to 10 minutes. You want it tender but not mushy.

Meanwhile, combine the celery and onion in a nonreactive mixing bowl (stainless steel, glass, or plastic).

Uncover the cauliflower as soon as the microwave beeps to stop the cooking. Drain and let it cool to the point where it won't cook the celery and onion. Add to the mixing bowl. Add the salt and vinaigrette and stir to coat. Let the vegetables marinate in the vinaigrette for a good hour or two. When the vegetables are well acquainted with the vinaigrette, stir in the mayo.

Peel and chop the eggs and stir them in gently, so as to preserve some hunks of yolk. Chill until serving time.

½ of a head of cauliflower

8 ounces (225g) bacon, cooked until crisp and crumbled

2 medium tomatoes, diced

1 bunch of scallions, including the crisp green part, sliced

½ cup (115g) mayonnaise

Salt and pepper

YIELD: 6 servings – Per serving: 371 calories; 34g fat (81.3% calories from fat); 13g protein; 5g carbohydrate; 2g dietary fiber; 3g net carbohydrate.

BACON, TOMATO, AND CAULIFLOWER SALAD

This recipe originally called for cooked rice, so I tried it with Cauli-Rice. I liked it so much I ate it all and made it again the very next day. It's great for potlucks and barbecues.

Shred and cook the cauliflower as instructed under Cauli-Rice, page 107.

When the cauliflower has cooled, combine it with the bacon, tomatoes, scallions, and mayonnaise in a big bowl. Stir to coat. Season with salt and pepper to taste and mix again.

If you're feeling fancy, you can pack this into a custard cup and then turn it out, molded, onto a lettuce-lined plate.

---

1 green bell pepper

2 cucumbers, scrubbed but not peeled

½ of a large red onion

½ of a head of cauliflower

2 teaspoons salt or Vege-Sal

1½ cups (345g) sour cream

3 tablespoons (45ml) cider vinegar

1 tablespoon (3g) dried dill (unless you have fresh on hand—then use a few tablespoons, [12g] minced)

YIELD: 10 servings – Per serving: 97 calories; 7g fat (65.3% calories from fat); 2g protein; 7g carbohydrate; 2g dietary fiber; 5g net carbohydrate.

SOUR CREAM SALAD

This is one of those great salads that actually benefits from a day in the refrigerator. That lets you make your salad way in advance!

Slice the vegetables as thinly as you can—I use my food processor's slicing blade.

In a big, nonreactive mixing bowl—I use stainless steel, but glass or plastic will do—toss the vegetables with the salt. Chill for 1 to 2 hours.

In a smaller bowl, combine the sour cream, cider vinegar, and dill.

Pull the vegetables out of the fridge and drain off the water that will have collected at the bottom of the bowl. Stir in the sour cream dressing.

½ of a head of cabbage, shredded

½ cup (115g) mayonnaise

2 tablespoons (28ml) heavy cream

1 teaspoon yellow mustard

½ teaspoon salt

½ teaspoon pepper

½ of a clove of garlic, crushed

6 drops of liquid stevia, plain

YIELD: 6 servings – Per serving: 152 calories; 17g fat (96.8% calories from fat); trace protein; 1g carbohydrate; trace dietary fiber; 1g net carbohydrate.

GARLICKY SLAW

The recipe from which I adapted this billed it as "The Best Coleslaw You'll Ever Eat." I don't know about that—I still like my Classic Coleslaw Dressing best—but it's awfully good. Of course, I've made very few kinds of slaw I didn't like!

Follow the classic coleslaw procedure: add your cabbage to a mixing bowl. Stir together everything else, pour it over the cabbage, and stir until it's all evenly coated. Chill for a few hours for the flavors to marry.

NOTE: You can make this with bagged coleslaw mix if you like, but because of the carrots, the carb count will be slightly higher.

5 cups (350g) shredded cabbage (about ¼ of a head)

5 scallions, sliced

1 cup (120g) thinly sliced celery

½ cup (115g) mayonnaise

¼ cup (60ml) hot sauce (Frank's or Tabasco)

1 clove of garlic, crushed

4 ounces (115g) crumbled mild blue cheese

YIELD: 6 servings – Per serving: 222 calories; 21g fat (81.1% calories from fat); 6g protein; 6g carbohydrate; 2g dietary fiber; 4g net carbohydrate.

BUFFALO SLAW

Do you love Buffalo wings? You'll love Buffalo Slaw, too! It's an obvious side dish with grilled chicken, but it would be great with a steak, too.

Combine the cabbage, scallions, and celery in a mixing bowl.

In a small bowl, stir together the mayonnaise, hot sauce, and garlic. Pour over the vegetables and stir until they're evenly coated. Add the blue cheese and gently stir it in—you want there to be actual chunks of blue cheese in your slaw.

You can serve this right away, but consider chilling for an hour or two to let the flavors blend.

---

1 head of cabbage

¼ of a red onion

1 jalapeño, large or small, depending on how hot you like things!

1 cup (16g) chopped cilantro

3 tablespoons (45ml) lime juice

3 tablespoons (45ml) red wine vinegar

¼ cup (60ml) extra-virgin olive oil

¼ cup (60ml) MCT oil

1 teaspoon salt

½ teaspoon pepper

12 drops of liquid stevia, plain

YIELD: 10 servings – Per serving: 123 calories; 11g fat (76.7% calories from fat); 1g protein; 6g carbohydrate; 2g dietary fiber; 4g net carbohydrate.

JALAPEÑO VINEGAR SLAW

Are you tired of creamy coleslaw? How about a tangy, spicy version to serve alongside chicken or ribs?

Quarter your cabbage, cut out the core, and shred it—I'd run it through the slicing blade of my food processor, but if you'd rather use a knife and cutting board, go to it. Throw it in the biggest darned mixing bowl you've got.

Mince the onion quite fine—again, I'd use my food processor, running it through my fine shredding blade. Add it to the cabbage. Remove the stem, seeds, and pith from the jalapeño, mince it, and add it to the cabbage as well. Now wash your hands with soap and water!

Chop the cilantro and add it to the mix.

Put everything else in a clean jar, seal tightly, and shake hard. Pour over the vegetables and stir to coat. Let the whole thing marinate for an hour or two and then stir it up again before serving.

1 cup (235ml) extra-virgin olive oil

⅓ to ½ cup (80 to 120ml) red wine vinegar, to taste

1 clove of garlic, crushed

1 teaspoon Dijon mustard

¼ teaspoon salt

⅛ teaspoon pepper

YIELD: 1⅓ (315ml) cups, **11 servings** – Per serving: 175 calories; 20g fat (98.7% calories from fat); trace protein; 1g carbohydrate; trace dietary fiber; 1g net carbohydrate.

¼ cup (60ml) red wine vinegar

¼ cup (60ml) lemon juice

1 tablespoon (3g) dried oregano

2 cloves of garlic

½ teaspoon salt

¼ teaspoon pepper

1 cup (235ml) extra-virgin olive oil

½ cup (120ml) MCT oil

YIELD: 2 cups (475ml), **16 servings** – Per serving: 183 calories; 20g fat (98.0% calories from fat); trace protein; 1g carbohydrate; trace dietary fiber; 1g net carbohydrate.

¼ cup (60ml) raspberry vinegar

¼ cup (60ml) MCT oil

3 tablespoons (42g) mayonnaise

1 teaspoon Dijon mustard

6 drops of liquid stevia, plain or berry flavored

1 pinch each of salt and pepper

YIELD: ⅔ cup (175ml), **6 servings** – Per serving: 132 calories; 15g fat (97.8% calories from fat); trace protein; 1g carbohydrate; trace dietary fiber; 1g net carbohydrate.

BASIC VINAIGRETTE

This is about as basic as salad dressing gets and a beautiful thing it is, too. This is pretty French-like. Add a teaspoon or two of dried oregano or Italian seasoning, and you can give it a Greek or Italian accent.

Put everything in a clean jar. Seal tightly and shake hard. Store in the refrigerator and shake again before using.

NOTE: The olive oil will thicken with refrigeration. It's no big deal; just take the dressing out of the fridge 10 to 15 minutes before you need it. Are you in a hurry? Put your jar in a bowl of hot tap water for a few minutes.

OREGANO VINAIGRETTE

This is a good, all-around vinaigrette dressing. It complements any Mediterranean cuisine and makes a good marinade, too.

Put the red wine vinegar, lemon juice, oregano, garlic, salt, and pepper in your food processor and run until the garlic is pulverized. With the processor running, pour in the oils in a steady stream. When all the oil is in, run another 5 to 10 seconds. Store in a tightly lidded jar in the fridge. Shake well before using.

RASPBERRY VINAIGRETTE

Read labels carefully when buying raspberry vinegar—some have added sugar. Obviously, you're looking for the stuff that does not.

Put it all in a jar, seal it, and shake!

½ cup (120ml) extra-virgin olive oil

3 tablespoons (45ml) lemon juice

1 clove of garlic, crushed

1 teaspoon Dijon mustard

¼ teaspoon salt

¼ teaspoon pepper

12 drops of liquid stevia, Valencia orange

YIELD: ¾ cup (175ml), 6 servings – Per serving: 163 calories; 18g fat (97.5% calories from fat); trace protein; 1g carbohydrate; trace dietary fiber; 1g net carbohydrate.

ORANGE VINAIGRETTE

Lemon juice is often used in place of vinegar in salad dressings, especially in Mediterranean cuisine. Orange is a nice twist, complementing many flavors.

Put everything in a clean jar, seal tightly, and shake like mad. That's it!

Store in the refrigerator. Yes, the olive oil will thicken up on you—just get it out of the fridge before you start assembling your salad so it has time to warm a little and shake again hard before using it.

NOTE: If you don't have Valencia orange liquid stevia on hand, use plain or lemon drop flavor, plus a few drops of orange extract.

¼ cup (60ml) olive oil

¼ cup (60ml) melted bacon grease

¼ cup (60ml) cider vinegar

4 teaspoons (20g) brown mustard

1 shallot

¼ teaspoon maple flavoring

½ teaspoon chopped garlic

½ teaspoon salt

24 drops of liquid stevia, English toffee

YIELD: ⅔ cup (175ml), 6 servings   Per serving: 165 calories; 18g fat (96.4% calories from fat); trace protein; 1g carbohydrate; trace dietary fiber; 1g net carbohydrate.

MAPLE-BACON VINAIGRETTE

Try this over a spinach salad with crumbled bacon and chopped hard-boiled eggs! Or just use it to liven up some bagged salad greens.

Simply assemble everything in your blender or food processor and run until it's creamy. Pour over your salad and toss.

½ cup (120ml) extra-virgin olive oil

½ cup (120ml) lemon juice

½ cup (30g) minced parsley

18 drops of liquid stevia, English toffee

Salt and pepper to taste

YIELD: 1½ cups (355ml), 12 servings   Per serving: 83 calories; 9g fat (94.6% calories from fat); trace protein; 1g carbohydrate; trace dietary fiber; 1g net carbohydrate.

LEMON VINAIGRETTE

Tangy yet subtly sweet, this is a great choice for green salads or cucumber salads. Try mixing it half and half with mayonnaise for chicken salad, too.

Its the usual drill: Assemble everything in a clean jar. Seal tightly and shake hard. That's it! Store in the fridge and shake again before using.

⅓ cup (80ml) extra-virgin olive oil

3 tablespoons (45ml) red wine vinegar

1 teaspoon paprika

½ teaspoon ground cumin

1 clove of garlic, crushed

¼ teaspoon salt

⅛ teaspoon pepper

YIELD: ½ cup (120ml), 4 servings – Per serving: 165 calories; 18g fat (96.3% calories from fat); trace protein; 1g carbohydrate; trace dietary fiber; 1g net carbohydrate.

PAPRIKA-CUMIN VINAIGRETTE

The warmth of the paprika and cumin make this a good pairing with any Tex-Mex meal. It's great as a marinade for fish or seafood, too.

Assemble everything in a clean jar. Seal tightly and shake. Store in the refrigerator and shake again before using.

½ cup (115g) mayonnaise

2 teaspoons no-sugar-added ketchup

2 sugar-free bread-and-butter pickle slices

2 teaspoons Creole seasoning

½ teaspoon onion powder

1 clove of garlic

2 dashes of Worcestershire sauce

2 dashes of Tabasco sauce

YIELD: ⅔ cup (160ml), 6 servings – Per serving: 137 calories; 16g fat (95.5% calories from fat); trace protein; 1g carbohydrate; trace dietary fiber; 1g net carbohydrate.

CAJUN DRESSING

I came up with this for the Cajun Chicken Salad, but surely you can think of other things to do with it. How about shrimp salad? Or a spicy coleslaw?

I'd probably throw everything in my little food processor and pulse until the pickle was finely chopped. But if you prefer, you can measure stuff into a bowl, mince that pickle by hand, and stir it all up. It works either way.

¼ cup (60ml) MCT oil

2 tablespoons (28ml) soy sauce

2 tablespoons (30g) grainy mustard, such as Dijon or spicy brown

4 teaspoons (20ml) dark sesame oil

4 teaspoons (20ml) lemon juice

6 drops of liquid stevia, plain

YIELD: ⅝ cup (145ml), 4 servings – Per serving: 174 calories; 19g fat (93.8% calories from fat); 1g protein; 2g carbohydrate; trace dietary fiber; 2g net carbohydrate.

SOY AND MUSTARD DRESSING

I first made this for the Egg and Avocado Breakfast Bowl on page 81, but surely you can find other uses! To start with, it's a great marinade for chicken. But how about using it on a slaw of shredded Napa cabbage and sesame seeds? Or using it as a stir-fry sauce?

Follow your basic salad dressing procedure: Put everything in a clean jar, seal tightly, and shake hard. Store in the refrigerator and shake again before using. That's it!

CAESAR DRESSING

2 to 4 anchovy fillets, to taste

2 tablespoons (30g) Dijon or spicy brown mustard

1 tablespoon (15ml) white balsamic vinegar

2 tablespoons (28ml) Worcestershire sauce

2 cloves of garlic, crushed

1 tablespoon (15ml) lemon juice

1 egg

½ cup (120ml) extra-virgin olive oil

¼ cup (25g) grated Parmesan cheese

Bottled Caesar dressing is so often harsh, but this is rich and mellow. I used two anchovies because I only like a hint of them, but my husband, an anchovy fiend, said he'd love it with another anchovy or two.

Assemble everything from the anchovies through the egg in your food processor, with the S-blade in place. Run for a minute or so until the anchovies are pulverized. Now, with the processor running, slowly pour in the olive oil in a stream about the diameter of a pencil lead. Your dressing should emulsify. Add the Parmesan and pulse to mix it in. That's it. Store in a tightly lidded container in the fridge and use it up within a few days because of that egg.

YIELD: 1 cup (235ml), **6 servings** – Per serving: 198 calories; 20g fat (89.6% calories from fat); 3g protein; 2g carbohydrate; trace dietary fiber; 2g net carbohydrate.

LOUIS DRESSING

1 cup (225g) mayonnaise

⅓ cup (80g) no-sugar-added ketchup

2 scallions, minced

2 teaspoons lemon juice

1 teaspoon prepared horseradish

½ teaspoon hot sauce (Tabasco, Louisiana, or Frank's), or to taste

¼ cup (60ml) heavy cream, chilled

Add this to some lump crabmeat with a little diced celery and you've got classic cuisine. But feel free to serve this with lobster, shrimp, or any seafood. Hey, serve it on catfish or tilapia! Why not?

In a bowl, stir together everything but the heavy cream.

In another bowl with an electric mixer or a whisk, whip the cream until stiff. Fold it gently into the dressing. Refrigerate for an hour or two before serving.

YIELD: 1⅔ cups (395ml), **14 servings** Per serving: 130 calories; 15g fat (97.1% calories from fat); trace protein; 1g carbohydrate; trace dietary fiber; 1g net carbohydrate.

½ cup (120ml) buttermilk
½ cup (115g) sour cream
¼ cup (60g) mayonnaise
¼ cup (25g) sliced scallion
1 or 2 cloves of garlic, crushed
2 teaspoons lemon juice
1½ teaspoons dried dill
½ teaspoon salt
¼ teaspoon pepper
2 dashes of hot sauce
(Tabasco, Louisiana, or Frank's)

YIELD: 1½ cups (355ml),
12 servings – Per serving:
63 calories; 6g fat (85.1%
calories from fat); 1g protein;
1g carbohydrate; trace dietary
fiber; 1g net carbohydrate.

RANCH DRESSING

Ranch dressing is beloved by many, but bottled varieties too often have bad oils. We won't even talk about the fat-free stuff, which is pretty much spicy corn syrup. This is easy and will get some veggies into your kids.

It's so simple! Assemble everything in your blender and process until it's well blended. Chill for at least a few hours for the flavors to combine.

---

1 lemon, at room temperature
½ of a shallot, minced
2 tablespoons (8g) minced parsley
1 tablespoon (2g) fresh thyme
1 pinch of nutmeg
½ cup (120ml) extra-virgin olive oil
1½ teaspoons salt
¼ teaspoon pepper

YIELD: About ¾ cup (175ml),
6 servings – Per serving:
163 calories; 18g fat (96.2%
calories from fat); trace protein;
1g carbohydrate; trace dietary
fiber; 1g net carbohydrate.

REBECCA SAYS MAKE THIS DRESSING!

This dressing started out as part of the Mushroom Salad recipe. But Rebecca, my trusted tester, insisted that the dressing was so good I needed to include it as a separate recipe so you'd use it on other salads. So here it is!

Grate 1 teaspoon of lemon zest and then squeeze the juice. You want about 2 tablespoons (28ml). Put both in a clean jar. Add the shallot, parsley, thyme, nutmeg, olive oil, salt, and pepper. Seal the jar tightly and shake it hard for 20 to 30 seconds. Store in the refrigerator. Shake again before using.

½ cup (115g) mayonnaise
½ cup (115g) sour cream
1 chipotle chile canned in adobo
1 clove of garlic, crushed
2 teaspoons lime juice

YIELD: 1 cup (235ml),
8 servings – Per serving:
130 calories; 15g fat (95.3%
calories from fat); 1g protein;
1g carbohydrate; trace dietary
fiber; 1g net carbohydrate.

CREAMY CHIPOTLE DRESSING

This would be great over a grilled chicken salad and would make a truly—I was going to say "cool"—hot and funky version of coleslaw. How about using it to top a burger? Or a steak?

Just throw everything in your blender and run it for a minute or so. That's it!

3 cloves of garlic

1 tablespoon (15ml) melted bacon grease

½ cup (115g) mayonnaise

½ cup (115g) sour cream

½ cup (120ml) buttermilk

2 teaspoons lemon juice

1 teaspoon cider vinegar

4 scallions, sliced

1 tablespoon (4g) minced parsley

1 tablespoon (4g) minced fresh dill

⅛ teaspoon pepper

¼ teaspoon salt

YIELD: 1½ cups (355ml), 12 servings – Per serving: 103 calories; 11g fat (91.8% calories from fat); 1g protein; 1g carbohydrate; trace dietary fiber; 1g net carbohydrate.

BACON-ROASTED GARLIC RANCH DRESSING

This dressing originally appeared in *200 Low-Carb, High-Fat Recipes*, but demanded to be included here. I was looking for a dressing for the Turkey-Avocado Salad, and this one jumped up, waved frantically, and shouted, "ME! ME!"

Preheat your oven to 350°F (180°C, or gas mark 4). Poke a hole in each unpeeled garlic clove with the tip of a knife and put 'em in a little baking dish. Bake for 20 minutes, let them cool, and then peel.

Combine all the ingredients in your blender or food processor. Process until the garlic and scallions are pulverized.

½ cup (115g) mayonnaise

½ cup (115g) sour cream

1 teaspoon brown mustard

1 tablespoon (15ml) apple cider vinegar

8 drops of liquid stevia, plain

⅛ teaspoon salt or to taste

YIELD: 1 cup (235ml), 5 servings – Per serving: 208 calories; 24g fat (95.9% calories from fat); 1g protein; 1g carbohydrate; trace dietary fiber; 1g net carbohydrate.

CLASSIC COLESLAW DRESSING

Cabbage is a very low-carbohydrate vegetable; it's also reliably cheap. Sadly, commercial coleslaw dressings are full of both bad oils and sugar—often so much sugar I find them downright nasty. Make your own!

Measure everything and stir it all together in a bowl. Done. Once you've done this a few times, you'll be able to just eyeball it.

NOTE: I've made a lot of versions of coleslaw in my day, but the 50/50 mayonnaise–sour cream combo is still my favorite. I'll add: In 2016, I broke my left wrist not just once, but twice, in six months. Cooking one-handed is darned near impossible. I subsisted mainly on rotisserie chicken and coleslaw made from packaged coleslaw mix and this dressing, which I could, indeed, whip up one-handed.

CHAPTER 7

Hot Side Dishes

Everybody needs an elevator speech, a catchy way of summing up what one does in the length of an elevator ride. One of mine is, "If you've just gone low carb and you don't have a clue what goes on that third of the plate where the potato used to be, I'm your girl."

That said, I'm going to commit heresy here: You are not required to eat your vegetables with every meal. Depending on your own personal carbohydrate tolerance and the macros you need to stay in ketosis, there may be meals where you do best to just eat a protein-and-fat dish or just shirataki with a fatty sauce. Indeed, there is a growing zero carb movement—people who eat only meat and eggs—and while I know of no clinical research, I have read enthusiastic reports. And, of course, we crazy folks who shun carbohydrates love to cite the Inuit, who traditionally lived for much of the year on animal foods alone yet enjoyed good health.

It wouldn't suit me, though. To state the obvious, I'm a cook. I like variety. I like all kinds of flavors and textures. When I see my friend Shawn post photos on Twitter of yet another meal of nothing but steak with a side of bacon, I don't worry about his health. I just wonder if he ever gets bored.

Also, not all proteins come with sufficient fat, and some of us have to limit our protein intake. Side dishes can improve the ratios of a meal based on poultry, fish, or one of the leaner cuts of beef, pork, or lamb. They can also serve as a meal all on their own if you've already had sufficient protein for the day.

I'll start with the fundamentals, a couple of ideas that I certainly didn't invent, and that have been around since... well, since before I started writing low-carb cookbooks, at any rate. I'll follow each with variations.

½ of a large head of
cauliflower

1 ounce (28g) cream cheese

3 tablespoons (42g) butter

Salt and pepper

YIELD: 3 servings – Per serving:
159 calories; 15g fat (80.9%
calories from fat); 3g protein;
5g carbohydrate; 2g dietary fiber,
3g net carbohydrate.

FAUXTATOES

These have been a standard in low-carb circles for twenty years, with
good reason. Any time you are making a main dish with a good, rich
gravy, think Fauxtatoes. Do you automatically grab a sack of potatoes
at the grocery store? You're going to start grabbing a head or two of
cauliflower instead.

Trim the leaves and the very bottom of the stem from your cauliflower and whack
it into chunks. Steam until tender; I put mine in a microwave steamer and give it
12 to 14 minutes on high in the microwave. If you don't have a microwave steamer,
a microwavable casserole dish with a lid will work fine; just add a few tablespoons
(45ml) of water and cover. Or, you can steam it on the stove. When your cauliflower
is tender, drain it very well. This is essential.

Now, puree your cauliflower; I put mine in a deep, narrow bowl and use my stick
(immersion) blender, but a food processor will do the trick, too.

When your cauliflower is getting to the pureed stage, add the cream cheese and
butter and work them in. Add salt and pepper to taste. These are fine as is, or with
gravy, or just a little steak juice spooned over them.

½ of a head of cauliflower

1 chipotle chile canned in
adobo plus 1 teaspoon sauce

2 tablespoons (28ml) olive oil

2 tablespoons (28ml) heavy
cream

2 cloves of garlic, crushed

2 ounces (55g) cream cheese

YIELD: 4 servings – Per serving:
155 calories; 15g fat (80.7%
calories from fat); 3g protein;
5g carbohydrate; 2g dietary fiber;
3g net carbohydrate.

CHIPOTLE FAUXTATOES

Yes, it's true. I like hot peppers in everything, especially chipotles.
This would definitely jazz up "hamburgers, again." This is four servings
because the chipotle ups the carbohydrates a little bit.

Cook your cauliflower as for standard Fauxtatoes (above).

When time comes to puree the cauliflower, simple add everything else and puree
it together.

½ of a head of cauliflower

½ cup (115g) cream cheese
with chives and onions

2 tablespoons (28g) butter

1 clove of garlic, crushed

Salt and pepper

YIELD: 3 servings – Per serving:
227 calories; 20g fat (77.9%
calories from fat); 5g protein;
0g carbohydrate; 2g dietary fiber;
6g net carbohydrate.

NANCY'S CREAMY
GARLIC-CHIVE FAUXTATOES

Nancy O'Connor contributed this to *500 More Low-Carb Recipes*.
Due to missing data, I had to rewrite and reanalyze, but here it is. Yum.
What a great substitute for a loaded baked potato with your steak!

Cook your cauliflower as per Fauxtatoes (above) and then simply puree with the
rest of the ingredients.

1 head of cauliflower

1 small onion

3 tablespoons (42g) butter

1 tablespoon (3g) finely minced fresh sage

2 ounces (55g) cream cheese, softened

2 tablespoons (30g) sour cream

½ teaspoon salt

¼ teaspoon pepper

YIELD: 6 servings – Per serving: 126 calories; 10g fat (69.5% calories from fat); 3g protein; 7g carbohydrate; 3g dietary fiber; 4g net carbohydrate.

1 recipe Fauxtatoes (page 105)

3 eggs

4 teaspoons (9g) coconut flour

¼ cup (52g) lard, bacon grease, (60ml) MCT oil, or olive oil, plus more as needed

---

YIELD: 6 servings – Per serving: 203 calories; 19g fat (81.0% calories from fat); 5g protein; 5g carbohydrate; 3g dietary fiber; 2g net carbohydrate.

NOTE: Don't try to substitute coconut flour one-for-one in baking. The results are darned near inedible. The stuff has quite a learning curve. But if you'd like to learn, a quick Google search will turn up recipes and advice.

SAGE AND ONION FAUXTATOES

Says recipe tester Rebecca, "It would be quite nice as a side dish to some fancy meat dish in a high-priced restaurant. I am already thinking of taking this to the next Thanksgiving meal."

Cook your cauliflower as per Fauxtatoes (page 105).

In the meanwhile, peel and chop the onion. In a medium-size skillet over medium-low heat, melt the butter and start the onion sautéing. Add the sage and keep sautéing until the onion is soft and starting to turn golden. Remove from the heat.

When the cauliflower is soft, drain it very well. Now, you can either put it in your food processor and do the rest there or put it in a big, deep mixing bowl and use your stick blender. I'm a stick-blender girl.

Either way, add the onion and sage to the cauliflower, along with the cream cheese, sour cream, salt, and pepper. Puree everything together until it's a mashed potato consistency.

Serve with more butter to melt on top!

FAUXTATO PANCAKES

It's worth making extra Fauxtatoes to make these the next night! They make a good side or can stand alone as a light supper for, say, three people. The widely distributed Bob's Red Mill brand packages coconut flour; my local groceries carry it. Certainly, a health food store could order it.

This is darned simple: Put your Fauxtatoes in a mixing bowl, add the eggs and coconut flour, and whisk it up.

Put your big, heavy skillet over medium heat and add the fat—I used lard. When the skillet's hot, add the batter by the ¼ cup (60ml). Fry until nicely browned on the bottom, flip, and brown the other side. Serve hot!

½ of a large head of cauliflower

YIELD: 4 servings – Per serving: 18 calories; trace fat (trace % calories from fat); 1g protein; 4g carbohydrate; 2g dietary fiber; 2g net carbohydrate.

CAULI-RICE

Here's another reason to buy cauliflower every time you're at the grocery store. Cookbook author Fran McCullough came up with the original idea, and I have used it a hundred ways since. It's become so popular that many grocery stores now sell riced cauliflower, which you certainly may use if you like. I like the texture of this better.

Trim the leaves and the very bottom of the stem from your cauliflower and cut the rest into pieces that will fit in the feed tube of your food processor. Run it through the shredding blade.

Steam the resulting shreds lightly; I cook mine for about 7 or 8 minutes on high in the microwave. Uncover immediately to avoid mushiness and drain well. Season and use in a million ways!

½ of an onion, diced

3 tablespoons (45ml) olive oil

½ of a head of cauliflower

1 cup (235ml) dry white wine

3 teaspoons (15ml) chicken bouillon concentrate

1 clove of garlic, crushed

⅔ cup (200g) canned artichoke hearts, drained and chopped

½ cup (50g) grated Parmesan cheese

2 tablespoons (28ml) heavy cream

Salt and pepper

YIELD: 5 servings – Per serving: 195 calories; 13g fat (69.4% calories from fat); 6g protein; 7g carbohydrate; 2g dietary fiber; 5g net carbohydrate.

ARTICHOKE "RISOTTO"

I love artichokes, but they're carbier than some other vegetables. By combining them with the lower-carb cauliflower, we can enjoy them. Pair this with a rotisserie chicken from the grocery store and the family will ask if company is coming.

First, start the onion sautéing in the olive oil, in a big, heavy saucepan over medium-low heat.

Trim the leaves and the very bottom of the stem off your cauliflower and run it through the shredding blade of your food processor. Go stir your onions! Now, dump the resulting Cauli-Rice into a microwavable casserole dish with a lid (or you can place a microwavable plate on top.) Add a couple of tablespoons (28ml) of water, cover, and nuke it for 6 minutes on high.

Okay, back to your sautéing onions. By now they should be turning translucent. Add the white wine, the bouillon concentrate, and the garlic and turn the heat up to high. You want to bring it to a boil and then turn the burner down just enough to keep the mixture boiling without boiling over.

Somewhere in here, your microwave will beep. Remove your Cauli-Rice and uncover it to stop the cooking.

When your wine has cooked down to about one-fourth of its original volume, add the cauli-rice, artichoke hearts, Parmesan, and cream. Stir it all up, season with salt and pepper to taste, and serve.

1½ pounds (680g) cauliflower, riced (Jen uses purchased riced cauliflower.)

6 tablespoons (85g) butter

⅔ cup (82g) pistachio nuts, coarsely chopped

1 tablespoon (12g) Greek Seasoning (Jen uses Penzeys.)

2 tablespoons (28ml) lemon juice

1 tablespoon (10g) chopped garlic

¼ teaspoon pepper

YIELD: 8 servings – Per serving: 163 calories; 14g fat (72.6% calories from fat); 4g protein; 8g carbohydrate; 3g dietary fiber; 5g net carbohydrate.

JEN HOBERER'S CAULIFLOWER COUSCOUS

When cyberpal and fellow low-carber Jen Hoberer posted this recipe, I pounced! I asked her immediately if she'd be okay with my analyzing and sharing it. She kindly agreed—and said this was so good she could have "eaten a pound!" Thanks, Jen!

Steam the cauli-rice briefly—Jen microwaves hers in the bags it comes in, 4 minutes on high per bag.

Uncover the cauliflower immediately and drain if needed.

In a wok or big darned skillet, over medium heat, melt the butter. Add the cauli-rice, then everything else. Sauté, stirring often, for 4 to 5 minutes.

NOTE: Having looked at other "Greek seasonings," it appears that their ingredients are different from Penzeys—they often include MSG and/or starch of some kind. They also have a different blend of spices. I suspect this recipe would be awesome with whatever Greek seasoning you favor, but will note that Penzeys Greek Seasoning contains only coarse salt, Turkish oregano, garlic, lemon, black pepper, and marjoram. There is a Greek Seasoning recipe on page 255.

½ of a head of cauliflower

1 tablespoon (15ml) olive oil

1 tablespoon (14g) butter

1 cup (70g) sliced mushrooms

3 anchovy fillets, minced

1 clove of garlic, crushed

3 tablespoons (15g) grated Parmesan cheese

YIELD: 3 servings – Per serving: 136 calories; 11g fat (65.8% calories from fat); 6g protein; 7g carbohydrate; 3g dietary fiber; 4g net carbohydrate.

VENETIAN "RICE"

Simple yet intensely flavorful, with umami from the mushrooms, anchovies, and Parmesan, this is a great side dish with almost anything. In the unlikely event you have leftovers, try them warmed up with a fried egg or two on top for a great breakfast.

Run the cauliflower through the shredding blade of your food processor. Put it in a microwavable casserole dish with a lid, add a couple of tablespoons (28ml) of water, cover, and nuke on high for 5 to 6 minutes. When it's done, uncover immediately!

Combine the olive oil and butter in your big heavy skillet over medium heat, swirling together as the butter melts. Add the mushrooms and sauté until they're soft and changing color. If your mushroom slices are quite large, you may want to break them up a bit with the edge of your spatula as you stir.

When the mushrooms are soft, stir in the minced anchovies and garlic. Add the cauli-rice, undrained—that little bit of water is going to help the flavors blend. Stir well to distribute all the flavors. Stir in the Parmesan and serve.

½ of a head of cauliflower

⅓ cup (37g) slivered almonds

2 tablespoons (28g) butter

3 scallions

¼ cup (16g) chopped fresh parsley

2 teaspoons chicken bouillon concentrate

YIELD: 3 servings – Per serving: 196 calories; 17g fat (70.6% calories from fat); 6g protein; 10g carbohydrate; 4g dietary fiber; 6g net carbohydrate.

RICE-A-PHONY

My husband and I were just finishing up supper when my brother John and his family arrived to drop off the kids for a few days. Sitting at the dining room table chatting, John idly tasted this dish. He said, "I know that some of this is cauliflower, but how much is cauliflower and how much is real rice?" When I told him it was all cauliflower, no rice, he exclaimed, "Wow, it's Rice-a-Phony!" And so it has been named ever since.

Do the cauliflower "rice" thing—trim your cauliflower, chunk it, run it through the shredding blade of your food processor, and microwave-steam the resulting cauliflower rice for 6 minutes.

In the meanwhile, put your big, heavy skillet over medium heat and start sautéing the almonds in the butter.

While the almonds and the cauliflower are cooking, slice your scallions, including the crisp part of the green. Don't forget to stir your almonds!

Okay, the almonds are golden, and the microwave has beeped. Drain the cauliflower and dump it into the skillet with the almonds. Stir in everything else, mixing until the chicken bouillon concentrate is dissolved and everything is well distributed. You're done!

½ of a head of cauliflower

¼ cup (55g) butter

2 tablespoons (28ml) extra-virgin olive oil

8 ounces (225g) small portobello mushrooms, sliced

½ cup (80g) diced onion

2 cloves of garlic, crushed

¼ cup (60ml) dry white wine

½ teaspoon pepper

¼ cup (20g) shredded Parmesan cheese

YIELD: 6 servings – Per serving: 156 calories; 13g fat (76.4% calories from fat); 3g protein; 6g carbohydrate; 2g dietary fiber; 4g net carbohydrate.

MUSHROOM-PARMESAN PILAF

I use mushrooms more and more! They add great flavor, and they absorb and hold fat beautifully. If you can't find small portobellos presliced—around here they come labeled "baby bellas"—sliced cremini mushrooms will do just fine.

Trim the cauliflower, whack it into chunks, and run it through the shredding blade of your food processor. Put the resulting cauli-rice in a microwavable casserole dish with a lid (if it's a round casserole, a plate works fine as a lid) or a microwave steamer. Add a couple of tablespoons (28ml) of water, cover, and nuke on high for 8 minutes.

In the meanwhile, melt the butter in your big heavy skillet over medium heat. Add the olive oil and swirl 'em together. Throw in the mushrooms, onion, and garlic and sauté until the mushrooms have changed color and softened and the onion is translucent. Add the wine and pepper and let it cook until most of the wine has evaporated.

Now, stir in the cauli-rice (you remembered to uncover it when the microwave beeped, right?), combining well. At the last minute, stir in the Parmesan and serve.

½ of a head of cauliflower

10 ounces (280g) frozen chopped spinach, thawed and drained

2 tablespoons (28g) butter

½ cup (80g) chopped onion

1 clove of garlic, crushed

4 eggs

½ cup (120ml) heavy cream

1½ teaspoons salt or Vege-Sal

¼ teaspoon pepper

½ cup (50g) grated Parmesan cheese

1 cup (115g) shredded mozzarella cheese

YIELD: 6 servings – Per serving: 256 calories; 21g fat (72.4% calories from fat); 13g protein; 5g carbohydrate; 2g dietary fiber; 3g net carbohydrate.

¼ cup (55g) butter

20 ounces (560g) frozen chopped spinach, thawed and well drained

½ cup (120ml) heavy cream

¼ cup (25g) grated Parmesan cheese

⅛ teaspoon ground nutmeg

Salt and pepper

YIELD: 8 servings – Per serving: 131 calories; 12g fat (80.1% calories from fat); 3g protein; 3g carbohydrate; 2g dietary fiber; 1g net carbohydrate.

MACADANGDANG

Longtime readers know that I'm a big fan of Peg Bracken and her cookbooks. This is my de-carbed version of Macadangdang Spinach Medley, which appeared in Peg's *I Hate to Cook Almanac*. It is named for her Aunt Henry Macadangdang, who married a Filipino gentleman of that name. I found the name so charming and euphonious, I thought I'd just call this version Macadangdang. My husband rates this a perfect 10 (and I like it too)! I've adapted this a bit from the version that originally appeared in *300 Low-Carb Slow Cooker Recipes*.

Run the cauliflower through the shredding blade of your food processor. Dump the resulting Cauli-Rice into a mixing bowl. Drain the thawed frozen spinach really well —I actually squeeze mine—and add it to the cauli-rice.

Melt the butter in a medium skillet over medium-low heat and sauté the onion until it's just translucent. Add the garlic, sauté for another minute or two, and then dump the whole thing in the bowl with the cauliflower and spinach.

Add the eggs, cream, salt, pepper, and grated Parmesan and stir the whole thing up quite well. Put it in a 1½- to 2-quart (1½ to 2L) Pyrex casserole dish that you've sprayed with nonstick cooking spray. Cover the whole thing with foil and place it in your slow cooker. Pour water around it up to 1 inch (2.5cm) of the rim. Cover, set the slow cooker on low, and let it cook for 2½ hours.

Open the slow cooker and remove the foil. Sprinkle the mozzarella over your Macadangdang, put the foil back on, re-cover the pot, and let it cook for another 20 minutes to melt the cheese. Then, turn off the pot, uncover it, take off the foil, and let the whole thing cool just to the point where you can remove it from the water bath without scalding yourself—20 more minutes.

Should you be unlucky enough to be stuck with an oval, rather than round, slow cooker and be unable to fit a casserole dish down into it, you can bake this for 30 minutes at 325°F (170°C, or gas mark 3). And start haunting the local Goodwill, searching for a proper round slow cooker.

CREAMED SPINACH WITH BROWNED BUTTER

Our tester Christina Robertson rated this a 10. She also says that a dash of jalapeño sauce does not go amiss here. I am not the sort to object to a dash of hot sauce!

In a large saucepan over medium heat, melt the butter. Let it cook until it turns golden brown and nutty smelling, about 6 to 8 minutes. Don't let it burn!

Mix in the spinach and cream and bring to a simmer. Let cook for 5 minutes. Stir in the Parmesan and nutmeg and season with salt and pepper to taste.

3 small zucchini

Salt

3 tablespoons (45ml) olive oil

1 clove of garlic, crushed (optional)

2 teaspoons oregano (optional)

YIELD: 4 servings – Per serving: 113 calories; 10g fat (80% calories from fat); 2g protein; 5g carbohydrate; 2g dietary fiber; 3g net carbohydrate.

ZOODLES

These zucchini noodles have taken the low-carb world by storm! You'll need a spiral cutter, which you can get at any housewares store or online. Choose zucchini small enough in diameter to fit in your cutter. Serve them as you would noodles; you can simply add Parmesan, top them with no-sugar-added spaghetti sauce, or use them as a bed for a main dish with a tasty gravy—use your imagination!

Simply run your zukes through the spiral cutter, piling your Zoodles into a mixing bowl.

Salt the Zoodles, tossing as you go. Let them sit for 15 to 20 minutes.

Now, use clean hands to squeeze your Zoodles to get out the excess liquid and drain well. The liquid will take much of the salt with it.

Put a big, heavy skillet over medium-high heat and add the olive oil. When it's hot, add the Zoodles, tossing just until they are thoroughly good and hot. Stir in the garlic and oregano, if using, and cook for just another minute. Don't let them get mushy!

---

1 large eggplant

Salt

2 ounces (55g) pork rinds

⅓ cup (27g) shredded Parmesan cheese

1 teaspoon Italian seasoning

½ teaspoon onion powder

¼ teaspoon granulated garlic

¼ teaspoon paprika

1 egg

½ cup (120ml) olive oil

YIELD: 5 servings – Per serving: 314 calories; 28g fat (78.2% calories from fat); 11g protein; 6g carbohydrate; 2g dietary fiber; 4g net carbohydrate.

NOTE: The nutrition statistics are approximate because I don't know exactly how much oil the eggplant absorbs. Also, the slices are different sizes. It's definitely low carb and high fat, though. Eggplant sucks up oil like frat boys suck down beer.

CRISPY FRIED EGGPLANT

That Nice Boy I Married is convinced he doesn't like eggplant. Then I serve it to him fried in plenty of oil and he decides it's a-okay. He yummed this right down.

Slice your eggplant into rounds ½ inch (1.3cm) thick. Lay them on your cutting board and salt them on both sides. Let them sit for half an hour or so.

Meanwhile, put the pork rinds, Parmesan, Italian seasoning, onion powder, garlic, and paprika in your food processor. Pulse until the mixture is the texture of bread crumbs. Dump the mixture out onto a plate.

On another plate—one with a rim—beat the egg with 1 teaspoon of water until well blended.

Return to your eggplant. You will see that water has collected on the surfaces of the slices. Pat them dry with paper towels.

Dip each eggplant slice in the egg wash, then in the pork rind crumbs, coating both sides. Stash the coated slices on a plate.

Put your large, heavy skillet over medium heat. Let it get hot and then add the olive oil.

Fry the eggplant slices until browned and crisp, about 5 minutes per side. Add more oil if needed. Serve immediately!

1½ cups (120g) Pork Rind Crumbs (page 63)

2 teaspoons Tajin Clasico

1 egg

1 teaspoon water

1 avocado

½ cup (103g) bacon grease, divided

YIELD: 3 servings – Per serving: 662 calories; 59g fat (80.3% calories from fat); 27g protein; 5g carbohydrate; 2g dietary fiber; 3g net carbohydrate.

1 cup (235ml) chicken broth

½ cup (120ml) dry vermouth

1 package (8 ounces, or 225g) of Miracle Rice

2 ounces (55g) pork rinds

1 teaspoon red pepper flakes

4 anchovy fillets, plus 1 teaspoon oil from the can

3 tablespoons (45ml) olive oil, divided

4 tablespoons (55g) butter, divided

½ of a medium onion

1 celery rib

1 clove of garlic

½ of a head of cauliflower

2 teaspoons bouillon concentrate

¼ cup (60ml) heavy cream

½ cup (40g) shredded Parmesan cheese

YIELD: 6 servings – Per serving: 293 calories; 23g fat (75.5% calories from fat); 11g protein; 6g carbohydrate; 2g dietary fiber; 4g net carbohydrate.

MEXICAN-SPICED CRUNCHY AVOCADOS

Tajin Clasico is a Mexican seasoning of ground chiles, sea salt, and powdered lime juice. I picked mine up in Playa del Carmen on the Low Carb Cruise—seasonings and hot sauces are my favorite souvenirs. Thanks to the Internet, you don't have to go that far, though if there's a Latino market or an Aldi in your area, I'd check there, first. You could try this with Creole seasoning, too.

On a rimmed plate, mix the Pork Rind Crumbs with the Tajin.

On another plate, use a fork to beat the egg with the water until the white and yolk are well blended.

Whack your avocado in half, remove the pit, and cut into ½-inch (1.3cm) slices. Peel the slices. (I find this easier than peeling first.)

Put your large, heavy skillet over medium heat. Add ¼ cup (52g) of the bacon grease. Let it get hot while you do the next step.

Dip the avocado slices in the egg wash, then the crumbs, and then repeat, making a double layer of crumbs.

Fry until crunchy, adding more bacon grease as needed, about 5 minutes per side.

CAULIFLOWER "RISOTTO"

I saw a recipe for risotto with cauliflower in it and knew I had to adapt it. This is not the quickest recipe in the book, but it is a worthy side dish for your most elegant dinners. It's also good warmed up for breakfast, especially with a fried or poached egg on top.

First, combine the chicken broth and vermouth in a nonreactive saucepan—stainless steel, ceramic nonstick, or enamelware—and bring to a boil. Turn down to a simmer and let it sit there and reduce while you proceed with your recipe.

Prepare your Miracle Rice as explained on page 23.

Put your pork rinds, red pepper flakes, and anchovies in your food processor and pulse until you have coarse crumbs.

In a medium-size skillet over medium heat, combine 1 tablespoon (15ml) of the olive oil and 1 tablespoon (14g) of the butter. Add the pork rind crumbs and stir them over the heat until browned and super-crispy. Set aside.

Now, back to the food processor. Add the onion and celery, cut into chunks, and then add the garlic. Pulse until finely chopped.

Put your large, heavy skillet over low heat. Add the remaining 2 tablespoons (28ml) of olive oil and remaining 3 tablespoons (42g) of butter and start sautéing the onion and celery mixture. You want to cook it until soft without browning it, about 12 to 15 minutes.

Swap your processor's S-blade for the shredding blade and turn your cauliflower into Cauli-Rice as described on page 107. Put it in a microwave steamer or micro-wavable casserole dish, add a couple of tablespoons (28ml) of water, cover, and microwave on high for 8 minutes—you want it just tender.

CAULIFLOWER "RISOTTO" *(continued)*

Go check your broth/vermouth mixture! If it hasn't reduced to one-fourth of its original volume, turn up the heat a little. You'll want it pretty soon.

Throw the prepped Miracle Rice in the skillet with the onion and celery and stir the whole thing up. When the Cauli-Rice is done, drain it very well and add it to the skillet, too.

When your broth/vermouth mixture has reduced to one-fourth its original volume, add the bouillon concentrate to it, stirring until dissolved, and then add it to the skillet. Stir it in. Finally, stir in the cream and the Parmesan.

Serve and pass the dish of seasoned pork rind crumbs to scatter over each serving.

MAPLE-GLAZED BRAISED TURNIPS

Recipe tester Rebecca says, "It was nicely sweet but not too much. This replaces the syrupy sweet potatoes that we remember from bygone days." She adds that she could see this being served at a fancy restaurant!

¼ cup (55g) butter

1½ cups (355ml) chicken broth

1½ tablespoons (18g) erythritol

24 drops of liquid stevia, English toffee

¼ teaspoon maple flavoring

1½ pounds (680g) small white turnips, peeled and halved

1 tablespoon (15g) brown mustard

Guar or xanthan (optional)

Salt and pepper

1 tablespoon (4g) minced parsley

YIELD: 6 servings – Per serving: 102 calories; 8g fat (69.7% calories from fat); 2 g protein; 6g carbohydrate; 2g dietary fiber; 4g net carbohydrate.

In your large, heavy skillet over medium heat, melt the butter. Stir in the broth, erythritol, liquid stevia, and maple flavoring. Bring to a simmer.

Add the turnips, reduce the heat to medium-low, and cover the skillet. Let cook until the turnips are tender, about 15 minutes, but test them with a fork.

Use a slotted spoon to transfer the turnips to a bowl. Turn the heat under the skillet to medium-high, bring it to a boil, and reduce the liquid by half, about 3 to 5 minutes.

Whisk in the mustard and then thicken just a little with your guar or xanthan shaker if you feel it's needed. Season with salt and pepper to taste. Turn the heat down.

Return the turnips to the sauce and reheat. Spoon into a serving dish, along with the sauce, and sprinkle with parsley.

GARLICKY SNOW PEAS

Quick and easy, this is a great alternative to Salad Again. Recipe tester Alan Blues rates this a 10 and says simply, "Love it!"

2 cups (126g) fresh snow pea pods

4 cloves of garlic, crushed

3 tablespoons (45ml) MCT oil

¼ teaspoon salt

¼ teaspoon pepper

YIELD: 4 servings – Per serving: 58 calories; 5g fat (78.6% calories from fat); 1g protein; 2g carbohydrate; 1g dietary fiber; 1g net carbohydrate.

Pinch the ends off the snow peas, pulling off any strings as you go. Have your garlic crushed and ready to go in a small dish by the stove—once you start cooking, this goes lightening-fast.

If you have a wok, use it. Otherwise, use your large, heavy skillet, having given it the usual shot of cooking spray. Put the pan over medium-high heat.

When the pan is good and hot, add the MCT oil, then the snow peas and salt and pepper. Stir-fry 'em for just 2 to 3 minutes—you want them crisp-tender, with a few brown spots appearing.

Add the garlic and stir-fry for just another 10 seconds—if you burn the garlic, all is lost, so get 'em out of the pan and plated, quick!

½ of a head of cauliflower

8 ounces (225g) cheddar cheese, half sharp, half extra-sharp, shredded

1 cup (235ml) heavy cream

3 eggs

1 teaspoon dry mustard

½ teaspoon salt or Vege-Sal

¼ teaspoon pepper

YIELD: 6 servings – Per serving: 323 calories; 29g fat (81% calories from fat); 13g protein; 2g carbohydrate; trace dietary fiber; 2g net carbohydrate.

3 slices of bacon

½ cup (120ml) chicken broth

2 ounces (55g) cream cheese

½ cup (120ml) heavy cream

2 tablespoons (28ml) dry white wine

½ cup (40g) shredded Parmesan cheese, divided

Guar or xanthan

1½ pounds (680g) Brussels sprouts

Salt and pepper

YIELD: 8 servings – Per serving: 148 calories; 11g fat (63.3% calories from fat); 6g protein; 8g carbohydrate; 3g dietary fiber; 5g net carbohydrate.

ERIC'S BIRTHDAY MAC AND CHEESE

This is so cheesy good, no one's going to care that it's cauliflower instead of macaroni. Certainly, Eric didn't!

Preheat the oven to 350°F (180°C, or gas mark 4). Grease a 3-quart (28L) casserole dish.

Trim the leaves and the very bottom of the stem off your cauliflower. Now cut the rest into bits about ½ inch (1.3cm) or so.

Mix the two kinds of shredded Cheddar together. Set aside ½ cup (60g) and layer the rest in the casserole dish starting with the cauliflower.

Whisk together the cream, eggs, dry mustard, salt, and pepper and pour it over the cauliflower and cheese. Sprinkle the reserved ½ cup (58g) cheese over the top. Bake for 45 to 50 minutes or until the cauliflower is tender.

BRUSSELS SPROUTS WITH PARMESAN-BACON CREAM SAUCE

My sister and brother-in-law introduced me to a San Diego restaurant called Bistro 60 where a dish very much like this is a standard on the menu. We ate two batches. I don't know their recipe, but these are just as good!

Chop your bacon or use your kitchen shears to snip it into bits. Put a large saucepan over medium heat and fry the bacon bits until crisp. Remove to a plate and reserve.

Pour all but a film of the bacon grease out of the pan, reserving it for other uses. Add the chicken broth and cream cheese to the pan and turn the heat to medium-low. Use a spoon, fork, or whisk to break the cream cheese up into bits to help it melt.

When your cream cheese is good and soft, grab your stick blender. (If you don't have one, transfer the mixture to your regular blender.) Blend in the heavy cream, wine, and ¼ cup (20g) of the Parmesan cheese. Thicken to the texture of heavy cream using your guar or xanthan shaker. Turn the heat off and cover the pan to keep warm.

Trim the stems of the Brussels sprouts and remove any bruised leaves. Halve them and then steam until just tender—I gave mine 8 minutes in my microwave steamer. Drain well. Put them in your serving dish.

Stir the remaining shredded ¼ cup (20g) of Parmesan into your sauce and pour over the Brussels sprouts. Season with salt and pepper. Top with the bacon bits and serve immediately.

1 pound (455g) radishes, trimmed

6 tablespoons (78g) bacon grease, chicken fat, duck fat, tallow, or lard, divided

Salt and pepper

YIELD: 4 servings – Per serving: 198 calories; 20g fat (91.7% calories from fat); trace protein; 4g carbohydrate; 2g dietary fiber; 2g net carbohydrate.

SMASHED RADISHES

These radishes are tasty, fun to make, and interesting to look at on the plate. Buy the pre-trimmed radishes in the 1-pound (455g) bag and this is a snap.

It's just so simple! Throw your radishes in a Pyrex casserole dish or microwave steamer, add a few tablespoons (45ml) of water, cover, and nuke 'em on high for 12 minutes. You want them tender but not mushy.

When the microwave beeps, pull the radishes out and uncover them to stop the cooking. Let them cool for 10 minutes or so.

Are the radishes cool enough to handle? Time for the next part: One at a time, place your radishes on your cutting board and press down on each with your thumb or the heel of your hand, smashing it pretty flat, but not breaking it into little pieces. (You'll probably get a few pieces anyway. That's okay. Fry them up with the rest.)

Put your large, heavy skillet over medium heat. Add 3 tablespoons (39g) of the bacon grease and lay your smashed radishes in it. Let them fry until they're good and brown on the bottom, about 5 to 7 minutes. Turn, add the remaining 3 tablespoons (39g) of bacon grease, and brown the other side. Season with salt and pepper, and they're done.

¼ cup (55g) butter

¼ cup (29g) hazelnuts, chopped medium-fine

1 tablespoon (15ml) white balsamic vinegar

1 pound (455g) asparagus

YIELD: 4 servings – Per serving: 171 calories; 17g fat (84.8% calories from fat); 3g protein; 4g carbohydrate; 2g dietary fiber; 2g net carbohydrate.

ASPARAGUS WITH HAZELNUT-BALSAMIC BUTTER

You've heard of "gilding the lily," right? Well, this is about as gilded as this lily gets! This recipe is sure to impress.

In a medium-size skillet over medium-low heat, melt the butter. Dump in your hazelnuts and stir them in the butter until they're golden brown, about 5 minutes or so. Add the balsamic vinegar—it will hiss furiously. Stir it in, turn off the heat, and deal with your asparagus.

Snap the ends off the asparagus where it wants to break naturally. Place the spears in a glass pie plate, spoke-fashion, the tips pointing out toward the rim, add a couple of tablespoons (20ml) of water, and cover with a plate or plastic wrap. Alternatively, put the asparagus in a microwave steamer—again, with a couple of tablespoons (28ml) of water. Either way, microwave for just 4 minutes.

Plate your lovely crisp-tender asparagus, divide the nuts and butter among the plates, and you're done.

4 tablespoons (55g) butter, divided

1 pound (455g) frozen green beans, French cut, thawed

1 tablespoon (15ml) balsamic vinegar

Salt and pepper

YIELD: 4 servings – Per serving: 140 calories; 12g fat (70.6% calories from fat); 2g protein; 9g carbohydrate; 3g dietary fiber; 6g net carbohydrate.

BALSAMIC GREEN BEANS

Early in my cooking career, I favored green beans with lemon butter. Green beans with butter and balsamic vinegar is an echo of the same concept. If you take your frozen beans out in the morning and place them in the fridge to thaw, they'll be ready to cook by suppertime. You can make this with fresh beans if you insist, but I am not hard-core enough to French cut my own green beans.

I had leftover beans, so the next day, I sautéed some sliced almonds in even more butter, then threw the leftover beans in, and mixed it up. It's fabulous!

Put your large, heavy skillet over medium heat. Melt 3 tablespoons (42g) of the butter and add the green beans. Stir until they're all coated with the butter. Now, cover the skillet with a lid, tilted to make a crack to let the steam out. Let them cook for 10 to 12 minutes, stirring every 4 to 5 minutes.

When the beans are tender, stir in the balsamic vinegar and the remaining 1 tablespoon (14g) of butter. Season with salt and pepper, and you're done.

2 pounds (910g) broccoli

¼ cup (35g) pine nuts

¼ cup (25g) olives (kalamatas or green, or a combo)

¼ cup (55g) butter

2 tablespoons (28ml) lemon juice

YIELD: 6 servings – Per serving: 135 calories; 12g fat (70.8% calories from fat); 4g protein; 6g carbohydrate; 3g dietary fiber; 3g net carbohydrate.

BROCCOLI WITH OLIVES AND PINE NUTS

As the melodic name suggests, broccoli hails from Italy—before it was Italy. Adding olives, pine nuts, and lemon juice not only honors that heritage, it tastes great, too.

Start by cutting the stems off the broccoli, not to discard them, but to make them easier to peel. Use a paring knife to peel the tough skin from the stems and then cut them into bite-size pieces. (If you've never done this before, you may be startled to discover the stems are the best part!) Cut up the florets into similar-size bites, again, peeling any tough skin. Set this to steam—I gave mine 10 minutes in the microwave, but feel free to do yours on the stove top, if you prefer.

While the broccoli is steaming, stir your pine nuts in a medium-size dry skillet over medium heat until they're golden.

Next, chop your olives—I used a combination of kalamatas and green olives packed in olive oil, with a few hot peppers in the mix—though I didn't chop up and add the peppers. Just be sure to use good, strong-flavored olives. Chop them fairly fine.

Okay, 10 minutes are up. Check your broccoli for doneness—you want it tender but not mushy. If it needs another minute or two, do that. Otherwise, uncover while you finish the sauce.

Remove the pine nuts from the skillet to a small plate and keep them close at hand. Turn the heat back on under the skillet, this time to medium-low, and add the butter. Let it melt and then stir in the lemon juice and the olives.

Put your broccoli in a big bowl and pour the butter-lemon-olive mixture over it. Toss to coat thoroughly. Sprinkle the pine nuts over it, toss again, and serve.

12 ounces (340g) broccoli

¼ cup (55g) butter

3 anchovy fillets

1 clove of garlic, crushed

1 tablespoon (6g) chopped black olives

3 tablespoons (15g) shredded Parmesan cheese

YIELD: 3 servings – Per serving: 189 calories; 18g fat (80.4% calories from fat); 5g protein; 4g carbohydrate; 2g dietary fiber; 2g net carbohydrate.

BROCCOLI WITH ANCHOVY BUTTER, OLIVES, AND PARMESAN

I used pedestrian canned chopped black olives for this. They made this side dish quick and easy, and the whole thing tasted great. Still, you may pit and chop more elevated olives if you prefer.

Cut your broccoli into florets. Peel the stems and include them, too! Steam lightly; about 5 to 6 minutes in the microwave is about right.

In the meanwhile, put a small saucepan over very low heat and melt the butter. Mince the anchovies and throw 'em in, along with the garlic. Cook them together, stirring and mashing the bits of anchovy, for about 5 minutes, keeping the heat very low—you don't want to brown the butter or the garlic.

When your broccoli is brilliantly green, drain it well and transfer it to a mixing bowl. Pour on the anchovy butter and add the chopped olives. Toss to coat and then plate. Top each serving with 1 tablespoon (5g) of Parmesan.

1 pound (455g) broccoli (I'd use frozen, but go with fresh if you prefer.)

4 tablespoons (55g) butter, divided

3 tablespoons (15g) Pork Rind Crumbs (page 63)

3 tablespoons (18g) almond meal

1 teaspoon lemon zest

½ teaspoon red pepper flakes

2 tablespoons (28ml) olive oil

1 tablespoon (15ml) lemon juice

YIELD: 6 servings – Per serving: 152 calories; 14g fat (78.3% calories from fat); 5g protein; 4g carbohydrate; 1g dietary fiber; 3g net carbohydrate.

BROCCOLI WITH CRUNCHY LEMON TOPPING

I grew up eating broccoli with lemon butter, so I have a great fondness for the flavor combination. If you're using fresh broccoli, peel the stems and cut them up and steam them with the florets—they're delicious!

Steam your broccoli until crisp-tender—how long will depend some on how large or small your pieces are. If you use frozen broccoli, there will likely be instructions on the bag. Fresh broccoli will need no more than 5 to 6 minutes.

While the broccoli is steaming, melt 2 tablespoons (28g) of the butter in a small skillet over medium heat. Add the Pork Rind Crumbs, almond meal, lemon zest, and red pepper flakes and stir them in the butter for 4 to 5 minutes until very crisp.

When the broccoli is crisp-tender and brilliantly green, drain it well and put it in a serving bowl. Add the remaining 2 tablespoons (28g) of butter and the olive oil and toss to coat. Add the lemon juice and toss again.

Plate the broccoli and top each serving with 1 tablespoon (5g) of the crumb mixture. Serve immediately, before the crumbs can get soggy!

1 pound (455g) frozen broccoli

⅓ cup (80ml) vinaigrette, store-bought or homemade (pages 98–100)

1 tablespoon (15g) Dijon mustard

3 scallions

YIELD: 3 servings – Per serving: 173 calories; 15g fat (69.9% calories from fat); 5g protein; 9g carbohydrate; 5g dietary fiber; 4g net carbohydrate.

BROCCOLI DIJON

I like to use broccoli "cuts" for this, but use spears or florets if that's what you have on hand; it'll be fine. If it's frozen in a clump, throw the bag on the floor, hard, a few times to break it up, or, if it's a box, slam all sides of it against the counter. This will make sure it's separated and cooks evenly.

Put your smashed-apart (see headnote) broccoli, still frozen, in a microwavable casserole dish with a lid. Add a couple of tablespoons (28ml) of water, cover, and nuke on high for 7 minutes. It should be crisp-tender by then, but if there are still cold spots, stir it and give it another minute or two. Don't overcook it!

While the broccoli is cooking, add the vinaigrette and Dijon mustard to a bowl and whisk together. Slice your scallions thin, too, including the crisp part of the green shoot.

Okay, the broccoli's done! Drain it and then pour the dressing over it and toss. Add the scallions, toss again, and serve immediately.

---

2 tablespoons (28ml) olive oil

1 tablespoon (14g) butter

1 pound (455g) frozen broccoli, thawed

1 clove of garlic, crushed

1 teaspoon red pepper flakes

¼ cup (20g) shredded Parmesan cheese

¼ teaspoon salt

YIELD: 3 servings – Per serving: 182 calories; 15g fat (69.8% calories from fat); 7g protein; 8g carbohydrate; 5g dietary fiber; 3g net carbohydrate

PARMESAN BROCCOLI

I would use what is labeled "cut" broccoli or "broccoli cuts" for this— smaller than spears, but larger than chopped broccoli. They're just the right size for sautéing. If you take your broccoli out of the freezer in the morning, and leave it in the fridge, it'll be thawed by suppertime.

Put your big, heavy skillet over high heat and add the olive oil and butter. When they're hot, add the broccoli. Stir-fry until it's crisp-tender, with a few brown spots.

Stir in the garlic and red pepper flakes and stir-fry for another minute or two. Stir in the Parmesan and salt and serve.

---

1 recipe Lemon-Balsamic Mayonnaise (page 237)

1 bunch of broccoli

YIELD: 4 servings – Per serving: 515 calories; 53g fat (89.0% calories from fat); 6g protein; 9g carbohydrate; 5g dietary fiber; 4g net carbohydrate.

NOTE: You won't need all the Lemon-Balsamic Mayonnaise for this. You can make a half batch, or you can just figure it's nice to have Lemon-Balsamic Mayonnaise in the fridge.

BROCCOLI WITH LEMON-BALSAMIC MAYO

A nice twist on broccoli with lemon-butter! You can use this as a dip, or if you prefer, you can chill the broccoli spears after steaming and serve this as a salad rather than a hot side dish.

Make your Lemon-Balsamic Mayonnaise first, which is super-quick and easy to do.

Cut your broccoli into spears. Don't discard the stems—peel them! Once you peel off the tough skin, the stems are the best part.

Steam for 5 to 7 minutes or until brilliantly green and crisp-tender. Serve with little dishes of the Lemon-Balsamic Mayonnaise to dip it in.

1 pound (455g) broccoli, frozen or fresh, as you prefer

1½ tablespoons (21g) butter

1½ tablespoons (23ml) olive oil

1 clove of garlic, crushed

3 slices of bacon, cooked and crumbled

2 tablespoons (18g) pine nuts, toasted

YIELD: 3 servings – Per serving: 207 calories; 19g fat (77.8% calories from fat); 6g protein; 6g carbohydrate; 3g dietary fiber; 3g net carbohydrate.

BROCCOLI WITH BACON AND PINE NUTS

I came up with a version of this before packaged real bacon bits became common. This would be a great place to use them! About 2 tablespoons (14g) should do it. Give them a few seconds on a plate in the microwave to refresh them.

Steam your broccoli until it is just crisp-tender and brilliantly green.

While the broccoli is steaming, melt the butter with the oil in a skillet or saucepan over medium-low heat. Sauté the crushed garlic in it, without browning.

Drain your broccoli very well and put it in a mixing bowl. Pour in the garlicky butter and oil combination and toss to coat.

Serve up the broccoli and top with crumbled bacon and pine nuts.

---

6 tablespoons (84g) mayonnaise

2 chipotle chiles, canned in adobo

6 large portobello mushroom caps

6 ounces (170g) Swiss cheese, sliced

YIELD: 6 servings – Per serving: 237 calories; 20g fat (71.4% calories from fat); 11g protein; 7g carbohydrate; 2g dietary fiber; 5g net carbohydrate.

CHEESE AND CHIPOTLE PORTOBELLOS

I invented this for *300 15-Minute Low-Carb Recipes*, which is why it uses an electric grill—it's super-quick. But you can do these on your barbecue grill or under the broiler if you prefer. And, come to think of it, Monterey Jack would be good in this in place of the Swiss. Suit yourself.

Preheat your electric tabletop grill to 350°F (180°C).

Run the mayo and chiles through your food processor. Brush the convex sides of the mushroom caps with a little of the chipotle mayo and then fill the cavities with a spoonful of the mayo. Put 'em in the grill filled-side up. Set a timer for 5 minutes.

When the timer beeps, open the grill and cover each mushroom with Swiss cheese—if the slices are bigger than the mushroom caps, tear and overlap them to fit. Use a cup or jar to prop the grill lid just far enough open that it's not touching the cheese and give the mushrooms another 60 to 90 seconds—just long enough to melt the cheese.

Plate the mushrooms, spoon the rest of the chipotle mayo on top, and serve.

---

2 tablespoons (28g) butter

8 ounces (225g) sliced mushrooms

1 clove of garlic, crushed

¼ cup (50g) whipped cream cheese

¼ cup (30g) crumbled blue cheese

Salt and pepper to taste

YIELD: 3 servings – Per serving: 175 calories; 16g fat (79.1% calories from fat); 5g protein; 5g carbohydrate; 1g dietary fiber; 4g net carbohydrate.

BLUE CHEESE MUSHROOMS

How fantastic would this be spread on a steak? I'd use a mild blue for this—Gorgonzola would be perfect, or perhaps Dana Blue, though I may be biased there.

Put your large, heavy skillet over medium heat and melt the butter. Sauté the mushrooms, stirring often, until they've softened and turned dark, about 7 to 8 minutes. Stir in the garlic and let it cook for another minute or two.

Add the cream cheese and stir until it's melted in. Now, add the blue cheese and stir, but only for a minute. You want some nice hunks of blue cheese to remain. Season with salt and pepper, and it's done!

3 tablespoons (42g) butter

1 clove of garlic, crushed

10 ounces (280g) frozen chopped spinach, thawed and drained

¼ cup (20g) shredded Parmesan cheese

3 tablespoons (45ml) heavy cream

⅓ cup (80g) Porcini, Portobello, and Button Mushrooms in Cream (page 241)

YIELD: 4 servings – Per serving: 188 calories; 17g fat (80.1% calories from fat); 5g protein; 5g carbohydrate; 2g dietary fiber; 3g net carbohydrate.

1 cup (235ml) heavy cream

2 ounces (55g) cream cheese, softened

½ teaspoon salt or Vege-Sal

¼ teaspoon pepper

¼ teaspoon ground nutmeg

3 medium turnips

1 small onion

8 ounces (225g) shredded Colby Jack cheese

YIELD: 6 servings – Per serving: 194 calories; 18g fat (81.7% calories from fat); 2g protein; 7g carbohydrate; 1g dietary fiber; 6g net carbohydrate.

CREAMED SPINACH AND MUSHROOMS

I got the idea for this when I was making Shirred Eggs Florentine (page 81). I thought, "Wow, I bet this spinach mixture would be good mixed with my Porcini, Portobello, and Button Mushrooms in Cream." Yup. It's seriously tasty.

Put a medium-size skillet over low heat. Melt the butter and add the garlic. Let it cook gently while you make sure your spinach is thoroughly drained.

Stir the spinach into the butter and garlic and let it heat through. Add the Parmesan, heavy cream, and Porcini, Portobello, and Button Mushrooms in Cream and stir it all together well.

Let the whole thing simmer for 5 minutes, and it's done.

NOTE: To forestall the inevitable question: Yes, you can make this with two bags of fresh baby spinach instead. The texture will be different, but the flavor should be the same. And you'll need a much bigger skillet.

TURNIPS AU GRATIN

Mild, sweet, and creamy, these turnips would be equally at home next to a Thanksgiving turkey or an Easter ham or with Saturday night pork chops.

Preheat the oven to 350°F (180°C, or gas mark 4). Coat a 2-quart (2L) casserole dish with nonstick cooking spray.

In a medium-size, heavy-bottomed saucepan, combine the heavy cream, cream cheese, salt, pepper, and nutmeg. Put it over the lowest heat and let it sit while you do the next couple of steps.

Trim and peel your turnips and onion and then slice them thin—I used my food processor's 2 mm blade, but you can use a mandoline or a good ol' knife and cutting board.

Layer the turnips and onion in the prepared casserole dish—a few layers of turnip, a light layer of onion, then repeat. When your casserole dish is half filled, add a layer of half of the shredded cheese. Continue the layers of turnips and onion, finishing with turnips.

Now, go back to that saucepan. Use your stick blender to blend the cream and cream cheese into a sauce. (If you don't have a stick blender, you can transfer the sauce to a regular blender or food processor.) Pour the sauce evenly over the turnips. Top with the rest of the cheese.

Cover the casserole dish—with a lid if it has one, or foil if it doesn't—and bake for 40 minutes. Then uncover and bake for another 20 minutes or until bubbly.

1 celeriac

¾ cup (75g) grated Parmesan cheese

¾ cup (72g) almond meal

2 teaspoons paprika

1 teaspoon garlic powder

¼ teaspoon pepper

2 eggs

1 teaspoon water

2 cups (475ml) MCT oil, melted bacon grease, beef tallow, or chicken fat

Salt

YIELD: 5 servings – Per serving: 954 calories; 97g fat (89.1% calories from fat); 16g protein; 10g carbohydrate; 1g dietary fiber; 9g net carbohydrate.

NOTE: This analysis is way off on calories because you will not eat anywhere near all the oil.

CELERY FRIES

This sounds crazy, no? But my celery-hating husband loved these. Celery root, aka celeriac, has a much milder flavor than stalk celery.

Grab a good, strong, sharp paring knife—celeriac is a knobby, tough thing that needs some serious peeling. A slit-blade vegetable peeler is not up to the task. Peel off the outside surface. You'll find that bits of the outer surface have folded in a bit; cut those out, too.

When you have a nice, pristine celeriac, you are ready to proceed. Grab a bigger knife. Whack your celeriac in half, lay each half flat-side down, and cut it into ¼-inch (6mm) slices. Cut those into ¼-inch (6mm) strips. Cut out and discard any pithy bits.

In a mixing bowl, combine the Parmesan—you can use the cheap stuff in the green shaker—almond meal, paprika, garlic powder, and pepper. Stir together well and then transfer half of the mixture to another bowl. (This is because, inevitably, some raw egg will drip into your coating mixture, gooking it up. If you keep half of the mixture aside and pristine, it'll be there when the first bowl is too cakey to continue.)

In another bowl, beat the eggs with the water until the yolks and whites are well combined.

Put your big, heavy skillet over medium-high heat—I used my electric induction burner set to 370°F (188°C). Add ¼ inch (6mm) of oil or fat and let it get good and hot before you go on.

Okay, throw a handful of celery root strips in the egg and mess them around with a fork until they're coated. Scoop them out and drop them in one of the bowls of Parmesan-almond meal coating. Shake the bowl until the strips are coated. Lift 'em out with a fork to a plate. Repeat the process.

When you have enough coated strips to cover the bottom of your skillet, transfer them to the hot fat. Fry for a good 5 minutes and as long as 7—I found I needed to fry them a little longer than I thought to get them good and crisp. Flip them with a spatula once or twice during cooking time. When they're nicely browned and crisp, transfer to a plate—line it with paper towels to drain, if you want, but I didn't bother —season with salt and shovel in your face.

While the first batch is cooking, you will, of course, be coating the second batch, and you'll coat the third batch while the second is cooking. Eat them as they come out! They're best hot, right out of the skillet.

1 pound (455g) very fresh, thin asparagus spears

3 scallions

⅓ cup (40g) chopped walnuts

1 tablespoon (15ml) soy sauce

2 teaspoons grated ginger

1 teaspoon dark sesame oil

1 clove of garlic, crushed

12 drops of liquid stevia, English toffee

½ teaspoon sriracha, or to taste

3 tablespoons (45ml) MCT oil, divided

YIELD: 3 servings – Per serving: 247 calories; 23g fat (79.7% calories from fat); 6g protein; 7g carbohydrate; 3g dietary fiber; 4g net carbohydrate.

STIR-FRIED ASPARAGUS WITH WALNUTS

This is about as far from steamed asparagus with lemon butter as you can get and still be eating asparagus, and it's wonderful. Feel free to increase or decrease the sriracha, or skip it altogether, according to your taste.

First, prep everything: Snap the ends off of your asparagus where it wants to break naturally. Lay it on your cutting board and cut it into 1½-inch (4cm) lengths. Pile them into a bowl and prep the scallions. Trim the roots and the limp part of the green shoot and then slice the rest into ¼-inch (6mm) lengths. Add that to the bowl with the asparagus. Place your walnuts in a separate bowl.

In a custard cup, mix together the soy sauce, ginger, sesame oil, garlic, liquid stevia, and sriracha.

Okay, you're ready to cook! If you've got a wok, this would be a fine time to use it, but a large skillet will do nicely. Put it over high heat. Add 1 tablespoon (15ml) of the MCT oil and throw in the walnuts. Stir-fry them for about 3 minutes until they smell toasty. Scoop them out and put them back in the little bowl you had them in before.

Add the remaining 2 tablespoons (28ml) of MCT oil to the skillet and throw in the asparagus and scallions. Stir-fry, stirring constantly, for 4 to 5 minutes or until the asparagus is brilliantly green and just crisp-tender.

Add the soy sauce mixture, scraping the custard cup to get it all, and stir it in. Add the walnuts next. Keep stirring for about another minute, and you're done.

1½ pounds (680g) small, firm zucchini

3 tablespoons (42g) butter, divided

3 tablespoons (45ml) olive oil, divided

½ cup (60g) chopped walnuts

1 shallot, minced

Salt and pepper

YIELD: 6 servings – Per serving: 190 calories; 19g fat (83.0% calories from fat); 4g protein; 5g carbohydrate; 2g dietary fiber; 3g net carbohydrate.

SAUTÉED ZUCCHINI WITH WALNUTS

Zucchini is ridiculously low carb and easy to come by in late summer. Keep an eye on your favorite home gardeners; you may well score a free zucchini or two come August. Our tester, Wendy, says, "My family raved about this and there wasn't anything left! This would be elegant enough for company as well as easy enough to make for every day."

Scrub your zucchini, trim the ends, and then slice into rounds about ¼ inch (6mm) thick.

Put your large, heavy skillet over medium-low heat and add 1 tablespoon each of the (14g) butter and (15ml) olive oil. Dump in the walnuts and sauté them, stirring often, for 5 to 6 minutes or until they smell toasty. Scoop the walnuts out and stash them on a nearby plate.

Add the remaining 2 tablespoons each of the (28g) butter and (28ml) olive oil to the skillet and turn the heat up to medium-high. Throw in the zucchini and shallot and sauté, stirring frequently, for 5 to 6 minutes until just tender. Stir in the walnuts and season with salt and pepper to taste.

1 pound (455g) green beans

1 pound (455g) wax beans

¼ cup (60ml) olive oil

2 tablespoons (28ml) MCT oil

½ of a medium red onion, finely diced

3 cloves of garlic, crushed

4 anchovy fillets

2 teaspoons red pepper flakes, or more or less, to taste

¼ cup (60ml) lime juice

YIELD: 10 servings – Per serving: 106 calories; 8g fat (66.9% calories from fat); 2g protein; 7g carbohydrate; 3g dietary fiber; 4g net carbohydrate.

SPICY SUMMER BEANS

This could not get much farther from that sticky casserole made with canned green beans and mushroom soup! Spicy and savory, these would go well with grilled chicken or fish.

If using fresh beans, trim them and cut them in half. Put your beans in a microwavable casserole dish with a lid or a microwave steamer. Add a few tablespoons (45ml) of water, cover, and microwave for 6 minutes. Then, drain them well. If using frozen beans, you just have to thaw them, drain them, and cut them if they're not already cut.

Put your large, heavy skillet over medium-high heat and add the olive oil and MCT oil. Add the onion, garlic, anchovy fillets, and red pepper flakes. Sauté until the onions are turning golden. As you sauté, mash up the anchovies into the oil until they've disintegrated.

Now, add the green beans and sauté them for 4 to 5 minutes until they're hot through and completely coated with the seasoned oil. Stir in the lime juice and serve 'em up.

6 tablespoons (85g) butter, divided

¼ cup (35g) pine nuts

1½ pounds (680g) thin green beans, trimmed

1 yellow bell pepper

1 tablespoon (15ml) lemon juice

¼ teaspoon salt

¼ teaspoon pepper

¼ cup (16g) minced parsley

YIELD: 8 servings – Per serving: 129 calories; 11g fat (71.3% calories from fat); 3g protein; 7g carbohydrate; 3g dietary fiber; 4g net carbohydrate.

GREEN BEAN AND YELLOW PEPPER SAUTÉ

Julie, my ace tester, said, "Solid 10, Dana. Once again, everyone in the family came back for seconds. Austin was over the moon. Glen, who thinks of potatoes and corn as 'eating his vegetables,' ate two servings. Katie ate hers and came back for more, attempting to steal as many pine nuts as she could."

In a small skillet over medium-low heat, melt 1 tablespoon (14g) of the butter. Add the pine nuts and sauté, stirring often, until they're golden. Remove from the heat and reserve.

Put the green beans in a microwavable casserole dish with a lid or a microwave steamer. Add a couple of tablespoons (28ml) of water, cover, and microwave on high for 10 minutes.

In the meanwhile, whack your pepper in half, remove the seeds and pith, and cut it into matchstick strips.

When the microwave beeps, grab your big heavy skillet and put it over medium heat. Melt the remaining 5 tablespoons (70g) of butter in it.

Drain the green beans and put them and the pepper in the skillet. Sauté, stirring often, until the green beans are just tender and the pepper is crisp-tender.

Stir in the lemon juice, salt, pepper, parsley, and half the pine nuts. Pile them into a serving dish, sprinkle the rest of the pine nuts on top, and you're done.

1½ large heads of cauliflower, about 2½ pounds (1.1kg) total

1 cup (235ml) chicken broth

½ cup (120ml) heavy cream

4 ounces (115g) cream cheese, softened

1 cup (115g) shredded sharp cheddar cheese, divided

2 tablespoons (28g) butter

¼ cup (16g) minced parsley

4 scallions, sliced, including the crisp part of the green shoot

1 clove of garlic, crushed

1 teaspoon salt, or to taste

¼ teaspoon pepper

½ cup (115g) sour cream

Guar or xanthan (optional)

YIELD: 10 servings – Per serving: 200 calories; 17g fat (74.5% calories from fat); 7g protein; 7g carbohydrate; 2g dietary fiber; 5g net carbohydrate.

CREAMY, CHEESY CAULIFLOWER CASSEROLE

This makes a lot! That makes it the perfect side dish for parties, potlucks, or holidays or to make over the weekend to warm up during the week. Leftovers are the busy person's friend.

Preheat the oven to 350°F (180°C, or gas mark 4). Coat a rectangular 2-quart (2L) baking dish with nonstick cooking spray.

Trim the leaves and the very bottom of the stem from your cauliflower and then cut the rest into bite-size pieces. Put them in a microwavable casserole dish with a lid or a microwave steamer, add a few tablespoons (45ml) of water, cover, and microwave on high for 12 minutes or until nearly tender.

Put a large, heavy-bottomed saucepan over medium heat and add the chicken broth. As it is coming to a simmer, add the heavy cream and cream cheese and whisk or blend with a stick blender until the cream cheese has entirely melted in. Now, add ½ cup (58g) of the shredded cheddar, a tablespoon (7g) at a time, whisking or blending each addition in thoroughly before adding more.

Now, whisk in the butter, parsley, scallions, garlic, salt, and pepper. Turn off the heat and whisk in the sour cream. Thicken a little with your guar or xanthan shaker if you feel it needs it.

By now, your microwave has beeped. Drain the cauliflower very well and transfer it to the prepared baking dish. Pour the sauce evenly over the cauliflower. Put 'er in the oven and set a timer for 20 minutes.

When the timer beeps, top with the remaining ½ cup (58g) of cheese. Bake for 5 minutes more or until the cheese is melted.

½ of a head of cauliflower

1 ounce (28g) cream cheese, at room temperature

1 tablespoon (14g) butter

1 teaspoon salt

½ teaspoon pepper

¼ teaspoon granulated garlic

1 egg

⅔ cup (77g) shredded cheddar cheese

¼ cup (28g) bacon bits

1 scallion, minced

½ recipe Pork Rind Crumbs (page 63)

Refined coconut oil or MCT oil, for frying

LOADED CAULI TOTS

These are fried and crunchy and so yummy! Don't tell the kids it's cauliflower again, and they may not even notice. These actually are higher in fat than the numbers suggest, because Mastercook can't figure the quantity of oil absorbed. I was left with less than ¼ inch (6mm) of oil in my skillet by the time I was done.

Trim the very bottom of the stem and the leaves from the cauliflower and then whack the rest into chunks. Put 'em in a microwavable casserole dish or microwave steamer, add a few tablespoons (45ml) of water, cover, and nuke on high for 10 to 12 minutes or until tender.

Drain the cauliflower quite well and put it in a deep, narrow bowl. Add the cream cheese, butter, salt, pepper, and granulated garlic and use a stick blender to mash it into Fauxtatoes. Blend in the egg.

Add the shredded cheese, bacon bits, and scallion and blend them in, stopping before they've vanished into the mix—you want to be able to see actual bacon

LOADED CAULI TOTS *(continued)*

bits, shreds of cheese, and flecks of scallion. Now, blend in the Pork Rind Crumbs quickly—the mixture will thicken as you do.

In a large, heavy skillet, over medium-high heat, melt ½ inch (1.3cm) of coconut oil. You want to bring it to 375°F (190°C); I use a countertop electronic induction burner for this because it lets me hold a precise heat.

Drop in the cauliflower mixture in spoonfuls. Fry until a fairly deep brown, flip, and fry the other side. Serve hot!

My husband liked no-sugar-added ketchup with these, but they're great with just an additional sprinkle of salt.

YIELD: 4 servings – Per serving: 257 calories; 18g fat (62.5% calories from fat); 18g protein; 6g carbohydrate; 3g dietary fiber; 3g net carbohydrate

NACHO MAC AND CHEESE

I made the Nacho Cheese Powder to flavor pork rinds, but I had some left over. It's a sign of how long it's been since I ate packaged mac and cheese that it took me longer than 30 seconds to think of this! It worked great. By the way, once you have cheddar cheese powder on hand, you can simply use it, cream, and butter on shirataki to make macaroni and cheese reminiscent of your youth.

1 package (8 ounces, or 225g) of tofu shirataki, preferably macaroni

3 tablespoons (18g) Nacho Cheese Powder (page 247)

2 tablespoons (28ml) heavy cream

2 teaspoons butter

Prepare the shirataki according to the instructions on page 23.

When they've been drained for the last time, simply add everything else and stir until you have a sauce. That's it!

YIELD: 1 serving – Per serving: 291 calories; 25g fat (72.6% calories from fat); 12g protein; 9g carbohydrate; 3g dietary fiber; 6g net carbohydrate.

FETTUCCINI WITH ARTICHOKE PESTO

You don't have to use fettuccini; use whatever shape you like. It just appealed to me in this context. Throw in a bottle of Pinot Grigio and you've got a company supper—and you can do most of it in advance!

⅔ cup (67g) walnuts

8 ounces (225g) frozen artichoke hearts, thawed and drained

1 cup (60g) lightly packed chopped flat-leaf parsley

Zest and juice of 1 lemon

1 clove of garlic

½ teaspoon salt

½ teaspoon pepper

¾ cup (175ml) olive oil

⅔ cup (53g) shredded Parmesan cheese

4 packages (8 ounces, or 225g each) of tofu shirataki, fettuccini

Preheat the oven to 350°F (180°C, or gas mark 4). Spread the walnuts in a shallow baking dish and roast for 7 to 8 minutes until toasty.

Put the walnuts, artichoke hearts, parsley, lemon zest and juice, garlic, salt, and pepper in your food processor and pulse, stopping now and then to scrape down the sides until it's all finely chopped.

With the processor running, drizzle in the olive oil. Add the Parmesan in 3 additions, pulsing just enough to mix it in.

You can do all of this in advance, if you like, and stash the pesto in the fridge. If you do this, take it out of the refrigerator ahead of time to reach room temperature.

When it's time to eat, simply prepare the shirataki as directed on page 23. When it's hot and thoroughly drained, toss with the pesto.

YIELD: 6 servings – Per serving: 385 calories; 38g fat (84.8% calories from fat); 8g protein; 7g carbohydrate; 3g dietary fiber; 4g net carbohydrate.

2 large turnips

6 ounces (170g) shredded
Swiss cheese

½ of a medium onion

1 teaspoon salt or Vege-Sal

½ teaspoon pepper

3 tablespoons (42g) butter

YIELD: 6 servings – Per serving:
172 calories; 14g fat (70.2%
calories from fat); 9g protein;
4g carbohydrate; 1g dietary fiber;
3g net carbohydrate.

CHEESY NEEPS

Americans are so potato-centric that we often seem to forget that there are other root vegetables in the world. Turnips were a European staple for centuries before potatoes ever made it across the Atlantic. This will help make it clear why.

Peel the turnips, whack 'em into hunks, and run 'em through the shredding disk of your food processor. Run the Swiss cheese through, too. Chop your onion pretty fine—I find my shredding disk doesn't work for this, so I just used a knife and a cutting board, but you could swap out the shredding disk for the S-blade and use it to chop your onion fine, if you like.

Coat your slow cooker with nonstick cooking spray. Put the turnips, cheese, and onion in there and sprinkle the salt and pepper over it all. Toss until everything is well combined.

Smooth the top. Now, cut your butter into little bits and dot the top of the turnip mixture evenly with it. Cover the pot, set to low, and let it all cook for 5 hours or so.

---

2 turnips

½ of a head of cauliflower

1 onion

2 tablespoons (28g) butter

½ cup (120ml) heavy cream

1 tablespoon (15g) anchovy
paste

¼ teaspoon salt or Vege-sal

¼ teaspoon pepper

YIELD: 5 servings – Per serving:
167 calories; 14g fat (72.4%
calories from fat); 3g protein;
9g carbohydrate; 3g dietary fiber;
6g net carbohydrate.

JANSONN'S TEMPTATION

This Swedish favorite is traditionally made with potatoes. I have no idea how this de-carbed version compares, but it's utterly delicious.

Preheat the oven to 400°F (200°C, or gas mark 6). Coat an 8 × 8-inch (20 × 20cm) baking dish with nonstick cooking spray.

Peel your turnips and cut them into smallish strips—about the size of fast food French fries. Cut up your cauliflower, too—cut it into strips as much as possible (include the stem), but of course, being cauliflower, it'll crumble some. It's no biggie. Combine the turnips and cauliflower in a bowl. Slice your onion quite thin.

Melt the butter in your heavy skillet over medium heat and sauté your onions until they're limp and turning translucent.

Layer the turnip/cauliflower mixture and the onions in the prepared baking dish.

Combine your cream, anchovy paste, salt, and pepper in a cup and stir until the anchovy paste is dissolved. Pour this mixture over the vegetables. Bake for 45 minutes or until bubbly.

---

3 tablespoons (42g) coconut
oil

4 turnips, about baseball size

4 tablespoons (55g) Maple
Butter (page 251)

2 teaspoons brown mustard

MUSTARD-MAPLE GLAZED TURNIPS

These are really good, fitting for a holiday dinner. Roasting brings out the natural sweetness of the turnips, and the Maple Butter complements it.

Preheat the oven to 350°F (180°C, or gas mark 4). While it's heating, put the coconut oil in a baking pan and slide it into the oven to melt.

Peel the turnips and cut 'em into chunks—I went with strips about ½ inch (1.3cm) square and 1 to 1½ inches (2.5 to 4cm) long.

Toss the turnips in the coconut oil, coating them all over. Put them in the oven and set the timer for 15 minutes.

When the timer beeps, stir up your turnips and use a spatula to turn them over so they brown evenly. Give them another 15 minutes.

Repeat the stirring/turning over routine and give them yet another 15 minutes.

By now, your turnips should be softened and getting browned all over. Stir in the Maple Butter and mustard.

Give your turnips another 10 to 15 minutes and serve.

THE SIMPLEST EGGPLANT

My husband didn't much care for eggplant until, in an attempt to come up with a 15-minute recipe (and failing), I tried cooking it this way. Then, he yummed it down and asked for more!

When I say "simple," I mean simple. Slice your eggplant into rounds about ½ inch (1.3cm) thick.

Put your big, heavy skillet over medium-high heat. Pour in a bunch of olive oil and get it hot. Throw in the eggplant, however many rounds your skillet will fit. Fry until brown on one side, flip, and fry until brown on the other side. Remove from the skillet and repeat—adding more oil as needed, and you'll need plenty—until all the eggplant is used up. But go ahead and eat the first batch while the second batch is frying; no use letting it get cold. We put nothing on this but salt and pepper, and it was wonderful.

PARMESAN CAULIFLOWER PACKET

Foil packets are a great way to cook vegetables if you're grilling outside. If you're not, you can do them in the oven and save on dishwashing! If you want to double this, make two packets rather than making one huge one.

Tear off a 20-inch (50cm) length of aluminum foil—preferably nonstick foil—and lay it on your counter.

Trim the very bottom of the stem and the leaves from your cauliflower. Cut the rest into bite-size chunks. Put them in a mixing bowl.

Dice the onion fine, crush the garlic, and mince the rosemary. Add them to the cauliflower along with the Parmesan. Stir everything together, sprinkling in the salt and pepper as you go.

Pile it all in the center of your foil. Cut the butter into small bits and distribute them over the cauliflower. Drizzle the olive oil evenly over the whole thing.

Fold the long ends over the cauliflower and roll them down, making as tight a seam as you can. Roll in the sides, making them as tight as possible, too.

Throw the packet on the grill. Give it 10 to 12 minutes per side.

YIELD: 4 servings – Per serving: 327 calories; 34g fat (89.0% calories from fat); 2g protein; 8g carbohydrate; 2g dietary fiber; 6g net carbohydrate.

---

1 eggplant

About ¾ cup (175ml) olive oil

Salt and pepper

YIELD: 4 servings – Per serving: 388 calories; 41g fat (91.9% calories from fat); 1g protein; 7g carbohydrate; 3g dietary fiber; 4g net carbohydrate.

NOTE: As I say, that quantity of olive oil is approximate and so is the nutritional analysis. Still, eggplant might as well be named "oil sponge plant." It'll suck up plenty. By the way, feel free to fry it in bacon grease instead, for a totally different flavor.

½ of a head of cauliflower

½ of a small onion

3 cloves of garlic

2 teaspoons fresh rosemary

½ cup (40g) shredded Parmesan cheese

½ teaspoon salt

¼ teaspoon pepper

2 tablespoons (28g) butter

2 tablespoons (28ml) olive oil

YIELD: 4 servings – Per serving: 179 calories; 15g fat (74.7% calories from fat); 6g protein; 6g carbohydrate; 2g dietary fiber; 4g net carbohydrate.

2 packages (8 ounces, or 225g each) of shirataki noodles, spaghetti

4 cloves of garlic, crushed

2 tablespoons (28g) coconut oil

2 tablespoons (32g) natural peanut butter

4 tablespoons (60ml) rice vinegar

4 tablespoons (60ml) soy sauce

2 tablespoons (28ml) dark sesame oil

36 drops of liquid stevia, plain

½ teaspoon chili garlic paste

2 scallions

YIELD: 4 servings – Per serving: 205 calories; 18g fat (76.1% calories from fat); 4g protein; 9g carbohydrate; 3g dietary fiber; 6g net carbohydrate.

SESAME NOODLES

Pining for take-out Chinese? Try this quick and easy side dish.

Drain and rinse the shirataki. Snip across them a few times, put them in a microwavable bowl big enough to eventually toss them in, and nuke 'em for 90 seconds.

In the meanwhile, combine the garlic, coconut oil, peanut butter, rice vinegar, soy sauce, sesame oil, liquid stevia, and chili garlic paste in a small saucepan over low heat.

When the microwave beeps, re-drain the noodles, put them back in the bowl, and give them another 90 seconds on high.

Whisk your sauce over low heat until it's smooth and thick—it won't take long.

When the microwave beeps again, drain the noodles one last time and put them back in their bowl. Pour on the sauce and toss.

Slice up the scallions really quick. Serve the noodles with the scallions scattered on top.

1 package (8 ounces, or 225g) of Miracle Rice

1 egg

¼ cup (60ml) olive oil, divided

3 tablespoons (27g) pine nuts

⅓ cup (23g) chopped mushrooms

¼ cup (40g) diced onion

¼ cup (75g) jarred artichoke hearts, drained and chopped

¼ cup (25g) pimento-stuffed olives, sliced (or you can use "salad olives," which are the same thing, but presliced)

2 tablespoons (8g) minced parsley

1½ teaspoons chicken bouillon concentrate

YIELD: 3 servings – Per serving: 260 calories; 25g fat (83.6% calories from fat); 5g protein; 6g carbohydrate; 2g dietary fiber; 4g net carbohydrate.

MEDITERRANEAN FRIED "RICE"

I was going to improvise a Mediterranean-influenced Miracle Rice dish and throw a fried egg on top, when it hit me: Why not stir in strips of egg, like in Chinese fried rice? It was awesome. Add a second egg and this is filling enough for a main dish.

Prepare the Miracle Rice as explained on page 23. Take that time to chop and slice what needs chopping and slicing.

If your medium-size skillet isn't nonstick, give it a shot of cooking spray. Put it over medium-high heat. Break the egg into a bowl and scramble it up. When the skillet is hot, add 1 tablespoon (15ml) of the olive oil, slosh it around to coat the skillet, and then pour in the egg. Pull back the edges of the egg as it sets, letting the raw egg run underneath, as you would make an omelet. When there's not enough raw egg to run underneath, use a spatula to flip the whole egg disk over. Let it cook for another minute and then remove to a plate and reserve.

Put the medium-size skillet back over the heat, turned to medium-low. Add the pine nuts and stir until touched with gold, about 4 to 5 minutes.

Now, you need your large, heavy skillet. Put it over medium-high heat and pour in the remaining 3 tablespoons (45ml) of olive oil. Throw in the mushrooms and onion and sauté for 4 to 5 minutes until the mushrooms have softened and changed color and the onion is turning translucent. Add the artichoke hearts, olives, and parsley and sauté the whole shebang together for another 2 to 3 minutes.

Add your Miracle Rice and the chicken bouillon concentrate and stir everything together until the bouillon concentrate has dissolved and everything is evenly distributed. Turn the heat to low.

MEDITERRANEAN FRIED "RICE" *(continued)*

Remember your egg disk? Grab it, throw it on your cutting board, and roll it up. Slice across the roll at ½-inch (1.3cm) intervals, making strips, and then cut in the other direction once or twice. Stir your egg strips into the Miracle Rice mixture.

Grab your toasted pine nuts and stir 'em in. Done!

FETTUCCINI WITH ARUGULA AND CREAMY LEMON SAUCE

I was surprised how many grams of carb arugula contributed to this recipe! That's why the portions are side dish sized. It's a great choice with something low fat, such as a simple fish dish.

2 packages (8 ounces, or 225g each) of tofu shirataki, fettuccini

2 lemons

3 cups (60g) arugula

½ cup (115g) sour cream

¾ cup (150g) whipped cream cheese

Salt and pepper

5 ounces (140g) shredded Parmesan cheese, divided

YIELD: 4 servings – Per serving: 323 calories; 26g fat (71.3% calories from fat); 17g protein; 7g carbohydrate; 1g dietary fiber; 6g net carbohydrate.

Prepare the shirataki as described on page 23.

In the meanwhile, grate the zest from your lemons and then squeeze out their juice. (If you warm them slightly and roll them firmly under the heel of your hand for a few seconds before cutting them open, you'll maximize juice yield.) Coarsely chop your arugula.

Stir together the sour cream, whipped cream cheese, lemon juice, and zest—you can do this with a bowl and whisk or in your food processor. Season with salt and pepper to taste.

When the noodles are done, toss them with the sauce and arugula and half of the Parmesan.

Divide among 4 plates and top with the rest of the Parmesan.

SHIRATAKI WITH FETA-CAPER PESTO

This, of course, started as a very high-carb recipe. Shirataki to the rescue! You could make this with Zoodles (page 111), too.

2 packages (8 ounces, or 225g each) of tofu shirataki (I'd use macaroni, but any shape will do.)

1 clove of garlic

3 anchovy fillets

1 tablespoon (9g) capers

1 teaspoon lemon zest

⅔ cup (100g) plus 2 tablespoons (19g) crumbled feta cheese, divided

¼ cup (16g) chopped parsley

1 tablespoon (15ml) lemon juice

¼ cup (60ml) extra-virgin olive oil, plus more for drizzling

Salt and pepper

YIELD: 3 servings – Per serving: 277 calories; 27g fat (86.0% calories from fat); 7g protein; 3g carbohydrate; trace dietary fiber; 3g net carbohydrate.

Prepare the shirataki according to the instructions on page 23.

While that's happening, put the garlic, anchovies, capers, lemon zest, ⅓ cup (100g) of the feta, parsley, and lemon juice in your blender or a small food processor. Turn it on and drizzle in the olive oil through the feed tube. When it's all in, season with salt and pepper to taste—how much salt will depend on how salty your feta is.

When the shirataki is done, toss it with the pesto, thinning it with a little more olive oil if need be, and pile it into 3 bowls.

Crumble the remaining 2 tablespoons (19g) of feta over the top. Done!

1 medium onion, finely diced

3 tablespoons (42g) butter

2 cups (460g) sour cream

2 tablespoons (28ml) beef stock

2 teaspoons beef bouillon concentrate

20 ounces (560g) frozen chopped spinach, thawed and drained

YIELD: 8 servings – Per serving: 185 calories; 17g fat (77.6% calories from fat); 4g protein; 7g carbohydrate; 2g dietary fiber; 5g net carbohydrate.

SPINACH CASSEROLE

This is a great side dish for a crowd. If you like caramelized onions, try cooking a batch in your slow cooker and stashing them in baggies in your freezer.

Preheat the oven to 350°F (180°C, or gas mark 4). Coat a 1-quart (1L) baking dish with nonstick cooking spray.

Put a medium-size, heavy skillet over medium-low heat and start sautéing the onion in the butter. You want to sauté it until it caramelizes—turns brown and sweet. This takes time. Pour yourself a cup of tea or coffee. Put on your favorite music or podcast. Stir 'em every 5 minutes or so. Do not turn up the heat to hasten the process! Figure you're in for a 15- to 20-minute wait.

In a mixing bowl, combine the caramelized onions with the sour cream.

Put the skillet back on the burner, add the beef stock and beef bouillon concentrate, and stir it around, scraping up all the nice browned stuff from the bottom of the skillet and making sure the bouillon concentrate is dissolved. Add to the mixing bowl and stir the whole thing up.

Make sure your spinach is really well drained—I either pick it up with clean hands and squeeze it dry or put it in a strainer and press it hard with the back of a spoon. Stir it into the rest of the stuff in the mixing bowl, combining thoroughly.

Put the mixture into the prepared baking dish. Bake for 30 minutes until bubbly.

6 large portobello mushroom caps

1 clove of garlic

¼ cup (4g) minced cilantro

6 drops of liquid stevia, plain

1 tablespoon (15ml) soy sauce

1 tablespoon (15ml) MCT oil

½ teaspoon sriracha

⅓ cup (75g) Sriracha Mayonnaise (page 237)

YIELD: 6 servings – Per serving: 150 calories; 13g fat (72.2% calories from fat); 4g protein; 8g carbohydrate; 2g dietary fiber; 6g net carbohydrate.

GRILLED PORTOBELLOS

These make a great side dish at a cookout. Or you can get fancy and grill filets mignons along with them and serve each tiny, expensive steak on top of a grilled mushroom, with the mayo on top of that. It makes the filets seem a bit bigger.

Lay your mushrooms in a nonreactive pan—glass or stainless steel are good—ribbed-side down.

Run the garlic, cilantro, liquid stevia, soy sauce, MCT oil, and sriracha through your food processor until the garlic and cilantro are largely pulverized.

Brush this mixture over the tops of the portobellos. Flip them over and brush the rest over the ribbed side. Let the mushrooms marinate for at least 20 minutes.

Grill the mushrooms for about 3 minutes per side, basting with any marinade left in the pan.

Plate the mushrooms and spoon Sriracha Mayonnaise into the center of each. Garnish with a little more cilantro, if you have it.

4 medium artichokes (about 2 pounds, or 910g)

YIELD: 4 servings – Per serving: 171 calories; 1g fat (2.4% calories from fat); 12g protein; 38g carbohydrate; 20g dietary fiber; 18g net carbohydrate.

ARTICHOKES

Okay, this isn't really a recipe so much as simple instructions. But still, artichokes are yummy and fun to eat. They're also a great transport device for fats!

Put a big pot of water on to boil. In the meantime, trim the stems from your artichokes. Lay them on their sides and trim off about the top ¾ inch (2cm). Use kitchen shears to trim the points from the leaves.

By now, your water's boiling! Put your artichokes in, base-side down, and cover, leaving a crack. Cook for 25 to 30 minutes or until you can pierce them easily with a knife. Scoop them out with a slotted spoon and sit them upside down on a plate to drain and cool a bit.

While those artichokes have been boiling, you should have given some thought to your sauce. The Lemon-Anchovy Sauce on page 239 would be good; so would olive oil with a little garlic crushed into it and salt and pepper, with piles of grated Parmesan to dip into; or one of the flavored mayonnaises; or the classic, never to be outdone—lemon butter. Whatever you've chosen, put it in 4 little dishes, so each diner can have his or her own.

When you can handle the artichokes, place each one on a salad plate. Spread the leaves and use the tip of a spoon to scrape out the fuzzy "choke." Then, place a dish of your chosen sauce on each plate and bear them forth, rejoicing.

Have you not had the pleasure, you eat them thusly: Peel off a leaf. Most of it will be inedible, but there will be a tiny, tender, delicious bit where the leaf attached to the artichoke. Dip it in your sauce and then pull it between your teeth to scrape off the flesh, discarding the leaf. Repeat until all the leaves are gone. Eat the heart with a knife and fork and the remains of your sauce.

1 tablespoon (15ml) dry sherry

1 tablespoon (15ml) soy sauce

4 drops of liquid stevia, plain

½ teaspoon salt

1 pound (455g) romaine lettuce hearts

3 tablespoons (45ml) MCT oil

3 cloves of garlic, peeled and smashed with the side of a knife, but not crushed

1 teaspoon dark sesame oil

YIELD: 4 servings – Per serving: 125 calories; 12g fat (81.8% calories from fat); 2g protein; 4g carbohydrate; 2g dietary fiber; 2g net carbohydrate.

STIR-FRIED LETTUCE

Do yourself a favor: Buy organic romaine hearts and trust that they're clean enough to not need washing. It's hard to get them completely dry, and any water clinging to the leaves will cause furious—and possibly painful—oil spitting.

In a small dish, combine the sherry, soy sauce, liquid stevia, and salt. Put this by the stove.

Slice across your romaine hearts, cutting them into 1-inch (2.5cm) strips.

Put a wok or huge frying pan over high heat. Let it get good and hot. Add the MCT oil, then the garlic, and swirl it around. Add the lettuce and stir-fry for just 1 to 2 minutes.

Stir in the sauce, cooking just another 30 seconds. Remove from the heat, drizzle the sesame oil over it, and stir before serving.

CHAPTER 8

Poultry

I f you've been eating boneless, skinless chicken breast, it's time to move on!
It's time to buy chicken on the bone—you can save them for bone broth. With its
collagen-rich skin, it's not just higher in fat, thus closer to our macros, but it's
also more nutritious—and cheaper, too.

You'll find I have used chicken thighs a lot. There are a few reasons for this:
They're my favorite part of the chicken, they're fattier than breasts, and I often get
them for as little as 69 cents per pound (455g). If you're dead-set on using breasts or
drumsticks, however, you certainly may.

When you do use boneless, skinless chicken—say, for kebabs—you'll want to
lavish them with oil or a tasty sauce. Regardless, it can be hard to get poultry, with
the exception of duck, up to a high enough fat percentage for us. You'll want a salad
or a rich side dish.

One 6-pound (2.7kg) whole chicken

¼ cup (60ml) MCT oil, divided

2 teaspoons pepper

2 teaspoons Virtue or Natural Mate, or 4 tablespoons (60ml) erythritol

1 teaspoon ground cinnamon

1 teaspoon ground ginger

1 teaspoon dried thyme

1 teaspoon salt

½ teaspoon cayenne

½ teaspoon ground cloves

¼ cup (60ml) dark rum

2 tablespoons (28ml) lime juice

18 drops of liquid stevia, English toffee

½ cup (120ml) chicken broth

YIELD: 8 servings – Per serving: 613 calories; 45g fat (69.6% calories from fat); 43g protein; 2g carbohydrate; trace dietary fiber; 2g net carbohydrate.

TRADEWINDS CHICKEN

While looking for something new to do with a huge roasting chicken, I wound up with this. That Nice Boy I Married declared it "unusual"—while reaching for more of the basting sauce. You could use cut-up chicken instead, if you prefer. I like whole chickens—they often come cheap, they offer the choice of white or dark meat, and there's something festive about serving a whole bird. Also, you get that carcass to add to the bone bag for making broth. However, it cannot be questioned that cut-up chicken cooks faster. Feel free to substitute the cut-up chicken parts of your choice for the whole chicken. If you do, start basting at 20 minutes and figure on about 1 hour total cooking time.

If you're thinking ahead—and with a bird that takes a couple of hours to roast, you might well be—try rubbing your chicken with oil and sprinkling it with the spice mixture a day before and let it sit in the refrigerator soaking up the flavor.

If you prefer, you may substitute 2 tablespoons (28ml) of rum extract for the dark rum. However, keep in mind that rum extract usually also contains some alcohol, though I believe the concentration is lower.

Preheat the oven to 350°F (180°C, or gas mark 4). Place a rack in a roasting pan and put the chicken on it. Rub the chicken all over with 2 tablespoons (28ml) of the MCT oil.

In a small bowl, mix together the pepper, Virtue or Natural Mate, cinnamon, ginger, thyme, salt, cayenne, and cloves. Sprinkle half of this mixture all over the skin of your chicken, reserving the remaining spice mixture in the bowl. Place the chicken in the oven. Set the timer for 1 hour.

In the meanwhile, grab that bowl of reserved spice mixture. Add to it the rum, lime juice, liquid stevia, chicken broth, and remaining 2 tablespoons (28ml) of MCT oil. This will be both your baste and your sauce.

When the timer beeps, baste your chicken all over with the sauce you've made. Continue roasting for another 45 to 60 minutes or until a meat thermometer inserted into the thickest part of the thigh reads 165°F (74°C) or until the pop-up timer, should your bird have one, pops, basting every 10 to 15 minutes with the sauce.

Remove the chicken from the oven and let it rest on a platter for 15 minutes before carving. Serve with the remaining sauce.

One 3-pound (1.4kg) whole chicken

¼ cup (60ml) lemon juice

½ cup (120ml) olive oil

½ teaspoon salt

¼ teaspoon pepper

YIELD: 5 servings – Per serving: 49g fat (75.6% calories from fat); 35g protein; 1g carbohydrate; trace dietary fiber; 1g net carbohydrate.

4 chicken thighs, bone in, skin on

Salt and pepper

1 tablespoon (15ml) olive oil

6 tablespoons (90ml) dry vermouth

2 tablespoons (28ml) lemon juice

5 ounces (140g) bagged baby spinach

2 scallions, sliced, including the crisp part of the green shoot

2 tablespoons (8g) minced parsley

6 tablespoons (84g) mayonnaise

¼ cup (60g) horseradish

YIELD: 4 servings – Per serving: 422 calories; 35g fat (77.3% calories from fat); 18g protein; 6g carbohydrate; 2g dietary fiber; 4g net carbohydrate.

GREEK ROASTED CHICKEN

Greek restaurants do a brisk carry-out business in chickens roasted this way, and it's no wonder—they're terrific. If you happen to have a rotisserie, this is a perfect dish to cook in it, but the oven works fine.

Combine the lemon juice, olive oil, salt, and pepper in a small bowl. Put your chicken in a 1-gallon (3.8L) resealable bag sitting in a mixing bowl (for neatness) and pour the lemon juice–olive oil mixture over it. Pour some of it right into the body cavity. Seal the bag, carefully pressing out the air as you go. Turn the chicken this way and that to coat. Stick 'er in the fridge.

Let your chicken marinate for several hours, and all day is great. Any time you're in the fridge, turn the bag. This helps the chicken marinate evenly.

A good 90 minutes before suppertime, preheat the oven to 375°F (190°C, or gas mark 5). Pull your chicken out of the fridge and pour the marinade into a saucepan; place on the stove and bring to a boil, then remove from heat. Arrange the chicken on a rack in a roasting pan.

Roast, basting now and then with the reserved marinade, for about 1 hour or until the juices run clear when it's pierced to the bone. A meat thermometer stuck in the thickest part of the thigh should read 165°F (74°C). Discard the rest of the marinade.

When your chicken is done, let it rest on a platter for 10 to 15 minutes before carving.

CHICKEN BRAISED IN VERMOUTH WITH SPINACH-HORSERADISH SAUCE

Dry vermouth, spinach, and horseradish add up to a rich and sophisticated flavor for these simple chicken thighs. It is quick, too! Yes, you can use breasts if you prefer. I'm just a big fan of thighs.

Put your large, heavy skillet over medium heat. Season your chicken all over with salt and pepper. When the pan is hot, add the olive oil, sloshing it around to coat the skillet. Then put in the chicken, skin-side down.

Sauté until the skin is a nice golden brown—this may take as much as 10 minutes. While it's browning, cover the skillet with a lid tilted to let out steam. I needed to rotate my skillet from time to time to keep the chicken browning evenly.

When the skin is nicely golden, flip your chicken and let the bottom brown for another 5 minutes, again with a tilted lid.

Add the vermouth and lemon juice to the skillet. Let it come to a boil and then turn down the heat until it's just simmering. Cover the skillet tightly this time and set a timer for 20 minutes.

The timer beeped! Go pierce the biggest piece of chicken to the bone. If the juice runs clear, it's done. If it runs pink, put the lid back on and give it another 5 minutes or so.

CHICKEN BRAISED IN VERMOUTH *(continued)*

A meat thermometer stuck in the thickest part of the thigh should read 165°F (74°C).

When the chicken is done through, remove to a platter. Add the spinach, scallion, and parsley to the skillet. Sauté until the spinach is limp, a few minutes.

Transfer the spinach mixture to your food processor using a rubber scraper to get all of the flavorful drippings from the skillet. Add the mayonnaise and horseradish to the food processor and process until the spinach is chopped. Season with salt and pepper to taste and serve over the chicken.

CHICKEN LIVER "RICE" BOWL

You will enjoy this dish if you like chicken liver and mushrooms, and you won't enjoy it if you don't. I love 'em both, and this made a fast, fabulous, and super-filling breakfast. Plus, liver is nature's own vitamin pill.

1 package (8 ounces, or 225g) of Miracle Rice

2 chicken livers

2 tablespoons (28g) butter

⅓ cup (80g) Porcini, Portobello, and Button Mushrooms in Cream (page 241)

YIELD: 1 serving – Per serving: 422 calories; 38g fat (78.4% calories from fat); 13g protein; 10g carbohydrate; 2g dietary fiber; 11g net carbohydrate.

Drain, rinse, and microwave your Miracle Rice as described on page 23.

While the Miracle Rice is in the microwave, use your kitchen shears to snip your livers into bite-size bits.

Put a medium-sized skillet, preferably nonstick, over medium heat. Melt the butter and when it's hot, throw in the bits of liver. Sauté, stirring often, until the surfaces change color and they stop running red. *Do not overcook.*

Stir in the hot Miracle Rice and the Porcini, Portobello, and Button Mushrooms in Cream. Heat through, dump into a bowl, and stuff in your face.

As I write this up, it occurs to me that a sprinkle of grated Parmesan might be nice on this, but it's hardly necessary.

CHICKEN LIVER MARSALA

This is a throwback to the mid-twentieth century, and a fine one, too. I served this over Miracle Rice, but that's not essential. You could serve this with a green salad or even use it to fill omelets.

¼ cup (55g) butter

4 slices of bacon

2 shallots, minced

1 teaspoon dried sage

8 ounces (225g) chicken livers (about 12)

¼ cup (60ml) Marsala wine

YIELD: 3 servings – Per serving: 298 calories; 22g fat (71.0% calories from fat); 17g protein; 4g carbohydrate; trace dietary fiber; 4g net carbohydrate.

Put your large, heavy skillet over medium-low heat. Start the butter melting while you use your kitchen shears to snip the bacon into pieces right into the skillet. Throw in the shallots and the sage. Sauté it all together, stirring frequently, until the bacon bits are getting crisp.

While that's happening, use your kitchen shears to snip your livers into bite-size pieces. When the bacon bits are crisp, add the liver to the skillet and sauté, stirring frequently, until the liver bits are just done—they should still be pink in the middle. Use a slotted spoon to remove the livers and bacon from the skillet to a plate.

Pour the Marsala into the skillet and stir it around, scraping up all the tasty residue, and let it simmer until it has reduced to half the original volume. Pour over the livers.

2 large boneless, skinless chicken breasts (1½ pounds, or 680g)

4 ounces (115g) smoked Gouda cheese

4 ounces (115g) thinly sliced deli ham

½ cup (15g) fresh baby spinach

1 cup (110g) pecans

1 teaspoon Creole seasoning

½ teaspoon guar or xanthan

2 eggs

4 tablespoons (55g) butter

YIELD: 4 servings – Per serving: 671 calories; 48g fat (63.4% calories from fat); 55g protein; 7g carbohydrate; 2g dietary fiber; 5g net carbohydrate.

CHICKEN CORDON BLUES

Chicken cordon bleu has been around for a long time. I've jazzed it up with pecans and Creole seasoning, adding a Southern note that rates it the title "Chicken Cordon Blues."

Using a sharp knife, cut each chicken breast in half horizontally, leaving them attached at one side—you want to open them up like a book.

Layer half of the smoked Gouda, ham, and spinach on one side of each chicken breast. Close the "books" and use a couple of toothpicks to hold them shut.

Run the pecans, Creole seasoning, and guar or xanthan through your food processor until the pecans are finely chopped. Spread them on a plate.

On a rimmed plate, scramble up the eggs with a teaspoon of water until the whites and yolks are well blended.

Dip each stuffed breast in the egg, then in the pecans, coating them all over. Let them sit for a few minutes.

If you have a large nonstick skillet, use it. If not, coat your skillet with nonstick cooking spray. Either way, put it over medium-low heat and throw in the butter.

When the butter is completely melted, add the chicken breasts and cover with a tilted lid—you want to reflect the heat back at the chicken, but let the steam escape. Cooking time will depend on how thick your breasts are—mine took about 8 minutes per side. Flip once, carefully, so as not to disturb the pecan crust.

When the chicken is done through, split each stuffed breast into 2 portions and plate.

1 pound (455g) boneless, skinless chicken thighs

6 ounces (170g) mushrooms

1 shallot

3 tablespoons (42g) butter

1 clove of garlic, crushed

¼ cup (60ml) dry white wine

¼ cup (60ml) chicken broth

1 teaspoon chicken bouillon granules

½ cup (115g) sour cream

Guar or xanthan (optional)

Salt and pepper to taste

YIELD: 4 servings – Per serving: 285 calories; 21g fat (67.4% calories from fat); 18g protein; 4g carbohydrate; trace dietary fiber; 4g net carbohydrate.

CHICKEN STROGANOFF

I adore chicken, and, of course, in its native state it is zero carb. But it is also lower in fat than red meats. This scrumptious recipe gets us closer to our macros. If you prefer white meat, you can use boneless, skinless chicken breast, but it will lower the percentage of fat. Serve over tofu shirataki fettuccini or Zoodles (page 111).

Dice your chicken into 1-inch (2.5cm) cubes. Chop your mushrooms if you didn't buy them sliced. (Why didn't you buy them sliced?!) Mince your shallot.

Put your large, heavy skillet over medium heat and add the butter. When it's melted, swirl it to cover the whole bottom of the skillet and then throw in the chicken, mushrooms, shallot, and garlic. Sauté the whole thing, using a spatula to turn everything over now and then, until most of the pink is gone from the chicken and the mushrooms have softened and changed color.

Add the wine, chicken broth, and chicken bouillon concentrate. Stir it up and turn the heat down to medium-low. Now, cover it with a tilted lid—leave a crack for steam to escape—and let it simmer for 15 minutes.

After 15 minutes, uncover and let it simmer for another 5 to 10 minutes until the liquid has cooked down to ⅛ inch (3mm) in the bottom of the skillet.

CHICKEN STROGANOFF *(continued)*

Turn the heat to its lowest setting—once you add the sour cream, you do not want it to boil. Stir in the sour cream. If your sauce seems a trifle thin to you, add a sprinkle of guar or xanthan, but it shouldn't need much. Season with salt and pepper to taste.

POLLO RIVIERA MAYA

4 chicken thighs
1½ cups (355ml) water
1 tablespoon (15g) salt
½ cup (120ml) lemon juice
½ cup (120ml) lime juice
½ teaspoon liquid stevia, Valencia orange
1 tablespoon (3g) dried oregano
2 teaspoons chili powder
1½ teaspoons granulated garlic
1½ teaspoons salt or Vege-Sal
1 teaspoon ancho chile powder
1 teaspoon ground cumin
½ teaspoon pepper
½ teaspoon smoked paprika –hot or sweet, as you prefer
¼ teaspoon ground allspice
¼ teaspoon ground coriander
¼ teaspoon ground cinnamon
2 tablespoons (28ml) red wine vinegar
2 tablespoons (28ml) MCT oil

YIELD: 4 servings – Per serving: 293 calories; 22g fat (65.0% calories from fat); 17g protein; 9g carbohydrate; 2g dietary fiber; 7g net carbohydrate.

This chicken takes a few steps, but none of them is particularly hard, and it adds up to huge flavor. I broiled this, but in cookout weather, this is a natural for grilling.

Put your chicken in a 1-gallon (3.8L) resealable plastic bag. In a bowl, mix together the water, salt, lemon juice, lime juice, and liquid stevia, stirring until the salt dissolves, and then pour it into the bag. Seal the bag, pressing out the air as you go (while being careful not to press out the brining solution!). Refrigerate for 1 to 2 hours.

After an hour or two, drain off the brine—it can go down the sink. Put a wire rack over a plate or large bowl, set your chicken on it, and place it in the fridge to drain for an hour or so. If you like, at this point, you can put the chicken back in its plastic bag and refrigerate until dinnertime or even the next day.

In a smallish bowl, mix together the oregano, chili powder, garlic, salt, ancho chile powder, cumin, pepper, smoked paprika, allspice, coriander, and cinnamon. Now, add the red wine vinegar and MCT oil and stir to make a paste. This is your "wet rub."

Use a spoon or clean hands to spread the wet rub over every millimeter of your chicken, even working it up under the skin. Once again, let your chicken sit in the fridge for an hour or so—again, at this point you could keep your chicken in the refrigerator to hold for a day.

It's finally time to cook your chicken! Turn on your broiler. Coat your broiler rack with nonstick cooking spray and arrange the chicken, bone-side up, down the middle, staggering pieces a little as needed to get them all to fit. Broil about 6 inches (15cm) from the heat for 12 to 15 minutes, turning the broiler pan end to end halfway through to ensure even cooking. Flip the chicken to skin-side up and broil for another 12 to 15 minutes or until the juices run clear when it's pierced to the bone.

NOTE: Mastercook can't account for the brine you drain off, so the actual carb count will be a bit lower.

1 cup (235ml) MCT oil, melted butter, bacon grease, or a combination

1 cup (80g) Pork Rind Crumbs (page 63)

6 tablespoons (90g) horseradish mustard

1 tablespoon (15ml) hot sauce (I used Frank's but Tabasco or Louisiana will do fine.)

4 chicken thighs

YIELD: 4 servings – Per serving: 809 calories; 76g fat (84.5% calories from fat); 30g protein; 2g carbohydrate; 1g dietary fiber; 1g net carbohydrate.

CRUNCHY DEVILED CHICKEN

I've used chicken thighs again because I love them and they're inexpensive, but feel free to use breasts or drumsticks. I think coleslaw or creamy cucumber salad would be perfect with this!

Put your big, heavy skillet over medium-low heat—you want it hot when you're ready to cook. Add the oil and swirl to coat the pan.

Place the Pork Rind Crumbs in a paper bag.

Stir the horseradish mustard and hot sauce together in a small bowl. Spread it all over the chicken, coating all sides liberally. As each piece of chicken is coated with the mustard–hot sauce mixture, drop it into the bag of crumbs and shake to coat.

When all the chicken is coated, place bone-side down in the hot oil. Cover with a tilted lid—leave a crack for steam to escape. (I have a lid with a built-in strainer. It's perfect for this job; no need to tilt.)

Let the chicken cook for 15 minutes. Turn it skin-side down and let it cook for another 15 minutes.

Pierce to the bone at the thickest part. If the juices run clear, it's done. If they still run pink, give it another 5 minutes or so and test again. A meat thermometer stuck in the thickest part of the thigh should read 165°F (74°C).

Serve this immediately! The coating is nicely crunchy when fresh, but will grow soggy if allowed to sit.

NOTE: The measurements here are approximate because I can't know how large your pieces of chicken are. You want your hot oil to come up about ½ inch (1.3cm) on the chicken.

The calorie count and fat percentage are skewed by the fact that you'll leave much of the grease in the pan. The carb count is correct, and certainly this will be a low-carb/high-fat dish.

If you have leftovers, deal with the inevitably sogginess by simply refrying each side for about 5 minutes. It will crisp back up nicely.

3 pounds (1.4kg) boneless, skinless chicken breast or thighs, as you prefer

1 cup (235ml) olive oil

½ cup (120ml) lemon juice

¼ cup (7g) fresh rosemary

¼ cup (16g) minced parsley

5 cloves of garlic

2 teaspoons salt

1½ teaspoons red pepper flakes

YIELD: 6 servings – Per serving: 597 calories; 42g fat (63.7% calories from fat); 51g protein; 3g carbohydrate; trace dietary fiber; 3g net carbohydrate.

LEMON-HERB CHICKEN SKEWERS

This is actually lower in both carbohydrates and fat than the numbers would suggest because you discard most of the marinade. I recommend you serve this with or next to a big green salad with plenty of full-fat dressing. I think a Greek salad would be perfect.

Cut your chicken into cubes about ¾ to 1 inch (2 to 2.5cm). Put them into a 1-gallon (3.8L) resealable plastic bag.

Put everything else in your food processor and process until you're sure the rosemary and garlic are pretty close to pulverized. Pour this mixture into the bag with the chicken cubes and seal it, pressing out the air as you go. Turn the bag a few times to make sure all of your chicken is coated with the marinade. Throw the bag in your refrigerator, where it will sit happily for a minimum of half an hour, but all day would be awesome.

At least 30 minutes before you're going to cook your chicken, put a dozen bamboo skewers in water to soak.

LEMON-HERB CHICKEN SKEWERS *(continued)*

If you're grilling out, get your fire going; you'll want well-ashed coals. Make sure the grill is good and clean; you might want to grease it, too. You don't want your chicken to stick. You can also cook these on an electric grill or under the broiler.

Drain the marinade into a saucepan and bring to a boil on the stove before setting aside. Thread the chicken cubes onto the now well-saturated skewers.

Grill the chicken for about 10 minutes. Halfway through, baste with the reserved marinade, turn them, and baste the other side.

---

8 slices of bacon

2 very large boneless, skinless chicken breasts (2 pounds, or 910g)

½ cup (120ml) Porcini, Portobello, and Button Mushrooms in Cream (page 241)

½ cup (120ml) heavy cream

1 ounce (28g) cream cheese, cut into several chunks, at room temperature

½ cup (115g) sour cream

Guar or xanthan

Paprika

YIELD: 4 servings – Per serving: 582 calories; 36g fat (57.0% calories from fat); 57g protein; 4g carbohydrate; trace dietary fiber; 4g net carbohydrate.

MOM'S 1960s CHICKEN GOES UPSCALE

Back in the 1960s, my mother used to dazzle dinner guests with chicken breasts wrapped in bacon and baked in a sauce of cream of mushroom soup and sour cream. People have become somewhat harder to dazzle, but this should suffice.

Preheat the oven to 300°F (150°C, or gas mark 2). Coat an 8 × 8-inch (20 × 20cm) baking dish with nonstick cooking spray.

Lay your bacon on a microwave bacon rack or in a Pyrex pie plate. Microwave for 5 minutes—you're parcooking it. It should still be limp when it comes out.

Cut your chicken breasts in half so you have 4 portions. Wrap each portion in 2 bacon slices, covering as much of the surface as you can. Tuck the ends underneath to hold them in place as you lay them in the prepared pan.

In a saucepan over medium-low heat, combine the Porcini, Portobello, and Button Mushrooms in Cream with the heavy cream and cream cheese. As it warms, use a spoon or whisk not only to stir, but also to continue smooshing and breaking up the cream cheese to melt it in entirely.

When the cream cheese is all melted in, add the sour cream and stir it in. Spoon the sauce over the bacon-wrapped breasts and bake for 1 hour.

When the hour is up, use a spatula to remove the chicken to plates. You will notice the sauce looks a mess. Do not panic. When this happened to me, I realized instantly that it was because my homemade sauce lacked the thickening power of the tremendous quantity of cornstarch in canned cream of mushroom soup. Here's what you do: Grab a whisk and your trusty guar or xanthan shaker. Whisking madly, sprinkle in just enough guar or xanthan to bind the sauce again. Spoon over the chicken. Sprinkle a little paprika over it for expression, and you're done.

3 packages (8 ounces, or 225g each) of tofu shirataki, angel hair or spaghetti

4 boneless, skinless chicken breasts (1 pound, or 455g)

¼ cup (60ml) olive oil

Salt and pepper

3 tablespoons (42g) butter

2 cloves of garlic

3 tablespoons (26g) capers, drained and chopped

¾ cup (175ml) chicken broth

2 tablespoons (28ml) lemon juice

¼ cup (16g) chopped parsley, divided

2 ounces (55g) cream cheese

Guar or xanthan (optional)

YIELD: 4 servings – Per serving: 393 calories; 30g fat (69.8% calories from fat); 28g protein; 2g carbohydrate; trace dietary fiber; 2g net carbohydrate.

SPAGHETTI WITH CREAMY CHICKEN PICCATA SAUCE

The bright, sunny flavors of chicken piccata are terrific, and it's very low carb, but I wanted to add more fat. This was my solution. Our tester Rebecca proclaimed this "nice and easy, and very tasty."

Prepare the shirataki according to the instructions on page 23.

Cube your chicken into ½-inch (1.3cm) pieces. This is easiest if the chicken is half-frozen.

Put your large, heavy skillet over medium heat. When it's hot, add the olive oil and the chicken. Sauté, salting and peppering as you stir the chicken, until it's done through, about 5 minutes. Scoop the chicken out of the skillet with a slotted spoon and reserve on a plate or in a bowl.

Turn the heat down to medium-low. Add the butter to the oil remaining in the skillet. Crush in the garlic and sauté it for just a minute or two, but don't let it brown. Add the capers, chicken broth, lemon juice, and 2 tablespoons (8g) of the parsley. Stir it around, dissolving any nice browned stuff the chicken may have left in the skillet. Let the whole thing simmer for 5 minutes.

Cut your cream cheese into small chunks and add them to the sauce one at a time, whisking as you do it. Melt each bit of cream cheese in completely before adding another. If you think it needs it, thicken the sauce a little with your guar or xanthan shaker—you want it about the texture of heavy cream.

Stir the cooked chicken and the remaining 2 tablespoons (8g) of parsley into the sauce. Serve over the shirataki.

12 ounces (340g) boneless, skinless chicken breasts

¼ cup (60ml) caper brine

4 tablespoons (60g) mayonnaise, divided

Salt and pepper

2 tablespoons (17g) capers

10 pimento-stuffed green olives

1½ tablespoons (14g) pine nuts

1 tablespoon (4g) minced parsley

YIELD: 2 servings – Per serving: 461 calories; 33g fat (64.0% calories from fat); 40g protein; 2g carbohydrate; 1g dietary fiber; 1g net carbohydrate.

CAPER-BRINED CHICKEN BREASTS WITH CAPER SAUCE, OLIVES, AND PINE NUTS

Honestly, I am not a fan of the boneless, skinless chicken breast. But, as I have repeatedly said, I don't write recipes for me, I write them for you, and many people simply love boneless, skinless chicken breast. I had a few aims, here: to lend flavor and moisture to a cut that is too frequently both bland and dry, yet to get a nice golden sear on the chicken. And, of course, to add fat to a very low-fat protein. I have succeeded in all—I enjoyed this very much. I hope you do, too!

Twelve ounces (340g) is about one big boneless, skinless breast. You'll want to start by subdividing that breast into 2 portions. Put 'em in a resealable bag. Pour in the caper brine and then seal the bag, pressing out the air as you go. Throw the bag in the fridge for just an hour or so.

Pull out your bag. Drain the caper brine and pat the chicken dry with paper towels.

Tear off 2 pieces of aluminum foil, each about 12 inches (30cm) long. Lay a piece of chicken on one of the sheets of foil to one side of the center and coat it with 2 teaspoons of the mayonnaise—just spread it all over that chicken. Sprinkle it with a

CAPER-BRINED CHICKEN BREASTS *(continued)*

little salt and pepper while you're at it. Fold the foil over it and roll it up at the side, then at the ends—you want the foil smooth over the broad surfaces of the chicken, with the seams at the edges. Repeat with the second piece of foil, piece of breast, and 2 more teaspoons of mayo.

Put your large, heavy skillet over medium-high heat. Let it get good and hot before you add your packets of chicken. Press them down so they make good, solid contact with the pan—this will give you a nice, golden color when you open the packet. I gave my chicken 6 minutes per side, but it will depend some on how thick your breast is. Mine was a bit over 1 inch (2.5cm) at the thickest point.

While your chicken is cooking, place the remaining 2 tablespoons plus 2 teaspoons (40g) of mayonnaise in a small bowl. Measure the capers and then drain the brine from your measuring spoon into the mayonnaise. Chop the capers and stir them into the mayonnaise with the brine.

Chop your olives and set aside.

If you didn't buy toasted pine nuts, stir them in a dry skillet over medium heat for 3 to 4 minutes until they're touched with gold.

The chicken's done! Pull a packet out of the skillet and put it on a plate before opening it. Plate it, pouring all the liquid from the packet over it. Repeat with the second packet.

Top each serving with half of the caper sauce, chopped olives, parsley, and pine nuts.

APPLE-BRINED GRILLED CHICKEN

Brining enssures that this grilled chicken stays juicy, while also adding flavor. I served this with the Barbecue Sauce on page 242, and it was ideal. I used thighs, but breasts or drumsticks will work, too.

1 quart (946ml) hot tap water

2 tablespoons (28g) salt

¼ cup (60ml) cider vinegar

¼ teaspoon liquid stevia, English toffee

½ teaspoon pepper

6 chicken thighs (3 pounds, or 1.4kg)

2 tablespoons (28ml) olive oil

YIELD: 6 servings – Per serving: 420 calories; 32g fat (69.3% calories from fat); 31g protein; 1g carbohydrate; trace dietary fiber; 1g net carbohydrate.

In a bowl, combine the water, salt, cider vinegar, liquid stevia, and pepper, stirring until the salt dissolves.

Put the chicken in a 1-gallon (3.8L) resealable plastic bag and pour in the brine. Seal the bag, carefully pressing out the air as you go. Let the chicken brine for 1 to 2 hours, flipping the bag once or twice if you happen to be wandering through the kitchen.

Now, it's getting on toward time to cook! Pour off the brine and discard it. Pat the chicken dry with paper towels. Let it sit on a wire rack while you get your grill going—I used charcoal.

When the grill is good and hot—if you're using charcoal, you want a bed of well-ashed coals—rub the chicken lovingly all over with the olive oil and then place it on the grill, bone-side down. Close the lid, leaving the vent open just enough that the fire doesn't go out. Cook for 15 minutes.

Flip the chicken, close the lid again, and give it another 12 to 14 minutes. Then, turn it over again. Pierce the biggest piece to the bone—if the juices run clear, it's done. If they're still pink, close the lid and give it another 10 minutes or until a meat thermometer inserted into the thickest part of the thigh reads 165°F (74°C).

4 chicken thighs

Salt and pepper

1 tablespoon (15g) butter

1 tablespoon (15ml) olive oil

½ cup (120ml) dry white wine

1 tablespoon (15ml) raspberry vinegar

18 drops of liquid stevia, plain

1 clove of garlic, crushed

1 teaspoon chicken bouillon granules

½ teaspoon spicy mustard

¼ cup (40g) chopped onion

¼ cup (31g) raspberries

YIELD: 4 servings – Per serving: 285 calories; 21g fat (70.8% calories from fat); 17g protein; 3g carbohydrate; 1g dietary fiber; 2g net carbohydrate.

4 chicken thighs

Salt and pepper

2 tablespoons (28g) butter

3 tablespoons (36g) erythritol

1 chipotle chile canned in adobo, minced, plus 1 tablespoon of the (15ml) adobo sauce

2 teaspoons balsamic vinegar

1 teaspoon ground sage

1 teaspoon soy sauce

½ teaspoon salt or Vege-Sal

½ teaspoon hot paprika

2 drops of liquid stevia, plain

YIELD: 4 servings – Per serving: 252 calories; 20g fat (72.4% calories from fat); 17g protein; 1g carbohydrate; trace dietary fiber; 1g net carbohydrate.

CHICKEN WITH RASPBERRY SAUCE

Rebecca, who tested this, warns that she couldn't find raspberry vinegar at her grocery store. She says, "I never did find the raspberry vinegar. You can find raspberry vinaigrette in every store in town, but I went to five different stores and called another, and nobody had raspberry vinegar. I ended up using a nice mild rice vinegar. The sauce did taste sweet and fruity, but not obviously raspberry. Perhaps a little berry stevia instead of just plain? It was really fine, though. Everybody was saying, 'Yumm, yumm.'" That said, I bought my raspberry vinegar right here in Bloomington, Indiana, so surely some of you can find it!

Sprinkle your chicken all over with salt and pepper.

In your large, heavy skillet over medium-high heat, melt the butter with the olive oil. When the skillet it hot, brown the chicken all over. You want it a nice golden shade.

While the chicken is browning, stir together the wine, raspberry vinegar, liquid stevia, garlic, bouillon concentrate, and mustard, stirring until the bouillon concentrate is dissolved.

When the chicken is a pretty brown, remove it to a plate for a minute. Throw the onion in the skillet and sauté for just a minute or two. Pour in the wine mixture and stir it around with the onions. Put the chicken back in, skin-side up. Cover the skillet, turn the heat to low, and let it simmer for 20 minutes.

Add the raspberries, re-cover the skillet, and let it cook for another 5 minutes.

Plate the chicken and stir the sauce, mashing the berries a little as you do—you want them to flavor the sauce, but you should still be able to see some bits of berry on your plate. Season with salt and pepper to taste and spoon the sauce over the chicken.

MAPLE-CHIPOTLE GLAZED CHICKEN THIGHS

You have no doubt noticed my fondness for chicken thighs. It has only a little to do with them being reliably cheap, a little more with them being higher in fat than breasts, and everything to do with them being juicy and flavorful.

Preheat the oven to 350°F (180°C, or gas mark 4).

Season the chicken all over with salt and pepper and arrange in a roasting pan—mine fit nicely in an 8 × 8-inch (20 × 20cm) pan. Put it in the oven and set the timer for 30 minutes.

In the meanwhile, in a small saucepan over low heat, combine everything else. Bring to a low simmer and stir until you have a nice glaze, about 3 to 5 minutes.

When the timer beeps, baste the chicken with the glaze, reserving about one-third of it for later. Return it to the oven and set the timer for another 10 minutes. Baste again, give it another 5 minutes, and you're done. Serve the reserved glaze spooned over the chicken.

2 pounds (910g) boneless, skinless chicken breasts

7 ounces (200g) pork rinds (2 big bags)

2 tablespoons (24g) Creole seasoning

4 eggs

2 tablespoons (28ml) water

Lard or other fat

YIELD: 6 servings – Per serving: 231 calories; 7g fat (28.3% calories from fat); 38g protein; 2g carbohydrate; trace dietary fiber; 2g net carbohydrate.

NOTE: Since Mastercook can't figure for fat absorbed in frying, the actual fat percentage will be considerably higher.

CHICKEN NUGGETS

Or, if you prefer, make tenders. Just cut 'em into strips instead of squares. Crunchy on the outside, moist on the inside, these are sure to please the whole family. These can be served with the dipping sauce of your choice— half mayonnaise and half brown mustard, with a few drops of liquid stevia, is good, or any of the flavored mayonnaises in chapter 14.

Set your oven to its lowest temperature.

Cut your chicken breast into chunks—mine were about 1½ × 2 inches (4 × 5cm), but it's up to you—the smaller the bits, the more coating you'll use.

Run your pork rinds through your food processor until they're crumbs and then add the Creole seasoning and pulse to mix it in. Dump this into a pie plate.

In another pie plate, beat the eggs with the water until they're well blended.

Put your big heavy skillet over medium heat and add fat—you want it to be about ½ inch (1.3cm) deep, and should you have a thermometer, you're shooting for 375°F (190°C). (I bought one of the new induction burners largely because it lets me hold a specific temperature. That's very helpful.)

Okay, make an assembly line: chicken chunks, egg wash, and pork rind crumbs, with a plate on the end for the coated nuggets. Use a fork to dip each nugget in the egg wash, then the crumbs, coating each completely. When you've got enough to fill your skillet without crowding it—you want about 1 inch (2.5cm) between nuggets —go put 'em in and set your oven timer for 3 to 4 minutes. Go start breading the next batch.

When the timer beeps, flip the frying nuggets and reset the timer. Go bread more nuggets!

As each batch is done, transfer to a shallow baking pan in the oven to keep warm or just serve them in batches, which is what I did.

Add more lard to the skillet as it is needed to maintain that ½ inch (1.3cm) depth and keep frying nuggets until they're all done.

SWEET AND TANGY GRILLED CHICKEN

3 pounds (1.4kg) chicken pieces

¾ cup (175ml) olive oil

⅓ cup (80ml) soy sauce

¼ cup (60ml) red wine vinegar

¼ cup (60ml) lemon juice

3 tablespoons (33g) yellow mustard

2 cloves of garlic, crushed

¼ teaspoon liquid stevia, lemon drop

YIELD: 6 servings – Per serving: 592 calories; 51g fat (77.1% calories from fat); 30g protein; 4g carbohydrate; trace dietary fiber; 4g net carbohydrate.

This dish is easy and tasty, and the marinade cooks down into a citrusy sauce. I used thighs, but use what you like.

Put your chicken in a 1-gallon (3.8L) resealable bag. Mix together everything else in a bowl and pour it into the bag. Seal the bag, carefully pressing out the air as you go. Turn several times to coat the chicken and then throw it in the fridge. Let it marinate for a good 5 to 6 hours.

Get your grill going! I used charcoal, but whatever you have should do. Pour the marinade into a small, nonreactive saucepan—stainless steel or ceramic nonstick. Put that saucepan of marinade over medium heat, bring it to a boil and then turn down to a simmer. Let it reduce by about one-half.

When your fire is ready, throw your chicken on the grill bone-side down. Close the lid, leaving the vent open.

Grill your chicken, turning every 12 to 15 minutes, and basting with the marinade when you do. I can't tell you exactly how long it will take because I don't know how big your pieces of chicken are, but I can tell you that a meat thermometer inserted into the thickest part of the chicken should read 165°F (74°C).

Serve the grilled chicken with the remaining marinade as a sauce.

TURKEY BREAST WITH SAGE, CAPERS, AND CREAM

3 tablespoons (45ml) extra-virgin olive oil

2 cloves of garlic, crushed

2 pounds (910g) turkey breast cutlets

½ cup (120ml) dry vermouth

⅔ cup (160ml) heavy cream

2 tablespoons (17g) capers, drained

2 teaspoons dried sage, crumbled

1 teaspoon white balsamic vinegar

Salt and pepper

YIELD: 6 servings – Per serving: 328 calories; 18g fat (54.2% calories from fat); 33g protein; 2g carbohydrate; trace dietary fiber; 2g net carbohydrate.

Okay, this uses boneless, skinless white meat. Sadly, it's one of the few forms of turkey regularly available outside of the holiday season. But it's amazing what a little heavy cream can do, both for flavor and for the macros. Still, you'll want a rich side dish or well-dressed salad with this.

If your large, heavy skillet isn't nonstick, give it a coating of cooking spray. Put it over medium heat, add the olive oil, and throw in the garlic. Cook it for just a minute or two.

Add the turkey breast cutlets and sauté them 3 to 4 minutes per side until they're just getting a little golden at the edges and are done through. Plate them and keep them in a warm spot or tent with foil.

Add the vermouth, cream, capers, sage, and white balsamic vinegar to the skillet and stir it around, scraping up any nice browned bits. Let the sauce cook for 2 to 3 minutes until it thickens a little. Season with salt and pepper to taste and serve over the turkey cutlets.

1½ pounds (680g) ground turkey

¼ cup (40g) plus 2 tablespoons (26g) chopped onion, divided

2 tablespoons (26g) bacon grease, divided

4 teaspoons (20g) chili garlic sauce, divided

1 teaspoon salt

2¼ teaspoons (8g) garam masala, divided

2 teaspoons coconut oil

1 clove of garlic, crushed

½ cup (120ml) unsweetened coconut milk

3 tablespoons (48g) peanut butter

1 tablespoon (15ml) soy sauce or coconut aminos

2 tablespoons (18g) chopped roasted, salted peanuts

1 lime, cut into wedges

YIELD: 4 servings – Per serving: 500 calories; 37g fat (66.1% calories from fat); 35g protein; 8g carbohydrate; 2g dietary fiber; 6g net carbohydrate.

TURKEY BURGERS WITH SPICY COCONUT-PEANUT SAUCE

Many thanks to my friend Amanda, who fixed this for me! The way I originally wrote it, the sauce separated. She fixed it, and added coconut aminos for umami, but soy sauce works, too.

In a mixing bowl, combine the ground turkey, ¼ cup (40g) of the onion, 1 tablespoon (13g) of the bacon grease, 2 teaspoons of the chili garlic sauce, the salt, and 1 teaspoon of the garam masala. Use clean hands to smoosh it all together really well and then form into 4 patties. If you have the time, it's nice to chill the burgers at this point, but it won't be fatal if you don't.

When cooking time comes, put your large, heavy skillet over medium heat and melt the remaining 1 tablespoon (13g) of bacon grease. Cook the burgers, turning once, for about 5 minutes per side until a meat thermometer inserted into the thickest part of the burger reads 165°F (74°C).

While the burgers are cooking, put a saucepan over medium heat and melt the coconut oil. Sauté the remaining 2 tablespoons (20g) of onion and the garlic until the onion is translucent. Add the coconut milk and bring to a simmer. Let it cook for 2 to 3 minutes and then remove from the heat.

Whisk in the peanut butter, soy sauce, and remaining 1¼ teaspoons of chili garlic sauce, stirring until smooth.

Plate the burgers, pour on the sauce, and top with the chopped peanuts. Add lime wedges for diners to squeeze over the burgers.

---

1 pound (455g) ground turkey

2 tablespoons (20g) minced onion

½ teaspoon salt or Vege-Sal

¼ teaspoon pepper

2 tablespoons (26g) bacon grease

½ cup (116g) Boursin cheese

¼ cup (45g) chopped roasted red peppers

YIELD: 4 servings – Per serving: 352 calories; 29g fat (73.3% calories from fat); 22g protein; 2g carbohydrate; trace dietary fiber; 2g net carbohydrate.

TURKEY BURGERS WITH BOURSIN

It's amazing what a rich, creamy cheese can do to jazz up ground turkey—and up the fat content. Alouette cheese would work here, too.

Put your turkey in a mixing bowl and add the onion, salt, and pepper. Use clean hands to smoosh it all together really well. Form into 4 patties, ½ inch (1.3cm) thick.

Put your big, heavy skillet over medium heat. When it's hot, melt the bacon grease and start the burgers cooking, about 5 minutes per side, until a meat thermometer inserted into the thickest part of the burger reads 165°F (74°C).

When the burgers have another minute or so to go, top each with 2 tablespoons (29g) of the Boursin. It'll melt as they finish cooking.

Top each burger with 1 tablespoon (11g) of roasted red pepper to make it pretty!

1 pound (455g) frozen
broccoli, thawed

1 pound (455g) roasted turkey
or chicken

1 cup (225g) mayonnaise

1¼ cups (125g) grated
Parmesan cheese, divided

1 cup (235ml) heavy cream

2 tablespoons (28ml) dry
vermouth

YIELD: 6 servings – Per serving:
630 calories; 55g fat (76.4%
calories from fat); 32g protein;
6g carbohydrate; 2g dietary fiber;
4g net carbohydrate.

One whole duck, about
6 pounds (2.7kg)

1 medium onion

1 large celery rib

1 large carrot, peeled

Fresh rosemary and/or sage
(optional)

1 clove of garlic, cut in half
(optional)

YIELD: 6 servings – Per serving:
1334 calories; 129g fat (87.6%
calories from fat); 38g protein;
3g carbohydrate; 1g dietary fiber;
2g net carbohydrate.

NOTE: If you like, swap that carrot
in the body cavity for a quartered
orange.

SUPER-EASY TURKEY DIVAN

This is far and away both my and my husband's favorite leftover turkey
recipe—very handy for the weekend after Thanksgiving. Double it and
feed a crowd a fresh new meal with your leftovers.

Preheat your oven to 350°F (180°C, or gas mark 4). Coat an 8 × 8-inch
(20 × 20cm) baking dish with nonstick cooking spray.

Cover the bottom of the pan with the broccoli—I use broccoli "cuts," which are
bigger than chopped broccoli, but much smaller than spears. Cover with slices of
leftover turkey or chicken. I like to put the white meat on one side and the dark on
the other, so people can choose.

In a mixing bowl, combine the mayo, 1 cup (100g) of the Parmesan, cream, and
vermouth. Pour over the turkey and broccoli, sprinkle the remaining ¼ cup (25g) of
Parmesan on top, and bake until it's getting golden, about 30 minutes.

BASIC ROAST DUCK

If you're looking for fatty meats—I prefer them—you can't do better than
duck. Don't forget to keep the fat for roasting vegetables!

Preheat the oven to 450°F (230°C, or gas mark 8).

Prick your duck's skin all over, especially the areas with a thick layer of fat underneath. Don't pierce the meat, just the skin. Prick liberally—you're letting the excess
fat out so your duck won't be greasy. You can use the tip of a sharp knife for this or
the tines of a carving fork; I find my dinner forks are not sharp enough for this job.

Cut the onion, celery, and carrot into chunks. Stuff these into the body cavity. If
you have some fresh herbs on hand, you can put a few sprigs in there, too. You can
rub your duck with a cut clove of garlic, too, if you like.

Truss your duck—tuck the wing tips underneath and tie the legs together. Put it on
a rack in a roasting pan.

When the oven's up to 450°F (230°C, or gas mark 8), put the duck in, turning
the temperature down to 350°F (180°C, or gas mark 4). Now, roast your duck for
20 minutes per pound, about 2 hours for a 6-pounder (2.7kg). Every 30 minutes or
so, pull your duck out and repeat the pricking of the fatty areas.

When your duck is done, remove it to a platter and let it rest for 10 to 20 minutes.
In the meanwhile, take the rack out of the roasting pan and pour off the duck fat to
use for cooking. Pull the veggies out of the body cavity and discard.

If you like, you can make Giblet Gravy according to the recipe on page 258.

One whole duck, about
6 pounds (2.7kg)
Salt and pepper

YIELD: 6 servings – Per serving:
1321 calories; 129g fat (88.5%
calories from fat); 38g protein; 0g
carbohydrate; 0g dietary fiber; 0g
net carbohydrate.

UNSIGHTLY BUT DELICIOUS DUCK

I read about this method of cooking a duck and always wanted to try
it. It takes forever and involves turning the sucker over a few times, but,
as advertised, it does yield a very moist, flavorful, un-greasy duck with
crispy skin. It also yields a whole lot of duck fat, which is exceedingly
delicious for cooking with.

However, unlike the illustrations I saw when I read about this, my duck
did not come out picture perfect. Instead, it was so tender that the wings
had started coming off. Still, it tasted so good, and I got so much yummy
duck fat, I thought I'd tell you about it.

Preheat your oven to 300°F (150°C, or gas mark 2).

Using a very sharp, thin, straight-bladed knife, slash the breast skin of your duck
into roughly 1-inch (2.5cm) diamonds. Be careful—you want to cut the skin and fat,
but not the flesh of the duck. This is a little tricky. Turn the duck over and do the
same wherever the skin is thick, with a goodly layer of fat under it. Then, use the
point of your knife to pierce the skin all over.

Truss your duck—tuck the wing tips underneath and tie the legs together. Put it on
a rack in a roasting pan, placing it breast-side down. Put the duck in the oven and
set a timer for 1 hour.

When the timer goes off, pull your duck out of the oven. Pierce the skin all over
again and turn the duck breast-side up. Put the duck back in the oven and set the
timer for another hour.

Repeat this performance twice more: Remove the duck from the oven, pierce the
skin all over, turn it over, and put it back. You're roasting it for a total of 4 hours.

Remove the duck from the oven and turn the heat up to 400°F (200°C, or gas
mark 6).

While the oven is heating, lift the rack, duck and all, out of the pan, and set it
somewhere safe—I think the sink is ideal because drips are easy to clean up.
Carefully, pour the accumulated duck fat into an old glass jar. (If you want to know
how much you get, you could pour it into a Pyrex measuring cup instead. I got a bit
more than 1 cup [235ml].) Save the fat for cooking: it's delicious!

Put the rack back in your roaster, with the duck breast-side up. You can now
sprinkle with salt and pepper or otherwise season your duck—you didn't do it earlier
because you wanted that duck fat to be pristine. I sprinkled mine with Chicken
Seasoning Redux (page 255), which is great on any poultry. Put the duck back in
the oven. Let him crisp for 10 minutes. A meat thermometer inserted into the thigh
should read 165°F (74°C).

You can then glaze your duck if you like. The Maple-Chipotle Glaze for Maple-
Chipotle Glazed Chicken Thighs (page 142) would be good and so would the Plum
Sauce on page 253.

Remove to a platter, let it rest for 10 minutes, and then carve and serve with any
remaining glaze or sauce.

4 boneless, skin-on duck breasts (about 1½ pounds, or 680g)

½ teaspoon salt

¼ teaspoon pepper

¼ teaspoon dry mustard

1 pinch of ground rosemary

1 tablespoon (13g) bacon grease

2 tablespoons (28ml) olive oil

1 recipe Plum Sauce (page 253)

YIELD: 4 servings – Per serving: 643 calories; 62g fat (87.2% calories from fat); 15g protein; 6g carbohydrate; 1g dietary fiber; 5g net carbohydrate.

NOTE: This is calculated on 6-ounce (170g) duck breasts, but that's not a big deal—if your butcher has bigger ones, so much the better!

PAN-SEARED DUCK BREAST WITH PLUM SAUCE

If time is short and you want to impress, it's hard to beat duck breast. Pairing duck with a fruit sauce is traditional—it complements the richness of the meat. Here, we've kept the quantity small enough so as not to skew our macros.

Preheat the oven to 375°F (190°C, or gas mark 5).

Using a very sharp, thin-bladed knife, score the skin on each duck breast into 1½-inch (4cm) diamonds.

Mix together the salt, pepper, dry mustard, and rosemary in a small bowl. Rub the breasts with the seasoning mixture.

Put your big, heavy skillet over medium-high heat. Let it get good and hot and then add the bacon grease and olive oil. Swirl them together and let them heat for a minute. Then, add the duck, skin-side down. Let it cook without disturbing it until the skin is brown and crunchy, about 5 minutes.

Now, put the skillet in the oven and let it cook for another 12 minutes or so. Timing will depend a bit on how thick your breasts are and how rare you like your duck.

Plate the duck breasts skin-side up and let rest for 5 minutes. Slice and serve with the Plum Sauce.

Two 6-ounce (170g) boneless duck breasts, skin on

1 tablespoon (8g) grated ginger

2 tablespoons (28ml) soy sauce

2 tablespoons (28ml) dry sherry

2 teaspoons Virtue or Natural Mate sweetener, or 2 teaspoons erythritol plus 12 drops of liquid stevia, plain

YIELD: 2 servings – Per serving: 716 calories; 67g fat (86.9% calories from fat); 21g protein; 2g carbohydrate; trace dietary fiber; 2g net carbohydrate.

GINGER DUCK BREAST

Roast whole duck is great, but it's hardly a spontaneous meal. With a couple of duck breasts in the freezer, you're never more than a few minutes away from a romantic dinner for two. And duck is so gloriously rich!

Use a thin, sharp knife to slash the skin on the duck breasts about 1½ inches (4cm) apart, into diamonds, cutting through the skin, but not into the meat.

Divide the grated ginger between the 2 breasts and rub it all over them, both sides, and down into the cuts in the skin. Let it sit while you heat your skillet.

If you don't have a large nonstick skillet, coat your skillet with cooking spray. Put it over medium-high heat. Let it get good and hot before you add the duck, skin-side down. Let it cook for 4 to 5 minutes until the fat is rendered and the skin is getting crisp and golden.

In the meanwhile, mix together the soy sauce, sherry, and sweetener in a small dish. Have this standing by the stove.

Flip your duck breast and give it about 4 minutes on the other side.

Now, pour in the sauce and flip the breast once or twice to coat. Let it simmer in the sauce for about 2 minutes per side until the sauce cooks down and starts becoming syrupy.

Plate and pour the rest of the sauce from the skillet over the duck.

Two 6-ounce (170g) boneless duck breasts, skin on

Salt and pepper

1 tablespoon (14g) butter

1 tablespoon (15ml) olive oil

1 tablespoon (10g) minced onion

1 tablespoon (15g) chipotle chile canned in adobo, minced

¼ cup (80g) Polaner Sugar Free Raspberry Preserves

1 tablespoon (15ml) balsamic vinegar

YIELD: 2 servings – Per serving: 626 calories; 61g fat (85.0% calories from fat); 14g protein; 10g carbohydrate; 6g dietary fiber; 4g net carbohydrate.

SEARED DUCK BREAST WITH RASPBERRY CHIPOTLE SAUCE

This makes a wonderful quick romantic supper. Try it for Valentine's Day. If you can't find the Polaner Sugar Free Raspberry Preserves, there's an easy recipe on page 246.

Use a sharp, straight-bladed knife to score the skin on the duck breasts about 1 inch (2.5cm) apart, into squares or diamonds. Cut through the skin, but not into the meat. Season with salt and pepper and let them sit for 10 minutes.

Preheat the oven to 300°F (150°C, or gas mark 2). Have a small baking pan standing by.

Put your big, heavy skillet over medium-high heat. Add the butter and olive oil and swirl them together as the butter melts. Let the pan get thoroughly hot.

Lay the duck breasts skin-side down in the skillet. Let them cook until the skin is brown and crisp, about 5 to 10 minutes. Flip the breasts and let them continue cooking until the juices are no longer running red, but still a bit pink. Remove to the baking pan and put in the oven to stay warm.

Pour off about half the fat in the skillet, which will now include duck fat as well as butter and olive oil. Don't discard this! Save it for cooking; it's delicious.

Put the pan back over the heat and turn the heat down to medium. Throw in the onion and sauté for a minute or two until it's turning translucent. Stir in the chipotle preserves and balsamic vinegar, whisking until smooth. Let it cook for another minute until syrupy. Turn off the heat.

Slice the duck breasts on the bias and arrange on 2 plates. Top with the sauce, dividing it between them, and serve immediately.

CHAPTER 9

Fish and Seafood

Fish and seafood are an interesting issue on a ketogenic diet. On the one hand, they are, of course, low- or no-carb. (Some shellfish contain a few carbohydrates in the form of glycogen.) On the other hand, as the nutrition gurus of the past few decades have hastened to point out, they are quite low in fat—even salmon, often labeled a "fatty fish," derives only 28 percent of its calories from fat. White fishes like cod drop down as low as 8 percent.

This calls for some planning. There are a few options: You can cook your fish with plenty of fat, you can top it with a fatty sauce, or you can pair it with a high-fat side dish—or a combination of these strategies. A 6-ounce (170g) lobster tail has only 153 calories, 9 percent of them from fat, and 1 gram of carbohydrate. Add a couple of tablespoons (28g) of lemon butter, and you're up to 359 calories and 62 percent fat. Have 2 cups (94g) of romaine with a couple of tablespoons (28g) of vinaigrette on the side, and you're up to 515 calories and 70 percent fat—and still only 5 grams of total carbohydrate for the whole meal.

If you choose one of the lower fat recipes from this chapter, keep this in mind.

Creamed Tuna ingredients

2 tablespoons (28g) butter

¼ cup (40g) minced onion

4 ounces (115g) mushrooms, chopped

¾ cup (175ml) stock (I used beef, but chicken or seafood stock would work fine.)

10 ounces (280g) canned light tuna in olive oil

½ cup (120ml) heavy cream

¹⁄₃ cup (80ml) half-and-half

2 ounces (55g) cream cheese, cut into small cubes

¼ teaspoon pepper

Salt or Vege-Sal

Guar or xanthan (optional)

¼ cup (25g) grated Parmesan cheese

YIELD: 3 servings – Per serving: 538 calories; 42g fat (70.1% calories from fat); 34g protein; 6g carbohydrate; 1g dietary fiber; 5g net carbohydrate.

CREAMED TUNA

This is the ultimate comfort food! Serve over shirataki or Zoodles (page 111).

In a good-size saucepan, over medium heat, melt the butter and start sautéing the onion and mushrooms. As I generally do, I started with sliced mushrooms and broke them up with the edge of the spatula as they sautéed. It's easier than chopping them in advance.

When the vegetables have softened a bit, add the stock and bring to a simmer. Let it simmer for 15 minutes or so.

Drain the tuna a bit—no need to stamp on it to get all the oil out or anything—and add it to the broth. Stir in the cream, half-and-half, and cream cheese. Whisk until the cream cheese melts, and you have a creamy sauce.

Whisk in the pepper and salt to taste. You can thicken this a little more with guar or xanthan if you want, but it really doesn't need it.

You're probably expecting this: Along with serving this over shirataki or Zoodles, it would make a great omelet filling. Yes, I'm predictable. Don't forget the Parmesan cheese!

NOTE: Do take the time to look for light, not white, tuna, canned in olive oil, not soy oil. Olive oil is far more healthful than soy oil, which is nasty stuff, full of inflammatory omega-6 fats. And light tuna is far less likely to be contaminated with mercury than white tuna is.

Skillet Tuna Casserole ingredients

2 packages (8 ounces, or 225g each) of tofu shirataki, macaroni

¼ cup (40g) finely diced onion

2 tablespoons (28ml) olive oil

½ cup (120ml) chicken broth or seafood stock, store-bought or homemade (page 221 or 222)

2 teaspoons Dijon or spicy brown mustard

2 tablespoons (28ml) lemon juice

1 pound (455g) frozen broccoli "cuts," thawed

1 cup (230g) sour cream

½ cup (50g) grated Parmesan cheese

12 ounces (340g) canned tuna in olive oil

YIELD: 6 servings – Per serving: 293 calories; 20g fat (59.6% calories from fat); 23g protein; 7g carbohydrate; 2g dietary fiber; 5g net carbohydrate.

SKILLET TUNA CASSEROLE

Here's a quick and easy skillet supper for the whole family! I found this was creamiest when first made, less so when I warmed up the leftovers, so consider halving the recipe if you're only serving one or two people.

Prepare the shirataki according to the instructions on page 23.

In the meanwhile, put your large, heavy skillet over medium heat and sauté the onion in the olive oil for 3 to 4 minutes.

Add the chicken broth to the skillet and stir in the mustard and lemon juice. Bring to a simmer and then turn down the heat to just hold that simmer. Throw in the broccoli, cover the skillet tightly, and let the broccoli cook until crisp-tender, about 8 minutes.

It's time to assemble the final product! Turn the heat to its lowest setting. Stir in the sour cream, Parmesan, and tuna, breaking the tuna up a bit as you blend it in. Stir in the prepared shirataki, and it's ready to serve.

PASTA WITH OLIVE-RED PEPPER-TUNA SAUCE

2 packages (8 ounces, or 225g each) of tofu shirataki, macaroni

¼ cup (60ml) olive oil

2 cloves of garlic, crushed

1 cup (100g) chopped kalamata olives

½ cup (90g) diced roasted red peppers

2 tablespoons (14g) oil-packed sun-dried tomatoes, chopped, plus 1 tablespoon (15ml) of the oil

10 ounces (280g) canned tuna in olive oil

2 tablespoons (8g) minced parsley

Salt and pepper

Grated Parmesan, for serving (optional)

This is super quick, yet it would be hard to find a dish with more flavor. It's colorful, too!

Prepare the shirataki according to the instructions on page 23.

Put a large saucepan over medium-low heat. Add the olive oil and sauté the garlic for just a minute or two. Add the chopped olives, roasted red peppers, sun-dried tomatoes, and the oil from them. Stir until heated through.

Add the tuna and stir it in, breaking it up a bit, but still leaving good hunks of it you can sink your teeth into. When the tuna is warmed through, stir in the parsley. Season with salt and pepper to taste, let the whole thing cook for another 4 to 5 minutes, and then toss with the shirataki.

Feel free to add a sprinkle of Parmesan, but it's not essential.

YIELD: 4 servings – Per serving: 319 calories; 24g fat (67.5% calories from fat); 21g protein; 5g carbohydrate; 2g dietary fiber; 3g net carbohydrate.

TUNA KEDGEREE

1 package (8 ounces, or 225g) of Miracle Rice

1 tablespoon (14g) butter

1 teaspoon curry powder

2 tablespoons (8g) minced parsley

1 scallion, sliced, including the crisp part of the green shoot

¼ cup (60ml) heavy cream

5 ounces (140g) canned tuna in olive oil, drained

2 hard-boiled eggs

Kedgeree is a traditional English dish, usually made with rice and smoked fish. We've gone pretty far afield here, what with the tuna and the Miracle Rice, but it's still quick, tasty, and filling. This is considered a breakfast dish, by the way. It's a long way from Pop-Tarts, that's for sure.

First, prepare the Miracle Rice as explained on page 23.

In a saucepan over very low heat, melt the butter. Add the curry powder and let it cook in the butter for just a minute. Then, add the parsley and scallion and sauté with the curry powder for another 1 to 2 minutes.

Add the cream and the canned tuna. Stir everything up, flaking the tuna as you go. Slowly heat the whole thing through and let it cook, stirring frequently, for about 5 minutes.

Stir in the Miracle Rice.

Peel the eggs and chop them coarsely. Stir them in gently so as to preserve some hunks of yolk and serve.

YIELD: 2 servings – Per serving: 378 calories; 28g fat (66.5% calories from fat); 28g protein; 4g carbohydrate; 1g dietary fiber; 3g net carbohydrate.

12 ounces (340g) cod fillet

Salt and pepper

2 tablespoons (28g) butter

2 tablespoons (28ml) olive oil

½ of a lemon

4 tablespoons (16g) minced parsley

2 tablespoons (28ml) dry white wine

20 pitted kalamata olives

YIELD: 2 servings – Per serving: 475 calories; 36g fat (69.7% calories from fat); 31g protein; 5g carbohydrate; trace dietary fiber; 5g net carbohydrate.

FISH WITH WINE, LEMON, AND OLIVES

I asked That Nice Boy I Married what I should call this recipe, and he said, "Excellent Fish," but I thought I'd be a tad more descriptive. You'd be hard-pressed to take more than ten minutes to make this. I used cod, 'cause it was on sale, but any mild white fish should be good this way—sole, flounder, stuff like that. Your butter/olive oil mixture will brown a little. Don't sweat it; it gives the sauce a nice nutty tone. You can increase this recipe, but I just figure most of you don't have a skillet big enough for 4 servings of fish.

Divide your fish into portions, with an eye to thickness—you want to put the thicker pieces in to cook first. Season with salt and pepper on both sides.

Use a nonstick skillet or spray your skillet with nonstick cooking spray. Put it over medium-low heat and add the butter and olive oil. Swirl them together as the butter melts.

When the fat is hot, lay the thick pieces of fish in it—my thickest pieces were about ¾ inch (2cm). Set the timer for 2 minutes. While that's happening, quarter your lemon and flick out the seeds.

When the timer beeps, turn the pieces of fish already in the skillet and add the thinner pieces to the pan. Set the timer again for 2 minutes.

By the time the second 2 minutes is up, the thick pieces should be flaky clear through; remove from the pan and plate them. The thinner pieces may be done, too, but I like to flip them and give them just a little heat on the other side so they get just a little gold. Plate those, too. Place in a low oven to keep warm or tent with foil.

Throw the parsley and wine into the skillet and squeeze in the lemon juice. As that's cooking down a little, add the olives; you want to just warm them through.

When the sauce has reduced a little—just a minute or two—divide the olives between the plates and then pour the sauce over them. Serve immediately.

3 catfish fillets

1 recipe Dill Pickle Sauce (page 245)

Paprika, for garnish

YIELD: 3 servings – Per serving: 527 calories; 45g fat (74.8% calories from fat); 28g protein; 6g carbohydrate; 1g dietary fiber; 5g net carbohydrate.

DILL PICKLE BAKED CATFISH

This was the first thing I did with the Dill Pickle Sauce. My husband loved it! Fried catfish is nice, but there's a limit to how much you can fit in the skillet at once. With this, all you need to feed more people is a double batch of sauce and another pan.

Preheat the oven to 350°F (180°C, or gas mark 4). Coat a 9 × 13-inch (23 × 33cm) baking pan with nonstick cooking spray.

Lay the catfish fillets in the prepared pan. Spread the sauce over them, coating them evenly. Sprinkle lightly with paprika.

Bake for 25 minutes. Serve.

4 slices of bacon

⅔ cup (67g) pecans

4 teaspoons (13g) Creole seasoning

1 egg

1 teaspoon water

2 catfish fillets (1 pound, or 455g)

¼ cup (60g) mayonnaise

2 teaspoons horseradish mustard

1 teaspoon lemon juice

YIELD: 3 servings – Per serving: 521 calories; 42g fat (70.5% calories from fat); 32g protein; 8g carbohydrate; 3g dietary fiber; 5g net carbohydrate.

½ of a large head of cauliflower

1 cup (235ml) water

2 pounds (910g) small clams, in the shell but scrubbed

3 tablespoons (45ml) extra-virgin olive oil

2 cloves of garlic, crushed

1 shallot, minced

1 cup (235ml) clam juice, no-carb (read the labels!)

1 cup (235ml) dry white wine

1 bay leaf

10 ounces (280g) frozen artichoke hearts, thawed and drained

2 tablespoons (8g) minced parsley

2 tablespoons (6g) minced fresh dill

Salt and pepper

YIELD: 4 servings – Per serving: 358 calories; 13g fat (36.3% calories from fat); 33g protein; 17g carbohydrate; 6g dietary fiber; 11g net carbohydrate.

BACON-PECAN CRUSTED CATFISH

I happened to invent this on a day when That Nice Boy I Married had eaten soggy, steam-table catfish at a buffet at lunch. He took one bite of this, sighed deeply, and said, "This is sooooo much better." This may be his favorite catfish ever—and that's saying something. I realize that making this for three servings requires you to subdivide those pretty fillets, but the husband insists that a whole fillet is just too big a serving, and who wants to waste it?

First, cook your bacon crisp in your large, heavy skillet. Crumble it into your food processor and add the pecans and Creole seasoning. Pulse until you have "crumbs." Dump this mixture into a pie plate.

In another rimmed plate, beat the egg with the water until it's evenly mixed.

Dip the catfish in the egg wash, then in the crumbs, coating well.

Do you see that bacon grease left in your skillet? Put it over medium heat. When it's hot, throw in the catfish. Cook until crisp and done through, about 5 to 6 minutes per side.

In the meanwhile, stir the mayonnaise, horseradish mustard, and lemon juice together in a bowl. Serve as a sauce with the fish.

ARTICHOKE AND CLAM "RISOTTO"

If you'd like this to have a creamy texture more like real risotto, the solution is simple: stir in some heavy cream. I just was trying to come up with some recipes that didn't include dairy for a change!

Turn the cauliflower into cauli-rice as described on page 107. While it's cooking, prepare the clams.

Put the water in a large saucepan and bring to a boil. Add the clams to the boiling water. Cover the pot and let them cook for about 5 minutes or until opened. Remove with a slotted spoon, discarding any clams that have not opened.

Strain the water from the clams and reserve. Somewhere in here, your Cauli-Rice will be done steaming—uncover it or you'll have unappealing mush.

Put your saucepan back over medium-low heat. Add the olive oil, then add the garlic and shallot, and sauté them for 3 to 4 minutes. Now, add the strained clam broth, clam juice, wine, and bay leaf. Bring this to a simmer. Reduce it to one-fourth its original volume, about 10 to 15 minutes.

While that's happening, remove the clams from their shells, discarding the shells. Quarter your artichoke hearts, too.

When your liquid has reduced nicely, remove the bay leaf. Now, stir in the Cauli-Rice, clams, artichoke hearts, parsley, and dill. Heat everything through and season with salt and pepper to taste.

½ of a large head of cauliflower

2 cans (6.5 ounces, or 185g) clams, no sugar added

3 tablespoons (45ml) extra-virgin olive oil

2 cloves of garlic, acrushed

1 shallot, minced

1 cup (235ml) clam juice, no-carb (Read the labels!)

1 cup (235ml) dry white wine

1 bay leaf

10 ounces (280g) frozen artichoke hearts, thawed and drained

2 tablespoons (8g) minced parsley

2 tablespoons (6g) minced fresh dill

Salt and pepper

YIELD: 4 servings – Per serving: 190 calories; 12g fat (46.4% calories from fat); 19g protein; 13g carbohydrate; 6g dietary fiber; 7g net carbohydrate.

ARTICHOKE AND CLAM "RISOTTO" THE EASY WAY

Some of you are avoiding all processed foods and will use the previous recipe. Some of you are looking for quick and easy. My tester asked for a version of this using canned clams, and here it is.

Turn the cauliflower into Cauli-Rice as described on page 107.

Strain the water from the clams and reserve.

Put a large saucepan over medium-low heat. Add the olive oil, garlic, and shallot and sauté them for 3 to 4 minutes. Now, add the strained clam broth, clam juice, wine, and bay leaf. Bring this to a simmer. Reduce it to one-fourth its original volume, about 10 to 15 minutes. Somewhere in here, your Cauli-Rice will be done steaming —uncover it or you'll have unappealing mush.

Quarter your artichoke hearts, if you didn't buy 'em that way.

When your liquid has reduced nicely, remove the bay leaf. Now, stir in the Cauli-Rice, clams, artichoke hearts, parsley, and dill. Heat everything through and season with salt and pepper to taste.

2 eggs, beaten

3 tablespoons (42g) mayonnaise

2 teaspoons Dijon or spicy brown mustard

1½ teaspoons Worcestershire sauce

1 teaspoon Old Bay Seasoning

¼ teaspoon salt or Vege-Sal

¼ cup (30g) finely diced celery

2 tablespoons (8g) minced parsley

1 pound (455g) crabmeat—lump or claw, as you prefer, claw is stronger flavored

½ cup (40g) Pork Rind Crumbs (page 63)

3 tablespoons (45ml) MCT oil, for frying

1 recipe Tartar Sauce (page 237)

YIELD: 6 servings – Per serving: 246 calories; 17g fat (63.3% calories from fat); 22g protein; 1g carbohydrate; trace dietary fiber; 1g net carbohydrate.

CRAB CAKES

Our tester Rebecca rates this a 10 and says it wasn't at all hard for such a nice dish. She says she'd be glad to pay plenty for this in a restaurant. Once again, I must warn you not to use fake crab. It virtually always has added carbohydrates.

In a mixing bowl, combine the eggs, mayo, mustard, Worcestershire, Old Bay, and salt. Stir it all together. Add the celery, parsley, crabmeat—which, we hope, you have picked over for bits of shell—and Pork Rind Crumbs. Stir together gently, preserving as many good big hunks of crabmeat as you can. Form into 8 patties, about ⅓ cup (85g) of the mixture for each.

If your large, heavy skillet isn't nonstick, give it a good coating of cooking spray. Put it over medium heat. When it's hot, add the MCT oil, then the crab cakes. Cook until golden, about 3 to 5 minutes per side.

Serve with tartar sauce.

3 saffron threads

1 tablespoon (15ml) boiling water

2 egg yolks

1 clove of garlic, crushed

¼ teaspoon salt

⅛ teaspoon pepper

2 pounds (910g) trout fillets (6 fillets)

2 tablespoons (28g) butter

2 tablespoons (28ml) MCT oil

10 ounces (280g) bagged baby greens

⅔ cup (160ml) vinaigrette

4 lemon wedges

YIELD: 6 servings – Per serving: 460 calories; 34g fat (66.7% calories from fat); 34g protein; 4g carbohydrate; 2g dietary fiber; 2g net carbohydrate.

TROUT WITH SAFFRON

The saffron lends a warm flavor and golden glow to the trout, a nice contrast to the cool greens. Do look for saffron that is in actual threads; that's the way it grows. Our tester Rebecca says she used the Rebecca Says Make This Dressing on page 102, but if you have another vinaigrette you prefer it should do nicely. She also says, "I served it to a guest and she couldn't stop exclaiming how delicious it was."

Put the saffron threads in a small bowl and pour the boiling water over them. Let this sit until the water is lukewarm.

Add the egg yolks, garlic, salt, and pepper and whisk it all together well.

Put the trout fillets in a resealable plastic bag and pour in the yolk mixture. Seal the bag, pressing out the air as you go. Turn the bag over and over until the fillets are evenly coated with the yolk mixture. Throw the bag in the fridge. Let it sit there for an hour or so. You get bonus points for flipping it halfway through.

Grab your large, heavy-bottomed skillet. If it's not nonstick, coat it with cooking spray. Put it over medium-high heat and add the butter and MCT oil.

While the fat is heating, grab your bag of fish. Turn it over once or twice, evening out the coating.

When the butter-oil mixture is hot, fry your fish for 3 to 4 minutes per side, depending on the thickness of your fillets. Don't crowd the pan—it's better to do it in batches. If you need extra butter and oil, add 'em.

While the fish is frying, toss the bagged salad with the vinaigrette and distribute it among 4 plates. Serve the fish atop the salad, with a wedge of lemon on the side.

---

3 pounds (1.4kg) lobster tails

1 quart (946ml) seafood stock

½ cup (112g) butter

¼ cup (60ml) Cognac

¼ cup (60ml) dry white wine

2 tablespoons (28ml) lemon juice

1 cup (235ml) heavy cream

¼ cup (50g) whipped cream cheese

Guar or xanthan (optional)

Salt and pepper

YIELD: 4 servings – Per serving: 794 calories; 52g fat (62.2% calories from fat); 66g protein; 5g carbohydrate; trace dietary fiber; 5g net carbohydrate.

BEST THING HE'S EVER HAD AFTER ALFREDO (aka Lobster in Cream)

Hand to God, that's how That Nice Boy I Married described this: "It's the best thing I've ever had after Alfredo." That seems like an endorsement to me.

Put the lobster tails and seafood stock in a large saucepan. Bring to a simmer, turn the heat down so it stays just at a simmer, and cover the pot. How long you'll poach them depends on how big they are—and, as in my case, if you start with them still frozen solid. I can tell you that rock-hard-frozen 12-ounce (340g) (big!) lobster tails take about 25 minutes.

Remove the lobster tails to a plate and let them cool a bit. Check to be sure there are no bits of shell in your stock and then put it back over the heat and reduce it by about two-thirds.

When your lobster tails have cooled enough to handle, use kitchen shears to crack them open and remove the meat. Cut it into bite-size pieces.

NOTE: That Nice Boy I Married ate this as a stew, licking every drop of the sauce out of the bowl. If you prefer, you could serve this over shirataki noodles, Miracle Rice, Cauli-Rice (page 107), or Zoodles (page 111). Take your pick.

If you can't afford lobster, do not use fake seafood! It nearly always has added carbohydrates. Consider making it with monkfish fillets, sometimes called "poor man's lobster," instead.

4 lobster tails (6 ounces or 170g, each)

½ cup (112g) butter, at room temperature

4 teaspoons (20ml) lemon juice

1 teaspoon Creole seasoning

1 teaspoon Old Bay Seasoning

YIELD: 4 servings – Per serving: 360 calories; 25g fat (61.8% calories from fat); 32g protein; 2g carbohydrate; trace dietary fiber; 2g net carbohydrate.

LOBSTER IN CREAM *(continued)*

Put your large, heavy skillet over medium heat and melt the butter. Add the lobster meat and let it sauté, stirring often, soaking up the butter, for about 5 minutes or until it's turning golden in just a few spots.

Add the Cognac, wine, and lemon juice to the reduced seafood stock. Let it simmer together for a minute or two. Stir the heavy cream and whipped cream cheese into the stock and keep stirring until it's smooth.

Pour the sauce over the lobster and stir it in. Thicken a little with your guar or xanthan shaker if you think it's needed. Season with salt and pepper to taste.

BROILED LOBSTER TAIL WITH SEASONED BUTTER

These don't look like the restaurant lobster tails, with the meat popped up on top. Frankly, that's a two-fisted job. I went with easy. And anyway, this way the shell holds the butter against the meat as it cooks.

Start by brining your lobster tails. Use kitchen shears to snip all the way down both the top and bottom of the shells. Use brute force to bend them open a bit. Fill a bowl with enough water to submerge your tails and dissolve about 1 teaspoon salt per cup (235ml) of water in it. Throw in your lobster tails and let them soak for just 15 to 20 minutes. Then, remove from the brine and let them drain in the fridge until time to cook—at least 30 minutes.

It's cooking time! Turn on the broiler. Arrange a rack 6 inches (15cm) beneath the broiler.

Arrange the lobster tails in a shallow pan, top-side up.

Put the butter, lemon juice, Creole seasoning, and Old Bay in the food processor and process to blend thoroughly.

Stuff 1 tablespoon (14g) of the butter into each lobster tail—down the center and under the edges of the shells. Broil the tails for 15 to 17 minutes, turning the pan a few times to even out the heat.

Spoon the remaining seasoned butter over them to serve.

4 slices of bacon

2 tablespoons (28g) butter

¾ teaspoon sweet smoked paprika

1½ pounds (680g) bay scallops

3 tablespoons (45ml) clam juice, no-carb (Read the labels!)

¼ teaspoon salt

1 pinch of pepper

YIELD: 3 servings – Per serving: 319 calories; 14g fat (39.5% calories from fat); 41g protein; 6g carbohydrate; trace dietary fiber; 6g net carbohydrate.

BACON SCALLOPS

I was looking at a recipe for sea scallops wrapped in bacon, but around here, sea scallops were running $22.99 per pound (455g), while bay scallops were only $8.99 per pound (455g). But who can wrap a teeny bay scallop in bacon? So, I just cooked 'em together.

Put your large, heavy skillet over medium heat. Use your kitchen shears to snip in the bacon and cook the bacon bits until they're crisp. Scoop 'em out with a slotted spoon and reserve on a plate, leaving the bacon grease in the skillet.

Add the butter to the bacon grease. Stir the paprika into the fat and then add the scallops. Sauté until cooked through, about 3 to 4 minutes. Add the clam juice and let the whole thing simmer for another minute or two.

Add the salt and pepper, stir in the bacon bits, and you're done. Eat before the bacon goes soggy!

¼ cup (30g) chopped walnuts

½ cup (120ml) extra-virgin olive oil, divided

2 tablespoons (28ml) lemon juice

1 teaspoon lemon zest

½ teaspoon salt

½ teaspoon pepper

8 ounces (225g) bacon (or enough so you have ½ strip for each scallop)

12 ounces (340g) sea scallops (16 to 20)

2 tablespoons (28ml) MCT oil

1 pound (455g) fresh spinach

YIELD: 4 servings – Per serving: 776 calories; 67g fat (77.2% calories from fat); 37g protein; 8g carbohydrate; 4g dietary fiber; 4g net carbohydrate.

SCALLOPS ON SPINACH WITH WALNUT SAUCE

Originally donated by Tanya Rachfal for *500 Low-Carb Recipes*, this recipe was tweaked just a bit to fit our macros. If you can't afford sea scallops, try chopping the bacon and pan-frying it together with bay scallops like in the recipe above.

In a skillet over medium-low heat, sauté the walnuts in 2 teaspoons of the olive oil for 5 minutes until they smell toasty.

Put them in a bowl and add ¼ cup (60ml) of the olive oil, lemon juice and zest, salt, and pepper. Mix well. Alternatively, you could run this briefly through the blender or a small food processor, but don't turn the walnuts into paste!

Cut the bacon slices in half. Wrap a half slice around each scallop and hold it in place with a toothpick. Arrange on your broiler rack. Baste with the MCT oil. Preheat the broiler.

Put your large, heavy skillet over high heat and add the remaining 3 tablespoons and 1 teaspoon (50ml) of olive oil. Put in the spinach to sauté.

Run the scallops under the broiler. Give them about 5 minutes per side or until the bacon is done. Sauté your spinach until it's just wilted.

Plate the spinach, place scallops on the spinach, and then give the walnut sauce a final stir and spoon it over the top.

6 ounces (170g) salmon fillet

Salt and pepper

1 tablespoon (15g) butter

Lemon juice (optional)

Parsley (optional)

YIELD: 1 serving – Per serving: 299 calories; 17g fat (53.4% calories from fat); 34g protein; trace carbohydrate; 0g dietary fiber; trace net carbohydrate.

BUTTERED SALMON SEARED IN FOIL

I saw an article somewhere about combining the searing of fish and cooking en papillote by wrapping fish tightly in foil and then throwing it in a hot skillet. So I tried it. This is extremely simple and quick, yet yields a flavorful and moist fillet. I assume you can look at this and figure out that there's no reason not to do this with as many salmon fillets, tablespoons of butter, and sheets of foil as will fit in your skillet, right?

My husband doesn't like to eat the salmon skin, so for him, I put both squares of butter on the fleshy side of the salmon, so the butter soaks in there.

Tear off a piece of foil about 15 inches (38cm) long. Lay the salmon on it. Season with salt and pepper on one side, flip, and season the other side.

Cut your butter into 2 squares. Put one on each side of the salmon. Fold the foil up over the salmon and roll down the edges. Then, fold in the ends, making a sealed packed.

Put your large, heavy skillet over high heat. When it's good and hot—not before!—throw in your salmon packet. Set the timer for 5 minutes. When it beeps, use tongs to flip the packet and give it another 5 minutes.

That's it. Serve it right from the foil. If you want, you can add a squeeze of lemon juice or a sprinkling of parsley, but it's not really needed. Some recipes are born simple, and this is one of them.

1½ pounds (680g) salmon fillet, cut into 4 pieces

Salt

½ scant teaspoon pepper, plus more for sprinkling

¼ cup (55g) butter

¼ cup (60ml) lemon juice

16 drops of orange extract

12 drops of liquid stevia, lemon drop

YIELD: 4 servings – Per serving: 304 calories; 17g fat (50% calories from fat); 34g protein; 1g carbohydrate; trace dietary fiber; 1g net carbohydrate.

ORANGE-PEPPER SALMON

Lemon and lime are often used with fish, but the orange flavor goes wonderfully with the richness of salmon. This is, however, low enough in fat that you'll want a rich side dish or a salad with a good, oily dressing.

Season the salmon lightly on both sides with salt and pepper.

Put a skillet, preferably nonstick, over medium-high heat and melt the butter. Throw in the salmon, skin-side down. Give it about 4 minutes and then flip and give it another 4 minutes or so; how long will depend on the thickness of your fillets.

While the fish is cooking, stir together the lemon juice, orange extract, liquid stevia, and ½ scant teaspoon of pepper.

When the salmon is done to your liking, transfer to a serving plate. Now, pour the lemon juice mixture into the hot skillet and stir it around, scraping up all the nice browned stuff. Let this simmer for a minute or two and then pour over the fish and serve immediately.

12 ounces (340g) salmon fillet

Salt and pepper

2 tablespoons (28g) butter

1 shallot, minced

4 cups (120g) packed fresh baby spinach

⅔ cup (160ml) heavy cream

2 tablespoons (28ml) vodka

4 tablespoons (60ml) lime juice

YIELD: 2 servings – Per serving: 630 calories; 47g fat (69.9% calories from fat); 38g protein; 8g carbohydrate; 2g dietary fiber; 6g net carbohydrate.

1½ pounds (680g) salmon fillet, cut into 4 pieces

Salt

¼ cup (60ml) MCT oil

2 tablespoons (12g) packed mint leaves

2 tablespoons (5g) packed cilantro leaves

2 scallions, trimmed and cut into 1-inch (2.5cm) lengths

2 tablespoons (28ml) soy sauce

2 tablespoons (16g) sesame seeds

YIELD: 4 servings – Per serving: 352 calories; 22g fat (56.3% calories from fat); 35g protein; 3g carbohydrate; 1g dietary fiber; 2g net carbohydrate.

PAN-FRIED SALMON WITH SPINACH AND LIME-VODKA CREAM SAUCE

This dish is quick and easy, yet fancy-schmancy. And it almost makes it to 70 percent of calories from fat! You can increase this if you like, but you'll need a bigger skillet than my cast-iron one.

If your large, heavy skillet isn't nonstick, coat it with cooking spray. Put it over medium heat.

Season the meaty side of the salmon fillets with salt and pepper. When the pan is hot, throw in the butter. As soon as it's melted, add the salmon. Give it about 4 minutes—you want it turning golden on the meaty side. Remove the salmon to a plate.

Throw the shallot in the pan and sauté it for 2 to 3 minutes. Add the spinach and sauté just until it's going limp. Stir in the heavy cream, vodka, and lime juice. Use your spatula to make spaces for your salmon. Lay the fillets in the sauce skin-side down.

Cover the skillet with a tilted lid. Let the whole thing cook for 4 to 5 minutes until your salmon looks cooked through at the thickest spot.

Divide the spinach between 2 plates, making 2 beds, and place a fillet, skin-side down, on each.

Turn up the heat under the skillet and reduce the sauce for another minute and then divide between the servings, pouring it over the salmon.

EASY ASIAN-ISH SALMON

I stole the idea of mixing mint and cilantro from a Vietnamese cookbook, which suggested it as a substitute for an Asian herb rarely found in this country. I love it! Our tester, Rebecca, calls this "very special."

Sprinkle the salmon lightly with salt and set aside.

Put the MCT oil, mint leaves, cilantro leaves, scallions, and soy sauce in your blender or food processor and process until you have a paste. Set aside 2 table-spoons (28g) of this mixture.

Pat your salmon filets dry, place them on a rimmed baking dish or sheet, and spread the remaining herb paste all over both sides. Let them sit for 10 to 15 minutes.

While the salmon is marinating, put a small skillet over medium heat. Add the sesame seeds. Shake the pan to keep the seeds from sticking and burning. Cook until they're golden and smell toasty. Remove from the heat.

Now, you have a choice: You can grill your salmon on a barbecue or in an electric grill, you can pan-fry it in a nonstick skillet, or you can broil it about 4 inches (10cm) from the heat source. Regardless, go with medium-high heat and about 3 to 4 minutes per side or until cooked through. (Timing will depend on the thickness of your fillets.)

Plate the salmon and top with the reserved marinade and the toasted sesame seeds.

1 teaspoon hot smoked paprika

½ teaspoon ground cumin

½ teaspoon salt

1½ pounds (680g) salmon fillet, cut into 4 pieces

2 tablespoons (28g) butter

12 drops of liquid stevia, English toffee

YIELD: 4 servings – Per serving: 261 calories; 12g fat (43% calories from fat); 34g protein; trace carbohydrate; trace dietary fiber; 0 net carbohydrate.

SWEET AND SMOKY SALMON

Here's something quick, easy, and beguilingly different. This will need a fatty side dish, but with zero net carbohydrate, you can afford it!

In a small dish, mix together the paprika, cumin, and salt. Sprinkle this mixture evenly over both sides of the salmon fillets.

Put a big, heavy skillet, preferably nonstick, over medium-low heat. Melt the butter and stir in the liquid stevia. Add the salmon and sauté until done, about 4 to 5 minutes per side, depending on thickness. Transfer to plates and scrape every last drop of that seasoned butter over each serving!

---

2 packages (8 ounces, or 225g each) tofu shirataki, angel hair

⅓ cup (80ml) olive oil

2 tablespoons (8g) minced parsley

1 clove of garlic, crushed

½ teaspoon red pepper flakes

¼ cup (60ml) dry white wine

¼ teaspoon ground nutmeg

12 ounces (340g) small shrimp, peeled and deveined

Grated Parmesan, for serving

YIELD: 2 servings – Per serving: 524 calories; 39g fat (70.3% calories from fat); 35g protein; 3g carbohydrate; trace dietary fiber; 3g net carbohydrate.

ANGEL HAIR WITH SHRIMP

Do you want a super-quick supper that will impress a date? Try this. Throw in a green salad and a good bottle of wine, and you may even get a proposal. Our tester Julie says, "So incredibly easy and very good. Another winner for sure!"

Prepare the shirataki according to the instructions on page 23.

In the meanwhile, put your big, heavy skillet over medium-high heat. Add the olive oil, then the parsley, garlic, and red pepper flakes. Sauté for 2 to 3 minutes.

Add the wine, nutmeg, and shrimp. Turn the heat down to a low simmer, cover the skillet, and let the whole thing cook for 5 minutes.

Toss the angel hair with the shrimp mixture, and you're done!

You can pass grated Parmesan at the table, but it's not essential.

---

1 pound (455g) medium shrimp, peeled and deveined

½ cup (120ml) olive oil

Salt and pepper

1 cup (225g) flavored mayonnaise (pages 235-237), Remoulade (page 238), or Lemon-Anchovy Sauce (page 239)

YIELD: 4 servings – Per serving: 753 calories; 76g fat (87.4% calories from fat); 23g protein; 1g carbohydrate; 0g dietary fiber; 1g net carbohydrate.

OIL-POACHED SHRIMP

Fish and seafood are naturally low fat, so when I heard about poaching shrimp in oil I thought, "Perfect for a keto diet!" Adding a high-fat sauce is the crowning touch.

Preheat the oven to 225°F (110°C).

Put your shrimp in a casserole dish just big enough to hold them in a single layer. Pour in the olive oil and sprinkle them with salt and pepper. Bake for 20 to 25 minutes until cooked through.

Give everyone a plate of shrimp and a dish of sauce to dip them in.

6 tablespoons (112g) Sriracha Butter (page 243), divided

1 pound (454g) large shrimp, peeled and deveined

2 tablespoons (2g) minced cilantro (optional)

YIELD: 3 servings – Per serving: 282 calories; 19g fat (63.1% calories from fat); 25g protein; 1g carbohydrate; trace dietary fiber; 1g net carbohydrate.

SRIRACHA BUTTER SHRIMP

There was that leftover Sriracha Butter (page 243); there were those shrimp—what else could I do? They're still a little low on fat, so serve a salad with a good vinaigrette alongside. But there are almost no carbohydrates here and a metric boatload of flavor.

Put your large, heavy skillet over medium heat. Melt 4 tablespoons (60g) of the Sriracha Butter.

Lay your shrimp in the melted butter and let them cook until pink and firm clear through—mine took about 4 minutes per side, but it will depend on how big your shrimp are.

Melt in the remaining sriracha butter just before you plate the shrimp. Sprinkle each serving with cilantro, if desired.

2 tablespoons (28ml) olive oil

2 tablespoons (28ml) MCT oil

8 ounces (225g) large shrimp, peeled and deveined

2 tablespoons (28ml) dry sherry

1 teaspoon Tabasco sauce

Salt and pepper

YIELD: 2 servings – Per serving: 345 calories; 28g fat (76.8% calories from fat); 19g protein; trace carbohydrate; 0g dietary fiber; trace net carbohydrate.

SHRIMP IN SHERRY

This would make a great date-night supper—just add a salad or some asparagus and maybe a bottle of dry white wine, well chilled. Or, you can divide it four ways and call it an appetizer.

This is so quick and easy! Put your large, heavy skillet over medium heat and add the oils. When it's hot, throw in the shrimp. Sauté for 3 to 4 minutes per side.

Add the sherry and Tabasco and stir them in. Cook the shrimp, stirring often, for another 2 to 3 minutes. Season with salt and pepper to taste.

1 shallot

7 tablespoons (98g) butter, softened, divided

Zest and juice of ½ of a lime

3 dashes of hot sauce (I used Frank's.)

2¼ pounds (1kg) cod fillets

1 tablespoon (15ml) olive oil

Salt and pepper

YIELD: 6 servings – Per serving: 281 calories; 17g fat (54.6% calories from fat); 31g protein; 1g carbohydrate; trace dietary fiber; 1g net carbohydrate.

PAN-SEARED COD WITH LIME BUTTER

Quick and easy, this preparation lends needed fat to the very lean fish. Feel free to substitute another firm white fish.

Put the shallot in your food processor and pulse until it's finely chopped. Add 6 tablespoons (85g) of the butter, lime zest and juice, and hot sauce. Pulse to blend.

If you have a large nonstick skillet, use it. If not, coat your large skillet with nonstick cooking spray. Put it over medium-high heat and add the remaining 1 tablespoon (14g) of butter and the olive oil.

As the skillet heats, season your cod with salt and pepper. When the pan is hot, swirl the butter and oil together and then add the fish. Cook it quickly, about 5 to 7 minutes, turning once. You want it flaky and touched with gold.

Plate your fish and scoop a dollop of the lime butter onto each portion.

1½ pounds (680g) cod fillet, cut into 4 pieces

2 tablespoons (28ml) olive oil

Salt and pepper

2 small tomatoes, diced

4 tablespoons (25g) chopped olives

4 tablespoons (40g) diced red onion

8 teaspoons (23g) chopped capers

4 tablespoons (38g) crumbled feta cheese

8 teaspoons (10g) minced parsley

YIELD: 4 servings – Per serving: 254 calories; 11g fat (39% calories from fat); 32g protein; 5g carbohydrate; 1g dietary fiber; 4g net carbohydrate.

COD WITH TOMATOES, OLIVES, CAPERS, AND FETA

Add a salad tossed with vinaigrette and a bottle of dry wine, and you've got a great quick supper.

Preheat the oven to 350°F (180°C, or gas mark 4). Grease 4 gratin dishes, if you have them, or a Pyrex baking dish if you don't.

Brush each fillet with the olive oil and season with salt and pepper on both sides. Lay them in the prepared dishes or baking dish. Now layer the rest of the ingredients on top of the fish in the order given, dividing them evenly.

Bake for 10 to 15 minutes or until flaky all the way through. If you've used gratin dishes, just serve them as is. If you used a Pyrex baking dish, you'll want to put the fish on serving plates, scooping out any stray bits of yumminess that have escaped and dividing them among the servings.

NOTE: Gratin dishes are really quite useful and are great for baking individual servings of fish, eggs, or fruit. They're worth having on hand.

2 pounds (910g) fish fillets (Mahi-mahi or red snapper are good.)

2 tablespoons (28ml) lemon juice

1 teaspoon garlic powder

1 teaspoon salt

¼ teaspoon pepper

1 can (14½ ounces, or 410ml) of unsweetened coconut milk

2 teaspoons grated ginger, divided

1 medium green chile pepper

Salt and pepper

¼ cup (56g) coconut oil, divided

¼ of a medium red onion, finely diced

2 cloves of garlic, crushed

1 tablespoon (2g) minced cilantro (optional)

YIELD: 4 servings – Per serving: 520 calories; 37g fat (62.4% calories from fat); 43g protein; 7g carbohydrate; trace dietary fiber; 7g net carbohydrate.

FISH IN COCONUT-CHILE SAUCE

Exotic! Mahi-mahi is a tropical fish, and so is especially appropriate with coconut milk.

Place your fish in a shallow nonreactive dish or pan—glass or stainless steel. Rub it all over with the lemon juice. Mix together the garlic powder, salt, and pepper and sprinkle evenly over the fish. Stick the dish in the fridge and let your fish marinate for at least 30 minutes, and longer is better. Turn the fish over when you're in there grabbing a sparkling water.

Make your sauce next. Put your coconut milk in a saucepan over medium-low heat. As it's warming, add 1 teaspoon of the ginger.

Remove the stem, seeds, and pith from your chile pepper. Wash your hands thoroughly with soap and water before you do anything else!

Bring the coconut milk to a simmer and then turn it down to just below a simmer and let it cook for 15 minutes. Add salt and pepper to taste and turn the heat to its very lowest setting.

Go grab your fish out of the fridge. Coat your large, heavy skillet with nonstick cooking spray—unless it's nonstick, of course—and put it over medium heat. Melt 2 tablespoons (28g) of the coconut oil and throw in the onion, garlic, and chile. (Use your spatula to transfer the chile from your cutting board, or you'll have to go wash your hands again.) Sauté for 2 to 3 minutes. Scoop them out with your spatula and stir them into your sauce, leaving the coconut oil in the skillet.

Add the remaining 2 tablespoons (28g) of coconut oil to the skillet. Pat your fish fillets dry with paper toweling and throw them in. Let them fry for 3 to 4 minutes per side. Add the sauce and let the fish simmer in it for another 6 to 8 minutes.

Plate the fish with the sauce, sprinkling cilantro over each serving, if desired.

CHAPTER 10

Beef

Whenever someone looks horrified by the idea of giving up starches and sugars, I say, "Yeah, but I can have a rib-eye steak and a glass of dry red wine any time I want to and not feel guilty about it. It's health food."

For so long, we who gain easily have been told to eat boneless, skinless chicken breast (snore . . .), turkey burgers, and broiled fish. What a joy to know that beef is not just okay, but also one of our best possible choices. If you're concerned about the environmental impact of beef, I recommend you look up the work of Peter Ballerstedt, Ph.D., a forage agronomist, and particularly his lecture, "Red Meat Is Green," available on YouTube. The truth is that ruminants—cows, sheep, goats, and the like—are the best way to make use of much of the land, especially that which is unsuited for crops.

Dr. Ballerstedt also tells me that even grain-fed beef steers are grass-fed for most of their lives, only being penned and grain-fed for the last few weeks. Yes, grass-fed is more nutritious, with higher levels of omega-3 fatty acids. (Indeed, I have had some grass-fed beef that tasted a little fishy due to those high levels of omega-3s), but grain-fed is still nutritious stuff.

So, hey, have a steak. Have a burger. Tell 'em it's health food.

1½ pounds (680g) steak, 1 inch (2.5cm) thick

1 tablespoon (13g) bacon grease or (15ml) olive oil

YIELD: 4 servings – Per serving: 403 calories; 33g fat (73.7% calories from fat); 24g protein; 0g carbohydrate; 0g dietary fiber; 0g net carbohydrate.

PAN-BROILED STEAK

This is a method rather than a recipe, but it's become our favorite way of cooking a steak. It's quicker than broiling and makes for a crustier outside. Don't worry about the measurements much, by the way; I just included them because they were needed for a nutritional breakdown. You know steak's got no carbohydrates, so don't worry. We like rib eye, but T-bone, sirloin, or strip will do.

Put your big, heavy skillet (cast iron is best) over highest heat and let it get good and hot. In the meanwhile, you can season your steak if you like. We like the Montreal Steak Seasoning that's currently popular, or you could use one of the rubs on pages 254–259. Or, instead, you could top it when done with butter and blue cheese, or sautéed onions and mushrooms, or go for classic simplicity and just salt and pepper it.

When the skillet's hot, add the bacon grease and slosh it around and then throw in your steak. Set a timer for 5 to 6 minutes—your timing will depend on your taste and how hot your burner gets. On my stove, 5 minutes per side with a 1-inch (2.5cm) thick steak comes out medium-rare. When the timer goes off, flip the steak and set the timer again. Let the steak rest for 5 minutes before devouring.

1 tablespoon (15ml) olive oil

1½ pounds (680g) rib-eye steak

2 shallots, chopped

½ cup (120ml) dry red wine

½ cup (120ml) beef stock, or ½ cup (120ml) water and ½ teaspoon beef bouillon concentrate

1 tablespoon (15ml) balsamic vinegar

1 teaspoon brown or Dijon mustard

1 tablespoon (2g) dried thyme

3 tablespoons (42g) butter

Salt and pepper

YIELD: 4 servings – Per serving: 428 calories; 28g fat (58.9% calories from fat); 35g protein; 2g carbohydrate; trace dietary fiber; 2g net carbohydrate.

RIB-EYE STEAK WITH WINE SAUCE

This is a classic. This would be perfect for an at-home date night.

Cook your steak as described in Pan-Broiled Steak (above).

In the meanwhile, in a bowl, combine the shallots, wine, beef stock, balsamic vinegar, mustard, and thyme in a measuring cup with a pouring lip. Whisk 'em up.

When the timer goes off, flip the steak and set the timer again.

When your steak is done, put it on a platter. Pour the wine mixture into the skillet and stir it around, scraping up the nice browned bits, and let it boil hard. Continue boiling your sauce until it's reduced by at least half. Melt in the butter, season with salt and pepper, and serve with your steak.

½ cup (120ml) lime juice

3 large chipotle chiles canned in adobo, plus 4 teaspoons (20ml) adobo sauce

2 cloves of garlic

⅛ teaspoon liquid stevia, English toffee (about 36 drops)

1 teaspoon salt

½ teaspoon pepper

½ teaspoon meat tenderizer

1 cup (235ml) olive oil

2 pounds (910g) beef chuck, 1½ inches (4cm) thick

YIELD: 6 servings – Per serving: 642 calories; 60g fat (83.3% calories from fat); 24g protein; 2g carbohydrate; 1g dietary fiber; 1g net carbohydrate.

CHIPOTLE-LIME CHUCK

It was a great day when I learned to marinate sale chuck roasts to make them tender enough for grilling! You can serve a big, tasty, impressive hunk of meat without breaking the budget.

I like Spike Tenderizer Magic!, formerly called Indo, from Modern Products, the same company that produces Vege-Sal. It's one of the few tenderizers I know that contains no sugar. It does have a little soy and a tiny bit of wheat in the powdered soy sauce—not enough to worry me, but if you have celiac disease or are otherwise extremely gluten-sensitive, use another tenderizer. Or just skip the tenderizer and let the meat marinate a bit longer; the lime juice has a tenderizing effect.

Simply combine everything but the beef—I ran my ingredients through the blender to pulverize the chipotle, but you could mince it if you prefer. Remember to wash your hands well with soap and water after handling that chile!

Grab a fork and stab your chuck viciously all over. Put your now thoroughly dead chuck in a 1-gallon (3.8L) resealable bag.

Pour the marinade you've made into the bag and seal it, carefully pressing out the air as you go. Turn the bag a few times to completely coat the meat and then throw it in the refrigerator. Let it marinate for at least a few hours, and all day is great.

Dinnertime has rolled around. Pull the steak out of the fridge, drain the marinade into a saucepan, and lay the steak on a platter to come up to room temperature. If you're going to grill your chuck, get the grill going. Or you can broil it—turn on the broiler and coat your broiler rack with cooking spray.

While you're waiting on your steak, place the saucepan with the reserved marinade on the stove and bring to a boil to kill off any raw meat germs. Remove from the heat and set aside.

Grill or broil your steak to your taste. Do keep it fairly far from the heat—you don't want the exterior to burn to charcoal while you're waiting for the middle to warm up. Baste the steak from time to time with the reserved marinade.

When the steak is done, let it rest on a platter for 5 minutes before carving.

3 pounds (1.4kg) chuck roast,
1½ to 2 inches (4 to 5cm) thick

½ of an onion

2 cloves of garlic

¼ cup (60ml) lime juice

¼ cup (60ml) olive oil

1½ teaspoons chili powder

1½ teaspoons ground cumin

1 teaspoon salt or Vege-Sal

½ teaspoon meat tenderizer

1 recipe Crema Caliente
(page 253)

YIELD: 9 servings – Per serving:
462 calories; 38g fat (74.2%
calories from fat); 25g protein;
4g carbohydrate; 1g dietary fiber;
3g net carbohydrate.

BORDER TOWN CHUCK WITH CREMA CALIENTE

This is best done on the grill, but it can be broiled, too. It's just another example of how proper marinating turns simple chuck into a steak tastier than a T-bone or strip.

Using a carving fork, stab your chuck roast all over. Stick it in a great big resealable bag.

In your food processor, combine the onion, garlic, lime juice, olive oil, chili powder, cumin, salt, and meat tenderizer. Run the food processor until the onion and garlic are finely chopped. Pour this mixture into the bag with your chuck and carefully seal the bag, pressing out the air as you go. Turn the bag a few times to coat. Refrigerate for at least an hour or two, and all day is fine.

Dinnertime is here! Fire up the grill. I'd use charcoal, but run with what you've got. With a piece of meat this thick, you're going to want to keep it as far from the fire as you can, to avoid charring the outside before the center is even warm. If you're using your broiler, set the rack a good 6 to 8 inches (15 to 20cm) from the heat.

Pour the marinade into a saucepan and place on the stove. Bring to a boil to kill off any raw meat germs, then remove from the heat and set aside.

Put the steak on the grill and close the lid, leaving the vent open just enough so that the fire doesn't go out. Let it cook for a good 10 minutes before you check—mine wound up taking 13 to 15 minutes per side. While you've got the grill or the oven open (You do know you should always broil meat with the oven door cracked, right? That's why it has that setting that holds the door open 4 to 5 inches.), baste that big, beautiful hunk of meat with the reserved marinade.

When is it done? An instant-read thermometer is your friend here, but a regular meat thermometer will serve. The USDA insists that you get your beef roast up to 145°F (63°C) at the center, but that's too well-done for my liking. I'm a medium-rare girl. That's somewhere between 120° and 130°F (49° to 54°C), but your risks are your own to take. Cook it to your preference, basting now and then with the marinade.

Okay, your chuck is done. Remove it to a platter and let it rest for 10 minutes to let the juices settle. Carve your steak and pass the Crema Caliente at the table.

2 teaspoons meat tenderizer

2 to 2½ pounds (910 g to 1.1kg) boneless chuck steak, 1½ to 2 inches (4 to 5cm) thick

½ cup (120ml) MCT oil

¼ cup (60ml) soy sauce

½ cup (120ml) dry red wine

1 tablespoon (8g) grated ginger

2 teaspoons curry powder

2 tablespoons (30g) no-sugar-added ketchup

¼ teaspoon pepper

1 teaspoon Tabasco sauce

YIELD: 6 servings – Per serving: 503 calories; 42g fat (77.4% calories from fat); 25g protein; 3g carbohydrate; trace dietary fiber; 3g net carbohydrate.

UPTOWN CHUCK

I have repeated this recipe in a few books because I know of no better way to cook a chuck steak. If you're hoping to impress cookout guests without breaking the bank, this is your recipe. You can broil this instead of grilling it if the weather is wretched, but this recipe cries out for charcoal.

Sprinkle half the tenderizer over one side of the steak, pierce it all over with a fork, turn it, and repeat with the rest of the tenderizer. This one works best with a shallow, flat, nonreactive pan—place the steak in it, mix together all the remaining ingredients in a bowl, and pour it over the steak. Then, turn the steak over to coat both sides with the marinade. Stick the whole thing in the fridge and let it marinate, turning it over when you think of it, for at least several hours, and overnight is even better.

Drain the marinade into a saucepan, then place on the stove and bring to a boil to kill the germs. Remove from the heat and set aside.

Once you have your grill going and your coals are white or your gas grill is heated, grill your steak for about 12 minutes per side, or to your liking, basting a few times with the marinade. Slice across the grain and serve.

NOTE: Those numbers are actually high because you won't consume most of the marinade. Figure about 375 calories, about 70 percent of calories from fat, and no more than 1g net carbohydrate.

4 pounds (1.8kg) chuck roast, 1½ inches (4cm) thick

¼ cup (60ml) sriracha

¼ cup (60ml) tequila

2 tablespoons (28ml) lime juice

2 tablespoons (28ml) lemon juice

2 tablespoons (13g) sliced canned jalapeño pepper, with the liquid

½ of a small onion, chopped

18 drops of liquid stevia, Valencia orange

½ cup (8g) minced fresh cilantro

¼ cup (60ml) olive oil

YIELD: 10 servings – Per serving: 444 calories; 34g fat (71.7% calories from fat); 29g protein; 1g carbohydrate; trace dietary fiber; 1g net carbohydrate.

GLOBAL CHUCK

Between the Asian sriracha, the Mexican tequila, and the citrus flavors, this chuck steak is all over the map. But the place it really belongs is on your grill!

Stab your chuck ruthlessly all over with a fork and put it in a big resealable plastic bag—perhaps a 1-gallon (3.8L) bag, but for a chunk of chuck this big you may need a 2-gallon (7.6L) bag.

Mix everything else together in a bowl, and pour it in with the steak. Seal the bag, carefully pressing out the air as you go. Turn the bag a few times to coat and then throw it in the fridge. Let it marinate for at least a few hours, and all day is just fine. Should you think of it, flip the whole thing halfway through the day.

When dinnertime rolls around, pull the bag out of the fridge. Drain the marinade off into a small saucepan and lay the steak on a plate for 20 minutes or so to come up to room temperature before grilling. If you're using charcoal, this is a great time to light it up. If you're cooking inside, get the broiler going and coat the broiler rack with cooking spray.

While you wait on your steak to warm up, place the saucepan with the reserved marinade on the stove and bring to a boil. Remove from the heat and set aside.

Grill or broil your steak a little way from the heat—set your grill well above the coals, or your broiler rack a good 6 inches (15cm) away from the heat element. You

GLOBAL CHUCK *(continued)*

don't want the outside to scorch before the center is done. I'd give it about 8 to 10 minutes per side, but do it to your liking. When you flip your steak, baste both sides with the reserved marinade.

When your steak is done, let it rest for 5 minutes before carving. Serve the remaining marinade as a sauce with the meat.

SLOW-COOKER TRI-TIP

You'll need a big slow cooker for this, but it will feed a crowd. Go ahead and use a 4-pound (1.8kg) tri-tip if you can fit it in your pot. Personally, I think this would be a great match with the Blue Cheese Slaw on page 90.

Put your large, heavy skillet over high heat and sear the tri-tip roast all over in the bacon grease. Get it nice and brown.

In the meanwhile, mix together your salt, both paprikas, pepper, garlic, onion powder, celery salt, and oregano.

Okay, your roast is nicely browned. Let it cool until you can handle it.

Stab your roast all over with a carving fork. Now, rub the roast all over with the chipotle hot sauce, then the liquid smoke. Now, sprinkle the spice mixture evenly all over the roast. Rub it in well.

Drop the roast into your slow cooker, slap on the lid, set it for low, and let it cook for a good 7 to 8 hours. Then, remove to a platter and let it rest for 15 minutes before carving.

You can thicken up the juice that will collect in the pot using your guar or xanthan shaker or serve it as is and say you're serving your tri-tip au jus.

---

3 pounds (1.4kg) tri-tip roast beef

2 tablespoons (26g) bacon grease

1 tablespoon (12g) salt or Vege-Sal

1 tablespoon (7g) sweet smoked paprika

1 tablespoon (7g) hot smoked paprika

1½ tablespoons (9g) pepper

1½ tablespoons (15g) granulated garlic

1½ teaspoons onion powder

1 teaspoon celery salt

1 teaspoon dried oregano

1 tablespoon (15ml) chipotle hot sauce

1 tablespoon (15ml) liquid smoke

Guar or xanthan (optional)

YIELD: 8 servings – Per serving: 474 calories; 36g fat (69.9% calories from fat); 32g protein; 3g carbohydrate; 1g dietary fiber; 2g net carbohydrate.

1 pound (455g) ground beef

6 slices of bacon

1 small onion, thinly sliced

1 tablespoon (15ml) cider vinegar

12 drops of liquid stevia, English toffee

8 drops of maple flavoring

3 ounces (85g) sharp cheddar cheese, sliced

YIELD: 3 servings – Per serving: 671 calories; 56g fat (75.7% calories from fat); 36g protein; 4g carbohydrate; 1g dietary fiber; 3g net carbohydrate.

4 ounces (115g) ground beef

1 tablespoon (16g) no-sugar-added pizza sauce

3 tablespoons (22g) shredded mozzarella cheese

2 teaspoons shredded Parmesan cheese

6 anchovy fillets

YIELD: 1 serving – Per serving: 491 calories; 39g fat (72.3% calories from fat); 32g protein; 2g carbohydrate; trace dietary fiber; 2g net carbohydrate.

SON OF VERMONSTER

Here's yet another adapted recipe: I saw a recipe for The Vermonster, a bacon cheeseburger with maple-glazed apples and onions—and a bun, of course. I axed the apples and the bun, added cider vinegar to get an apple note, and wound up with this.

Form your ground beef into 3 patties about ¾ inch (2cm) thick. Stash them on a plate in the fridge.

Snip your bacon in half, making 12 short strips. In your large, heavy skillet, over medium heat, fry 'em crisp. Remove to a plate and reserve.

Throw your onion into the bacon grease and sauté for 3 to 4 minutes until limp and starting to brown. Stir in the cider vinegar, liquid stevia, and maple flavoring. Cook for another 3 minutes or so until the onions are brown and glazed. Stash them on another little plate.

Grab those burgers! Turn the heat up a bit, to medium-high, and start pan-broiling your burgers. I gave mine 4 to 5 minutes per side. When you've flipped them, top each with the cheddar and let it melt while the second side is cooking.

Plate the burgers. Top each with one-third of the bacon and one-third of the onions and stuff in your face. Bun? What bun?

ERIC'S PIZZA BURGER

Eric is also known as That Nice Boy I Married, and he is devoted to anchovies. If you're not a fan, how about sausage? Or pepperoni? But Eric pronounced this "[obscenity redacted] awesome, just like this!"

This recipe calls for a 4-ounce (115g) hamburger patty because that's the size of the preformed, all-beef hamburgers I buy in sacks at Costco for quick and easy meals. You can make your own, of course, but the timing on this assumes a ¼-inch (6mm) pre-formed patty cooked from frozen.

Put a small, heavy skillet over medium-high heat and bring it up to temperature before putting in the burger. Once the skillet is hot, throw in the patty and set the timer for 3 minutes.

Warm your pizza sauce—I just took the lid off the jar and stuck it in the microwave for a minute.

When the timer beeps, flip the burger. Spread the pizza sauce over it and sprinkle on first the mozzarella, then the Parmesan. Arrange the anchovies in spoke-fashion. Set the timer for 2 minutes (we're figuring that topping the burger took you a minute) and cover the skillet—this will help melt the cheese. Serve to applause.

1½ pounds (680g) ground chuck

1 small onion

4 tablespoons (55g) butter

8 ounces (225g) sliced mushrooms

½ cup (60g) crumbled blue cheese

YIELD: 4 servings – Per serving: 635 calories; 52g fat (74.1% calories from fat); 35g protein; 5g carbohydrate; 1g dietary fiber; 4g net carbohydrate.

BLUE MOON BURGER

This is a burger that I suspect you will want to eat more often than once in a blue moon! Who needs a bun?

First, make 4 burgers no more than ¾ inch (2cm) thick—you want the middle to be done before the outside is overcooked. Put them on a plate and chill them while you work on the toppings.

Slice the onion quite thin. Put your large, heavy skillet over medium-low heat and melt the butter. Add the onion and mushrooms and sauté until the onions are limp and turning golden and the mushrooms are soft, about 6 to 7 minutes. Stash this mixture on a plate.

Turn the heat up to medium-high and let the skillet get hot. Grab your burgers and throw them in. Fry 'em about 6 minutes per side—this gave me a burger that was done through, but still slightly pink and juicy in the center.

When you're down to about 3 minutes left to cook on the second side of the burgers, top each with 2 tablespoons (15g) of the crumbled blue cheese. Cover the skillet with a tilted lid—leave a crack for steam to escape.

When they're done, plate your burgers and top them with the mushroom-onion mixture.

---

1 pound (455g) ground beef

2 tablespoons (28ml) bourbon

½ cup (120ml) heavy cream

½ teaspoon beef bouillon concentrate

Salt and pepper

YIELD: 3 servings – Per serving: 630 calories; 55g fat (81.9% calories from fat); 26g protein; 1g carbohydrate; 0g dietary fiber; 1g net carbohydrate.

BURGERS IN WHISKEY SAUCE

Bourbon and heavy cream combine to bring the humble hamburger into the spotlight. You could make the same sauce for a pan-broiled steak. Yum!

Form your ground beef into 3 patties about ¾ inch (2cm) thick.

Put your large, heavy skillet over medium-high heat. When it's hot, throw in your burgers, pressing each down firmly with your spatula just once. Cook for about 5 minutes per side or to taste.

Remove the burgers to plates. Pour most of the fat off the skillet, leaving 1 teaspoon. Put the skillet back over the heat.

Pour the bourbon into the skillet and stir it around for a minute, scraping up all the browned bits.

Add the cream and the beef bouillon concentrate. Stir it all together, making sure the bouillon concentrate dissolves. Simmer the sauce for a minute or two until it thickens to the texture of heavy cream. Season with salt and pepper to taste and pour over the burgers.

2 pounds (910g) ground chuck

⅔ cup (107g) minced red onion

1 tablespoon (15ml) olive oil

½ teaspoon ground cumin

1 tablespoon (6g) ground coriander

1 pinch of salt

1 teaspoon ground pepper

2 tablespoons (10g) grated Parmesan cheese

1½ tablespoons (23g) spicy mustard

YIELD: 6 servings – Per serving: 441 calories; 35g fat (72%% calories from fat); 28g protein; 3g carbohydrate; trace dietary fiber; 3g net carbohydrate.

2 pounds (910g) ground beef

6 chipotle chiles canned in adobo sauce, minced

½ cup (8g) chopped cilantro

2 cloves of garlic, crushed

¼ cup (40g) minced onion

½ teaspoon salt

6 ounces (170g) Monterey Jack cheese, sliced

1 recipe Chipotle Mayonnaise (page 236)

YIELD: 6 servings – Per serving: 581 calories; 49g fat (76% calories from fat); 33g protein; 1g carbohydrate; 1g dietary fiber; 0g net carbohydrate.

JAMIE'S ELVIS BURGERS

I must give credit where credit is due: This recipe was inspired by one demonstrated by Jamie Oliver on his Food Network show *Oliver's Twist*—he made some burgers for an Elvis impersonator friend. They looked very tasty, but had too much onion, and a pile of bread crumbs in them, and, of course, Jamie served his on a bun. Plus, he's a serious purist who grinds his own beef, not to mention his own spices. This version is both easier and considerably lower in carbohydrates—but still unusually tasty.

Just plop everything into a large mixing bowl and mush it all together with clean hands until it's well combined. Form into 6 burgers about 1 inch (2.5cm) thick. Put 'em on a plate and chill for at least an hour before grilling.

Get your fire going—you'll want your gas grill on medium, or a little lower, or well-ashed charcoal. Grill for 7 to 10 minutes per side, keeping flare-ups down with a squirt bottle of water, until the juices run clear. Serve with no-sugar-added ketchup and some dill pickles, if you like.

CHIPOTLE CHEESEBURGERS

These are truly great; my husband and I couldn't stop talking about how well this recipe worked out! Of course, because I have to keep cooking new stuff, we won't get to eat these again until next year. But still, they're just amazing.

Plunk everything but the cheese and sauce into a big bowl and using clean hands, mush everything together until very well blended. Form into 6 burgers, about 1 inch (2.5cm) thick. Put your burgers on a plate and stick 'em in the fridge to chill for a good hour—it makes them easier to handle on the grill.

Get your fire going—you'll want your gas grill on medium, or a little lower, or well-ashed charcoal. Grill for 7 to 10 minutes per side, keeping flare-ups down with a squirt bottle of water, until the juices run clear. Serve with the Chipotle Mayonnaise.

1½ pounds (680g) ground chuck

1 teaspoon granulated garlic

1 teaspoon salt or Vege-Sal

½ teaspoon pepper

1 small clove of garlic, crushed

¼ cup (60g) mayonnaise

¼ cup (58g) Boursin cheese

YIELD: 4 servings – Per serving: 612 calories; 53g fat (78.5% calories from fat); 31g protein; 1g carbohydrate; trace dietary fiber; 1g net carbohydrate.

GARLIC CHEESEBURGERS

Garlicky and rich, these burgers are guaranteed to please the family—and keep vampires away! Just more proof that burgers don't need buns to be fabulous.

In a mixing bowl, combine the ground chuck, granulated garlic, salt, and pepper. Use clean hands to smoosh it all together really well. Form it into 4 burgers about ½ inch (1.3cm) thick.

In a small bowl, combine the crushed garlic and mayonnaise.

Put your large, heavy skillet over medium heat. Throw in your burgers. Give them about 5 minutes per side.

Plate the burgers, spread each with 1 tablespoon (15g) of the cheese, and then top with 1 tablespoon (15g) of the garlic mayo.

2 cloves of garlic

¼ cup (60ml) olive oil

⅛ loaf of Soul Bread or Whole-Grain Soul Bread (page 61 or 62)

1½ pounds (680g) ground chuck

1 teaspoon pepper

½ teaspoon salt or Vege-Sal

4 romaine lettuce leaves

¼ cup (60ml) Caesar Dressing (page 101)

YIELD: 4 servings – Per serving: 811 calories; 68g fat (75.8% calories from fat); 44g protein; 4g carbohydrate; 1g dietary fiber; 3g net carbohydrate.

CAESAR BURGERS ON GARLIC TOAST

How many times have I ordered the chicken Caesar salad, hold the croutons? (Confession: When they give me croutons anyway, I've been known to build things with them.) I figured we could have a Caesar burger instead. These are big burgers—if you need to watch your protein intake, you could cut it back to 1 pound (455g) of ground chuck. They'll still taste great.

First, make you garlic toast: Peel your garlic and slice each clove in half the longest, flattest way you can to expose as much of the interior as possible. Put a large, heavy skillet over lowest heat and add the olive oil and the garlic cloves, cut-sides down. Let 'em sit for 5 minutes—they shouldn't brown; you're just making garlicky olive oil.

In the meanwhile, cut 4 slices of Soul Bread or Whole-Grain Soul Bread a little thinner than standard white bread.

After 5 minutes, fish the garlic cloves out of the oil. Reserve them; they still have a use! Turn the heat up to medium-low and lay your bread in the oil. Flip it to soak both sides. Now, fry it until golden and crisp on both sides.

While the bread's frying, mince your leftover garlic cloves as finely as you possibly can. Put the ground chuck in a mixing bowl and add the minced garlic, pepper, and salt. Use clean hands to smoosh it all together quite thoroughly, and then form it into 4 patties about ½ inch (1.3cm) thick.

Surely, your bread is crisp by now! Pull it out of the skillet and hold it on a plate. Turn up the heat to medium-high. When it's hot, throw in your burgers. Give them about 5 minutes per side.

While the burgers are cooking, place a slice of garlic toast on each of 4 plates. Put a romaine leaf on each.

When the burgers are done, put one on each lettuce leaf. Top each with 1 tablespoon (15ml) of the Caesar Dressing and you're done.

1⅓ pounds (600g) ground chuck

4 tablespoons (42g) crumbled blue cheese

4 tablespoons (60ml) blue cheese salad dressing (page 90)

4 tablespoons (40g) minced red onion

⅓ cup (37g) bacon bits, or 6 strips of bacon, cooked and crumbled

YIELD: 4 servings – Per serving: 546 calories; 44g fat (72.7% calories from fat); 33g protein; 4g carbohydrate; 1g dietary fiber; 3g net carbohydrate.

BLUE BACON BURGERS

We're talking bacon cheeseburgers with the bacon and the cheese on the inside! You can serve these with extra blue cheese, blue cheese dressing, or bacon bits on top, if you like. Gild that lily!

Just assemble everything in a bowl and smoosh it all together really well. Form into 4 patties about ½ inch (1.3cm) thick.

Put your large, heavy skillet over medium heat and cook 'em for about 5 minutes per side or to your preference. You can grill them if you prefer, but they're a bit soft. You might want to refrigerate the patties for 20 to 30 minutes first.

---

1 medium onion, thinly sliced

4 teaspoons (19g) butter, divided

¼ cup (30g) chopped walnuts

8 slices of bacon

4 ounces (115g) brie

24 ounces (680g) ground chuck

YIELD: 4 servings – Per serving: 708 calories; 58g fat (74.0% calories from fat); 42g protein; 4g carbohydrate; 1g dietary fiber; 3g net carbohydrate.

BRIE AND WALNUT BISTRO BURGERS

Okay, so this dirties up a few skillets. It's unusual and luscious! Asked to rate this recipe, our tester Virginia said, "More than 10 … YUUUUMMMMMM!" However, our tester Shayne pointed out that for those who need to limit their protein intake, perhaps a 4-ounce (115g) patty would be better. Pay attention to your body.

Put a medium-size skillet over medium-low heat and start sautéing the onions in 1 tablespoon (14g) of the butter. You want to caramelize them—let them get limp, brown, and sweet without burning them. This will take 15 minutes or so.

In the meanwhile, put a small skillet over medium-low heat and melt the remaining 1 teaspoon of butter. Sauté the walnuts in it just until they smell toasty, about 5 to 7 minutes. Remove from the heat.

Cook your bacon however you wish to cook your bacon—I often microwave mine, but feel free to do it in your large, heavy skillet. Whatever, just get it nice and crisp.

Slice your brie into 4 portions, removing the white rind. Slice it thinly enough that you can cover each burger.

Okay! Your toppings are prepared. Form your ground chuck into 4 patties about ½ inch (1.3cm) thick. Put your large, heavy skillet over medium heat and let it get good and hot. Throw in your burgers and cook them to your liking—I give mine about 5 minutes per side.

When you've flipped your burgers and the second side has just another minute or two to cook, spread a tablespoon (8g) of the walnuts on each, and then cover with Brie. Let it melt as the burgers finish cooking.

Plate your burgers, top with the bacon and caramelized onions, and try not to drool.

1 pound (455g) ground chuck

1 tablespoon (15g) prepared horseradish

1 clove of garlic, crushed

½ teaspoon salt or Vege-Sal

¼ teaspoon pepper

1 tablespoon (15g) butter

1 small onion, sliced

3 ounces (85g) Gruyère cheese, sliced

YIELD: 3 servings   Per serving: 569 calories; 44g fat (71.3% calories from fat); 36g protein; 4g carbohydrate; 1g dietary fiber; 3g net carbohydrate.

HORSERADISH BURGERS WITH GRUYÈRE AND ONIONS

That Nice Boy I Married would happily eat simple burgers with ketchup and mayo every night of the week. I, on the other hand, find them a tad dull. These are definitely not dull, and TNBIM rated them "outstanding."

In a mixing bowl, combine the ground chuck, horseradish, garlic, salt, and pepper. Use clean hands to smoosh it all together really well and then form into 3 patties about ½ inch (1.3cm) thick.

I cooked mine in my large, heavy skillet over medium-high heat, about 6 minutes per side, but you can broil or grill them if you prefer.

While your burgers are cooking, melt the butter in a medium-size skillet over medium heat and sauté the onion. You want it soft and starting to turn brown.

When you flip your burgers, top each with Gruyère and let it melt.

Plate your burgers, divide the onions among them, and dig in.

2 tablespoons (28g) coconut oil

12 ounces (340g) ground chuck

8 ounces (225g) mushrooms, sliced

1 shallot, minced

2 cloves of garlic, crushed

2 tablespoons (16g) grated ginger

⅔ cup (160ml) unsweetened coconut milk

1 cup (235ml) beef broth

1 tablespoon (15ml) soy sauce

Guar or xanthan gum

YIELD: 4 servings – Per serving: 384 calories; 32g fat (73.4% calories from fat); 20g protein; 6g carbohydrate; 1g dietary fiber; 5g net carbohydrate.

BEEF AND MUSHROOMS IN GINGER COCONUT MILK

Old cookbooks inspire me—the recipes often are too bland for today's palates, but they are unafraid of fat. The inspiration for this was a Hawaiian recipe in a cookbook written in 1960, though I've livened it up a bit.

I originally made this with leftover chuck that had been tenderized and broiled rare, but I daren't assume you have leftover steak lying around. Should you have such a thing, cut it into slices about ⅛ inch (3mm) thick and 1 inch (2.5cm) long, and start by sautéing the mushrooms, shallot, and garlic before adding the beef. I served this over tofu shirataki spaghetti, but it's not essential.

Put your large, heavy skillet over medium heat and melt the coconut oil. Add the ground chuck and start to brown and crumble it.

As fat starts to cook out of the beef, add the mushrooms, shallot, garlic, and ginger. Sauté it all together until the beef is browned and the mushrooms softened. Stir in the coconut milk, beef broth, and soy sauce. Turn the heat down so the mixture is just simmering. Let it cook for 5 minutes.

Thicken just a little with your guar or xanthan shaker and serve.

1 pound (455g) ground chuck

2 tablespoons plus 1 teaspoon (16g) Taco Seasoning (page 256)

¼ cup (60ml) beef broth or water

YIELD: 4 servings – Per serving: 314 calories; 24g fat (69.8% calories from fat); 21g protein; 2g carbohydrate; 1g dietary fiber; 1g net carbohydrate.

BEEF TACO FILLING

Confession: I made several attempts at low-carb, gluten-free tortillas, but failed. That, however, does not make taco filling useless! Make a taco salad, a taco omelet, or serve it over shirataki noodles.

This is a great recipe for families where some are eating keto and others are still carbivores. Stir up the taco filling and put it out with chopped lettuce, shredded cheese, sour cream, salsa, and taco shells. The carb eaters can assemble tacos, while you make a taco salad. Heck, throw in a can of vegetarian refried beans and you can even please the family vegetarian.

Put your big, heavy skillet over medium heat and start browning and crumbling your ground chuck.

When most of the pink is gone from your meat, you have a decision to make: to drain or not to drain? I keep the fat in mine—it's ketogenic and we like it that way. But if the greasiness bothers you, drain some or all of the fat from the pan.

Sprinkle the Taco Seasoning evenly over the meat and stir it in. Now, stir in the broth, turn the heat down to low, and let the whole thing simmer for 15 to 20 minutes. That's it!

3½ pounds (1.6kg) beef spareribs

⅓ cup (80ml) olive oil, divided

½ cup (85g) Beef Rub (page 254), divided

½ cup (120ml) beef broth

2 teaspoons liquid smoke

YIELD: 6 servings – Per serving: 957 calories; 84g fat (79.3% calories from fat); 45g protein; 4g carbohydrate; trace dietary fiber; 4g net carbohydrate.

OVEN-ROASTED BEEF RIBS

I am the first to admit that oven-roasting does not beat slow-smoking, but I am also not a person who is willing to cook out in lousy weather. These are terrific as is, but feel free to slow-smoke them outdoors in good weather.

Preheat the oven to 300°F (150°C, or gas mark 2).

Lay your ribs in a big ol' roasting pan, preferably dark metal. If you need to, cut your slab in half to fit in the pan. Slather them all over with 2 tablespoons (28ml) of the olive oil.

Put 2 tablespoons (21g) of the rub aside in a small bowl. Sprinkle the remaining 6 tablespoons (64g) over your ribs, coating both sides, pressing the rub into the oily surface with your hands. Put them in the oven and set the timer for 30 minutes.

In the meanwhile, add the remaining 3⅓ tablespoons (50ml) of olive oil, beef broth, and liquid smoke to the reserved rub. This is your mopping sauce.

When the timer beeps, baste your ribs on both sides with the mopping sauce, flipping them in the process. Put them back in.

Continue to roast for another 60 to 90 minutes, depending on the meatiness of your ribs, basting and flipping every 20 minutes. Look for the meat pulling back from the ends of the bones and the slab threatening to disconnect when you flip it.

It's easiest to pull them out when they're done, let them cool for 10 minutes or so and then cut between the ribs with kitchen shears to serve. My slab was nearly triangular—huge ribs at one end, little ones at the other, so allocate the ribs accordingly.

2 pounds (910g) ground beef

1 medium onion, finely chopped

2 scallions, minced

1 cup (80g) Pork Rind Crumbs (page 63)

2 eggs, beaten

¾ cup (180g) no-sugar-added ketchup, divided

2 tablespoons (30g) prepared horseradish

1 teaspoon dry mustard

1½ teaspoons salt or Vege-Sal

½ teaspoon pepper

YIELD: 6 servings – Per serving: 584 calories; 46g fat (72.0% calories from fat); 36g protein; 5g carbohydrate; 1g dietary fiber; 4g net carbohydrate.

SUSAN'S MEATLOAF

I don't know Susan, but her meatloaf sounded good—except for the 2 cups (230g) of bread crumbs! This version keeps all the flavor while eliminating a pile of carbohydrates.

Preheat the oven to 350°F (180°C, or gas mark 4). Coat a 9 × 5-inch (23 × 13cm) loaf pan with cooking spray.

Follow your usual meatloaf procedure: Plunk the ground beef, onion, scallion, Pork Rind Crumbs, eggs, ¼ cup (60g) of the ketchup, horseradish, dry mustard, salt, and pepper in a big mixing bowl and use clean hands to smoosh it all together quite well.

Pack this into the prepared loaf pan, smoothing the top with a damp hand. Spread the remaining ½ cup (120g) of ketchup over the top. Bake for an hour or until it reaches an internal meat temperature of 160°F (71°C). Let cool in the pan for 10 to 15 minutes before slicing.

1 pound (455g) ground chuck

8 ounces (225g) ground pork

1½ cups (120g) Pork Rind Crumbs (page 63)

1 egg, beaten

1 small onion, finely chopped

½ of a green bell pepper, finely chopped

1 large celery rib, finely diced

1 small carrot, grated

1½ teaspoons salt or Vege-Sal

½ teaspoon ground thyme

½ teaspoon pepper

¼ teaspoon dry mustard

⅛ teaspoon ground sage

⅛ teaspoon ground nutmeg

1 cup (245g) tomato sauce, divided

YIELD: 6 servings – Per serving: 448 calories; 31g fat (62.9% calories from fat); 34g protein; 7g carbohydrate; 2g dietary fiber; 5g net carbohydrate.

THE BEST MEATLOAF?

I adapted this from a recipe that billed itself as The Best Meatloaf. I have, of course, altered it to slash the carb count. Is it still the best? We loved it, but you be the judge. It's still a little south of the 70 percent mark, so serve with a richly dressed salad or a green vegetable with plenty of fat.

Preheat the oven to 350°F (180°C, or gas mark 4). Coat a 9 × 5-inch (23 × 13cm) loaf pan with cooking spray.

Follow your usual meatloaf procedure: Assemble everything except for ½ cup (123g) of the tomato sauce in a big mixing bowl and use clean hands to smoosh it all together, mixing thoroughly. I did all that chopping in my food processor, but use your cutting board and grater if you prefer.

Pack the meat mixture into the prepared loaf pan, smoothing the top with a wet hand.

Bake for 30 minutes. Pour the reserved tomato sauce over the meatloaf and bake for another 30 minutes or until it reaches an internal temperature of 160°F (71°C). Let it cool in the pan for 10 minutes before slicing.

1 tablespoon (15g) salt

1 teaspoon ground red pepper

1 teaspoon ground black pepper

½ teaspoon ground cumin

½ teaspoon ground nutmeg

½ of a medium onion

1 large celery rib, including leaves if fresh

½ of a green bell pepper

¼ cup (55g) butter

2 cloves of garlic, crushed

2 bay leaves

1 tablespoon (15ml) hot sauce (Tabasco, Frank's, or Louisiana)

1 tablespoon (15ml) Worcestershire sauce

1½ pounds (680g) ground beef

8 ounces (225g) ground pork

½ cup (120g) no-sugar-added ketchup

2 eggs, beaten

½ cup (40g) Pork Rind Crumbs (page 63)

YIELD: 6 servings – Per serving: 597 calories; 50g fat (75.6% calories from fat); 32g protein; 4g carbohydrate; 1g dietary fiber; 3g net carbohydrate.

CAJUN MEATLOAF

Funny enough—I adapted this from a recipe by celebrity Cajun chef Paul Prudhomme—he'd deliberately tried to make it a lower-fat recipe. I fixed that! Julie, my good friend and yeoman recipe tester, says, "This will become a regular in my family meal rotation. Definite winner! Give this baby a 10."

Preheat the oven to 350°F (180°C, or gas mark 4). Coat your broiler rack with nonstick cooking spray.

In a small dish, mix the salt, red pepper, black pepper, cumin, and nutmeg.

Cut your onion, celery, and bell pepper into a few chunks and throw them in the food processor. Pulse until they're finely chopped.

Put your large, heavy skillet over medium heat and melt the butter. Add the chopped vegetables, crushed garlic, and bay leaves and sauté for 5 minutes or so. Stir in the hot sauce, Worcestershire, and the spice blend you made. Keep sautéing until the vegetables are soft. Remove the bay leaves.

Put the ground beef and pork in a big darned mixing bowl. Add the sautéed vegetables, ketchup, eggs, and Pork Rind Crumbs. Use clean hands to smoosh it all together really, really well.

Turn the meat mixture out onto your broiler rack and form it into a loaf about 12 × 6 inches (30 × 15cm). Bake for 60 minutes or until it reaches an internal temperature of 160°F (71°C).

ZUCCHINI MEATLOAF ITALIANO

2 medium zucchini

1 medium onion

3 tablespoons (45ml) olive oil

2 cloves of garlic

1½ pounds (680g) ground chuck

¾ cup (75g) grated Parmesan cheese

1 egg, beaten

2 tablespoons (8) chopped fresh parsley

1 teaspoon salt

½ teaspoon pepper

YIELD: 6 servings – Per serving: 434 calories; 34g fat (71.4% calories from fat); 26g protein; 4g carbohydrate; 1g dietary fiber; 3g net carbohydrate.

This was in my very first cookbook, *500 Low-Carb Recipes*, and it's still one of my favorite meatloaf recipes—the zucchini keeps it moist and flavorful. This started as a recipe for "Zucchini Mold," in a terribly fancy Italian cookbook, and it had only a tiny bit of meat. I thought, "How could adding more ground beef be a problem here?" When I'm right, I'm right.

Preheat the oven to 350°F (180°C, or gas mark 4).

Dice your zucchini and onion, or, if you prefer, put them in your food processor and pulse until chopped medium-fine.

Place your large, heavy skillet over medium heat and add the olive oil. Sauté the zucchini and onion. When they're half-done, crush in the garlic. Keep sautéing until the onion is translucent, about 7 to 8 minutes total. Remove from the heat and let the vegetables cool for a few minutes.

Meanwhile, in a large mixing bowl, combine the ground chuck, Parmesan, egg, parsley, salt, and pepper. When the vegetables are cool enough to handle safely, throw them in, too. Use clean hands to smoosh everything together quite well.

Pack the meat mixture into a big loaf pan, smoothing the top with a wet hand. Bake for 75 to 90 minutes, or until the juices run clear or it reaches an internal temperature of 160°F (71°C). Let cool for 10 minutes in the pan before serving.

JOE

1½ pounds (680g) ground chuck

1 medium onion, diced

3 cloves of garlic, crushed

8 ounces (225g) sliced mushrooms

1 box (10 ounces, or 285g) frozen chopped spinach, thawed and drained

6 eggs, beaten

Salt and pepper

⅓ cup (33g) grated Parmesan cheese

YIELD: 6 servings – Per serving: 415 calories; 30g fat (64.7% calories from fat); 30g protein; 6g carbohydrate; 2g dietary fiber; 4g net carbohydrate.

I know of few quick one-pan meals better or more resilient than this. Don't like mushrooms? Leave 'em out. You'd rather use fresh spinach? Go ahead. Someone's bestie decides to stay for supper? Throw in an extra egg. It's all good.

Put your big, heavy skillet over medium heat and throw in your ground chuck. Start it browning and crumbling. When some fat has cooked out of your meat, throw in the onion, garlic, and mushrooms. Keep cooking and crumbling the meat until all the pink is gone. Use your spatula to break the mushrooms up into smaller bits as they cook.

When the meat is done and the onions are soft and translucent, stir in the thawed, drained spinach and the eggs and keep stirring until the eggs are set.

Season with salt and pepper to taste. Serve topped with the Parmesan.

12 ounces (340g) ground chuck

12 ounces (340g) Italian sausage

½ cup (80g) finely diced onion

1 clove of garlic, crushed

1 teaspoon Italian seasoning

1 cup (252g) no-sugar-added pizza sauce

8 ounces (225g) shredded mozzarella cheese or Italian cheese blend

¼ cup (20g) shredded Parmesan cheese (optional)

YIELD: 6 servings – Per serving: 505 calories; 40g fat (73.0% calories from fat); 28g protein; 5g carbohydrate; 1g dietary fiber; 4g net carbohydrate.

MEATZA!

This was my first pizza-like recipe, all the way back in 2002. It's still one of the best! It's so much more flavorful—and filling—than a carby crust.

Preheat the oven to 350°F (180°C, or gas mark 4).

In a large mixing bowl, combine the ground chuck, Italian sausage, diced onion, garlic, and Italian seasoning. Using clean hands, combine it all very well.

Pat the meat out into an even layer in a 9 × 13-inch (23 × 33cm) baking pan. Bake for 20 minutes.

When the meat comes out it will have shrunk because of the grease cooking off. Pour off the grease. Spread the pizza sauce over the meat and then sprinkle the mozzarella over that. If you're using plain mozzarella, you may want to add the Parmesan on top of that, but it's not necessary.

Turn on your broiler. Slide the pan about 4 inches (10cm) below the heat element and broil for 5 minutes or until the cheese is melted and starting to brown.

1½ pounds (680g) ready-to-cook stew beef, cut into 1-inch (2.5cm) cubes or chunks

⅓ cup (80ml) olive oil

½ of a medium onion, chopped

1 clove of garlic, crushed

1½ cups (355ml) beef broth

1 teaspoon beef bouillon concentrate

½ teaspoon caraway seed

1½ tablespoons (10g) chili powder

⅔ cup (67g) green olives, sliced

Guar or xanthan gum

Salt and pepper to taste

½ cup (115g) sour cream

YIELD: 4 servings – Per serving: 579 calories; 39g fat (61.0% calories from fat); 49g protein; 7g carbohydrate; 2g dietary fiber; 5g net carbohydrate.

BEEF AND OLIVE STEW

I adapted this from a James Beard recipe that he labeled "chili." This isn't chili in my book, but it's a darned good stew.

As an alternative, you can do this is a slow cooker—sear the meat in your skillet, transfer to the slow cooker, and then go from there. I just happened to be puttering around the house while this was cooking.

In your large, heavy skillet over medium-high heat, sear the stew meat in the olive oil. Don't crowd it—remove the cubes to a plate as they're browned to make room for more.

When all the meat is browned and on the plate, add the onion and garlic to the skillet. Sauté for just a couple of minutes.

Put the meat back in, along with the broth, bouillon concentrate, caraway seed, and chili powder. Stir until the bouillon concentrate dissolves. Stir in the olives. Place a lid on the skillet, turn the heat to low, and let simmer until the meat is tender—mine took 2 hours.

Thicken the gravy a little with your guar or xanthan shaker and season with salt and pepper to taste.

Ladle into bowls and top each serving with a dollop of sour cream.

2 pounds (910g) beef chuck, cubed

4 cloves of garlic, crushed

1 medium carrot, sliced

3 tablespoons (42g) butter

1 medium onion, diced

2 tablespoons (32g) tomato paste

1 tablespoon (7g) paprika

2 teaspoons ground cumin

1 teaspoon ground cardamom

¼ teaspoon ground cinnamon

2 cups (475ml) beef stock

1 teaspoon beef bouillon concentrate

3 tablespoons (45ml) lemon juice

Guar or xanthan

¾ cup chopped cilantro (12g) or (45g) parsley, or both

⅔ cup (153g) sour cream

YIELD: 6 servings – Per serving: 458 calories; 35g fat (70.0% calories from fat); 26g protein; 8g carbohydrate; 1g dietary fiber; 7g net carbohydrate.

SLOW COOKER BEEF STEW EXOTICA

I adapted this from a recipe in *Milk Street Magazine*–the original was both much higher carb and not for the slow cooker. This version is wonderful! But I don't know what cuisine this combination of spices comes from, so I'm just going with "exotica."

The original recipe called for lamb, but said beef would also work. Beef was what I had on hand, so that's what I used. But should you happen to have a chunk of lamb shoulder cluttering up the place, use it.

Assemble your cubed beef, crushed garlic, and sliced carrot in your slow cooker.

In your large, heavy skillet, over medium heat, melt the butter. Add the onion and sauté until just starting to turn golden, about 6 to 7 minutes. Add the tomato paste and the spices. Stir them with the butter and onion for 1 minute. Scrape this mixture into the slow cooker.

Pour the beef stock and bouillon concentrate into the skillet and stir it around until the bouillon concentrate dissolves. Pour this into the slow cooker as well. Give the whole thing a stir, then put on the lid, set it to low, and let it cook for 8 hours.

When dinnertime comes, stir in the lemon juice and then thicken the gravy a little with your guar or xanthan shaker.

Stir in the cilantro and ladle into bowls. Drop a big dollop of sour cream in the middle of each serving.

6 beef or lamb marrowbones, in 2-inch (5cm) lengths

Salt and pepper

YIELD: Per ½ ounce – (about 1 tablespoon, or 14g) serving: 126 calories; 7g fat (50.0% calories from fat); 0g protein; 0g carbohydrate; 0g dietary fiber; 0g net carbohydrate.

MARROW BONES

Wild animals go for the marrow first. If you haven't tried it, it's time to get over being grossed out. Not only is marrow highly nutritious, but it also tastes like meat-flavored butter. How can you resist that?

Preheat your oven to 350°F (180°C, or gas mark 4).

Arrange your bones on end in a pan just about the right size to hold them. (Obviously, they'll stand up more easily if you stand them thick end down.)

Roast your bones for about 20 minutes. Then scoop out the marrow—Victorian households had narrow spoons for just this purpose, but you'll probably have to use a butter knife. Season with salt and pepper and eat. That's it.

2 pounds (910g) skirt steak or chuck

2 teaspoons meat tenderizer

½ cup (120ml) red wine vinegar

¼ cup (60ml) olive oil

2 tablespoons (30g) no-sugar-added ketchup

1 tablespoon (15ml) soy sauce

2 cloves of garlic

2 teaspoons sage

½ teaspoon salt

1 teaspoon dry mustard

1 teaspoon smoked paprika

2 whole jalapeños, seeded and minced

¼ cup (4g) minced cilantro (optional)

YIELD: 6 servings – Per serving: 358 calories; 25g fat (63.4% calories from fat); 30g protein; 3g carbohydrate; trace dietary fiber; 3g net carbohydrate.

CARNE ASADA

This is not quite as high in fat as the analysis would have you believe because you don't eat all the marinade. That's okay! Just serve it with sliced avocados and sour cream, or maybe some Crema Caliente (page 253)!

Put your skirt steak in a resealable bag.

Mix together everything else—with or without cilantro. I'd throw it in my little food processor and run until the jalapeños were minced fine, but if you want to cut them up by hand, go for it. Don't forget to wash your hands well with soap and water after handling the jalapeños!

Pour this mixture into the bag with the steak and carefully seal it, pressing out the air as you go. Throw it in the fridge and let it marinate for several hours, even all day.

Get your grill going! When it's good and hot and the charcoal, if any, is well ashed, remove the steak from the marinade and sear it fairly close to the heat for 3 to 5 minutes per side, depending on the thickness and your preferred doneness.

Let it rest for 10 minutes and then slice thinly across the grain.

4 hot dogs, lowest carb you can find, preferably all-beef

½ of a Vidalia onion

3 tablespoons (45ml) olive oil

3 sugar-free bread-and-butter pickle spears

1 medium tomato

4 dill pickle spears

4 pepperoncini peppers or sport peppers, if you can get them

Yellow mustard

Celery salt

YIELD: 4 servings – Per serving: 296 calories; 27g fat (81.0% calories from fat); 7g protein; 7g carbohydrate; 1g dietary fiber; 6g net carbohydrate.

ALMOST CHICAGO DOGS

You may well need a full set of cutlery—a fork, knife, and spoon—to eat this without a bun. Hey, what is cutlery for? Once again, you can provide buns—aka Edible Napkins—for those who eat such things.

Get your grill heating.

While that's happening, slice your onion and sauté it in the olive oil until it's limp and translucent.

Put your bread-and-butter pickles in the food processor and pulse until they're about the consistency of relish.

Dice your tomato or cut it into thin wedges, whichever you prefer.

Okay, it's cooking time! Grill your dogs. Plate 'em and top them with everything: onions, your homemade relish, tomatoes, a pickle spear, a pepperoncini or two, and yellow mustard and celery salt to taste.

NOTE: The classic pepper for a Chicago dog is the "sport pepper," but I can't find them around me, while pepperoncini are in every grocery store. Use sport peppers if you can find them, but pepperoncini are yummy.

2 hot dogs, lowest carb you can find

1 slice of American cheese

2 slices of bacon

YIELD: 2 servings – Per serving: 431 calories; 37g fat (78.4% calories from fat); 21g protein; 2g carbohydrate; 0g dietary fiber; 2g net carbohydrate.

FRANCHEEZIE

This is just so old-school! My sister and I used to make these for ourselves when we were kids. They're a mid-twentieth-century classic. I put these in the beef chapter because all-beef hot dogs are so common, but feel free to use pork hot dogs instead.

Slice each hot dog down the middle, leaving a "hinge" so you can open it up like a book.

Cut the American cheese into strips and fill each hot dog with strips of cheese. Close 'em up and then wrap each in a spiral fashion with a strip of bacon, covering as much of the hot dog as you can. Hold in place with toothpicks.

You can grill these, but be aware that flare-ups from bacon grease will be an issue. Or you can broil them or cook them in your skillet. Regardless, cook until the bacon is crisp.

Need I tell you to serve these with yellow hot dog mustard?

1 jarred roasted red pepper

1 bunch of watercress

½ of a small red onion

⅓ cup (75g) mayonnaise

1 teaspoon prepared horseradish

1 pound (455g) deli roast beef, sliced, but not too thin

6 ounces (170g) blue cheese, crumbled

YIELD: 12 rolls – Per serving: 164 calories; 11g fat (60.4% calories from fat); 14g protein; 3g carbohydrate; trace dietary fiber; 3g net carbohydrate.

BEEF-AND-BLEU ROLLUPS

This makes a nice, cool supper for a hot night. If you cut the rolls in pieces, they'd make good party food, too. Warning: My ingredients didn't come out exactly even, and yours may not either.

Drain your roasted red pepper and cut it into strips. Chop your watercress and red onion together; you can do this in your food processor if you like, but I didn't bother. If you do, put the onion in and pulse a few times before you add the watercress, or the watercress will be pulp before the onion is finely chopped.

Mix the mayo and the horseradish together in a small bowl.

Okay, it's assembly line time: Lay a slice of roast beef on your cutting board. Spread it edge to edge with the horseradish mayo, sprinkle it evenly with some blue cheese, and then sprinkle with onion and watercress. Place a strip of roasted red pepper across one narrow edge and roll the whole thing up around it. Repeat the process until you run out of ingredients! I got about a dozen rolls. I don't guarantee your ingredients will come out exactly even because I don't know how thickly sliced your roast beef is and, therefore, how many rolls you'll get.

CHAPTER 11

Pork and Lamb

've said it before, I'll say it again: pork does not deserve its bad reputation. Pork is highly nutritious and a particularly good source of both niacin (vitamin B_3) and potassium. In fact, a pork chop contains as much potassium as a banana, with none of those banana carbohydrates.

The one real problem with pork is that because animal fat was demonized thirty-odd years ago, the pork producers have been breeding pigs to be leaner and leaner. As a result, cuts like loin are so low in fat as to be dry and flavorless.

Happily for us, fatphobia has held down the prices of the most succulent, fatty cuts—picnic shoulder, Boston butt (actually also a shoulder cut), shoulder steaks, and spareribs. These are my favorites; I use them in endless ways. When pork shoulder goes on sale, I put two or three in the freezer, so I rarely pay more than $1.99 per pound (455g). It's important to know that pork doesn't freeze well for more than about four months; purchase accordingly.

Sadly, lamb is consistently pricey. On the other hand, it's virtually all grass-fed. It also freezes well. When leg of lamb drops to $5.99 per pound (455g) (or lower!), I buy one or two and have the nice meat guys slice them into steaks ½ inch (1.3cm) thick. At home, I bag them individually, and into the freezer they go. I like these better than chops; they're both cheaper and meatier. Plus, they come with a little bonus of marrow in the bone—yum! However, if you prefer chops, all of my lamb steak recipes will adapt readily to their use.

2 pounds (910g) pork jowls

1 quart (946ml) chicken broth

1 medium onion, chunked

1 dried hot red chile pepper

1½ teaspoons peppercorns

1 clove of garlic, quartered

Guar or xanthan

Creole seasoning

YIELD: 8 servings – Per serving: 773 calories; 80g fat (93.2% calories from fat); 10g protein; 3g carbohydrate; 1g dietary fiber; 2g net carbohydrate.

BRAISED HOG JOWL

I'm putting this first out of sheer audacity: it's so fatty and delicious! We first had hog jowl at a very chic bistro here in Bloomington, Indiana, one that specialized in charcuterie. It was love at first bite! We ordered it every time we went in. Sadly, they changed their menu. So, I learned to cook it myself! It's crunchy, fatty, porky goodness. This takes a few steps, best done over a couple of days, but none of them is particularly hard. Warning: You may need to search a bit for hog jowl unless you live in a pretty cosmopolitan area or a region where it's popular. I had to order it from my specialty butcher. It's so worth it!

Cut your jowl into pieces of about 2 ounces (55g) each. Put them in a Dutch oven or other kettle with a tight-fitting lid.

Add the chicken broth, onion, chile, peppercorns, and garlic. Bring to a simmer, cover, and then turn the heat down to keep it just barely simmering. Let it cook for 3 to 4 hours until a fork slides in easily.

Scoop out your jowls with a slotted spoon, placing them in a large pie plate. You can, and if you like, refrigerate the broth, skim off the fat to use for cooking, and use the now even-more-flavorful broth for soup, or you can discard it. Take your pick.

Put a plate that will fit down into the pie plate on top of the jowls. Weight it—I used the heavy iron lid from my Dutch oven. Put them in the fridge and let them sit overnight. At this point, if you like, you can stash your jowls in a snap-top container for a day or two.

When the time comes to cook, use a fine-holed shaker to dust the bits of jowl lightly with guar or xanthan—this is not essential, but it increases the crispness. Sprinkle them all over with Creole seasoning.

Put your large, heavy skillet over medium-high heat. When it's good and hot, add bits of hog jowl, making sure not to crowd the pan. Fry them good and crisp all over, about 5 minutes per side.

NOTE: The nutrition count on these is inaccurate because quite a lot of fat cooks off the jowl—think bacon. Both the calorie and the fat count are actually lower. Still, it's good and fatty. Save the wonderfully flavorful fat for cooking!

1 pound (455g) ground pork

1 shallot, minced

2 teaspoons minced fresh sage

1 teaspoon orange zest

1 tablespoon orange juice

½ teaspoon salt or Vege-Sal

¼ teaspoon pepper

3 tablespoons (45ml) dry white wine

1½ tablespoons (23ml) rice vinegar

1 teaspoon Worcestershire sauce

12 drops of liquid stevia, Valencia orange

2 drops of orange extract

YIELD: 3 servings – Per serving: 418 calories; 32g fat (71.9% calories from fat); 26g protein; 3g carbohydrate; trace dietary fiber; 3g net carbohydrate.

½ cup (120ml) MCT oil

⅓ cup (80ml) soy sauce

¼ cup (60ml) red wine vinegar

3 tablespoons (45ml) lemon juice

2 tablespoons (28ml) Worcestershire sauce

1 clove of garlic, crushed

1 tablespoon (4g) chopped parsley

1 tablespoon (9g) dry mustard

1½ teaspoons pepper

2 teaspoons sriracha

18 drops of liquid stevia, English toffee

1½ pounds (680g) pork tenderloin

YIELD: 6 servings – Per serving: 318 calories; 22g fat (63.1% calories from fat); 25g protein; 4g carbohydrate; trace dietary fiber; 4g net carbohydrate.

ORANGE-SAGE PORK BURGERS

I grew up eating pork chops and applesauce, but the truth is that pork pairs well with almost any fruit. What to do with the rest of your orange? You could plan a second orange-scented recipe for tomorrow, or just feed it to any kid in the house.

In a big mixing bowl, combine the pork, shallot, sage, orange zest, orange juice, salt, and pepper. Use clean hands to smoosh it all together very, very well—it took me some kneading to get the orange zest to distribute evenly. Form into 3 patties roughly 1 inch (2.5cm) thick.

Put your large, heavy skillet over medium heat. Let it get up to temperature before adding the pork burgers. Let them cook for 6 to 7 minutes per side—you want them done through (160°F [71°C]), but don't want to dry them out.

While your burgers are cooking, stir together the wine, rice vinegar, Worcestershire, liquid stevia, and orange extract in a bowl.

When the burgers are done, plate them.

Pour the wine-vinegar mixture into the skillet and stir it around, scraping up all the nice browned stuff. Let this mixture cook down by about half before you pour it over the burgers.

GRILLED PORK TENDERLOIN

Our tester Rebecca rates this a 10 and says not to forget to boil the marinade and serve it as a sauce—it really helps make the dish. She also liked that most of the work could be done in the morning, letting her make side dishes while her husband grilled the pork.

Combine everything but the pork in a medium-size bowl. Put the tenderloins in a 1-gallon (3.8L) resealable plastic bag. Pour in the marinade and seal the bag, carefully pressing out the air as you go. Turn the bag a few times to coat and then throw it in the fridge. Let the pork marinate for at least 4 to 5 hours, and all day is fine.

When cooking time comes, fire up the grill. Pour the marinade off into a small saucepan, place on the stove, and bring to a boil. Remove from the heat and set aside.

Grill your tenderloins over well-ashed coals or a gas grill set on medium for about 15 to 16 minutes or until a meat thermometer stuck in the thickest part registers 160°F (71°C). Baste frequently with the reserved marinade.

Serve the remaining marinade as a sauce with the pork.

2 tablespoons (20g) espresso ground coffee beans

1 tablespoon (12g) erythritol or 1½ teaspoons Virtue sweetener

2 teaspoons salt

1 teaspoon chili powder

1 teaspoon hot smoked paprika

1½ pounds (680g) pork chops (4 chops)

1 tablespoon (13g) bacon grease

YIELD: 4 servings – Per serving: 296 calories; 20g fat (62.6% calories from fat); 26g protein; 1g carbohydrate; trace dietary fiber; 1g net carbohydrate.

COFFEE-RUBBED PORK CHOPS

Coffee-rubbed meat is kinda trendy, and with good reason—it adds a lovely dark, rich flavor. This is quick and easy, too. If you've got coleslaw in the fridge, or even a bag of coleslaw mix, dinner can be ready in 15 minutes.

Mix together the coffee, erythritol, salt, chili powder, and paprika in a small bowl. Rub both sides of your pork chops liberally with this mixture.

Put your biggest heavy skillet or possibly two, depending on the size of your skillet and the size of your chops, over medium heat. Let 'em get good and hot.

Throw in the bacon grease and slosh it about as it melts to coat the bottom of the skillet. Now, throw in your chops.

Cooking time will depend on the thickness of your chops. Mine were about ½ inch (1.3cm) and took about 7 minutes per side. You want them done through (160°F [71°C]), but not dried out. If your chops are thicker than mine, turn down the heat a bit, and cover the skillet with a tilted lid to reflect heat back at the chops. This way you can cook them through before they're scorched on the outside—browned, good; scorched, bad.

I think coleslaw would be a perfect side with this, but it's up to you.

3 pounds (1.4kg) pork spareribs

Salt and pepper

½ cup (120ml) lemon juice

½ cup (120ml) olive oil

5 anchovy fillets

3 cloves of garlic

1 tablespoon (3g) dried oregano

½ teaspoon pepper

1 teaspoon salt or Vege-Sal

1 teaspoon hot smoked paprika

YIELD: 6 servings – Per serving: 580 calories; 52g fat (80.4% calories from fat); 25g protein; 3g carbohydrate; 1g dietary fiber; 2g net carbohydrate.

RIBS À LA JANN'S MOM

I was musing about something new to do to ribs, when my Facebook pal Jann Briesacher mentioned that her mother, who dislikes barbecue sauce, bastes them with anchovy paste, lemon juice, oregano, and garlic. So I gave it a shot, and this is what came out.

Preheat your oven to 325°F (170°C, or gas mark 3). Season your ribs with salt and pepper on all sides and lay them in a roasting pan, cutting the slab into sections to make it fit if need be. Get them in the oven!

Put everything else in your food processor or blender and run until the anchovies and garlic are pulverized. This is your basting sauce.

Roast your ribs for a good 2½ to 3 hours or until tender, with the meat pulling back from the bone. While roasting, baste the ribs liberally on both sides every 15 to 20 minutes, flipping the ribs over in the process. Keep the baste in the fridge when not in use.

I find it easiest to use kitchen shears to cut up a slab, simply snipping between the bones. If you like, you can serve any leftover basting sauce with the ribs, but do bring it to a boil first to kill any possible raw pork germs.

6 pounds (2.7kg) pork spareribs

3 tablespoons (36g) Vege-Sal or (45g) salt (Vege-Sal makes a big difference here)

1 tablespoon (7g) onion powder

2 teaspoons dried thyme

1 teaspoon paprika

1 teaspoon pepper

1¾ cups (410ml) chicken broth, divided

¼ cup (60ml) melted bacon grease

½ cup (120ml) dry white wine

½ cup (120ml) heavy cream

1½ tablespoons (23g) Dijon mustard

8 drops of liquid stevia, English toffee

Guar or xanthan

YIELD: 12 servings – Per serving: 493 calories; 42g fat (77.9% calories from fat); 25g protein; 1g carbohydrate; trace dietary fiber; 1g net carbohydrate.

OVEN-ROASTED RIBS WITH DIJON PAN SAUCE

It was a snowy day, and I certainly did not feel like running back and forth to the backyard, slow-smoking ribs. I thought I'd do something completely different with them. This is what I came up with. That Nice Boy I Married pronounced these "excellent."

Preheat the oven to 300°F (150°C, or gas mark 2). Find a roasting pan or pans that will fit your ribs—you may need to cut your slab into sections and use two roasting pans.

In a small bowl, combine the Vege-Sal, onion powder, thyme, paprika, and pepper. Set aside 1 tablespoon (10g) of the mixture in a small bowl.

Sprinkle the ribs all over both sides with the seasoning mixture. Place in the oven and set the timer for 30 minutes.

Meanwhile, add 1 cup (235ml) of the chicken broth and all of the bacon grease to the reserved seasoning mixture.

When the timer beeps, baste the ribs with the broth-seasoning mixture, turn them over, and baste the other side. Put them back in the oven and set the timer for another 30 minutes.

Repeat this process—roast, baste, turn, roast—for a good 2½ to 3 hours. When you go to pick up the ribs to turn them and a rib starts to come off in your tongs, they're done. That's when you go to the next step.

Place the ribs on a platter and put them someplace warm. Place the roasting pan(s) on your stove top over medium-low heat (see Note if using more than one pan). Pour in the remaining ¾ cup (175ml) of chicken broth and the wine and stir with a spatula, scraping all the nice browned bits off the bottom of the pan(s).

When the broth and wine reach a simmer, add the cream, Dijon mustard, and liquid stevia. Whisk them in and let the whole thing simmer for 2 to 3 minutes.

Thicken just a tiny bit with your guar or xanthan shaker if you feel the sauce needs it—I made mine about the texture of heavy cream. Serve over the ribs.

NOTE: If you use two pans, do the deglazing step this way: Pour the broth and the wine into one pan and stir and scrape up the browned stuff until it's dissolved. Then, pour the whole thing into the other pan and repeat the whole stirring and scraping. Then, add the cream, etc.

If you don't want to use wine, add extra broth instead. The flavor will be different, of course, but still quite good.

2 pounds (910g) pork spareribs

2 tablespoons (28ml) soy sauce

2 tablespoons (28ml) dry sherry

18 drops of liquid stevia, English toffee

1 teaspoon chili garlic sauce

1 teaspoon no-sugar-added ketchup

1 clove of garlic, crushed

Lard, for frying

Salt and pepper

YIELD: 4 servings – Per serving: 417 calories; 33g fat (74.3% calories from fat); 25g protein; 1g carbohydrate; trace dietary fiber; 1g net carbohydrate.

SPICY CHINESE-Y RIBS

Okay, the English toffee stevia in place of brown sugar or bead molasses is inauthentic. They still taste good!

Your first direction comes at the grocery store: pick a 4-pound (1.8kg) rack of ribs and have the butcher slice it down the middle the long way, making 2 racks of shorter ribs. Ask the butcher to wrap them separately—you'll only be using one for this recipe, unless you're having a party, and then you may want to double it. Otherwise, freeze half for later.

Use a sharp knife or kitchen shears to cut your half-rack into individual ribs. Throw them into a 1-gallon (3.8L) resealable plastic bag.

Mix together the soy sauce, sherry, liquid stevia, chili garlic sauce, ketchup, and garlic in a small bowl. Pour this mixture into the bag and then seal it, pressing out all the air as you go. Turn the bag over to coat all the ribs with the marinade and then throw the bag in the refrigerator.

Let the ribs marinate for at least several hours, and overnight is awesome. Turn the bag over once or twice in that time, when you're in the fridge grabbing something else.

Cooking time has arrived. If you have a deep fryer, use it. I use a stockpot over an electronic induction burner that lets me set a specific temperature. If you're going low tech—a pot on the stove—you'll want a thermometer. Melt about 2 inches (5cm) of lard in the kettle over medium heat. Let it warm while you get the ribs ready to cook. Regardless of what cooking device you're using, you want your fat at 350°F (180°C).

Pull your ribs out of the fridge and drain off the marinade. Pat them dry with paper towels. Season with salt and pepper all over.

Fry as many as you can fit without crowding for about 3 minutes and then scoop out with a slotted spoon or Chinese skimmer and hold them on a plate. Repeat until all the ribs have been fried for 3 minutes.

Then, starting with the first batch, fry them again, for another 3 minutes or so, until they're getting a little crispy. Serve hot!

NOTE: The nutrition stats are a little off here because Mastercook can't account for the marinade drained off, nor for the lard absorbed. They're close, but, if anything, your ribs will be a little lower carb and higher in fat than the numbers say.

Lard is a good fat, as long as it hasn't been bleached or hydrogenated. Ask around at your local farmers' market—I can buy it in 5-pound (2.3kg) buckets, though sometimes I have to give the farmer a week's notice. Spoon as much as you're likely to use soon into a clean old jar and store the rest in the freezer.

4 pounds (1.8kg) pork spareribs

½ cup (73g) Spanish-oid Rub (page 256)

½ cup (120ml) chicken broth

½ cup (120ml) melted bacon grease

YIELD: 6 servings – Per serving: 721 calories; 63g fat (79.1% calories from fat); 34g protein; 4g carbohydrate; 1g dietary fiber; 3g net carbohydrate.

4 pounds (1.8kg) pork spareribs

Salt and pepper

½ cup (120ml) chicken broth

Melted bacon grease, MCT oil, or melted refined coconut oil, for frying

---

YIELD: 6 servings – Per serving: 540 calories; 44g fat (75.4% calories from fat); 32g protein; trace carbohydrate; 0g dietary fiber; trace net carbohydrate.

SPANISH-OID RIBS

These oven-roasted ribs will get you happily through not-barbecue season. They take time, but very little work—a great choice for a rainy weekend when you're getting chores done around the house.

Preheat your oven to 300°F (150°C, or gas mark 2).

Cut your ribs to fit in a roasting pan or roasting pans and arrange them therein.

Set aside 2 tablespoons (18g) of the rub in a small bowl. Sprinkle the rest over your ribs, coating them liberally. Put them in the oven and set your timer for 30 minutes.

See that bowl of rub? Add the chicken broth and bacon grease to it and set it on top of the stove along with a basting brush—the warmth will keep the bacon grease liquid. Go do something else until the timer beeps.

Baste the ribs with the mopping sauce you made, flipping them in the process. Put them back in the oven.

From here on out, baste your ribs every 20 to 30 minutes, turning them over as you do. They'll take at least 2 hours, and possibly 3, depending on how thick your slab is. You'll know they're done when you try to pick them up with your tongs to turn them over and they threaten to fall apart.

These don't need another darned thing—no barbecue sauce, nada. Maybe a salad or some slaw on the side.

THE EASIEST WAY I'VE FOUND TO COOK RIBS INDOORS

Why didn't I think of this before? Geez. It takes maybe 5 to 10 minutes to brown and crisp the ribs when you get 'em out of the slow cooker. By the way, I specify 4 pounds (1.8kg) of ribs to have something to analyze. Use whatever fits in your slow cooker.

Cut your ribs into sections that will fit in your slow cooker—this is easiest if you have the nice meat guys at the grocery store cut your rack of ribs in half lengthwise. Then cut between the ribs to make sections that fit in the slow cooker.

Season your ribs with salt and pepper and stack them in the slow cooker. Pour in the broth. Slap on the lid, set to low, and let them cook for 6 to 8 hours.

Use tongs to pull the ribs out of the slow cooker and stack them on a platter. Let them cool for 5 minutes. Now, use your kitchen shears to snip them into individual ribs.

Put your large, heavy skillet over medium-high heat and add about ¼ inch (6mm) of bacon grease or oil. Let it get good and hot.

Now, quickly brown and crisp your ribs on all sides in the hot fat. It's nice to have any sauce you want to use in a big bowl by the stove. Just toss the ribs in as they're browned, then put the bowl, the tongs, and a roll of paper towels on the table, and let people help themselves.

3 pounds (1.4kg) pork
spareribs

1 tablespoon (15g) salt or (12g)
Vege-Sal

2 teaspoons hot smoked
paprika

2 tablespoons (20g)
granulated garlic

2 teaspoons dried thyme

½ teaspoon pepper

2 tablespoons (28ml) liquid
smoke

YIELD: 4 servings – Per serving:
625 calories; 50g fat (73.1%
calories from fat); 37g protein;
4g carbohydrate; 1g dietary fiber;
3g net carbohydrate.

FOIL-WRAPPED RIBS

True pitmasters slow-smoke their ribs, and a fine thing it is, too. But it is also darned time-consuming. Wrapping your ribs in foil lets you put them right over the fire, cooking them in a fraction of the time of slow-smoking. Feel free to use this method with your favorite rub; this just happened to be the one I tried.

Get your grill going! I went with charcoal, but gas will do fine. Put the grill rack as far from the fire as it will go.

Tear off a piece of foil at least 12 inches (30cm) longer than your ribs. Lay it on the counter and center your ribs on it.

In a small dish, stir together the salt, paprika, garlic, thyme, and pepper.

Rub or brush the ribs all over with the liquid smoke and then sprinkle them liberally with the spice mixture on both sides.

Wrap the foil tightly around the ribs—if it takes another sheet to get them sealed up, that's fine. Place the ribs on the grill and close the lid, leaving the vent open, of course. Set a timer for 20 minutes and go do something else.

When the timer beeps, flip your rack of ribs and set the timer for another 20 minutes.

Repeat this routine twice more. They should be pretty done by then—open the foil a little and peek. Are they tender? Is the meat pulling away from the bone? Good!

Unwrap your slab—carefully, it's hot!—and give them 5 minutes per side over the direct flame and then serve.

NOTE: Three pounds (1.4kg) is about half a slab. I regularly have the nice meat guys saw all my slabs of ribs in half, lengthwise, making two narrower racks. It's better for my two-person household, and easier to handle, to boot.

3 pounds (1.4kg) Boston butt pork shoulder

Salt and pepper

6 tablespoons (90ml) olive oil, divided

1½ tablespoons (9g) fennel seed

1½ tablespoons (5g) red pepper flakes

¼ cup (60ml) lemon juice

4 cloves of garlic

YIELD: 8 servings – Per serving: 477 calories; 37g fat (70.2% calories from fat); 33g protein; 2g carbohydrate; 1g dietary fiber; 1g net carbohydrate.

1 medium onion, thinly sliced

3 pounds (1.4kg) Boston butt pork shoulder

Salt and pepper

½ cup (120ml) chicken broth

3 tablespoons (24g) grated ginger

¼ teaspoon liquid stevia, English toffee

2 tablespoons (28ml) DaVinci sugar-free pineapple syrup

2 tablespoons (28ml) cider vinegar

1 tablespoon (15ml) soy sauce

1 clove of garlic, crushed

1 head of cabbage, coarsely chopped

1 small onion, diced

YIELD: 6 servings – Per serving: 532 calories; 36g fat (61.3% calories from fat); 45g protein; 5g carbohydrate; 1g dietary fiber; 4g net carbohydrate.

SPICY SLOW COOKER PORK BUTT

This super-simple preparation yields incredibly tender and flavorful pork. A simple salad alongside is all you need.

Put your large, heavy skillet over medium heat. While it's heating, season your pork all over with salt and pepper.

Put 2 tablespoons (28ml) of the olive oil in the skillet and sear the pork on all sides.

While the pork is searing, put the remaining 4 tablespoons (60ml) of oil in your food processor, along with the fennel seeds, red pepper flakes, lemon juice, and garlic. Run the processor until the garlic is finely chopped.

When the pork is nicely brown all over, transfer it to your slow cooker. Use a carving fork to stab it viciously all over one side and then smear half the spice mixture all over that side. Flip it and repeat with the rest of the spice mixture.

Cover the slow cooker, set it to low, and let the pork cook for 8 hours.

DREAMING OF THE ISLANDS PULLED PORK

I saw a recipe purporting to be Hawaiian pulled pork. It looked good, but was loaded with pineapple, one of the sugariest of fruits. It also took all day smoking on the grill or in the smoker. I had DaVinci pineapple syrup on hand and long experience making variations of pulled pork in my slow cooker. This is the result—a super-easy, crowd-pleasing meal.

Cover the bottom of your slow cooker with the sliced onion.

Use a carving fork to stab your pork butt all over—really go full-tilt serial killer on the thing. Season it with salt and pepper all over and plunk it on top of the onion.

Stir together the broth, ginger, liquid stevia, pineapple syrup, cider vinegar, soy sauce, and garlic in a bowl and pour it over the roast. Slap on the lid, set it to low, and forget about it for a good 8 to 10 hours.

When cooking time is up, use tongs to fish out your pork and place it on a platter. Ladle out about ½ cup (120ml) of the liquid from the pot and pour it over the pork.

Stir the cabbage and onion into the liquid left in the pot. Put the lid back on, crank the pot to high, and let it cook for 45 minutes.

In the meanwhile, use 2 forks to shred the pork, discarding the bones. (Many recipes will tell you to remove and discard the fat. The heck with that! Shred it right in with the meat.) Cover the pork to keep it moist and keep it in a warm place, such as your oven on its lowest setting.

Serve the pork with the cabbage and onion. Yum.

ORANGE-FENNEL PORK STEAK

1 teaspoon fennel seed

½ teaspoon dried thyme

½ teaspoon salt or Vege-Sal

¼ teaspoon pepper

1 pound (455g) pork shoulder steak, ½ inch (1.3cm) thick

1 tablespoon (15ml) olive oil

2 tablespoons (28ml) white balsamic vinegar

6 drops of orange extract

YIELD: 2 servings – Per serving: 469 calories; 38g fat (72.9% calories from fat); 29g protein; 2g carbohydrate; 1g dietary fiber; 1g net carbohydrate.

This dish is quick and easy, but with a complex and intriguing flavor. You can purchase ground fennel seed, but I ground my own with a mortar and pestle. Some people keep an electric coffee grinder dedicated to grinding spices, which also works well.

Grind the fennel seed and thyme together and then add the salt and pepper. Rub this mixture all over both sides of your pork steak.

Put your large, heavy skillet over medium heat. When it's good and hot, add the olive oil and slosh it around to coat and then throw in your seasoned pork steak. Cook until it's nicely browned on both sides and the juices run clear when pierced, about 8 minutes per side. A meat thermometer inserted into the thickest part of the steak should read at least 145°F (63°C). Remove to a plate.

Turn down the heat to medium-low. Stir together the white balsamic vinegar and orange extract and pour them into the skillet. Stir them around, scraping up all the nice browned stuff.

Now, put the pork steak back into the skillet. Let it cook for another 2 to 3 minutes on each side until the vinegar mixture is becoming syrupy. Remove to a platter, scraping all the extra sauce over it, and carve.

GLAZED PORK STEAK WITH PECANS

⅓ cup (37g) chopped pecans

2 tablespoons (28g) butter, divided

1 teaspoon Creole seasoning

1 pound (455g) pork shoulder steak, ½ inch (1.3cm) thick

Salt and pepper

2 tablespoons (28ml) cider vinegar

1 tablespoon (15g) brown mustard

¼ teaspoon liquid stevia, English toffee

1 tablespoon (12g) erythritol

½ teaspoon hot sauce, such as Frank's, Louisiana, or Tabasco

YIELD: 2 servings – Per serving: 637 calories; 55g fat (76.8% calories from fat); 32g protein; 6g carbohydrate; 2g dietary fiber; 4g net carbohydrate.

Plenty of pecans add crunch, flavor, and fat to this already delicious glazed pork steak. They're a perfect pairing with the Southern note of the Creole seasoning.

Put your large, heavy skillet over medium heat and sauté the pecans in 1 tablespoon (14g) of the butter, stirring frequently, for about 5 minutes or until they smell toasty. Stir in the Creole seasoning and then transfer the pecans to a plate.

Season the pork steak on both sides with salt and pepper. Melt the remaining 1 tablespoon (14g) of butter in the skillet and throw in the pork steak. Let it cook for about 6 to 7 minutes per side until browned and nearly cooked through.

While the pork is cooking, stir together the cider vinegar, mustard, liquid stevia, erythritol, and hot sauce in a bowl. When the pork steak is nicely browned on both sides and nearly done, add the mixture to the skillet and flip the steak to coat. Let it cook for another 2 to 3 minutes per side until the glaze starts to thicken a bit. Cut into portions and plate, pouring the remaining glaze in the pan on top.

Spread the pecans on top and dig in.

1 pound (455g) pork shoulder steak

Salt and pepper

1 tablespoon (13g) lard or (15ml) MCT oil

1 tablespoon (15ml) lemon juice

1 tablespoon (15ml) rice vinegar

1 teaspoon chipotle hot sauce

½ of a clove of garlic, crushed

12 drops of liquid stevia, Valencia orange

5 drops of orange extract

YIELD: 2 servings – Per serving: 464 calories; 37g fat (73.1% calories from fat); 29g protein; 1g carbohydrate; trace dietary fiber; 1g net carbohydrate.

ORANGE-CHIPOTLE PORK STEAK

Could it get easier than this? Feel free to use loin chops instead, if you don't share my obsession with pork shoulder.

You know the drill: put your large, heavy skillet over medium-high heat. While it's heating, season your pork on both sides with salt and pepper. Melt the lard, throw in the pork, and let it brown on both sides.

While the pork is browning, mix together the lemon juice, rice vinegar, hot sauce, crushed garlic, liquid stevia, and orange extract in a bowl.

Is the pork nearly done? Remove the steak from the skillet to a plate and keep it by the stove. Turn the heat down to medium-low. Pour in the sauce and stir it all around, scraping the bottom of the skillet to get up the browned stuff.

Put the steak back into the skillet, flipping it once or twice to coat. Let the whole thing simmer for a few minutes and then serve with all the pan liquid scraped over it.

1 tablespoon (15ml) olive oil

1 shallot, minced

1 teaspoon minced fresh rosemary

1 pound (455g) bulk pork sausage

1 tablespoon (15g) whole-grain Dijon mustard, regular Dijon, or spicy brown mustard

6 drops of liquid stevia, English toffee

4 drops of maple flavoring

½ teaspoon pepper

Lard or MCT oil, for frying

YIELD: 12 servings – Per serving: 170 calories; 16g fat (87.7% calories from fat); 5g protein; 1g carbohydrate; trace dietary fiber; 1g net carbohydrate.

ROSEMARY-MUSTARD BREAKFAST SAUSAGE

Do you want something special for a weekend breakfast? Add some pizzazz to simple bulk sausage meat. It sure dresses up "Eggs again!" If you don't have fresh rosemary, ground dried rosemary will serve, but the fresh is livelier.

Heat the olive oil in a small skillet over medium heat and sauté the shallot for a few minutes. Add the rosemary and keep sautéing until it's all soft, about 7 to 10 minutes.

Put the sausage meat in a mixing bowl and add the shallot and rosemary. Stir the mustard together with the liquid stevia and maple flavoring and then add them, too, along with the pepper. Use clean hands to combine really well and then form into 12 patties.

Fry 'em up like any sausage patties! Consider serving these with a little Maple Butter (page 251) melted over them.

COFFEE-MAPLE GLAZED PORK STEAK

1 pound (455g) pork shoulder steak, ½ inch (1.3cm) thick

Salt and pepper

1 tablespoon (13g) bacon grease

½ cup (120ml) brewed coffee

1½ teaspoons Virtue or Natural Mate or 1 tablespoon (12g) erythritol

32 drops of liquid stevia, English toffee

YIELD: 2 servings – Per serving: 462 calories; 37g fat (73.9% calories from fat); 29g protein; trace carbohydrate; 0g dietary fiber; trace net carbohydrate.

Wow. I tried this glaze on bacon first. It tasted great, but left the bacon a trifle soggy. Then, I thought of pork steak. I hit it out of the park! This is amazing and so easy, especially if you make it with the new bottled cold-brew coffee.

Put your large, heavy skillet over medium heat. Season your pork steak on both sides with salt and pepper. Melt the bacon grease in the skillet and throw in your pork steak. Give it about 7 to 8 minutes per side.

In the meanwhile, stir together the coffee and the sweeteners.

When the steak is nicely browned on both sides and cooked most of the way through, remove it to a plate for a moment. Pour the coffee mixture into the skillet and stir it around, dissolving all the tasty browned bits.

Put the steak back in and let it simmer until the coffee has cooked down and is syrupy, about 6 to 7 minutes, turning once or twice in the process.

QUICK SOY-GLAZED PORK STEAK

1 pound (455g) pork shoulder steak, ½ inch (1.3cm) thick

2 tablespoons (28ml) MCT oil

1 tablespoon (15ml) soy sauce

1 clove of garlic, crushed

1 teaspoon Virtue sweetener or Natural Mate, or ½ tablespoon erythritol plus 9 drops of liquid stevia, plain

½ teaspoon sriracha (optional)

YIELD: 2 servings – Per serving: 529 calories; 44g fat (76.2% calories from fat); 30g protein; 1g carbohydrate; trace dietary fiber; 1g net carbohydrate.

This is a great example of how just a few simple ingredients can add up to something quite wonderful. And it's done in far less time than it would take to order a pizza.

In your large, heavy skillet over medium heat, start pan-broiling the pork in the MCT oil. Give it about 5 minutes per side until it's starting to get golden.

Meanwhile, mix together the soy sauce, garlic, sweetener, and sriracha (if using) in a small bowl.

Spread half of this mixture on top of the pork steak and let it keep cooking for another 2 to 3 minutes. Then, flip it and coat the other side with the rest of the mixture. Let it continue cooking until the juices run clear when you pierce the pork at the thickest point.

Plate the pork and scrape all the tasty bits from the skillet on top before carving.

1 pound (455g) pork shoulder steak, ½ inch (1.3cm) thick

2 tablespoons (28ml) cider vinegar

1 tablespoon (12g) erythritol

18 drops of liquid stevia, English toffee

⅛ teaspoon molasses

1 teaspoon ground cumin

1 teaspoon hot sauce, such as Tabasco, Frank's, or Louisiana

1 tablespoon (13g) bacon grease

YIELD: 2 servings – Per serving: 468 calories; 37g fat (73.0% calories from fat); 29g protein; 2g carbohydrate; trace dietary fiber; 2g net carbohydrate.

1½ pounds (680g) boneless pork shoulder

1 teaspoon salt

YIELD: 4 servings – Per serving: 301 calories; 23g fat (70.2% calories from fat); 22g protein; 0g carbohydrate; 0g dietary fiber; 0 net carbohydrate.

CUMIN-MARINATED PORK STEAK

If, heaven forfend, I were limited to only one cut of one kind of meat for the rest of my life, I think I'd choose the pork shoulder steak. It's delicious, not too lean, reliably inexpensive—often downright cheap— and endlessly, endlessly variable. This variation is one of my best; I'd be impressed if I got this at a nice restaurant.

Put your pork steak in a big resealable plastic bag. Mix together the cider vinegar, erythritol, liquid stevia, molasses, cumin, and hot sauce in a bowl and then pour it into the bag. Seal the bag, pressing out the air as you go. Turn the bag over a few times to coat the steak evenly and then toss it in the refrigerator. Let it marinate for at least 30 minutes, and all day is great.

When cooking time rolls around, put your large, heavy skillet over medium heat and melt the bacon grease. Remove the pork steak from the bag, pouring off the marinade into a small dish.

Pat the steak dry with paper towels and then throw it in the skillet. Let it cook for 6 to 7 minutes per side or until no longer pink near the bone. A meat thermometer should read at least 145°F (63°C).

When the pork steak is done, remove it to a platter. Add the reserved marinade to the skillet and stir it around, scraping up any tasty browned bits. Let the marinade come to a full boil and cook down until it gets a little syrupy—this will happen very quickly—and pour it over the pork steak.

CARNITAS

This traditional Mexican dish is very simple and easy, but not quick. It's perfect for a day you're puttering around the house getting things done. My favorite way to eat carnitas is piled on a big green salad, with plenty of guacamole and sour cream on top, and some diced tomato. But I'll bet you'll come up with other ways to eat them!

Cut your pork into chunks roughly 1½ to 2 inches (4 to 5cm).

Put the pork in your big heavy skillet—you want a single layer, but the pork cubes can be very close together, that's fine. Cover with water, add the salt, and put over medium-high heat. Bring the water to a boil and then turn the heat down to low—you want to keep the water barely simmering.

Now, let your pork cubes simmer. And simmer. And simmer. Mine took a good 3 or 4 hours. That's okay; the simmering makes them tender. If you happen to be wandering through the kitchen, grabbing a cup of coffee, turn the cubes over once or twice.

Let your pork simmer until the water has completely cooked away. Continue cooking, letting the pork cubes brown in the fat that has collected in the bottom of the skillet. When they're crisply brown, they're done!

3 ounces (85g) cream cheese, softened

¼ cup (60ml) heavy cream

¼ cup (60ml) unsweetened pourable coconut milk

4 jalapeño peppers

¼ cup (60ml) olive oil, divided

Salt and pepper

1 medium onion

¼ cup (60ml) Zevia or Blue Sky Free diet cola, divided

4 bratwurst links

YIELD: 4 servings – Per serving: 515 calories; 49g fat (84.4% calories from fat); 14g protein; 6g carbohydrate; 1g dietary fiber; 5g net carbohydrate.

NOTE: You must use a stevia- and erythritol-sweetened cola for this recipe; that's why I've specified Zevia or Blue Sky Free. Artificially sweetened cola won't give the caramelizing effect of the erythritol. Aspartame-sweetened sodas will lose their sweetness completely.

BRATS WITH CREAM CHEESE AND COLA ONIONS

The recipe I adapted this from claimed this is how brats are served in Seattle, though they serve them in buns. Use a fork—and a napkin tucked under your chin. You can, of course, toast some hot dog buns for any die-hard carb lovers in the crowd.

Our tester, Christina, says, "Love the idea of Zevia for the onions. Suggestion for leftover Zevia: muddle 2 quarters of lime with 5 mint leaves. Add ice and Zevia. Yummmm… (Add vodka if you so desire, but good on its own.)" If you want to cut a step, you can sauté the jalapeños and onions together.

Rebecca, who also tried this, adds: "There are several steps and components, but it was so delicious it was worth it. I can also see making a whole lot of this at once and then having it around for when we feel like putting it on a brat or a hot dog. If I were at a festival and saw brats being served with these possible toppings, I'd be in seventh heaven."

Fire up the grill or use an electric tabletop or stove-top grill. If you're using the back-yard grill, you'll need a small-hole grill rack for the peppers.

First, make your cream cheese sauce: use a small food processor, electric mixer, or whisk to combine the cream cheese with the heavy cream and coconut milk until you have a consistency in the neighborhood of ketchup or mustard. If you have a spare squeeze bottle hanging around, transfer the cream cheese sauce to it, but if you don't, no big deal. Put it in a resealable sandwich bag—you'll snip a corner off later so you can squeeze out the cream cheese sauce—and stash in the fridge.

Slice your jalapeños lengthwise, removing the stem, seeds, and ribs. Toss with 2 tablespoons (28ml) of the olive oil, plus a sprinkle of salt and pepper. Throw them on the grill for a few minutes until they just have a few blackened spots and are softening a little. Remove from the grill. (Don't forget to wash your hands thoroughly! Touching your nose or eyes with jalapeño-y hands is no joke.)

Slice your onion lengthwise. Put your large, heavy skillet over medium-low heat, add the remaining 2 tablespoons (28ml) of olive oil, and cook the onions, stirring often, until they're starting to brown. Add 1 tablespoon (15ml) of the cola and keep cooking as it reduces. Repeat, 1 tablespoon (15ml) at a time, with the rest of the cola until the onions are brown and caramelized.

Slice your brats lengthwise, leaving one side intact so that you can open them like a book. Grill them for a few minutes per side, to your liking. While that's happening, chop your roasted jalapeños a bit.

Okay, it's assembly time! Plate the brats. Squeeze a good squirt of cream cheese sauce right into the middle of each brat and then pile on the onions and roasted jalapeños.

1 package (8 ounces, or 225g) of Miracle Rice

1½ pounds (680g) hot Italian sausage

1 cup (70g) chopped cremini mushrooms

2 teaspoons Italian seasoning

2 cloves of garlic

¼ cup (40g) minced onion

½ teaspoon pepper

2 tablespoons (8g) chopped parsley

½ teaspoon salt

1½ cups (173g) shredded Italian blend cheese, divided

4 green bell peppers

YIELD: 4 servings – Per serving: 514 calories; 43g fat (75.0% calories from fat); 21g protein; 11g carbohydrate; 3g dietary fiber; 8 g net carbohydrate.

ITALIAN STUFFED PEPPERS

Thes are not your average stuffed peppers! Bursting with flavor, they will please the whole family and reheat nicely, too.

Preheat the oven to 350°F (180°C, or gas mark 4). Coat an 8 × 8-inch (20 × 20cm) baking pan with nonstick cooking spray.

Prepare the Miracle Rice according to the instructions on page 23.

While the Miracle Rice is microwaving, put your large, heavy skillet over medium heat. If your Italian sausage is in links, slit them and squeeze out the sausage meat—if it's bulk, there's no need. Either way, throw it in the skillet and start browning and crumbling it. Add the mushrooms—if you buy them sliced you can just throw them in and break them up with your spatula—the Italian seasoning, garlic, onion, and pepper. Cook until the pink is gone from the sausage, about 8 to 10 minutes.

Stir in the parsley, salt, ¾ cup (86g) of the cheese, and the Miracle Rice. Remove from the heat.

Whack the tops off the peppers, removing the seeds and membranes. Stuff the sausage mixture into the peppers, arranging them in the prepared baking dish. Top with the remaining ¾ cup (86g) of cheese.

Bake for 10 minutes until the cheese is melted. Serve hot!

1 pound (455g) pork sausage

1½ cups (355ml) heavy cream

2 ounces (55g) cream cheese, cut into small cubes

Guar or xanthan

Salt and pepper

YIELD: 6 servings – Per serving: 554 calories; 56g fat (90.3% calories from fat); 11g protein; 3g carbohydrate; 0g dietary fiber; 3g net carbohydrate.

SAUSAGE GRAVY

As I was figuring out Biffins (page 53), I knew that one of the aims was biscuits and gravy for That Nice Boy I Married. You've got the Biffins, here's the gravy. Keep in mind that, unlike white flour biscuits, the Biffins themselves are super-filling. One Biffin covered with this gravy should satisfy all but the largest appetites.

Put your large, heavy skillet over medium heat and start browning and crumbling the sausage.

When all the pink is gone from the sausage, add the cream and cream cheese. Stir until the cream cheese is completely melted in.

Thicken the gravy a tad with your guar or xanthan shaker. Season with salt and pepper to taste. Serve over hot, split Biffins.

1 pound (455g) bacon

¼ cup (60ml) strong brewed coffee

1 tablespoon (15g) Virtue or Natural Mate sweetener or 2 tablespoons (24g) erythritol

12 drops of liquid stevia, English toffee

⅛ teaspoon maple flavoring

YIELD: 6 servings – Per serving: 436 calories; 37g fat (78.2% calories from fat); 23g protein; trace carbohydrate; 0g dietary fiber; trace net carbohydrate.

COFFEE-MAPLE GLAZED BACON

O.M.G. I saw this idea on BuzzFeed and had to decarb it. I'm so glad I did! It's enough to make you want to throw a brunch. Or just eat bacon for dinner.

Put your large, heavy skillet over medium heat and start frying your bacon—you'll have to do it in batches. I snip mine in half because I can fit more in the skillet and cook it more evenly that way.

Mix together the coffee, sweetener, liquid stevia, and maple flavoring in a bowl.

When the bacon starts to brown a bit, baste it with the coffee mixture. Baste every few minutes and definitely every time you turn the bacon.

That's all—just keep cooking and basting your bacon until it's done to your liking. Repeat with the rest of your bacon.

---

10 ounces (280g) lamb leg steak, ½ inch (1.3cm) thick

Salt and pepper

1 tablespoon (14g) coconut oil

½ cup (120ml) beef broth

1 tablespoon (6g) curry powder (Caribbean is ideal, but standard grocery store curry powder will serve just fine.)

¼ teaspoon dried thyme

¼ teaspoon ground allspice

1 tablespoon (14g) butter

2 tablespoons (20g) minced onion

1 clove of garlic

1 bay leaf

Caribbean hot sauce (optional)

YIELD: 1 serving – Per serving: 799 calories; 64g fat (72.2% calories from fat); 47g protein; 9g carbohydrate; 3g dietary fiber; 6g net carbohydrate.

ISLAND LAMB STEAK

I had a lamb steak, and I had a bottle of curry powder I'd bought in St. Maarten. So, I found a recipe for a Caribbean curried goat stew, and went from there.

Put your large, heavy skillet over medium-high heat. While it's heating, season both sides of your lamb steak with salt and pepper.

Add the coconut oil to the skillet and swirl it around as it melts. Throw in the steak and give it about 5 minutes per side to sear.

While that's happening, combine the beef broth, curry powder, dried thyme, and allspice in a glass measuring cup.

When the steak is browned on both sides, sideline it to a plate for a couple of minutes while you turn the burner down to low and melt the butter (don't scrape out the coconut oil first! You're going for a combination, here). Throw in the onion and crush in the garlic. Sauté for 2 to 3 minutes.

Throw the steak back in the skillet. Add the broth and spice mixture, plus the bay leaf. Adjust the heat so the broth mixture is just simmering. Set the timer for 7 minutes and let it cook. Then, flip the lamb steak and set the timer for another 7 minutes.

When the timer beeps the second time, check the steak. If a meat thermometer reads 145°F (63°C), your lamb is done. Taste the sauce. Does it need hot sauce? Are you that type? If so, give it a shot of good Scotch bonnet sauce (Warning: Seriously hot!). Remove the bay leaf and discard. Then, plate the lamb steak, pour the sauce over it, and tuck in.

12 ounces (340g) lamb shoulder chops

Salt and pepper

2 tablespoons (28ml) olive oil

½ of a medium onion

½ of a fennel bulb

1 tablespoon (14g) butter

1 clove of garlic

¼ cup (60ml) beef broth

½ teaspoon harissa

1 teaspoon tomato paste

YIELD: 2 servings – Per serving: 566 calories; 48g fat (76.5% calories from fat); 25g protein; 8g carbohydrate; 2g dietary fiber; 6g net carbohydrate.

LAMB CHOPS WITH FENNEL

This is a spicy and sophisticated one-dish meal—quick, too!

Put your large, heavy skillet over medium heat. While it's heating, season your chops with salt and pepper.

When the skillet is hot, add the olive oil, then the chops. Sear them on both sides, about 10 minutes total. If they start to curl, use your kitchen shears to snip the edges where they're curling.

While the chops are browning, thinly slice the onion and fennel.

Remove the chops from the skillet, stashing them on a nearby plate. Melt the butter and throw in the onion and fennel. Crush in the garlic, too. Sauté, stirring often, for 3 to 5 minutes.

Add the broth, harissa, and tomato paste, stirring them in. Lay the chops on top, cover the skillet, and turn the heat to low. Let simmer for 15 minutes.

Serve the chops with the vegetables and pan liquid on top.

---

8 ounces (225g) lamb leg steak, ½ inch (1.3cm) thick

Salt and pepper

3 tablespoons (45ml) olive oil, divided

8 olives

1 scallion

1 clove of garlic

2 anchovy fillets

1 tablespoon (4g) minced parsley

1 tablespoon (9g) capers

3 tablespoons (45ml) beef broth

YIELD: 1 serving – Per serving: 850 calories; 76g fat (80.1% calories from fat); 37g protein; 5g carbohydrate; 2g dietary fiber; 3g net carbohydrate.

LAMB STEAK WITH EVERYTHING YUMMY!

That's how I described this when I posted the picture on my Facebook fan page. And it's true! It's hard to think of anything you could add. It's just over-the-top flavor!

Put your large, heavy skillet over medium-high heat. While it's heating, season your lamb steak on both sides with salt and pepper.

Add 2 tablespoons (28ml) of the olive oil to the skillet, slosh it around to cover the bottom, and throw in your lamb steak. Sear it for about 4 minutes per side.

While that's happening, pit and chop your olives, mince your scallion, including the crisp part of the green shoot, crush or mince the garlic, and mince the anchovies.

Okay, the lamb steak is browned on both sides. Remove it to a plate for a moment. Add the remaining 1 tablespoon (15ml) of olive oil to the skillet and throw in all that stuff you just chopped up, including the parsley. Drain and add the capers, too. Sauté all of this together for 1 to 2 minutes.

Add the broth to the skillet and stir everything up. Now, use your spatula to make room in the middle for your lamb steak and plunk it back in. Let it simmer for 4 to 5 minutes until the broth has reduced by about half.

Plate the steak, pile all the yummy chopped stuff on top, and pour the pan juices over it.

NOTE: The only problem I had with this recipe is that my lamb steak seemed large for one serving, but small for two. So, I've analyzed it for one serving, but must tell you I only ate about two-thirds of it when I made it. The rest was great warmed up that evening. So, call it one serving and a dividend.

2 pounds (910g) lamb leg steaks, ½ inch (1.3cm) thick

1 teaspoon salt or Vege-Sal

1 teaspoon granulated garlic

1 teaspoon dried oregano

¼ teaspoon ground cumin

1½ teaspoons smoked paprika, hot or sweet, as you prefer

2 tablespoons (28ml) olive oil

1 tablespoon (15ml) sherry vinegar

¼ cup (55g) butter, at room temperature

½ of a shallot, minced

1½ tablespoons (17g) minced roasted red pepper

YIELD: 4 servings – Per serving: 582 calories; 49g fat (76.2% calories from fat); 33g protein; 2g carbohydrate; trace dietary fiber; 2g net carbohydrate.

LAMB STEAKS WITH PEPPER-BUTTER SAUCE

When whole legs of lamb go on sale, I buy one and have it cut into steaks ½ inch (1.3cm) thick. I like these better than chops, and they're certainly cheaper!

Slash the edges of your lamb steaks every ½ inch (1.3cm) or so, to prevent curling.

In a small dish, combine the salt, garlic, oregano, cumin, and 1 teaspoon of the smoked paprika. Rub this mixture all over both sides of your lamb steaks.

Put your large, heavy skillet over medium-high heat. When it's hot, add the olive oil and throw in the steaks. (Whether your skillet will fit both steaks at the same time will depend both on your skillet and your steaks. Sometimes, my skillet will fit two; other times, it won't—it depends on the shape of the steak, which In turn depends on which part of the leg it came from.) Sear the steaks for about 3 minutes per side. Then, turn down the heat to medium-low and continue cooking for another 7 to 8 minutes or until just pink in the middle (145°F [63°C]).

When the steaks are done to your liking, remove to a platter and let them rest for 5 minutes before carving.

In the meanwhile, add the sherry vinegar to the skillet and stir it around, scraping up the nice browned stuff. Melt in the butter and add the shallot, roasted red pepper, and the remaining smoked paprika.

Carve the lamb steaks and pour the butter sauce over them.

6 ounces (170g) lamb leg steak, ½ inch (1.3cm) thick

Salt and pepper

2 tablespoons (28ml) olive oil

1 clove of garlic, crushed

1 tablespoon (15ml) balsamic vinegar

YIELD: 1 serving – Per serving: 555 calories; 50g fat (81.1% calories from fat); 24g protein; 2g carbohydrate; trace dietary fiber; 2g net carbohydrate.

QUICK BALSAMIC-GLAZED LAMB STEAK

I came up with this one morning when I simply didn't feel like the usual breakfast foods. I just used what I had on hand, and it came out quite wonderful.

Put your large, heavy skillet over medium heat. Sprinkle your lamb steak on both sides with the salt and pepper.

Add the olive oil to the skillet and throw in your lamb. Brown on both sides, about 5 minutes per side.

While the lamb is cooking, combine the garlic and balsamic vinegar in a small bowl.

When the lamb is well browned on both sides, pour in the balsamic vinegar and garlic, flipping the steak to coat. Cook for another couple of minutes on each side, letting the vinegar cook down to a glaze.

1½ pounds (680g) lamb shoulder chops, sometimes called "blade" (4 chops)

Salt and pepper

¼ cup (55g) butter

½ cup (120ml) dry white wine

¼ cup (60ml) lemon juice

24 drops of liquid stevia, Valencia orange

8 drops of orange extract

1 teaspoon dried thyme

YIELD: 4 servings – Per serving: 543 calories; 47g fat (81.6% calories from fat); 22g protein; 2g carbohydrate; trace dietary fiber; 2g net carbohydrate.

CITRUS LAMB

Citrus is commonly paired with poultry or pork, but this orange-y sauce is terrific with lamb. It helps to tenderize the chops, too.

Put your large, heavy skillet over medium-low heat. Season your lamb on both sides with salt and pepper.

When the skillet is hot, add the butter and slosh it around as it melts. Add the chops, and set the timer for 5 minutes.

In the meanwhile, combine the wine, lemon juice, liquid stevia, orange extract, and thyme in a small dish.

When the timer beeps, flip the lamb. Let it go another 5 minutes on each side.

Okay, your lamb is browned on both sides. Add the wine–lemon juice mixture to the skillet. Cover the skillet with a tilted lid and turn the heat down so the sauce is just simmering. Set the timer for 4 minutes.

Flip the lamb, re-cover—again, leaving a crack—and cook for another 4 to 5 minutes.

Plate the lamb. Turn the burner up just a little and simmer the sauce for another 1 to 2 minutes until it's getting a little syrupy. Pour over the lamb.

1 pound (455g) lamb leg steak, ½ inch (1.3cm) thick

2 tablespoons (28ml) olive oil

2 tablespoons (14g) minced sun-dried tomatoes in olive oil

2 anchovy fillets, minced

1 clove of garlic, minced

4 teaspoons (12g) capers, chopped

2 tablespoons (28ml) balsamic vinegar

2 tablespoons (28ml) water

YIELD: 2 servings – Per serving: 411 calories; 32g fat (69.9% calories from fat); 28g protein; 3g carbohydrate; trace dietary fiber; 3g net carbohydrate.

LAMB STEAK WITH SUN-DRIED TOMATOES AND CAPERS

This is one of those "Hmmm, what's in the house?" recipes, and boy, did it work out! I'd be happy to pay for something like this at a restaurant.

Put your big, heavy skillet over medium heat and start pan-broiling the lamb steaks in the olive oil. Give them a good 7 to 8 minutes on each side.

In the meanwhile, combine the sun-dried tomatoes, anchovies, garlic, and capers in a small bowl.

When the steaks are browned on both sides, but still pink in the center (145°F [63°C]), plate them.

Add the sun-dried tomato mixture to the skillet and sauté it for a minute. Then, add the balsamic vinegar and water and stir it all around, deglazing the pan. Let it boil down until the liquid's getting syrupy and then spoon over the steaks and serve.

1 pound (455g) lamb leg steak, ½ inch (1.3cm) thick

Salt and pepper

1 tablespoon (13g) bacon grease

¼ cup (60ml) beef broth

2 teaspoons prepared horseradish

¼ cup (60ml) heavy cream

YIELD: 2 servings – Per serving: 584 calories; 48g fat (75.1% calories from fat); 34g protein; 2g carbohydrate; trace dietary fiber; 2g net carbohydrate.

LAMB STEAK IN HORSERADISH CREAM GRAVY

This dish is simple, rich, and good. I posted a photo of this on Facebook and got a number of "I love horseradish!" posts. So do I!

Put your large, heavy skillet over medium heat. While it's getting hot, season your lamb on both sides with salt and pepper. Melt the bacon grease in the skillet, and throw in your steak. Give it about 7 minutes per side until it is nicely browned, but the juices still run pink when pierced (an internal temperature of 145°F [63°C]).

Stir together the broth and horseradish and pour this into the skillet. Let the steak simmer in the mixture for about 3 to 4 minutes per side. Remove the steak to a platter.

Pour the cream into the skillet and stir it around, scraping up any nice browned stuff and dissolving it. Let it cook for 2 to 3 minutes until it thickens up a bit.

Carve the steak and serve with the gravy.

---

5 pounds (2.3kg) leg of lamb

6 cloves of garlic, thinly sliced lengthwise

⅓ cup (80ml) olive oil

Juice of ½ of a lemon

1½ tablespoons (3g) minced fresh rosemary

1½ tablespoons (6g) minced fresh oregano

¼ teaspoon pepper

YIELD: 6 servings – Per serving: 800 calories; 63g fat (71.9% calories from fat); 54g protein; 2g carbohydrate; trace dietary fiber; 2g net carbohydrate.

THE EASTER LAMB

You don't have to serve this for Easter! I did because I grew up with leg of lamb for Easter, but this is a classic festive spring dish to be served on any lovely day.

Start several hours before you want to serve your lamb, so you can give it time to marinate.

Now, put your lamb on the cutting board, and using a paring knife, go all serial killer on it. Stab it about 2 inches (5cm) apart, all over, on both sides. Now, insert a sliver of garlic into each hole—push them in well. Put your garlic-studded lamb in a nonreactive pan—I used Pyrex.

Mix together the olive oil, lemon juice, minced herbs, and pepper. Rub this mixture evenly over both sides of your lamb. Now, let it sit in the fridge for at least 2 to 3 hours.

About 3 hours before dinnertime, preheat your oven to 400°F (200°C, or gas mark 6).

Put the lamb on a rack in a roasting pan. Insert a meat thermometer into the thickest part, but not touching the bone.

When the oven is up to temperature, put the lamb in and immediately turn the oven down to 325°F (170°C, or gas mark 3). Now, let it roast for about 30 minutes per pound (455g), a bit less if you prefer your lamb rare. (I like mine medium to medium-well.) Check the meat thermometer to be sure—145° to 150°F (63° to 66°C) will be rare; 160°F (71°C) will be well done.

Remove to a platter and let the lamb rest for 15 minutes while you make your gravy (see Simple Pan Gravy, page 257). Then, carve and serve.

3 pounds (1.4kg) lamb shank (2 shanks)

2 tablespoons (30g) harissa

2 teaspoons Virtue sweetener

½ teaspoon pepper

¼ cup (60ml) olive oil

½ of an onion, diced

2 cloves of garlic, crushed

1 cup (235ml) chicken broth

½ cup (120ml) dry white wine

1 tablespoon (7g) smoked paprika, hot or sweet, to your taste

1 tablespoon (16g) tomato paste

1 teaspoon beef bouillon granules

½ teaspoon ground cinnamon

1 bay leaf

1 tablespoon (15ml) lemon juice

Guar or xanthan

YIELD: 3 servings – Per serving: 956 calories; 68g fat (66.6% calories from fat); 70g protein; 6g carbohydrate; 1g dietary fiber; 5g net carbohydrate.

HARISSA LAMB

Lamb shanks are just the sort of tough, bony meat that turns rich and succulent with slow cooking. And this sauce is divine! One minor issue: one shank makes a huge portion, so you'll want to carve these or at least pick the meat off the bones and divvy it up. I also highly recommend scooping as much marrow as possible out of the bones; it's scrumptious. I was eating lamb marrow before I was old enough to know it was "icky," so I have always loved it—meat butter! A bed of Miracle Rice or Cauli-Rice (page 107) is a great idea, here, to catch all that yummy sauce. You won't want to miss a drop.

Place your lamb shanks on a plate. Mix together the harissa, sweetener, and pepper in a bowl. Set aside 1 tablespoon (10g) of the mixture and rub the rest all over your shanks.

In your large, heavy skillet over medium heat, sear the shanks in the olive oil, getting them nice and brown all over. Transfer them to your slow cooker.

Add the onion and garlic to the skillet and sauté for just a minute or two. Add the chicken broth, wine, paprika, tomato paste, bouillon concentrate, cinnamon, and reserved harissa mixture. Bring to a boil, stirring to dissolve all the nice browned stuff stuck to the skillet. Let it boil hard for 4 to 5 minutes and then pour over the shanks.

Throw in the bay leaf, making sure it lands in the liquid. Cover the pot, set it to low, and let it cook for 8 to 10 hours.

It's dinnertime! Fish out the lamb shanks with tongs and put them on a platter. Remove the bay leaf and discard.

Stir in the lemon juice. Use your guar or xanthan shaker to thicken the sauce to the texture of heavy cream.

Carve the shanks into portions and serve with the sauce.

NOTE: Unfortunately, Mastercook doesn't allow me to analyze for whole shanks by weight, only for portions of the meat, so the protein and calorie numbers here are off. The carb count, however, is correct.

1 pound (455g) ground lamb

1 tablespoon (12g) Mediterranean or Greek seasoning

6 tablespoons (56g) crumbled feta cheese

3 tablespoons (21g) chopped sun-dried tomatoes in olive oil

YIELD: 3 servings – Per serving: 485 calories; 40g fat (74.2% calories from fat); 28g protein; 3g carbohydrate; trace dietary fiber; 3g net carbohydrate.

MYTHIC LAMBURGERS

I came up with this for *Paleo/Primal in 5 Ingredients or Less*. Somewhere in the mists of time, a hunter killed a lamb and found cheese curds in its stomach. I'm betting he served the two together. I mean, why not?

Plunk your lamb in a mixing bowl. Add the Mediterranean seasoning and use your hands to squish it through the lamb really well. Make 3 patties, about ¾ inch (2cm) thick.

Put your big, heavy skillet over medium-high heat and let it get hot before you lay your lamburgers in it. Cook them until they're brown on both sides, but not all dried out—they should be a little pink in the center when you cut into them (an internal temperature of 160°F [71°C]).

Top each burger with 2 tablespoons (19g) of the feta, turn down the heat, and cover the skillet for a minute to let it melt a bit.

Plate the burgers and top with the sun-dried tomatoes. Drizzle just a little of the oil from the tomato jar over each and serve.

½ of a medium onion

½ of an apple

1 celery rib

¼ cup (55g) butter

2 cloves of garlic

2 tablespoons (13g) curry powder

3 cups (450g) cubed leftover lamb

½ teaspoon thyme

½ cup (121g) canned tomatoes with green chiles

1 cup (235ml) chicken broth

1 can (14½ ounces, or 410ml) of unsweetened coconut milk

Guar or xanthan

YIELD: 6 servings – Per serving: 383 calories; 29g fat (66.1% calories from fat); 26g protein; 7g carbohydrate; 1g dietary fiber; 6g net carbohydrate.

LEFTOVER LAMB CURRY

For as long as I can remember, Easter dinner has been roast leg of lamb. However, with only two people in the house, it is hard to eat the whole thing at one go. I created this the Monday after Easter.

Cut the onion, apple, and celery into a few chunks. Put 'em in the food processor and pulse until chopped medium-fine, about a dozen pulses in my little processor.

Put your large, heavy skillet over medium-low heat and melt the butter. Add the chopped onion, apple, and celery and sauté for 5 minutes.

Add the garlic and curry powder and continue to sauté for another 2 to 3 minutes.

Add the lamb, thyme, tomatoes, broth, and coconut milk and stir it all up. Turn the heat up to medium-high, bring to a simmer, and then turn the heat down to maintain just a simmer and let the whole thing cook for 45 minutes.

Thicken the sauce with your guar or xanthan shaker, and you're done.

You can eat this as is, like a stew, or serve it over Miracle Rice or Cauli-Rice (page 107).

CHAPTER 12

Main Dish Salads

love main dish salads; they're one of my favorite things to eat in the summer. Yet, despite their reputation as the dieter's mainstay, it can be tricky keeping the carbohydrates low enough for our macros. It really is possible to eat 20 to 30 grams' worth of vegetables in a single salad.

That's not the case with these! We've got plenty of cool, delicious, filling salads that should keep you right in the sweet spot, especially if you make your own mayonnaise. Please make your own mayonnaise (page 235)!

1 celery rib, diced

2 scallions, sliced, including the crisp part of the green shoot

½ of an avocado, peeled, pitted, and diced

3 hard-boiled eggs, diced

¼ cup (30g) crumbled blue cheese

3 tablespoons (45ml) vinaigrette (pages 98–100, or your favorite)

Lettuce, for serving

YIELD: 2 servings – Per serving: 370 calories; 32g fat (76.9% calories from fat); 14g protein; 7g carbohydrate; 2g dietary fiber; 5g net carbohydrate.

AVOCADO, EGG, AND BLUE CHEESE SALAD

Don't find your average egg salad inspiring? Try this unusual version. It's nothing like the mayonnaise-based eggs salads you're familiar with.

This is very simple. Just combine the celery, scallions, avocado, eggs, and blue cheese in a mixing bowl. Add the vinaigrette and toss. Serve on a bed of lettuce.

½ cup (60g) diced celery

½ cup (80g) chopped sugar-free bread-and-butter pickles

¼ cup (40g) finely diced red onion

5 ounces (140g) canned tuna in olive oil

⅓ cup (75g) mayonnaise

1 hard-boiled egg, peeled and chopped

YIELD: 2 servings – Per serving: 461 calories; 40g fat (75.2% calories from fat); 25g protein; 5g carbohydrate; 1g dietary fiber; 4g net carbohydrate.

GOOD OL' TUNA SALAD

In Fran McCullough's *The Low-Carb Cookbook*, she said that everyone was eating tuna salad for lunch. Here's my favorite!

I assume you know how to make tuna salad! Combine the vegetables in a mixing bowl. Add the tuna, draining it only if you feel it's really excessively oily—since it's olive oil, it's your friend. Add the mayo and stir to coat. Stir the chopped egg in gently, and you're done.

I'm generally alone at lunchtime, so I often eat my tuna salad straight out of the mixing bowl. But if you'd like to be a tad classier, you could wrap yours in lettuce leaves. Depending on your personal macros, you could even stuff it into a tomato.

NOTE: I've analyzed this for two servings, but because it's so high in fat, it's very filling. It could well feed three.

5 ounces (140g) canned tuna in olive oil

2 celery ribs, diced

2 hard-boiled eggs, peeled and chopped

1 recipe Dill Pickle Sauce (page 245)

YIELD: 3 servings – Per serving: 337 calories; 28g fat (72.6% calories from fat); 19g protein; 4g carbohydrate; 1g dietary fiber; 3g net carbohydrate.

OH, YEAH! TUNA SALAD

Dill Pickle Sauce was such a hit on catfish, I started musing about other ways to use it. The lightbulb came on—oh, yeah! Tuna salad! I usually put pickles, onion, and mayo in tuna salad, so it seemed a natural. It works great!

Follow your basic tuna salad procedure: assemble the ingredients in a mixing bowl. Stir it up. Done.

NOTE: I had half a batch of Dill Pickle Sauce left over when I first made this, so I used a half-size can of tuna in olive oil, one celery rib, and one egg. If you don't happen to have Dill Pickle Sauce in the fridge—though if you like it as much as we do, you might consider making a double batch and keeping it on hand—you could leave it out.

¼ cup (35g) pine nuts

2 cups (280g) diced chicken

½ cup (60g) diced celery

4 scallions, sliced

8 pepperoncini peppers, sliced

1 cup (225g) mayonnaise

1 tablespoon (15ml) lemon juice

1 tablespoon (4g) minced fresh tarragon

Salt and pepper

YIELD: 4 servings – Per serving: 700 calories; 68g fat (84.0% calories from fat); 24g protein; 5g carbohydrate; 1g dietary fiber; 4g net carbohydrate.

---

1 package (8 ounces, or 225g) of tofu shirataki, macaroni

¼ cup (40g) diced red onion

1 medium tomato, diced

¼ of a medium green bell pepper, diced

1 cup (140g) diced chicken

¼ cup (4g) minced cilantro, plus extra for garnish (optional)

5 slices of bacon

½ cup (115g) Chipotle Mayonnaise (page 236)

1 avocado

Salt and pepper to taste

Hot sauce to taste (I'd use Tabasco Chipotle, but do as you like.)

YIELD: 3 servings – Per serving: 693 calories; 65g fat (82.7% calories from fat); 21g protein; 10g carbohydrate; 3g dietary fiber; 7g net carbohydrate.

PEPPERONCINI CHICKEN SALAD

I used pepperoncini because I had them in the house, but fresh banana peppers would be terrific here. I'd go with about ½ cup (72g), diced.

Toast the pine nuts first—just stir them over low heat in a small, dry skillet until they're lightly golden, about 3 to 4 minutes.

Combine the chicken, celery, scallions, and pepperoncini in a mixing bowl.

Stir together the mayo, lemon juice, and tarragon. Pour over the salad and stir to coat. Season with salt and pepper to taste.

Stir in the pine nuts, or if you're into presentation, sprinkle 1 tablespoon (9g) over each serving.

CHICKEN-BACON-AVOCADO-PASTA SALAD

This is what happens when I have a few stray slices of bacon and a ripe avocado begging to be used up. It's fabulous, beautiful, and super-filling. As I write this, it's five hours since I ate this salad and I'm still stuffed. You could use Miracle Rice instead of the shirataki—the texture will be different, but still good.

Prepare the shirataki according to the instructions on page 23.

While that's happening, combine the red onion, tomato, green pepper, chicken, and cilantro in a mixing bowl.

Cook your bacon—I give mine 8 minutes on high in the microwave, but you can cook yours however you like, as long as it's nice and crisp.

Somewhere in here, your shirataki will be properly drained. Let it cool, stirring now and then to let the heat out. When it's cool enough not to cook the vegetables, add it to the mix. Add the mayonnaise and stir to coat. If you're not eating this right away, chill now and finish assembling your salad right before serving.

At the last minute before serving, halve, peel, pit, and dice your avocado and crumble the bacon. Add both to the salad. Stir and season with salt and pepper and hot sauce to taste. Garnish with a few cilantro leaves, if you're feeling fancy.

TRADEWINDS CHICKEN SALAD

2 cups (280g) diced chicken

½ cup (60g) sliced celery

1 bunch of scallions, sliced, including the crisp part of the green shoot

¾ cup (180g) mayonnaise

3 tablespoons (45ml) lime juice

2 teaspoons dark rum

½ teaspoon pepper

½ teaspoon salt

½ teaspoon ground cinnamon

½ teaspoon ground ginger

½ teaspoon dried thyme

⅛ teaspoon cayenne

⅛ teaspoon ground cloves

18 drops of liquid stevia, English toffee

5 cups (235g) shredded romaine or (360g) iceberg lettuce

½ cup (68g) chopped oil-roasted macadamia nuts

YIELD: 4 servings – Per serving: 688 calories; 65g fat (82.5% calories from fat); 24g protein; 7g carbohydrate; 3g dietary fiber; 4g net carbohydrate.

Looking to use up the leftover Tradewinds Chicken (page 133), I came up with this. You don't have to use Tradewinds Chicken, though. A rotisserie chicken from the grocery store will do just fine.

Put the chicken, celery, and scallions in a mixing bowl.

In a bowl, combine the mayonnaise, lime juice, rum, pepper, salt, cinnamon, ginger, thyme, cayenne, cloves, and liquid stevia, stirring it all up. Pour this dressing over the chicken mixture and stir to coat.

Create 4 beds of shredded lettuce and place scoops of the chicken mixture on them. Scatter 2 tablespoons (17g) of chopped macadamias over each serving.

NOTE: Two teaspoons of rum divided by four should not be enough to get anyone the slightest bit tipsy. However, use a teaspoon of rum extract if you prefer.

CREAMY AND TANGY CHICKEN SALAD

3 cups (420g) diced cooked chicken

1 cup (120g) diced celery

1 bunch of scallions, sliced, including the crisp part of the green shoot

⅓ cup (69g) capers, drained

2 tablespoons (8g) minced parsley

½ cup (115g) sour cream

¾ cup (180g) mayonnaise

1 tablespoon (15ml) red or white wine vinegar

Salt and pepper

YIELD: 6 servings – Per serving: 488 calories; 45g fat (80.5% calories from fat); 22g protein; 2g carbohydrate; trace dietary fiber; 2g net carbohydrate.

My pal and expert recipe tester, Julie, is a bona fide Southern belle (transplanted to Michigan). She warns that the Junior League will raise their eyebrows if you use anything but breast meat for your chicken salad. Me, I like thighs. But then, I'm an unregenerate Yankee.

Do your dicing and slicing and deposit your chicken, celery, scallions, capers, and parsley in a good-size mixing bowl.

Stir together the sour cream, mayonnaise, and white wine vinegar in another bowl, pour over the salad, and stir until everything is friendly. Season with salt and pepper to taste.

You can stuff this into tomatoes, should you have any ripe ones on hand, or wrap it in lettuce leaves. Or just eat it with forks.

⅓ cup (33g) pecans

1 cup (140g) diced chicken

¼ cup (25g) diced celery

2 scallions, sliced, including the crisp part of the green shoot

¼ cup (60g) mayonnaise

1 tablespoon (15g) prepared horseradish

1 teaspoon lemon juice

YIELD: 2 servings – Per serving: 572 calories; 53g fat (80.2% calories from fat); 23g protein; 6g carbohydrate; 2g dietary fiber; 4g net carbohydrate.

CHICKEN SALAD WITH HORSERADISH AND PECANS

Horseradish gives a nice zing to this easy chicken salad, while pecans add a toasty crunch. It's super-filling, too.

Preheat your oven to 350°F (180°C, or gas mark 4).

Spread the pecans in a shallow baking pan and put 'em in the oven. Since the oven won't be up to temperature yet, set the timer for 10 minutes.

In the meanwhile, combine your chicken, celery, and scallions in a mixing bowl.

In a small dish, combine the mayonnaise, horseradish, and lemon juice. Pour it over the chicken and vegetables and stir.

Your pecans are now toasted! Pull them out, let them cool to the point where you can handle them, and chop them.

You can stir the pecans into the salad if you like—I did. Or you can scoop the salad onto lettuce-lined plates and sprinkle the pecans over the top—or 50/50! It's up to you.

¼ cup (31g) sliced almonds

¼ cup (60ml) MCT oil, divided

2 tablespoons (30ml) Hoisin Sauce (page 246)

1 tablespoon (15ml) rice vinegar

1 cup (140g) diced chicken

2 scallions, thinly sliced, including the crisp part of the green shoot

½ cup (60g) sliced cucumber

½ cup (50g) diced celery

4 tablespoons (38g) diced red bell pepper

YIELD: 2 servings – Per serving: 651 calories; 58g fat (78.2% calories from fat); 27g protein; 10g carbohydrate; 3g dietary fiber; 7g net carbohydrate.

HOISIN CHICKEN SALAD

Once, I had a batch of hoisin sauce in the refrigerator and I just had to come up with things to do with it. I had all of these things in the house, and they combined happily. This would be nice served in cups of iceberg lettuce, but it was darned good right out of the mixing bowl. If you'd like to increase the size of these portions, double the dressing and toss the whole thing with angel hair shirataki that you've prepared according to the instructions on page 23 and let cool.

Put a medium-size skillet over medium heat and stir the almonds in 1 tablespoon (15ml) of the MCT oil until they're golden. Remove from the heat.

Put the remaining 3 tablespoons (45ml) of MCT oil in a clean jar, along with the hoisin sauce and rice vinegar. Lid it tightly and shake hard. This is your dressing.

Now, combine the chicken, scallions, cucumber, celery, and red pepper in a mixing bowl, pour on the dressing, and stir. Add the almonds, stir again, and it's done.

---

1 recipe Buffalo Slaw (page 97)

1½ cups (210g) diced chicken

YIELD: 4 servings – Per serving: 515 calories; 45g fat (75.6% calories from fat); 24g protein; 8g carbohydrate; 3g dietary fiber; 5g net carbohydrate.

BUFFALO CHICKEN SALAD

I made the Buffalo Slaw, and it was great. Then, I remembered I had leftover chicken in the refrigerator and thought, "Why not?" This is so good!

Combine the Buffalo Slaw and the chicken in a mixing bowl. That's it! It's a great dish for a hot summer night.

¼ cup (28g) chopped pecans

1 teaspoon butter

1 celery rib, diced

3 scallions, sliced, including the crisp part of the green shoot

½ of a green bell pepper, sliced

¼ cup (16g) chopped parsley

1½ cups (210g) diced chicken

1 medium tomato, diced

1 recipe Cajun Dressing (page 100)

YIELD: 3 servings – Per serving: 482 calories; 41g fat (74.3% calories from fat); 23g protein; 8g carbohydrate; 3g dietary fiber; 5g net carbohydrate.

CAJUN CHICKEN SALAD

Hey, with celery, green pepper, scallions, pecans, and a little heat—of course it's Cajun! What else would it be?

Follow your basic chicken salad procedure, here, with one little addition: the first thing you need to do is chop your pecans and start 'em sautéing over medium-low heat in the butter (they'll take about 5 minutes). Then, just cut everything up, throw it in a bowl, add the pecans, add the Cajun Dressing, and toss. It's easy-peasy—not to mention good.

---

1 package (8 ounces, or 225g) of tofu shirataki, fettuccini

2 tablespoons (14g) slivered almonds

½ tablespoon coconut oil

2 tablespoons (28g) mayonnaise

1 tablespoon (16g) almond butter

6 drops of sriracha

½ teaspoon grated ginger

2 teaspoons soy sauce

½ cup (70g) diced cooked chicken, in ½-inch (1.3cm) cubes

2 scallions, thinly sliced, including the crisp part of the green shoot

---

YIELD: 2 servings – Per serving: 298 calories; 26g fat (74.3% calories from fat); 15g protein; 5g carbohydrate; 2g dietary fiber; 3g net carbohydrate.

CHICKEN-ALMOND NOODLE SALAD

I used leftover roasted chicken; I always roast more than I need so I have cold chicken in the fridge for just such purposes. But you could, instead, throw a boneless, skinless chicken breast into your electric tabletop grill as you are starting. Or, you could buy a rotisserie chicken; they're great for chicken salad.

Snip open packet of tofu shirataki and pour into a strainer in the sink. Rinse well, and use your kitchen shears to snip across them a couple of times since they're so long. If you want, you can put them to soak in a bowl of fresh water, but I didn't bother.

In a small, heavy skillet, over medium-low heat, start your almonds sautéing in your coconut oil.

Combine your mayo, almond butter, sriricha, ginger, and soy sauce in a smallish dish and stir together. This is your dressing.

Go back and stir your almonds! In fact, stir 'em once in between measuring the dressing ingredients. You don't want them to burn. When they're just getting golden, take them off the heat.

Okay, it's time to assemble your salad. Dump the shirataki into a mixing bowl (drain them again first if you've been soaking them in water). Add the chicken, scallions, and toasted almonds, then the dressing. Stir it all up, and you're done!

3 cups (213g) chopped broccoli, in bite-size bits

2 cups (280g) diced chicken or turkey

¾ cup (180g) mayonnaise

2 tablespoons (28ml) vermouth

½ cup (40g) shredded Parmesan or Romano cheese, divided

YIELD: 4 servings – Per serving: 607 calories; 55g fat (80.3% calories from fat); 27g protein; 4g carbohydrate; 2g dietary fiber; 2g net carbohydrate.

1 pound (455g) cooked turkey, diced

1 avocado, peeled, pitted, and diced

½ cup (17g) alfalfa sprouts

⅓ cup (37g) bacon bits

¼ cup (40g) diced red onion

4 ounces (115g) Monterey Jack cheese, diced or shredded

4 radishes, thinly sliced

1 recipe Bacon–Roasted Garlic Ranch Dressing (page 103)

YIELD: 4 servings – Per serving: 731 calories; 57g fat (68.6% calories from fat); 47g protein; 11g carbohydrate; 3g dietary fiber; 8g net carbohydrate.

CHICKEN (OR TURKEY) DIVAN SALAD

I'm a huge fan of Chicken or Turkey Divan, so the idea of the same flavors in a salad struck me as awesome. And it is! If you're dairy-free, try mashing a couple of anchovy fillets into the mayonnaise-vermouth mixture in place of the Parmesan. It won't be the same, of course, but it will add that umami tang.

Steam your broccoli—I gave mine 8 minutes in the microwave, but do yours on the stove top if you prefer. You want it brilliantly green and crisp-tender.

In the meanwhile, place your chicken in a big bowl.

When the broccoli is done, uncover it immediately to stop the cooking, or you'll end up with nasty, gray, sulfurous mush. Let it cool for a few minutes.

Stir the mayonnaise and vermouth together in a small bowl.

When the broccoli is just warm, add it to the chicken. Pour on the mayo mixture and stir to coat.

Stir in ¼ cup (20g) of the cheese. Serve the salad and sprinkle 1 tablespoon (5g) of the remaining cheese over each serving.

TURKEY-AVOCADO SALAD

This is a great way to use up leftover turkey. Should you not have any leftover turkey on hand, use deli turkey. Just have the deli people slice it ½ inch (1.3cm) thick, and you can make nice, neat cubes. I have fallen in love with packaged genuine bacon bits, but they do tend to be a trifle flabby. I spread them on a plate and microwave them for 30 seconds or so to crisp them up. On the other hand, if you don't have bacon grease in the house to use in the Bacon–Roasted Garlic Ranch Dressing, you may as well fry up your bacon fresh; five to six slices should do it, depending on how thinly sliced your bacon is.

Combine everything in a mixing bowl, pour in the Bacon-Roasted Garlic Ranch Dressing, and stir to coat. If you can afford an extra gram or two of carbohydrate, it would be nice to eat this in iceberg lettuce cups.

½ of a head of cauliflower

3 cups (420g) diced cooked turkey or cubed deli turkey

1 heart romaine lettuce, cut crosswise in ½-inch (1.3cm) strips

1 large tomato, diced

2 tablespoons (28ml) cider vinegar

2 tablespoons (28ml) lemon juice

1 teaspoon brown mustard

½ cup (115g) mayonnaise

Salt and pepper

10 slices of cooked bacon

YIELD: 6 servings – Per serving: 326 calories; 26g fat (68.7% calories from fat); 21g protein; 5g carbohydrate; 2g dietary fiber; 3g net carbohydrate.

CLUB SANDWICH SALAD

I came up with this recipe before packaged real bacon bits became widely available. This would certainly be a fine place to use them! About ¾ cup (84g) should do it. I'd refresh them in the microwave before adding them; just spread them on a plate and give them 45 to 60 seconds. I used deli turkey and had the people at the deli slice it a full ½ inch (1.3cm) thick, which made for nice cubes.

Trim the leaves and the very bottom of the stem off your cauliflower, whack it into chunks, and run it through the shredding blade of your food processor. Put the resulting cauli-rice into a microwavable casserole dish with a lid, add a couple of tablespoons (28ml) of water, and nuke on high for 6 minutes.

Combine the turkey, lettuce, and tomato in a big salad bowl.

Somewhere in here, your microwave will beep. Pull out your cauli-rice and uncover it to stop the cooking. Let it cool for a few minutes, so it won't cook your lettuce and tomatoes!

Whisk together your cider vinegar, lemon juice, mustard, and mayonnaise in a small bowl. Season with salt and pepper and whisk again.

Use your kitchen shears to snip the bacon into the salad, cutting it every ¼ inch (6mm) or so. Now, add the cauli-rice, pour on the dressing, toss well, and serve.

2 pounds (910g) cooked medium-size shrimp, peeled and deveined

1 medium red onion, sliced paper-thin

2 medium pale, inner celery ribs, including the leaves, thinly sliced

¼ cup (60ml) olive oil

3 tablespoons (45ml) lemon juice

1 teaspoon chopped fresh tarragon

1 clove of garlic, crushed

¼ teaspoon salt

1 tablespoon (9g) capers, drained

1 head of butter lettuce

YIELD: 6 servings – Per serving: 248 calories; 11g fat (39.6% calories from fat); 32g protein; 4g carbohydrate; 1g dietary fiber; 3g net carbohydrate.

SHRIMP SALAD

So simple, cool, and elegant—consider this for a summer company luncheon or even a bridal shower. You can make this with teeny bay scallops in place of the shrimp, if you prefer. Steam and cool them first.

If you buy precooked shrimp, this is a snap! Put your shrimp, onion, and celery in a nonreactive bowl—stainless steel, glass, enamel, or even plastic will do.

Put the olive oil, lemon juice, tarragon, garlic, and salt in a clean old jar, lid it tightly, and shake it hard for 15 seconds or so. Pour this over the shrimp and vegetables and stir to coat. Stir in the capers.

You can serve your salad right away, or you can refrigerate it for a few hours, if you like. If you choose the latter, give it a stir before spooning into butter lettuce cups to serve.

3 tablespoons (26g) raw shelled pumpkin seeds

½ of a medium cucumber

½ of a medium fennel bulb

¼ of a medium red onion

1 recipe Orange Vinaigrette (page 99), divided

10 ounces (280g) mixed greens, including arugula and radicchio

1 avocado, just getting ripe

12 ounces (340g) cooked shrimp, peeled and deveined

YIELD: 4 servings – Per serving: 459 calories; 36g fat (69.3% calories from fat); 22g protein; 14g carbohydrate; 6g dietary fiber; 8g net carbohydrate.

CUCUMBER-FENNEL-AVOCADO SALAD WITH SHRIMP AND ORANGE VINAIGRETTE

One of the questions my recipe testers answer is "On a scale of one to ten, with ten being 'Wow, I'd be happy to pay big bucks for this in a restaurant,' where do you rate this recipe?" Angele said, "10! I'd definitely get this in a restaurant. The citrus came through loud and clear; it was perfectly sweet and tangy. Each element of the salad complemented the others; it was scrumptious!"

Put a small skillet over medium-low heat. Stir the pumpkin seeds in the dry skillet until they start to puff and turn golden, just a few minutes. Remove from the heat.

Peel the cucumber if you prefer it that way. Slice it lengthwise and use the tip of a spoon to scrape out the seeds. Slice it thinly. Put in a nonreactive mixing bowl, such as glass or stainless steel.

Cut the core from your fennel bulb and slice thinly lengthwise. Cut across the slices once. Add to the bowl.

Slice the onion paper-thin lengthwise and then cut across the slices once. Add to the bowl.

Pour ¼ cup (60ml) of the Orange Vinaigrette over the cucumber, fennel, and onion. Stir to coat.

Put the mixed greens in a salad bowl. Pour on the remaining Orange Vinaigrette dressing and toss to coat. Pile the greens on 4 salad plates. Divide the cucumber-fennel-onion mixture among them.

Quickly peel, pit, and slice the avocado. Artfully arrange one-fourth of the avocado slices and the shrimp on each salad. Scatter the toasted pumpkin seeds over the completed salads.

2 pounds (910g) cooked shrimp, peeled and deveined

1 avocado

10 scallions, thinly sliced, including the crisp part of the green shoot

⅔ cup (160ml) vinaigrette (pages 99–100 or your favorite)

1 head of romaine lettuce

YIELD: 6 servings – Per serving: 352 calories; 21g fat (52.4% calories from fat); 35g protein; 8g carbohydrate; 4g dietary fiber; 4g net carbohydrate.

SHRIMP AND AVOCADO SALAD

This salad is dead easy, especially if you buy your shrimp already cooked and peeled. I like to use little-bitty shrimp for this, but feel free to use medium-size shrimp, if that's what you prefer.

Put the shrimp in a big mixing bowl. Peel and pit your avocado and dice it, somewhere between ¼ and ½ inch (6 to 13mm) big. Put that in the bowl along with the scallions.

Pour on the vinaigrette, and gently stir the whole thing up to coat all the ingredients. Let that sit for a few minutes while you break or cut up the lettuce. Arrange it in beds on 6 serving plates.

Now, stir the shrimp salad one last time to get up any dressing that's settled to the bottom of the bowl and spoon it out onto the beds of lettuce. Serve immediately.

3 tablespoons (45ml) MCT oil, divided

2 teaspoons chili powder

2 shallots

2 poblano peppers

1 pound (455g) large shrimp, peeled and deveined

3 radishes

5 ounces (140g) mixed greens

3 tablespoons (45ml) lime juice

½ teaspoon salt

½ of a clove of garlic, crushed

1 pinch of ground cumin

1 avocado

YIELD: 4 servings – Per serving: 292 calories; 19g fat (56.8% calories from fat); 22g protein; 11g carbohydrate; 3g dietary fiber; 8g net carbohydrate.

GRILLED SHRIMP AND POBLANO SALAD

Our recipe tester Rebecca says, "A 10—very delicious. It's the quality I would expect in one of the finer Mexican restaurants." If you have an electric tabletop grill, use it! You could also do this in a grill basket or grill wok over a fire in your grill.

Prepare your grill for medium heat.

Mix 2 tablespoons (28ml) of the MCT oil with the chili powder.

Peel and thinly slice the shallots. Slice the poblanos in half lengthwise, remove the seeds and pith, and then slice crosswise. Toss the shallot and poblano with half the seasoned oil and then grill for 4 to 5 minutes.

In the meanwhile, toss the shrimp with the rest of the seasoned oil. When the shallots and poblano are starting to soften, add the shrimp and cook for 5 minutes, or until pink and firm. Set aside to cool slightly.

Slice the radishes thin and put them in a salad bowl with the mixed greens.

Put the remaining 1 tablespoon (15ml) of MCT oil in a small dish or jar. Add the lime juice, salt, garlic, and cumin. If using a dish, whisk well, or if a jar, lid tightly and shake. Pour over the lettuce and radishes and toss until it's all evenly coated. Pile the salad onto 4 plates.

Halve your avocado, remove the pit, and then peel and slice.

Top each salad with one-fourth of the grilled mixture and one-fourth of the sliced avocado and serve.

1 pound (455g) spinach leaves

¾ cup (175ml) Caesar Dressing (page 108)

8 ounces (225g) cooked shrimp, peeled and deveined (Buy them that way.)

2 hard-boiled eggs

3 tablespoons (15g) shredded Parmesan cheese

YIELD: 3 servings – Per serving: 457 calories; 35g fat (70.0% calories from fat); 24g protein; 9g carbohydrate; 3g dietary fiber; 6g net carbohydrate.

SHRIMP AND SPINACH CAESAR SALAD

Dark spinach, pink shrimp, white and yellow eggs—how pretty is this?! And with prewashed baby spinach and precooked and peeled shrimp, it's super-quick and easy, too.

Put your spinach in a salad bowl and pour on the Caesar Dressing. Toss until it's all evenly coated. Pile it onto 3 plates.

Arrange your shrimp decoratively on the spinach. Peel the eggs and use the coarse side of your grater to grate them over the top. Scatter the Parmesan over that. Done!

1½ pounds (680g) lump crabmeat

1½ tablespoons (13g) capers, chopped

⅓ cup (40g) finely diced celery

1 cup (235ml) Louis Dressing (page 101)

3 hard-boiled eggs

2 heads of butter lettuce

YIELD: 6 servings – Per serving: 459 calories; 36g fat (69.3% calories from fat); 22g protein; 14g carbohydrate; 6g dietary fiber; 8g net carbohydrate.

WARNING: Do not, for the love of all that is nutritious, use fake crab. The stuff is Festival of Added Carbohydrates. If you can't afford crab, go with a less expensive—but real—seafood or fish.

CRAB LOUIS LETTUCE WRAPS

Classically, Crab Louis is served unmixed on a bed of shredded iceberg lettuce, and you may certainly do that if you like. I just like lettuce wraps, and thought this would be fun. Our tester, Christina, says she plans to do this with little-bitty salad shrimp in place of the crab.

In a mixing bowl, assemble the crabmeat, capers, and celery. Add the Louis Dressing and stir, breaking up the crab a bit, but not completely mashing it.

Peel the eggs and chop them coarsely. Fold them into the salad gently to preserve some hunks of yolk.

Serve with lettuce leaves for wrapping.

NOTE: If you'd like to give a nod to tradition, you can serve iceberg lettuce for wrapping, instead. Since it's crisper than butter lettuce, use a good sharp knife to cut slices from the outside of a head, creating lettuce cups. You'll end up with a core of lettuce that looks a bit like a vegetable soccer ball, but you can always make a tossed salad tomorrow.

---

3 tablespoons (45ml) rice vinegar, divided

2 tablespoons (28ml) lemon juice, divided

½ teaspoon dark sesame oil

¼ cup (60ml) MCT oil, divided

10 asparagus spears

2 cups (110g) mixed greens

6 sea scallops

Salt and pepper

YIELD: 2 servings – Per serving: 317 calories; 29g fat (78.2% calories from fat); 8g protein; 10g carbohydrate; 4g dietary fiber; 6g net carbohydrate.

SAUTÉED SCALLOPS WITH ASPARAGUS AND GREENS

I used big sea scallops to be fancy here, but if, as is so often the case, the little bay scallops are half the price, feel free to substitute. Who's going to complain?

Whisk together 2 tablespoon (28ml) of the rice vinegar with 1 tablespoon (15ml) of the lemon juice, the sesame oil, and 2 tablespoons (28ml) of the MCT oil. Set aside.

Snap the ends off the asparagus where they want to break naturally. Put them in a microwavable casserole dish with a lid, add a couple of tablespoons (28ml) of water, cover, and microwave on high for just 3 to 4 minutes. Uncover immediately. Divide the asparagus spears between 2 salad plates, fanning them out artistically. Top with the salad greens.

Sprinkle the scallops with a little salt and pepper.

Spray your big, heavy skillet with nonstick cooking spray and put it over medium-high heat. Add the remaining 2 tablespoons (28ml) of MCT oil and let it get good and hot. Add the scallops and cook for about 2 to 3 minutes per side or until opaque in the center. Remove to a bowl.

Put the remaining 1 tablespoon (15ml) of rice vinegar and remaining 1 tablespoon (15ml) of lemon juice in the skillet and boil down until reduced to just a couple of teaspoons. Drizzle over the scallops.

Now, drizzle the dressing you made first thing over the salad greens, top each serving with 3 scallops, and serve.

5 ounces (140g) bagged romaine lettuce

5 ounces (140g) bagged mixed greens

4 scallions, sliced, including the crisp part of the green shoot

2 canned artichoke hearts, drained and sliced

6 ounces (170g) sliced mushrooms

1½ pounds (680g) sirloin steak, about 1 inch (2.5cm) thick

2 tablespoons (28ml) olive oil

Salt and pepper

¾ cup (180ml) vinaigrette (pages 98–100, or your favorite recipe)

2 medium tomatoes, diced

8 green olives

8 kalamata olives

YIELD: 4 servings – Per serving: 691 calories; 57g fat (73.5% calories from fat); 35g protein; 11g carbohydrate; 4g dietary fiber; 7g net carbohydrate.

STEAK SALAD

Made with bagged salad, presliced mushrooms, and pitted olives, this is a quick and easy summer dinner. It's pretty to look at and crazy nutritious, too. If you prefer, throw the steak on the grill.

Preheat the broiler.

Combine both kinds of greens in your salad bowl. Add the scallions, artichoke hearts, and sliced mushrooms.

Rub your steak with the olive oil on both sides and season with salt and pepper. Broil close to the heat element until done to your liking—I'd go with medium-rare, which should take 4 to 6 minutes per side, depending on how close to the heat you can get your steak. Remove from the heat and let rest for 5 minutes.

Shake up your vinaigrette, pour it over the salad, and toss until everything's evenly coated. Pile the salad onto plates. Sprinkle the diced tomatoes over the top of each serving.

Slice the steak thin, across the grain, and divide among the servings. Distribute the olives among the salads and dinner is served.

1 tablespoon (12g) Cajun seasoning (I use Tony Chachere's More Spice blend.)

12 ounces (340g) sirloin steak

1½ heads of romaine lettuce

¼ of a red onion, sliced paper-thin

1 cup (100g) grated Romano cheese

¾ cup (175ml) Caesar Dressing (page 101)

1 teaspoon hot sauce, such as Tabasco, Frank's, or Louisiana

YIELD: 3 servings – Per serving: 684 calories; 54g fat (72.4% calories from fat); 35g protein; 11g carbohydrate; 3g dietary fiber; 8g net carbohydrate.

CAJUN STEAK CAESAR SALAD

Are you bored of the eternal Chicken Caesar Salad, hold the croutons? Here's a fine alternative.

Preheat the broiler.

Sprinkle the Cajun seasoning on both sides of the steak and put the steak in to broil.

While the steak is broiling, break up the lettuce into your salad bowl. Add the onion and toss to combine.

Coat a microwavable plate with nonstick cooking spray and spread the Romano on it. Put it in the microwave for 1 minute on high.

Stir the Caesar Dressing and the hot sauce together. Pour over the romaine and onion and toss.

Okay, your steak should be done now. Pull it out and slice it thin across the grain. Pile the lettuce on 3 serving plates and top with the sliced steak.

Pull the cheese out of the microwave—it will be a crisp sheet. Crumble the crisp cheese over the salads and serve.

3 slices of bacon

12 ounces (340g) ground
chuck

½ cup (115g) mayonnaise

5 sun-dried tomato halves

1 chipotle chile canned in
adobo, plus 1 teaspoon adobo
sauce

½ teaspoon chopped garlic

1 tablespoon (15ml) cider
vinegar

2 tablespoons (28ml) olive oil

10 ounces (280g) Italian
lettuce blend

3 cups (60g) arugula

¼ of a red onion

YIELD: 3 servings – Per serving:
720 calories; 67g fat (81.7%
calories from fat); 25g protein;
9g carbohydrate; 3g dietary fiber;
6g net carbohydrate.

2 packages (8 ounces, or
225g each) of tofu shirataki,
macaroni

¼ cup (35g) pine nuts

4 ounces (115g) mozzarella
cheese, cubed

1 large tomato, good and ripe,
diced

¼ cup (10g) minced fresh basil

½ cup (115g) mayonnaise

2 tablespoons (28ml) red wine
vinegar

1 clove of garlic, crushed

1 teaspoon Dijon mustard

½ teaspoon dried oregano

Salt and pepper

HAMBURGER SALAD WITH SUN-DRIED TOMATO AND CHIPOTLE DRESSING

I'm old enough to remember when every diner had a "diet plate" consisting of a bunless hamburger, lettuce, and tomato, plus maybe a scoop of cottage cheese. That was back in the day when everybody knew that to lose weight you gave up starches and sweets. This is the somewhat more interesting grandchild of that diner diet plate. Feel free to do the burgers on your backyard grill, by the way. I just invented this in the wintertime. You could pan-broil them, too.

Start preheating your electric tabletop grill.

Lay your bacon on a microwave bacon rack or in a Pyrex pie plate and nuke on high for 4 to 6 minutes or until crisp.

Make 3 hamburger patties from the ground chuck and set them by the grill, ready to go.

Put the mayonnaise in your food processor with the S-blade in place. Snip your tomato halves into your food processor (you can chop them instead, but I find snipping them with my kitchen shears quicker and easier). Add the chipotle and adobo sauce, garlic, cider vinegar, and olive oil. Turn on the processor!

By now your grill is hot. Throw on the hamburgers and set a timer for 4 to 5 minutes.

Go turn off the food processor; you should have dressing.

Okay, we're getting to the finish line: dump the lettuce and arugula into a big salad bowl. Pour on most of the dressing, reserving a few spoonfuls to top the burgers. Toss-toss-toss until everything is coated. Pile the salad onto 3 plates.

Slice your onion quarter paper-thin and distribute it among the 3 plates. Crumble a slice of bacon over each salad. When the burgers reach an internal temperature of 160°F (71°C), put one on each salad, top with the reserved dressing, and serve.

CAPRESE PASTA SALAD

The better your mozzarella and your tomato, the better this salad is. Go with the mozzarella in water from the fancy cheese counter and the ripest tomato you can find. I have seen jars of mini bocconcino—balls of mozzarella about 1 inch (2.5cm) in diameter—marinating in olive oil and herbs. They'd be awesome in this salad, I bet.

Prepare the shirataki according to the instructions on page 23. Let it cool completely. You can even do this the day before and chill it.

Put a small skillet over medium-low heat and stir the pine nuts in it until they are lightly golden, about 4 to 5 minutes. Remove from the heat.

Put the cooled shirataki in a mixing bowl and add the mozzarella, tomato, basil, and toasted pine nuts.

YIELD: 6 servings – Per serving: 231 calories; 23g fat (85.5% calories from fat); 6g protein; 3g carbohydrate; 1g dietary fiber; 2g net carbohydrate.

1 small head of iceberg lettuce

1 head of radicchio

¼ of a small red onion, diced

1 cup (150g) cherry tomatoes, quartered

6 ounces (170g) provolone cheese, sliced

6 ounces (170g) salami, sliced

5 pepperoncini, stems removed, sliced

1 tablespoon (15ml) lemon juice

½ cup (120ml) Oregano Vinaigrette (page 98)

YIELD: 4 servings – Per serving: 473 calories; 41g fat (76.0% calories from fat); 19g protein; 10g carbohydrate; 3g dietary fiber; 7g net carbohydrate.

4 ounces (115g) mortadella

4 ounces (115g) sliced deli ham

¼ cup (45g) jarred roasted red pepper, drained and diced

¼ cup (40g) chopped dill pickle

¼ cup (40g) diced red onion

2 tablespoons (8g) minced parsley

2 tablespoons (28ml) extra-virgin olive oil

2 tablespoons (28ml) red wine vinegar

2 tablespoons (28g) mayonnaise

2 teaspoons no-sugar-added ketchup

¼ teaspoon brown mustard

YIELD: 3 servings – Per serving: 345 calories; 30g fat (78.5% calories from fat); 13g protein; 5g carbohydrate; 1g dietary fiber; 4g net carbohydrate.

CAPRESE PASTA SALAD *(continued)*

In a bowl, combine the mayo, red wine vinegar, garlic, Dijon mustard, and oregano and season with salt and pepper. Whisk well to combine. Pour the dressing on the salad and stir to coat. Stir again right before serving.

CHOPPED SALAD

Recipe tester Rebecca says, "It was so easy. I'm happy to have so much dressing left over too, so that I have it around when I want to throw some salad together another time." She also suggests throwing in a few capers and olives, should you have some on hand. This recipe assumes you'll be using a cutting board and knife, but if you have a mezzaluna knife and a chopping bowl, use them! And if you're a fan of chopped salads, you just might want to acquire that equipment.

Halve your iceberg lettuce and remove the core. Cut it into ½-inch (1.3cm) slices and then chop across the slices, transferring chopped lettuce to a salad bowl as it accumulates. Do the same with the radicchio. Add the onion and tomatoes to the bowl.

Lay your sliced cheese and salami on your cutting board and cut through all the layers, making small squares. Separate them as you add them to the salad bowl. Add your pepperoncini, too.

Pour on the Oregano Vinaigrette and toss until every single surface is coated. Pile high on 4 plates to serve.

MORTADELLA AND HAM SALAD

Tired of tuna and chicken salads? Here's an unusual twist for you! Our tester, Rebecca, says this would be great for a luncheon or a potluck.

Cut the mortadella and ham into 2-inch (5cm) julienne strips, and put them in a non-reactive mixing bowl—stainless steel, glass, or even plastic will do. Add the roasted red pepper, pickle, onion, and parsley.

Combine the olive oil, red wine vinegar, mayo, ketchup, and mustard in a clean jar, lid tightly, and shake like mad. Pour over the salad and stir until everything is evenly distributed and well coated.

If you have time, let the salad marinate in the refrigerator overnight and then give it another stir before serving. But if you're in a hurry—no harm, no foul.

CHAPTER 13

Soups

Ah, soup! It is the stuff of legend, from the tale of Stone Soup to the miracle-working Jewish Penicillin. It can take myriad guises: from humble to elegant, from delicate starter to hearty meal. Few other dishes are so able to turn a handful of disparate ingredients into something you'd be happy to put on your table.

Yet, many soups simply do not fit ketogenic macros. Obviously, we must rule out potato soup and all the legume soups, from black bean to split pea. They are too carby for our purposes. Even soups like vegetable-beef are often carb-laden, and perhaps a majority of soups are too low in fat. (Indeed, in my low-fat/high-carb days, soup, especially legume soups, were a staple of my diet.)

I have worked hard to bring you a selection of soups that are quite low in carbohydrates and, as much as possible, also high in good fats. We will start with the basics: broth. Quite a lot of the reason for soup's reputation as a healer lies in the nutritive value of good bone broth. I hope I can convince you to make your own broth. It's easy, cheap, and yields better results than anything you can purchase.

That said, I do also keep boxed stock in the house. I like Kitchen Basics brand, widely available in grocery stores. I also like the Costco house brand, Kirkland, though, of course, it being Costco and all, you have to buy six quarts (946ml) at a time. I tend to use these in sauces and such. If I need to fall back on them for soup making, I generally reduce them—that is, boil them down—by about a third, to strengthen the flavor. I also stir in a spoonful of unflavored gelatin powder to give them both additional texture and nutritional value.

CHICKEN BONE BROTH, OR SOMETHING FOR NOTHING

Bone broth is liquid gold, one of the most valuable foods you can add to your diet—heck, companies are now selling canisters of pricey "bone broth protein" supplements. Skip it! You can make this with stuff you would otherwise discard.

This is a rule, rather than a recipe, but it is one of the most valuable in the book. Whenever you eat chicken on the bone—wings, a rotisserie chicken, or just roasted thighs—stash the bones in a large resealable plastic bag in your freezer. Add any onion trimmings, scallion tops, or bits of celery you might have—go easy on celery leaves, though; they can get bitter in concentration.

When you have enough bones to fill your slow cooker—I use my big 5-quart (4.8L) slow cooker—dump them in. Cover with water, and add 1 teaspoon salt and 1 or 2 tablespoons (15 or 28ml) cider or wine vinegar. (The vinegar draws calcium out of the bones, making for a more nutritious broth.) Lid it, set it to low, and let it sit for a minimum of 24 hours, and 48 hours isn't excessive.

Let it cool, strain, toss the bones, and you're done. You can make soup immediately, or stash your broth in snap-top containers in the freezer.

If you're short on freezer space, or dislike the idea of using packaged bouillon concentrate, or both, put your strained broth back in the slow cooker, set it to low again, and leave the lid off. Do this on a day when you'll be puttering around the house, so you can keep an eye on it. Let your broth cook down until it's syrupy, scrape it into a container, and freeze. Use just as you would commercial bouillon concentrate, though you'll want to add a little salt along with it.

Obviously, I can't give exact serving or nutrition counts for this, but it will be darned close to zero carb. Simply drinking a hot cup of this broth every day will do you good!

FISH STOCK

My friend Chris was recovering from a car wreck and clearly was in need of the healing magic of homemade soup. Because she loves salmon, I made my own fish stock for the first time. Again, it's impossible to get an exact analysis of this, but it will be no more than a gram or so of carb per serving.

Ask your local specialty butcher or fishmonger to save you fish bones and even heads if they have 'em. I got huge halibut skeletons at Butcher's Block, my local specialty butcher. Indeed, the hardest part of this exercise was chopping up the skeletons to fit in my slow cooker. I filled my 5-quart (4.8L) slow cooker to the top with the bones, added 2 onions, cut into chunks, 1 cup (235ml) dry white wine, 2 tablespoons (12g) fennel seed, and 1 teaspoon salt, covered it, and let it cook on low for a good 8 hours. Strain and done. It's so easy and full of the gelatin and calcium that makes good bone broth so nutritious.

½ cup (120g) Porcini, Portobello, and Button Mushrooms in Cream (page 241)

½ cup (120ml) heavy cream

1 teaspoon beef bouillon concentrate

YIELD: 1 serving – Per serving: 624 calories; 62g fat (88.9% calories from fat); 5g protein; 12g carbohydrate; 2g dietary fiber; 10g net carbohydrate.

1 quart (946ml) chicken stock, divided

½ teaspoon guar or xanthan

1 cup (100g) minced black olives (You can buy black olives already minced, in cans.)

1 cup (235ml) heavy cream

¼ cup (60ml) dry sherry

Salt or Vege-Sal and pepper

YIELD: 6 servings – Per serving: 200 calories; 18g fat (84.4% calories from fat); 4g protein; 3g carbohydrate; 1g dietary fiber; 2g net carbohydrate.

CREAM OF MUSHROOM SOUP

This is not to be confused in any way with the gloppy condensed stuff that comes out of a can. This is rich and flavorful beyond belief.

If you have the Porcini, Portobello, and Button Mushrooms in Cream on hand—I make triple batches and freeze it in smallish containers—this is a matter of 5 minutes to put together. Simply put everything in a saucepan, bring to a simmer, stirring to dissolve the bouillon concentrate, and you're done. Heck, you could put everything in a bowl and microwave it for a minute or two, stir to blend, and have instant soup.

OLIVE SOUP

Olives are so good for you! This makes a fine first course.

Put ½ cup (120ml) of the chicken stock in the blender with the guar and blend for a few seconds. Pour into a saucepan and add the remaining 3½ cups (825ml) of stock and the olives. Heat to simmering and then whisk in the cream. Bring back to a simmer, stir in the sherry, and season with salt and pepper to taste.

1½ quarts (1.4L) chicken broth

1 chipotle chile canned in adobo, plus 2 teaspoons adobo sauce

1 pound (455g) boneless, skinless chicken breast

2 avocados

3 tablespoons (3g) minced cilantro (optional)

YIELD: 6 servings – Per serving: 236 calories; 14g fat (51.3% calories from fat); 23g protein; 6g carbohydrate; 2g dietary fiber; 4g net carbohydrate.

SIMPLE MEXICAN SOUP

This simple soup is quite similar to one I had as a starter every evening on a trip to Querétaro, Mexico. It makes the cut here because it's quite low carb. If you need to up the fat content to hit your macros for the day, add a handful of shredded Monterey Jack or a dollop of sour cream.

Put the broth in a large saucepan over medium heat.

Chop the chipotle fine and stir it into the broth, along with the adobo sauce. Wash your hands thoroughly with soap and water!

Dice the chicken and stir it into the broth as it heats. Do not just plunk it in and let it sit! It will congeal into a blob in the bottom of the pan. That's a lesson from The Voice of Experience.

Let the soup simmer for 10 to 15 minutes until the chicken is cooked through. In the meanwhile, halve the avocados, remove the pits, peel them, and dice the flesh.

Ladle out the soup and top each bowl with diced avocado and cilantro, if desired.

2 quarts (1.9L) strong chicken broth

3 star anise

10 slices of ginger (about 1½ inches, or 4cm)

1 large shallot, minced

2 tablespoons (28ml) fish sauce (nam pla or nuoc mam)

1 pound (455g) boneless chicken

2 packages (8 ounces, or 225g each) of shirataki noodles, spaghetti or angel hair

1½ cups (156g) mung bean sprouts

6 tablespoons (6g) minced cilantro

YIELD: 6 servings – Per serving: 180 calories; 4g fat (22.1% calories from fat); 27g protein; 8g carbohydrate; 2g dietary fiber; 6g net carbohydrate.

NOTE: I discovered long after creating this recipe that fully 10 carb grams in this soup come from the star anise, for which Mastercook counts 3.35 grams apiece. But you don't eat them! I can't imagine all of those carbohydrates cook out into the soup. I'm guessing this is a good 1.5 grams lower than the analysis suggests.

SNOWY DAY IN MARCH SOUP

The title is for real. It was a cold, snowy day in mid-March, and I just did not want to go out of the house. I put this together from stuff I had on hand, with That Nice Boy I Married bringing home the cilantro and bean sprouts. It was so soothing and warming.

This soup is low carb, but, as you can see, not high in fat. But, it was so easy and delicious, I had to include it anyway! Pair it with a high-fat dish—perhaps Stir-Fried Asparagus with Walnuts (page 122) or a rich dessert.

You don't have to use boneless chicken. I often make soup by dropping in a few skinned chicken thighs and letting them simmer until done. I scoop them out with a slotted spoon, let them cool a bit, then pick the meat off the bones, snip it up with my kitchen shears, and throw it back into the soup—and put the bones in my bone bag for the next batch of broth!

Put your stockpot over low heat. Add the chicken broth, star anise, ginger, shallot, and fish sauce.

Dice the chicken and add it to the soup. Let the whole thing simmer for a good 30 to 40 minutes.

Drain and rinse your shirataki and snip it if you like your noodles a little shorter. Stir them into the soup.

Ladle the soup into bowls and garnish each with ¼ cup (26g) bean sprouts and 1 tablespoon (1g) cilantro.

3 quarts (2.8L) chicken broth

2 pounds (910g) frozen cauliflower

1 large celery rib

1 large onion

1 small carrot

4 tablespoons (55g) butter, divided

2 pounds (910g) Oscar Meyer Selects Natural Smoked Sausage

1 pound (455g) shredded Colby Jack cheese

4 ounces (115g) cream cheese, cut into 1-ounce (28g) chunks

3 tablespoons (45g) horseradish mustard

Salt or Vege-Sal and pepper

Guar or xanthan (optional)

YIELD: 12 servings – Per serving: 334 calories; 26g fat (69.4% calories from fat); 18g protein; 8g carbohydrate; 2g dietary fiber; 6g net carbohydrate.

CREAM OF CAULIFLOWER AND CHEESE WITH SMOKED SAUSAGE

That Nice Boy I Married had an all-day event to go to and people were bringing food to fuel it, so I made this for him to take. It's a huge batch; feel free to cut it in half. Why am I specifying Oscar Meyer Selects Natural smoked sausage? Because most of the smoked sausage at my grocery store had at least 4 grams of carbohydrate—and that was in a teeny 2-ounce (55g) serving. The Oscar Meyer Selects Natural comes in at less than 1 gram, though for analysis I've entered it into my database as 1 gram per 2 ounces (55g).

First things first: dump your broth into your biggest stockpot and add the cauliflower. Put it over high heat until it starts to simmer and then turn it down to maintain that simmer.

While the broth is heating and the cauliflower thawing, whack your celery rib into a few big chunks, keeping any fresh leaves. Throw the celery in your food processor with the S-blade in place. Halve and peel the onion, whack it into chunks, and throw it in with the celery. Peel the carrot, chunk it, too, and add it to the little veggie-fest going on in your food processor. Now, pulse until everything is finely chopped.

Put your large, heavy skillet over medium heat and melt 2 tablespoons (28g) of the butter. Add the vegetables and sauté until they're starting to get soft and picking up just a few golden spots, about 7 to 8 minutes. Add them to the stockpot, using a rubber scraper to get it all.

Slice your smoked sausages in half lengthwise and then into ¼-inch (6mm) slices. Using the same skillet, again over medium heat, melt 1 tablespoon (14g) of the butter and start browning your sausage—unless your skillet is a lot bigger than mine, you'll need to do them in 2 to 3 batches, which is where you use up the remaining 1 tablespoon (14g) of butter. As your sausage slices are browned, transfer them to a plate and reserve.

After a good 30 minutes of simmering, test a piece of your cauliflower. You want it quite tender. Dip out a ladle full of the broth and pour it into the skillet. Stir it around, dissolving all the tasty browned stuff, and then pour it back into the pot.

Grab your stick blender and the shredded cheese. Start blending the soup, pureeing the vegetables. As you do this, start adding the shredded cheese a handful at a time, making sure each addition is melted before adding more.

When the whole thing is smoothly pureed and all the shredded cheese is melted in, add the cream cheese and blend it in, too, again, making sure each addition is blended in before adding the next.

Blend in the horseradish mustard. Now, season with salt and pepper to taste.

If you think your soup could be a little thicker, feel free to grab that stick blender again and sprinkle a little guar or xanthan over the top.

Stir in the browned sausage slices, and you're done!

1 small onion, diced

1 small carrot, shredded

4 cloves of garlic, crushed

¼ cup (60ml) olive oil

5 medium zucchini, sliced

1 tablespoon (2g) fresh thyme or 1 teaspoon dried

1 teaspoon grated ginger

1 teaspoon Greek seasoning

¼ teaspoon red pepper flakes

1½ quarts (1.4L) chicken broth

1½ cups (355ml) heavy cream

1 tablespoon (15ml) lemon juice

Guar or xanthan (optional)

Salt and pepper

YIELD: 8 servings – Per serving: 272 calories; 24g fat (79.0% calories from fat); 6g protein; 8g carbohydrate; 2g dietary fiber; 6g net carbohydrate.

CREME DE COURGETTE

When Jess signed up as a recipe tester, she asked for soups, so I gave her this. She called it "amazing!"

Put your stockpot over medium heat and sauté the onion, carrot, and garlic in the olive oil for 5 minutes. Add the zucchini and sauté for another 4 to 5 minutes.

Add the thyme, ginger, Greek seasoning, red pepper flakes, and chicken broth. Bring to a simmer and let it cook until the vegetables are tender, about 20 minutes.

Use your stick blender to puree the vegetables. Blend in the heavy cream and lemon juice. Thicken a little with your guar or xanthan shaker, if you think it needs it, and then season with salt and pepper to taste.

---

1 quart (946ml) chicken stock

2 cups (475ml) fish stock

2 cups (475ml) no-carb clam juice

½ cup (120ml) heavy cream

Salt

1 pinch of cayenne

2 tablespoons (6g) snipped chives

YIELD: 8 servings – Per serving: 92 calories; 7g fat (81.9% calories from fat); 2g protein; 2g carbohydrate; trace dietary fiber; 2g net carbohydrate.

CONSOMMÉ BELLEVUE

This soup is so simple and yet so elegant. Our tester, Angele, says, "It came together in less than eight minutes start to finish, and yet I'd serve it at my next dinner party." Another ringer brought in from an ancient cookbook. I would use my homemade chicken bone broth for this and purchase Kitchen Basics Seafood Stock. But if you'd like to make your own seafood stock, have at it! There's a description of how on page 222. It's surprising how many brands of clam juice have added carbohydrates. Read your labels.

In a large saucepan, combine the chicken stock, fish stock, and clam juice. Put over medium heat and heat to simmering.

In a bowl with a handheld mixer, whip the cream to soft peaks.

Season the stock with salt to taste and stir in the cayenne. Ladle into cups or soup plates, top each with a dollop of whipped cream and a sprinkle of chives, and serve immediately. Don't be dismayed when the whipped cream melts into the broth—it's supposed to.

3 tablespoons (45ml) olive oil

3 tablespoons (45g) butter

3 shallots, minced

1 tablespoon (8g) grated ginger

2 pounds (910g) sliced cremini mushrooms

1 quart (946ml) chicken broth

1 cup (230g) sour cream, divided

Salt and pepper

2 tablespoons (8g) minced parsley

YIELD: 8 servings – Per serving: 196 calories; 17g fat (73.2% calories from fat); 6g protein; 8g carbohydrate; 1g dietary fiber; 7g net carbohydrate.

4 ounces (115g) bacon

¼ cup (55g) butter

½ of a medium onion, diced

2 celery ribs, diced

20 ounces (560g) canned clams, no sugar added, do not drain!

1 pint (475ml) seafood stock

1 pound (455g) turnips

1 pound (455g) cauliflower (about ½ of a head)

½ teaspoon dried thyme

2 bay leaves

1½ cups (355ml) heavy cream

Guar or xanthan

Salt and pepper

2 tablespoons (8g) minced parsley

YIELD: 8 servings – Per serving: 318 calories; 31g fat (71.1% calories from fat); 19g protein; 10g carbohydrate; 3g dietary fiber; 7g net carbohydrate.

GINGER-CREMINI SOUP

Our tester, Christina, says, "This would be great as an appetizer for a steak dinner." She also warns that the recipe makes a lot—so feel free to halve the recipe.

In your biggest saucepan over low heat, warm the olive oil and butter, swirling them together. Sauté the shallots and ginger gently for 5 minutes, without browning, until the shallot softens.

Add the mushrooms and sauté, turning everything over often, for another 7 to 10 minutes, until the mushrooms have softened and turned dark. You might break up the mushrooms a bit more with your spatula—you'll be pureeing them later anyway.

Pour in the chicken broth and bring to a boil. Lower the heat to a bare simmer and let the whole thing simmer for 15 minutes. Now, use your stick blender to puree the soup in the pan.

Stir in ⅔ cup (153g) of the sour cream. Season with salt and pepper to taste.

Serve with a dollop of sour cream and a sprinkle of parsley in each bowl.

NEW ENGLAND CLAM CHOWDER

Our recipe tester Angele, rating this a 10, said, "Super-easy, super-quick (about thirty minutes), incredibly delicious and hearty. This is a winner! It felt like it had potatoes in it and it's chock-full of clams! The flavors are perfect." Do read the label on your clams. Shocking but true: many brands have added sugar. Why anyone thinks clams need sugar, I have no idea.

Put a large stockpot over medium heat. Use your kitchen shears to snip the bacon into it in small bits. Fry the bits crisp and then scoop them out with a slotted spoon, leaving the grease in the pot. Set the bacon aside. Turn the heat down to low.

Add the butter to the bacon grease and throw in the onion and celery. Sauté until soft, about 10 minutes.

Add the juice from the canned clams and the seafood stock. Let them heat while you cut up the vegetables.

Peel the turnips and cut into ½-inch (1.3cm) dice. Put 'em in the pot.

Trim the very bottom of the stem and the leaves from your cauliflower. Chop into ½-inch (1.3cm) chunks. Throw them into the soup, too, along with the thyme and bay leaves. Let the whole thing simmer until the vegetables are tender, about 20 minutes.

Remove the bay leaves. Use your stick blender to partially puree the soup—you want about half the vegetables pureed, the other half still in tangible bits. If you prefer, you can scoop out half the vegetables with a slotted spoon, put them in your blender or food processor with just enough of the stock to cover, puree, and add them back to the pot. But that means more things to wash.

NEW ENGLAND CLAM CHOWDER *(continued)*

Turn the heat to the lowest setting. Stir in the cream. Thicken your chowder a bit with your guar or xanthan shaker if you feel needs it. Season with salt and pepper to taste.

Stir in the drained clams. Ladle out the soup and then top with the reserved bacon bits and the parsley.

CREAM OF CAULIFLOWER

¾ cup (120g) diced onion

¾ cup (90g) diced celery

3 tablespoons (42g) butter

1 quart (946ml) chicken broth

1 package (10 ounces, or 280g) of frozen cauliflower

2 teaspoons guar or xanthan (optional)

2 cups (475ml) heavy cream

Salt and pepper

YIELD: 4 servings – Per serving: 250 calories; 21g fat (74.6% calories from fat); 7g protein; 9g carbohydrate; 3g dietary fiber; 6g net carbohydrate.

You'll be surprised how much this tastes like cream of potato soup!

In a large saucepan over low heat, sauté the onion and celery in the butter until they're limp.

Add the chicken broth and cauliflower and simmer until the cauliflower is tender, about 20 minutes.

Using a slotted spoon, transfer the vegetables to a blender and then pour in broth to cover. Add the guar or xanthan if you're using it. Remove the little cap to let steam escape and cover the hole with a kitchen towel. Be careful—hot soup will expand in the blender and splatter. You may need to do this in batches. Puree everything in the blender until smooth.

Pour back into the saucepan. Stir in the cream and season with salt and pepper to taste.

SOPA DE COCO Y AGUACATE

3 cups (700ml) chicken broth

¼ of a large onion, diced

1 dried chipotle pepper

1 clove of garlic

1 can (13½ ounces, or 380ml) of unsweetened coconut milk

1 avocado

Salt

YIELD: 4 servings – Per serving: 305 calories; 29g fat (80.5% calories from fat); 7g protein; 9g carbohydrate; 2g dietary fiber; 7g net carbohydrate.

For some reason, that chipotle didn't make my soup hot at all; it was mellow and very flavorful. You could pass hot sauce for those who want it, but we liked it this way. Also, you could add a little minced cilantro as garnish, but really, this doesn't need a thing.

Put your chicken broth and onion in a large saucepan over medium heat. Use your kitchen shears to snip in the chipotle and then crush the garlic and add it, too. Bring to a simmer, and let it cook until the onion is soft, about 20 minutes.

Use your stick blender to puree the onions and chipotle into the chicken broth. (I had some visible bits of chipotle. Don't sweat it; it adds character.) Now, blend in the coconut milk. Let the whole thing come to a boil.

Whack your avocado in half, remove the pit, and use a spoon to scoop the flesh into the soup. Now, blend the whole thing up—I quit while there were still some small bits of avocado, again, for texture and character. Season with salt to taste.

Serve immediately. This soup will not keep, but it's awfully good.

3 cups (700ml) chicken broth

4 ounces (115g) cream cheese

1 teaspoon chicken bouillon concentrate

Guar or xanthan

4 ounces (115g) shredded cheddar cheese

Salt or Vege-Sal and pepper

YIELD: 3 servings – Per serving: 324 calories; 27g fat (75% calories from fat); 17g protein; 3g carbohydrate; 0g dietary fiber; 3g net carbohydrate.

CHEESY CHICKEN SOUP

This started out as a sauce for a ham casserole I was making, but I quickly found that it was quite good enough to serve all on its own. It's a great way to get some bone broth into your diet!

In a medium-size saucepan, combine the broth and cream cheese. Put it over medium heat and bring it to a simmer. Use a whisk to break up the cream cheese into little bits.

If you have a stick blender, switch over to it. If not, you'll just have to keep whisking. Immerse the blender and mix in the cream cheese until it's completely smooth. Blend in the bouillon concentrate.

Now, use your guar or xanthan shaker to thicken the soup to the texture of heavy cream. Keep blending and add the shredded cheese a few tablespoons (22g) at a time, making sure each addition is well blended in before adding more. Season with salt and pepper to taste and serve.

---

3 tablespoons (42g) butter

½ cup (60g) finely diced celery

½ cup (80g) minced shallot

2 quarts (1.9L) fish stock

1 cup (235ml) dry white wine

1 lemon

2 tablespoons (6g) minced fresh dill

1½ pounds (680g) salmon fillet, skinned

1 teaspoon paprika

1½ cups (355ml) heavy cream

Guar or xanthan

Salt and pepper

YIELD: 8 servings – Per serving: 423 calories; 30g fat (71.7% calories from fat); 19g protein; 7g carbohydrate; 1g dietary fiber; 6g net carbohydrate.

SALMON BISQUE

Ideally, this pale-pink soup is made with homemade fish stock (page 222), but you can use Kitchen Basics Seafood Stock instead, if you like.

In your stockpot over low heat and melt the butter and sauté the celery and shallot, without browning, for 5 minutes.

Add the fish stock and wine and turn the heat up to medium. Slice the lemon in half, remove any seeds, and then drop the halves into the pot. Stir in the dill.

When the stock is warmed, gently lower the salmon into the pot. When the stock reaches a simmer, turn the heat down to hold it there and cook for 20 to 25 minutes.

Now, you have a decision to make: do you want chunks of salmon in your finished soup, or do you want to puree the whole thing? If you want chunks, carefully fish (hah!) out some of your salmon with a slotted spoon and lay it on a plate. Don't worry if some pieces fall off and remain in the soup. You do want to puree at least half of the salmon. (My salmon fillet still had some grayish connective tissue where I'd pulled the skin off. Once simmered, this scraped off easily with a paring knife. It's not essential, just a cosmetic thing. If you want to remove this, be sure to scoop out all the salmon from the pot before pureeing and then add a portion back in.)

Add the heavy cream and use your stick blender to puree everything. You could transfer the soup to your blender instead, but you'd have to work in batches. Obviously, if you don't want chunks of salmon in your finished soup, just puree the whole thing—you don't even need to remove the salmon from the pot if you don't care about scraping off any connective tissue.

Use your guar or xanthan shaker to thicken the soup a little—not quite as thick as heavy cream. Season with salt and pepper to taste.

If you have reserved salmon, flake it coarsely and stir into the finished soup before serving.

1 quart (946ml) chicken broth

½ cup (50g) walnuts

½ cup (16g) parsley sprigs, plus more, chopped, for garnish

2 tablespoons (5g) chopped fresh sage

1 clove of garlic

¼ cup (60ml) olive oil

5 tablespoons (35g) grated Parmesan cheese, divided

12 ounces (340g) boneless, skinless chicken breast

2 teaspoons chicken bouillon concentrate

Salt and pepper

1 package (8 ounces, or 225g) of tofu shirataki, fettuccini

YIELD: 3 servings – Per serving: 525 calories; 38g fat (64.4% calories from fat); 41g protein; 6g carbohydrate; 1g dietary fiber; 5g net carbohydrate.

CHICKEN NOODLE SOUP WITH SAGE PESTO

See? You can have chicken noodle soup. Just put yummy pesto in it to increase the fat content. Well, that and use shirataki, of course.

Pour your broth into a big saucepan over high heat.

Spread your walnuts in a Pyrex pie plate and nuke 'em on high for 2 minutes.

While that's happening, combine the parsley sprigs, sage, garlic, olive oil, and 4 tablespoons (30g) of the Parmesan in your food processor with the S-blade in place. When the nuts are toasted, add them to the food processor and process until you have a paste.

Dice your chicken breast into ¼-inch (6mm) cubes—this is easier if it's partially frozen. Stir them into the broth, which should be getting hot by now. Stir in the bouillon concentrate, too, and season with salt and pepper to taste.

Drain your shirataki and rinse. Snip across them a couple of times with your kitchen shears and then add them to the soup.

When it's simmering and the chicken cubes are white through, serve. Add a couple of tablespoons (30g) of the pesto to each bowl and top with a third of the remaining 1 tablespoon (5g) of Parmesan and the remaining chopped parsley.

---

1 pound (455g) Italian sausage links, hot or not, as you prefer

1 medium onion

1 green bell pepper

1 celery rib

1 tablespoon (15ml) olive oil

½ tablespoon oregano

½ tablespoon Italian seasoning

3 cloves of garlic

2 quarts (1.9L) chicken broth

¾ cups (175ml) heavy cream

YIELD: 6 servings – Per serving: 624 calories; 57g fat (82.5% calories from fat); 19g protein; 8g carbohydrate; 1g dietary fiber; 7g net carbohydrate.

ITALIAN SAUSAGE SOUP

This homey, warming soup is bound to please the whole family, and the slow cooker makes it so easy! Keep in mind that many Italian sausages contain a little sugar. Read the labels to find the lowest carb sausage you can, and you'll probably drop the carb count lower than the nutritional analysis says.

Put your big, heavy skillet over medium heat and brown the sausage all over. Let it cool a little, so you can handle it.

While it's cooling, chop your onion, pepper, and celery.

Transfer your sausage to your cutting board, throw the veggies into the skillet along with the olive oil, and sauté for a few minutes.

Slice your sausage. Dump it in the slow cooker. Throw the sautéed vegetables in, too. Add the oregano and Italian seasoning and crush in the garlic.

Pour a cup or two (235 to 455ml) of the broth into the skillet and stir it around to deglaze. Add to the slow cooker along with the rest of the broth. Cover the slow cooker and cook for 5 or 6 hours.

At dinnertime, stir in the cream. Let it heat for another 10 to 15 minutes and serve.

1 small leek

¼ cup (55g) butter

½ of a head of cauliflower

1 quart (946ml) chicken broth

1 bay leaf

1 teaspoon fresh thyme leaves

3 cups (700ml) heavy cream

Guar or xanthan (optional)

Salt and pepper

YIELD: 12 servings – Per serving: 262 calories; 26g fat (88.5% calories from fat); 3g protein; 4g carbohydrate; 1g dietary fiber; 3g net carbohydrate.

VICHYSSOISE

This makes a lot; it's just that you need that leek, you see, and I didn't want to leave you with half a leek left over. So share or freeze this in serving-size containers. By the way, these are appetizer-size servings, about 1 cup (235ml) each.

Cut the green leaves and the roots off the white part of your leek. Split the white part down the middle and rinse between the layers—leeks can hold bits of grit. Mince the leek.

In a stockpot, melt the butter over medium-low heat. Sauté the leek until soft.

While the leek is softening, break or cut your cauliflower into small chunks.

When the leek is soft, add the cauliflower, chicken broth, bay leaf, and thyme. Turn up the heat, bring the broth to a boil, and then immediately turn down to a bare simmer. Let it cook until the cauliflower is soft, about 30 minutes, depending on how small your cauliflower bits are.

Let your soup cool. Remove the bay leaf. Use your stick blender to puree the cauliflower and leek. Blend in the cream.

Thicken a touch with guar or xanthan if you think it needs it. Season with salt and pepper to taste.

Traditional vichyssoise is served chilled, with a few chives snipped on top. But if you like it better hot, who am I to argue?

2 quarts (1.9L) chicken broth

¼ cup (30g) finely diced celery

¼ cup (38g) finely diced green bell pepper

¼ cup (28g) shredded carrot

¼ cup (16g) chopped fresh parsley

½ teaspoon pepper

1 pound (455g) sharp cheddar cheese, shredded

3 ounces (85g) cream cheese, cut into small chunks

12 ounces (355ml) light beer

½ teaspoon salt or VegeSal

¼ teaspoon Tabasco sauce

Guar or xanthan

YIELD: 8 servings – Per serving: 320 calories; 24g fat (69.7% calories from fat); 20g protein; 3g carbohydrate; trace dietary fiber; 3g net carbohydrate.

TAVERN SOUP

If you use Corona Light, your soup will be gluten free. I wouldn't worry about the alcohol unless you're especially sensitive—it's divided eight ways, and some of it will cook off, anyway.

Before you head out the door, combine the chicken broth, celery, green pepper, carrot, parsley, and pepper in your slow cooker. Cover, set to low, and let it slow cook 6 to 8 hours—and even a bit longer won't hurt.

When you get home, either use a stick blender to puree the vegetables right there in the slow cooker pot or scoop them out with a slotted spoon, puree them in your blender, and return them to the pot.

Now, whisk in the cheddar cheese and cream cheese, a little at a time, until they're all melted in. Add the beer, salt, and Tabasco sauce and stir until the foaming stops. Use your guar or xanthan shaker to thicken your soup until it's about the texture of heavy cream. Re-cover the pot, turn to high, and let it cook for another 20 minutes before serving.

1 leek

¼ cup (55g) butter

8 ounces (225g) sliced mushrooms

1 clove of garlic, crushed

2 teaspoons garam masala

1 teaspoon pepper

¼ teaspoon cayenne

¼ teaspoon ground nutmeg

1 quart (946ml) chicken broth

12 ounces (340g) boneless, skinless chicken breast, cut into thin strips

1 cup (235ml) heavy cream

3 tablespoons (3g) chopped fresh cilantro (optional)

YIELD: 6 servings – Per serving: 318 calories; 25g fat (70.2% calories from fat); 18g protein; 6g carbohydrate; 1g dietary fiber; 5g net carbohydrate.

SPICY CHICKEN AND MUSHROOM SOUP

Garam masala is a spice blend common in India and Pakistan, and it includes pepper, cloves, cinnamon, mace, and cardamom. If you can't find it locally, you can, like everything else, buy it online. Top-flight spice mail-order house Penzeys offers one at www.penzeys.com.

Thinly slice the white, crisp part of your leek, discarding the green top. Wash well to remove all the grit.

Melt the butter in your big, heavy skillet over medium heat and sauté the leek with the mushrooms until they both soften. Stir in the garlic, garam masala, pepper, cayenne, and nutmeg and sauté for another minute or two. Transfer to your slow cooker.

Pour in the chicken broth and add the cut-up chicken breast. Cover the pot, set to low, and let cook for 6 to 7 hours.

When time's up, use a slotted spoon to scoop roughly two-thirds of the solids into your blender or food processor. Add a cup (235ml) or so of the broth and puree until smooth. Stir back into the rest of the soup (you may want to rinse out the blender or food processor with a little broth, to get all of the puree). Alternatively, you could use your stick blender right in the pot, but take care to leave some chunks of meat and veggies for texture.

Stir in the cream. Re-cover the pot and let the whole thing cook for another 30 minutes. Serve with chopped fresh cilantro on top. Or not, if you prefer—it's nice without it, too!

4 tablespoons (55g) butter

½ of a medium onion, diced

1 pound (455g) frozen broccoli, thawed

3 cups (700ml) chicken broth

1½ cups (355ml) heavy cream

4 ounces (115g) crumbled blue cheese, divided

Guar or xanthan (optional)

Salt and pepper

YIELD: 4 servings – Per serving: 573 calories; 54g fat (82.7% calories from fat); 15g protein; 10g carbohydrate; 4g dietary fiber; 6g net carbohydrate.

BROCCOLI-BLUE CHEESE SOUP

Rich and flavorful, this soup can stand on its own. If the carbivores are insistent, you can give them toast to dip in it. But it's really unnecessary. Our recipe tester Rebecca rated this a 10 and commented, "So easy!" For the broccoli, I'd use "cut" broccoli; these are smaller than spears, but larger than chopped.

In a large saucepan over medium heat, melt the butter. Add the onion and sauté until it's just soft.

Add the broccoli and broth. Bring to a simmer, cover, and let it cook for 15 to 20 minutes until the broccoli is soft but not gray. Use your stick blender to blend the broccoli until it's smooth.

Stir in the cream and half of the blue cheese, mixing until the cheese is just melted.

Thicken a little with your guar or xanthan shaker if you feel it's needed. Season with salt and pepper to taste.

Stir in the rest of the blue cheese and serve before it melts.

1 pound (455g) asparagus

4 tablespoons (55g) butter

½ of a medium onion, diced

3 cups (700ml) chicken broth

1½ cups (355ml) heavy cream

4 ounces (115g) crumbled blue cheese, divided

Guar or xanthan (optional)

Salt and pepper

YIELD: 4 servings – Per serving: 557 calories; 54g fat (85.3% calories from fat); 13g protein; 8g carbohydrate; 1g dietary fiber; 7g net carbohydrate.

ASPARAGUS-BLUE CHEESE SOUP

See the Broccoli–Blue Cheese Soup recipe above? Our tester Christina asked if she could try it with asparagus instead. Who am I to object to such creativity? She rated this version a 10 and said even her asparagus-hating husband liked it.

Snap the ends off your asparagus where it wants to break naturally and then cut the rest into 1-inch (2.5cm) lengths.

In a large saucepan over medium heat, melt the butter. Add the onion and sauté until it's just soft.

Add the asparagus and broth. Bring to a simmer, cover, and let it cook for 8 to 10 minutes until the asparagus is soft but not gray. Use your stick blender to blend the asparagus until it's smooth.

Stir in the cream and half the blue cheese, mixing until the cheese is just melted.

Thicken a little with your guar or xanthan shaker if you feel it's needed. Season with salt and pepper to taste.

Stir in the rest of the blue cheese and serve before it melts.

2 avocados, good and ripe

1½ cups (345g) sour cream, divided

1 tablespoon (15ml) lime juice

1 quart (946ml) strong chicken broth

1 teaspoon salt

⅓ cup (5g) minced cilantro (optional)

YIELD: 6 servings – Per serving: 258 calories; 20g fat (70.1% calories from fat); 6g protein; 8g carbohydrate; 2g dietary fiber; 6g net carbohydrate.

SOPA DE AGUACATE Y LIMON VERDE

This pretty, pale-green soup can be served hot, but consider it cold for a sweltering summer evening. It's very rich; you could divide this eight ways as a starter if you wanted to. There's not much point to making this soup hot and then chilling it. Instead, start with cold avocados and sour cream and your broth just warm enough that it's liquid, not jellied. (If you're using boxed stock from the grocery store, go ahead and stick it in the refrigerator and use it cold.) Just combine everything but the sour cream for garnish and the cilantro, if using, in your food processor and run it. This assumes you have a good-size food processor, of course.

Halve your avocados, remove the pits, and scoop the flesh into your food processor with the S-blade in place. Add ¾ cup (173g) of the sour cream and the lime juice and process until smooth.

In a large saucepan, heat the chicken broth. Bring it just to simmering then turn the heat down to its lowest setting—you want to keep the broth just below a simmer.

Whisk the avocado mixture into the hot broth in 3 or 4 additions. Make sure it is thoroughly blended in. Add the salt and adjust to your taste if needed.

Ladle into bowls, scooping 2 tablespoons (30g) of the remaining sour cream into the center of each serving and sprinkling 1 tablespoon (1g) of cilantro over each if desired.

I'd pass a bottle of chipotle hot sauce with this, but then, I put chipotle hot sauce on almost anything.

3 tablespoons (45ml) olive oil

2 tablespoons (28g) butter

½ of a medium onion, chopped

2 pounds (910g) small zucchini

1 teaspoon dried oregano

1 quart (946ml) chicken broth

1 cup (235ml) heavy cream, divided

4 ounces (115g) crumbled Gorgonzola cheese, plus more for garnish (optional)

Salt and pepper

Guar or xanthan (optional)

YIELD: 6 servings – Per serving: 348 calories; 32g fat (80.7% calories from fat); 10g protein; 7g carbohydrate; 2g dietary fiber; 5g net carbohydrate.

ZUCCHINI-GORGONZOLA SOUP

Do use Gorgonzola in this soup, instead of one of the more assertive blue cheeses. It's a good blend with the subtle flavor of zucchini.

In a large pot over medium heat, warm the olive oil and butter together. When the butter is melted, add the onion and sauté for 5 minutes until just turning translucent.

While that's happening, slice your zucchini. When the onion's soft, add the zucchini to the pot, along with the oregano. Sauté for 10 minutes, stirring often.

Add the chicken broth and bring to a simmer. Let it cook for 20 to 30 minutes until the zucchini is quite soft.

Add ¾ cup (175ml) of the cream and the Gorgonzola. Use your stick blender to blend the soup smooth and bring back to a simmer. Season with salt and pepper to taste and thicken with your guar or xanthan shaker if you feel it needs it.

Serve 1 tablespoon (15ml) of the remaining cream swirled into each dish. Garnish with additional Gorgonzola, if you like.

CHAPTER 14

Sauces, Condiments, and Seasonings

When you go on vacation, do you buy a T-shirt? Maybe a coffee mug? Not me. I buy condiments, hot sauces, and seasoning blends. I can never have too many! What easier way is there to vary the simple proteins we eat—the pork steaks, rib eyes, chicken, burgers? Just add a different sauce or sprinkle on a different seasoning blend and voilà! You have new and interesting food.

Also, sauces let us up the fat content of various dishes, bringing them closer to our desired macros. Keep in mind, it wasn't so long ago that spooning a good, rich béarnaise over a porterhouse steak was just good, classical cuisine. Let's make it so again.

2 egg yolks

1½ teaspoons lemon juice

1½ teaspoons wine vinegar
(or another 1½ teaspoons
lemon juice)

½ teaspoon dry mustard

2 dashes of hot sauce, such as
Tabasco, Frank's, or Louisiana

¼ teaspoon of salt

1 to 2 drops of liquid stevia,
plain

1 cup (235ml) MCT oil

YIELD: 1 cup (225g),
8 servings – Per 2 tablespoon
(28g) serving: 257 calories;
29g fat (98.5% calories from fat);
1g protein; trace carbohydrate;
trace dietary fiber; negligible net
carbohydrate.

2 eggs

3 egg yolks

1 tablespoon (15ml) red wine
vinegar

1 tablespoon (15ml) lemon
juice

1 teaspoon dry mustard or
2 to 3 teaspoons (10 to 15g)
Dijon or spicy brown mustard

½ teaspoon salt

2 dashes of hot sauce
(I use Frank's)

1 teaspoon water

3 cups (700ml) MCT oil

YIELD: 1 quart (946ml),
32 servings – Per serving:
191 calories; 21g fat (98.4%
calories from fat); 1g protein;
trace carbohydrate; trace dietary
fiber; negligible net carbohydrate.

MAYONNAISE IN A JAR

I'm putting this first because I devoutly hope you will, indeed, start making your own mayonnaise, especially if you use it often. Because of the MCT oil, this is highly ketogenic—and way healthier than the grocery store stuff loaded with soybean oil. It's a snap to make, too. It's far faster than running to the grocery store.

First, find a jar the mouth of which will fit your stick blender, such as an old salsa jar. Have your MCT oil measured and standing by in a measuring cup with a pouring lip.

Put everything but the oil in the jar. Now, take your stick blender and insert it all the way down to the bottom of the jar. Turn it on and give it a few seconds to blend the egg yolks with the seasonings.

Keep the blender running. Now, slowly start pouring in the oil; you want a stream about the diameter of a pencil lead. Work the blender up and down in the jar as you go.

When you can't get any more oil to incorporate, and it's puddling on the surface, stop! You're done. Any leftover oil can go back in the bottle. Cap your jar of mayo and stash it in the fridge.

MAYONNAISE BY THE QUART

I can use a lot of mayonnaise, especially in warm weather. This has become my go-to mayonnaise recipe—it fills a standard 1-quart (946ml) mayonnaise jar. You'll need a big food processor—mine holds 14 cups (3.3L). Why not make it in the jar, as I do with lesser quantities? Because my stick blender won't fit.

With the S-blade in place in your food processor, add the eggs, egg yolks, red wine vinegar, lemon juice, mustard, salt, and hot sauce. Turn the processor on. While it's running, add the water.

Pour the MCT oil into a glass measuring cup with a pouring lip. With the processor running, add the oil in a thin stream, about the diameter of a pencil lead. When it's all worked in, you're done! Transfer to a tightly lidded jar and stash in the fridge.

Theoretically, the shelf life of this is about a week in the fridge, but I've used mine after 10 to 12 days with no ill effects. Your risks are your own to take.

NOTE: Are you afraid of raw eggs? See the directions on page 21 for pasteurizing them.

1 egg
1 egg yolk
2 tablespoons (28ml) lemon juice
2 cloves of garlic, crushed
¼ teaspoon salt
1 cup (235ml) MCT oil
½ cup (120ml) olive oil

YIELD: 1 pint (475ml), **16 servings** – Per serving: 189 calories; 21g fat (98.2% calories from fat); 1g protein; trace carbohydrate; trace dietary fiber; negligible net carbohydrate.

½ cup (115g) mayonnaise
2 teaspoons soy sauce
3 drops of liquid stevia, plain
1 teaspoon lemon juice
1 teaspoon wasabi paste

YIELD: ½ cup (120ml), **8 servings** – Per serving: 100 calories; 12g fat (98.3% calories from fat); trace protein; trace carbohydrate; trace dietary fiber; negligible net carbohydrate.

1 cup (235g) mayonnaise
1 chipotle chile canned in adobo
½ teaspoon ground cumin
1 clove of garlic

YIELD: 1 cup (235ml), **16 servings** – Per serving: 99 calories; 12g fat (98.7% calories from fat); trace protein; trace carbohydrate; trace dietary fiber; negligible net carbohydrate.

½ cup (115g) mayonnaise
1 tablespoon (15ml) sriracha
2 teaspoons lime juice
½ teaspoon soy sauce
½ of a clove of garlic, crushed

YIELD: ½ cup (120ml), **4 servings** – Per serving: 199 calories; 23g fat (98.4% calories from fat); trace protein; trace carbohydrate; trace dietary fiber; negligible net carbohydrate.

AIOLI

This is also known as "garlicky mayonnaise." It's great with everything.

With the S-blade in place in your food processor, add the egg, egg yolk, lemon juice, garlic, and salt. Run the processor to combine.

With the processor running, add the oils slowly, in a stream about the diameter of a pencil lead. When it's all worked in, you're done! Scrape it into an old 1-quart (946ml) mayonnaise jar—surely a friend will save one for you!—and stash it in the refrigerator.

NOTE: Do those raw eggs scare you? Find the instructions for pasteurizing eggs on page 21.

WASABI MAYONNAISE

I first used this on steamed asparagus, but how about shrimp? Or little-bitty bay scallops on toothpicks?

Just combine everything in a bowl and whisk together well. It's unbelievably good.

CHIPOTLE MAYONNAISE

You can use this as a dip for veggies or pork rinds, sure. But it's also great as a dressing for chicken salad or as a sauce for chicken, fish, or steak.

Throw everything in the food processor and run until the chipotle and the garlic are pulverized.

SRIRACHA MAYONNAISE

This is great for dipping shrimp or bites of grilled chicken. Or how about tossed with shredded Napa cabbage for a fresh twist on slaw?

Throw everything in the food processor and run until the garlic is pulverized.

¾ teaspoon fenugreek seed

½ teaspoon cumin seed

1 cup (225g) mayonnaise

¼ cup (28g) sun-dried tomatoes in olive oil

¼ teaspoon pepper

Salt to taste

YIELD: 8 servings – Per serving: 206 calories; 24g fat (97.0% calories from fat); 1g protein; 1g carbohydrate; trace dietary fiber; 1g net carbohydrate.

2 egg yolks

1 tablespoon (15ml) white balsamic vinegar

1 tablespoon (15ml) lemon juice

½ of a clove of garlic, chopped

¼ cup (60ml) extra-virgin olive oil

⅔ cup (160ml) MCT oil

YIELD: ¾ cup (175ml), 6 servings – Per serving: 315 calories; 35g fat (98.1% calories from fat); 1g protein; 1g carbohydrate; trace dietary fiber; 1g net carbohydrate.

1 cup (240ml) mayonnaise

1 sugar-free bread-and-butter pickle spear, plus 1 teaspoon pickle juice

1 teaspoon Dijon or spicy brown mustard

1 tablespoon diced red onion

2 tablespoons (28ml) lemon juice

Salt and pepper to taste

YIELD: 1 ¼ CUP (300ML) 6 servings – Per serving: 266 calories; 31g fat (98.1% calories from fat); 1g protein; 1g carbohydrate; trace dietary fiber; 1g net carbohydrate.

SUN-DRIED TOMATO MAYONNAISE

This calls for toasting and grinding your spices, whether with a mortar and pestle or a spice grinder (or, for that matter, a coffee grinder dedicated to the purpose). It makes for fresh, full flavor!

In a dry skillet over medium-low heat, stir the fenugreek and cumin seeds for 4 to 5 minutes until fragrant. Transfer them to a spice grinder or mortar and grind them fine.

Put them in your food processor with everything else and run until the tomatoes are pulverized.

LEMON-BALSAMIC MAYONNAISE

This could have gone with the salad dressings, but I'm more inclined to use it as a dip for steamed vegetables, like broccoli or asparagus. It would be good with fish or seafood, too.

Put the egg yolks, white balsamic vinegar, lemon juice, and chopped garlic in the bottom of a clean glass jar with a wide enough mouth to fit your stick blender—those short, wide salsa jars are perfect. Have both oils measured and standing by. Add the extra-virgin olive oil. Submerge your stick blender, turn it on, and blend until it's incorporated. Now, keeping the stick blender on, slowly drizzle in the MCT oil until the mixture is thickened and the oil starts puddling on the surface. Done! Use right away or cap the jar and stash in the fridge for up to a week or so. (Okay, I've been known to keep mine a little longer, but I'm a daredevil—and get my eggs from my own backyard.)

TARTAR SAUCE

A great way to add fat to lean fish dishes! I've made this with sugar-free bread-and-butter pickles instead of relish because the pickles are easy to find, while sugar-free relish can be more elusive.

Just stir everything together. It's nice to make this first and refrigerate it for a while to let the flavors blend.

½ of a shallot

2 tablespoons (17g) capers, drained

1 tablespoon (4g) chopped parsley

1 tablespoon (4g) chopped fresh tarragon

1 tablespoon (9g) chopped dill pickle

2 anchovy fillets

1 teaspoon lemon juice

1 cup (225g) mayonnaise

YIELD: 8 servings – Per serving: 201 calories; 23g fat (98.3% calories from fat); 1g protein; trace carbohydrate; trace dietary fiber; negligible net carbohydrate.

REMOULADE

A classic of French cuisine, remoulade has become a world traveler. Most commonly, it is used on fish, but depending on the region, it is also served with beef, French fries, celery root, and even hot dogs! Surely, you can find a use. FYI, our tester, Amanda, who rates this a 10, suggested that if your shallot is especially large, you go with one-fourth instead of half.

Put the shallot, capers, parsley, tarragon, pickle, and anchovies in your food processor and pulse until it's all quite finely chopped.

Add the lemon juice and mayonnaise and run just long enough to blend.

Refrigerate for an hour or two before serving to let the flavors marry.

---

1 scallion

2 cloves of garlic, ends trimmed

2 tablespoons (15g) diced celery

1 tablespoon (9g) capers, drained

1 tablespoon (4g) chopped parsley

1 cup (225g) mayonnaise

1 tablespoon (15g) Dijon mustard

1 tablespoon (15g) horseradish mustard

1 tablespoon (15ml) hot sauce (Tabasco, Louisiana, or Frank's)

1 teaspoon Worcestershire sauce

1 teaspoon paprika, plus more for garnish

¼ teaspoon salt

⅛ teaspoon cayenne

YIELD: 1¼ cups (300ml), 10 servings – Per serving: 163 calories; 19g fat (96.8% calories from fat); 1g protein; 1g carbohydrate; trace dietary fiber; 1g net carbohydrate.

LOUISIANA REMOULADE

You know how it is—Louisiana has put its own spin on all things French. This is classically served with cold boiled shrimp, but if you can get crayfish—aka mudbugs—go for it. This will lend them the fat they lack. Our tester raves, "I served this to company with boiled shrimp… they all loved it and started talking about other uses for this sauce: topping a mushroom/crabmeat crepe, serving with beef because the horseradish stands out, or as a topping for omelets."

Trim the root and any limp green off the scallion and cut it into 1-inch (2.5cm) lengths. With the S-blade in place in your food processor, add the scallion, garlic, celery, capers, and parsley. Pulse until minced.

Add everything else and pulse until mixed. Or, if you prefer, dump the minced stuff into a bowl, add the rest, and stir. Either way, it should wind up in a covered bowl in the refrigerator for an hour or more for the flavors to blend. Sprinkle a little more paprika on top before serving to make it look snazzy.

LEMON-ANCHOVY SAUCE

2 egg yolks

3 tablespoons (45g) brown mustard

2 ounces (55g) canned anchovies in olive oil

Zest and juice of 1 lemon

1 shallot

1 clove of garlic

1 cup (235ml) olive oil

1 tablespoon (9g) capers, drained

Salt and pepper

YIELD: 1½ cups (350ml), 24 servings — Per serving: 92 calories; 10g fat (93% calories from fat); 1g protein; 1g carbohydrate; trace dietary fiber; 1g net carbohydrate.

I found this in a thirty-year-old *Bon Appétit* cookbook. It didn't need a lot of tweaking to be keto, just better oil. Oh, and I added garlic. It's basically a riff on mayonnaise. Our tester Rebecca liked this so much, she developed two recipes using it all on her own!

Put your egg yolks, mustard, anchovies (including the oil, so make sure they're canned in olive oil), lemon zest and juice, shallot, and garlic in your food processor. Run until the shallot and garlic are pulverized. In the meanwhile, measure your olive oil into a measuring cup with a pouring lip.

Now, with the processor running, very slowly pour in the oil. You want a stream about the diameter of a pencil lead. When the sauce is thickened up like mayonnaise and the oil starts to puddle on the surface, quit, even if it's not all in—you can pour the oil back into the bottle. Turn off the processor.

Add the capers and pulse just to mix them in—you don't want to chop them too much. Season with salt and pepper to taste.

Scrape into a serving dish, cover, and refrigerate for at least a few hours and of course, keep refrigerated until serving.

BÉARNAISE SAUCE

¼ cup (60ml) dry white wine

¼ cup (60ml) tarragon vinegar

1 tablespoon (4g) minced fresh tarragon

1 tablespoon (10g) minced shallot

2 egg yolks

½ cup (115g) butter

YIELD: 4 servings — Per serving: 247 calories; 26g fat (94.5% calories from fat); 2g protein; 2g carbohydrate; 0g dietary fiber; 2g net carbohydrate.

This is a riff on hollandaise—a classic, especially over steak.

In a small saucepan over low heat, reduce the wine to about a tablespoon (15ml). Put it in the top of a double boiler, along with the tarragon vinegar (find this in your grocery store with all the other vinegars), fresh tarragon, minced shallot, and egg yolks. Have your butter measured—I think it's easier if you melt it.

Okay, it's show time: Put the double boiler over simmering water. Turn on your stick blender, immerse it in the egg yolks and seasonings, and blend 'em up.

Keep blending! Start adding the butter about 1½ tablespoons (21g) at a time, blending the whole time. Keep blending for about 30 seconds between each addition of butter. Your sauce should start thickening and fluffing up. Keep blending!

When all the butter is in, keep blending for another minute or two, making sure your sauce is good and thick before you turn off the stick blender and take the pan off the heat. If it's not finished cooking, your sauce will fall apart.

Once it's done, it will be lovely over steak, and any leftovers will keep for a day or two in a snap-top container in the fridge.

2 tablespoons (20g) minced shallot

1 tablespoon (15ml) dry white wine

3 tablespoons (45ml) lemon juice

Scant ⅛ teaspoon orange extract

8 drops of liquid stevia, lemon drop

1 teaspoon chipotle chile canned in adobo, minced

4 egg yolks, at room temperature

½ cup (112g) butter

Salt

YIELD: ¾ cup (175ml), 6 servings – Per serving: 181 calories; 19g fat (92.1% calories from fat); 2g protein; 1g carbohydrate; trace dietary fiber; 1g net carbohydrate.

ORANGE CHIPOTLE HOLLANDAISE

Yowza! Want something new to dip asparagus in? Or shrimp? Or chicken? How awesome is this?!

In a small saucepan, combine the shallot, wine, and lemon juice and simmer until it's all reduced by half. Let cool. Stir in the orange extract and liquid stevia.

Transfer the mixture to your blender. Add the chipotle and the egg yolks—make sure they're at room temperature!

In a 2-cup (475ml) Pyrex measure, in the microwave, melt the butter and then heat until it's bubbling hot.

While the butter is heating, turn on the blender. When the butter is bubbling hot, keep the blender running and slowly pour the butter in. When all the butter's worked in, season with salt, and you're done.

---

500 KETOGENIC RECIPES

15 ounces (420ml) tomato sauce

½ cup (120ml) cider vinegar

3 tablespoons (45g) Virtue sweetener

1 teaspoon salt

½ teaspoon onion powder

¼ teaspoon garlic powder

YIELD: 2½ cups (570ml), 24 servings – Per serving: 6 calories; trace fat (3.5% calories from fat); trace protein; 2g carbohydrate; trace dietary fiber; 2g net carbohydrate.

EASY NO-SUGAR-ADDED KETCHUP

Heinz no-sugar-added ketchup is quite good and even easier than making your own. But it's pricier and includes artificial sweeteners some people avoid. This is a cinch, tastes great—a lot like Heinz, actually—and has no artificial sweeteners.

Simply combine everything in a nonreactive saucepan—stainless steel, ceramic nonstick, or enamelware—and bring to a simmer. Let it cook for 15 minutes, cool, and it's done. I used a funnel to pour mine into an old squeeze-type ketchup bottle for ease of use, but a jar or snap-top container will do just fine.

½ ounce (15g) dried porcini mushrooms

½ cup (120ml) boiling water

2 tablespoons (28g) butter

2 tablespoons (28ml) extra-virgin olive oil

½ of a medium onion, diced

4 ounces (115g) portobello mushrooms, sliced

4 ounces (115g) button mushrooms, sliced

5 cloves of garlic, crushed

2 teaspoons minced fresh rosemary

2 tablespoons (8g) minced parsley

¼ cup (60ml) dry red wine

¼ cup (60ml) heavy cream

½ teaspoon salt

¼ teaspoon pepper

YIELD: 2 cups (475ml), 8 servings – Per serving: 104 calories; 9g fat (78.9% calories from fat); 1g protein; 4g carbohydrate; 1g dietary fiber; 3g net carbohydrate.

PORCINI, PORTOBELLO, AND BUTTON MUSHROOMS IN CREAM

This is extraordinarily, intensely flavorful. Don't skip the porcinis—they're what really make the dish. Serve this with a steak, use it to fill an omelet, even toss it with shirataki noodles. It's amazing. I originally planned on this being a side dish, but quickly realized it was one of the most versatile seasonings I'd ever created. You'll find many uses for it throughout this book. I make it in double batches and freeze it in small containers to call upon when needed.

First, put your porcini in a dish and pour the boiling water over them. Let them sit for 10 minutes or so.

In the meanwhile, put your large, heavy skillet over medium-low heat and add the butter and olive oil, swirling them together as the butter melts. Add the diced onion, then the portobello and button mushrooms. I'm assuming you bought them sliced—I did. Use the edge of your spatula to break them up a bit more as they sauté.

Use a fork to lift the soaked porcini out of their water—reserve the water—chop them medium-coarse and add them to the other mushrooms.

As the fresh mushrooms start to soften, add the garlic, rosemary, and parsley. Keep sautéing, stirring often, until the mushrooms are dark and soft.

Now, add the wine and the soaking water from the porcini. Stir everything up, turn up the heat to medium, and let the mixture boil until most of the liquid has boiled away. Then, turn the heat back down.

Stir in the heavy cream, salt, and pepper. Let the whole thing cook for another minute or two. Done!

½ cup (115g) sour cream

2 teaspoons prepared horseradish

1 tablespoon (4g) minced fresh dill

Salt and pepper

YIELD: 2 servings – Per serving: 126 calories; 12g fat (84.7% calories from fat); 2g protein; 3g carbohydrate; trace dietary fiber; 3g net carbohydrate.

SOUR CREAM AND DILL SAUCE

Not only will this liven up any simple fish, but it also adds useful fats. It's especially nice on salmon. Indeed, our tester, Julie, served it on salmon and said it pleased both her—a low carber—and her picky salmon-loving fourteen-year-old, Katie.

Stir everything together. That's it!

15 ounces (420ml) tomato sauce

¼ cup (60ml) vinegar

3 tablespoons (36g) erythritol

¼ teaspoon liquid stevia, English toffee

2 teaspoons molasses

¼ teaspoon onion powder

¼ teaspoon paprika

¼ teaspoon granulated garlic

½ teaspoon chili powder

1½ teaspoons liquid smoke

¼ teaspoon cayenne

⅛ teaspoon celery seed

YIELD: 2 cups (475ml), 16 servings – Per serving: 12 calories; trace fat (5.1% calories from fat); trace protein; 3g carbohydrate; trace dietary fiber; 3g net carbohydrate.

¼ cup (60g) sour cream

2 teaspoons prepared horseradish

½ teaspoon Dijon mustard

Salt

YIELD: 4 servings – Per serving: 32 calories; 3g fat (82.6% calories from fat); 1g protein; 1g carbohydrate; trace dietary fiber; 1g net carbohydrate.

2 tablespoons (30g) sour cream

2 tablespoons (28g) mayonnaise

2 teaspoons horseradish mustard

1½ teaspoons Creole seasoning

YIELD: 2 servings – Per serving: 141 calories; 15g fat (90.1% calories from fat); 1g protein; 3g carbohydrate; 1g dietary fiber; 2g net carbohydrate.

BARBECUE SAUCE

If you prefer, you can skip the molasses and knock 1 gram of carb off of each serving. It does lend a nice brown sugar flavor to your sauce, but it's fine without it.

This couldn't be easier: combine everything in a nonreactive saucepan—stainless steel, ceramic nonstick, or enamelware. Bring to a simmer, turn the heat to low, and let it cook for 10 minutes. Done. Use like any barbecue sauce.

HORSERADISH CREAM

It's hard to get bored of really good steaks, perfectly cooked. But should you have that moment of ennui, this is a great way to spark new interest.

Just stir everything together and spoon a dollop over each serving of steak.

CREAMY HORSERADISH-MUSTARD SAUCE

You'll notice a certain similarity to the previous recipe, but the Creole seasoning gives it an extra kick. I created this to go with the Crunchy Deviled Chicken (page 138), but you'll find plenty of uses—how about over a burger? Or as a dip with pork rinds? It's a snap to mix up, too.

Just measure everything and stir it together!

2 cloves of garlic

½ cup (112g) butter, at room temperature

2 tablespoons (28ml) sriracha

YIELD: 10 tablespoons (140g), 8 servings – Per serving: 103 calories; 12g fat (98.1% calories from fat); trace protein; trace carbohydrate; trace dietary fiber; negligible net carbohydrate.

SRIRACHA BUTTER

Want to kick steak up a notch, both in flavor and in fat content? This easy compound butter packs quite a punch. It's great with seafood, too.

I did this in my small food processor, but if you only have a full-size processor it may be easier to do it by hand. I put the garlic in the little processor and pulsed until it was chopped fine, but you can just crush it into a mixing bowl, if you like.

Add the butter and the sriracha and either run the processor—scraping down the sides a few times—until it's all well blended or work it with a fork or spoon until you achieve the same.

Lay a 12-inch (30cm) piece of wax paper on the counter and spoon/scrape your butter onto it, making a pile about the length and height of a stick of butter, although less rectangular, obviously. Wrap the wax paper around it and working through the paper, use your fingers to form the butter into a roll. Chill.

Now, you can simply unwrap and slice as you need it to melt over hot steak or hot chicken, or anything else, for that matter.

½ cup (112g) butter, at room temperature

2 tablespoons (30g) sun-dried tomato pesto

1½ tablespoons (23g) prepared horseradish

YIELD: ½ cup (120g), 8 servings – Per serving: 119 calories; 13g fat (92.5% calories from fat); 1g protein; 2g carbohydrate; trace dietary fiber; 2g net carbohydrate.

SUN-DRIED TOMATO AND HORSERADISH STEAK BUTTER

So, I had sun-dried tomato pesto in the fridge, and I wanted a new compound butter to embellish a steak. This is what happened! Although I put this on a nice, rich rib eye, steak butters are particularly useful for adding a hit of healthy fat to leaner cuts, like sirloin or flank.

Run everything through your food processor—I used my little one—until well blended.

Lay a 12-inch (30cm) piece of wax paper on your counter. Spoon/scrape the butter mixture into the center, forming it into a log roughly the dimensions of a stick of butter. Roll it up in the paper and refrigerate until you have a freshly grilled or broiled steak to embellish!

6 tablespoons (85g) butter, softened

3 tablespoons (25g) crumbled blue cheese

1½ tablespoons (23g) pesto

YIELD: ½ cup (120g), 6 servings – Per serving: 136 calories; 14g fat (94.2% calories from fat); 2g protein; trace carbohydrate; trace dietary fiber; negligible net carbohydrate.

BLUE CHEESE PESTO BUTTER

How simple is this? Not only is it good on steak, but it's also wonderful melted over shirataki or Zoodles (page 111) as a sauce.

This is so easy! Just run everything through your food processor. Put a dollop on each serving of hot steak.

2 shallots

2 tablespoons (30g) Dijon or brown mustard

1 teaspoon lemon juice

¼ teaspoon salt (optional)

½ cup (112g) butter, at room temperature

YIELD: ½ cup (120g), **4 servings** – Per serving: 214 calories; 24g fat (95.6% calories from fat); 1g protein; 1g carbohydrate; trace dietary fiber; 1g net carbohydrate.

MUSTARD SHALLOT BUTTER

In *Kitchen Confidential*, chef Anthony Bourdain has a section on why restaurant food tastes better than what you make at home. One of his answers is butter—restaurants use real butter and a whole lot more of it than most home cooks do. Another is shallots, which restaurants use frequently, while home cooks are largely using the more familiar onions and garlic. Here's a great way to use them both.

Put the shallots in your food processor with the S-blade in place and run until they're finely chopped. Add everything else, with or without the salt, and run until it's all well mixed. The classical way to serve something like this is to chill it in a roll and then slice it. But who's got that kind of time? Just scoop it into a little dish and let everyone spoon a dollop or two over their steak.

10 tablespoons (140g) butter, at room temperature

¼ cup (40g) minced shallot (about 1)

2 anchovy fillets

1 tablespoon (4g) minced parsley

YIELD: 10 servings – Per serving: 106 calories; 12g fat (95.7% calories from fat); trace protein; 1g carbohydrate; trace dietary fiber; 1g net carbohydrate.

ANCHOVY SHALLOT BUTTER

It was a great day for me when I realized that disliking anchovies all by themselves didn't mean I wouldn't love them as a seasoning. They're a great source of umami. You just have to control the intensity.

In a medium-size skillet over medium-low heat, melt 2 tablespoons (28g) of the butter and sauté the shallot until it's soft and golden.

Transfer the shallot and melted butter to the food processor and add the remaining 8 tablespoons (112g) of butter and the anchovy fillets. Process until the anchovies disappear. Add the parsley and pulse until it's mixed in.

If you want to be classical about this, turn the mixture out onto a piece of plastic wrap and form into a roll 1½ inches (4cm) in diameter. Wrap it up and chill. Then slice nice, pretty round pats to melt over steaks.

If that sounds like too much trouble, just keep it in a snap-top container and scoop it out by the spoonful. It's going to melt anyway, you know.

¼ cup (60ml) dry white wine

½ of a shallot, minced (about 2 teaspoons)

3 tablespoons (42g) butter

YIELD: 2 servings – Per serving: 174 calories; 17g fat (97.7% calories from fat); trace protein; 1g carbohydrate; 0g dietary fiber; 1g net carbohydrate.

WHITE BUTTER SAUCE

A riff on beurre blanc, a traditional French sauce, this is rich and delicious and will make any simple white fish very special. I served it to my husband over cod, and he licked the plate.

In a small, nonreactive saucepan over medium-low heat, combine the wine and shallot. Bring to a simmer and cook until the wine is reduced to about 1 tablespoon (15ml).

In the meanwhile, cut your butter into 1-tablespoon (14g) pats, and then quarter each of those.

When your wine is reduced, grab your stick blender. Start blending your wine mixture as you add one little lump of butter at a time, letting it melt completely before you add another. Your sauce should thicken and emulsify a bit, becoming creamy. When all the butter is in, it's done!

Serve over fish or scallops. A little parsley on top would make it look particularly spiffy, but it's not necessary if your focus is on taste.

½ cup (100g) whipped cream cheese

½ cup (115g) mayonnaise

2 tablespoons (28ml) dill pickle juice

1 cup (143g) finely diced dill pickle

2 shallots, minced

2 small cloves of garlic, crushed

½ teaspoon Old Bay Seasoning

½ teaspoon pepper

YIELD: 6 servings – Per serving: 188 calories; 20g fat (91.7% calories from fat); 1g protein; 3g carbohydrate; trace dietary fiber; 3g net carbohydrate.

DILL PICKLE SAUCE

This sauce is great with fish in myriad forms. I first used it on baked catfish for my husband, but quickly realized it would be just as good with salmon. It also makes a great dressing for tuna salad.

In a small mixing bowl, thoroughly combine the cream cheese, mayonnaise, and pickle juice. Stir in the chopped dill pickle, minced shallot, crushed garlic, Old Bay, and pepper, blending well.

10 ounces (280g) frozen raspberries, no sugar added

1 tablespoon (15ml) water

4 teaspoons (20g) Virtue sweetener or Natural Mate

1 teaspoon pectin (Use Sure-Jell in the pink box for low-sugar recipes.)

YIELD: 1 cup (235ml), 16 servings – Per serving: 19 calories; trace fat (1.3% calories from fat); trace protein; 5g carbohydrate; 1g dietary fiber; 4g net carbohydrate.

⅓ cup (80ml) lime juice

⅓ cup (80ml) MCT oil

3 cloves of garlic, minced

2 tablespoons (28ml) rice vinegar

2 tablespoons (28ml) fish sauce

2 tablespoons (28ml) soy sauce

¼ teaspoon liquid stevia, plain

YIELD: 1 cup (235ml), 4 servings – Per serving: 185 calories; 19g fat (85.8% calories from fat); 2g protein; 5g carbohydrate; trace dietary fiber; 5g net carbohydrate.

¼ cup (60ml) MCT oil

4 cloves of garlic, crushed

⅔ cup (160ml) soy sauce

⅓ teaspoon liquid stevia, plain (Fill your ¼ teaspoon and then half-fill it again.)

¼ cup (60ml) distilled vinegar

¼ cup (60g) tahini

4 teaspoons (20g) chili garlic sauce

YIELD: 1½ cups (355ml), 12 servings – Per servings: 81 calories; 7g fat (76.7% calories from fat); 2g protein; 3g carbohydrate; 1g dietary fiber; 2g net carbohydrate.

RASPBERRY PRESERVES

Sadly, I could not find no-sugar-added raspberry preserves at my local grocery stores. They had strawberry, blackberry, grape, even orange marmalade, but no raspberry—and raspberries are one of the lowest sugar fruits! Luckily, this is a snap to make.

Put the raspberries and water in a nonreactive saucepan—I used stainless steel. Bring to a simmer and mash the berries up with a fork. Stir in the sweetener and pectin and let it simmer for another 5 minutes. Done! Cool and store in the fridge in a clean old jam jar.

SWEET LIME AND GARLIC SAUCE

This Asian-influenced sauce is great with chicken or shrimp. It's even better if you add minced basil, cilantro, and mint!

It's just like making salad dressing: Put everything in a clean jar, lid it tightly, and shake hard. Store in the fridge.

HOISIN SAUCE

This super-popular Chinese condiment sparks all sorts of dishes! Sadly, authentic hoisin contains sugar, but that needn't concern us. Try this as a dip for chicken wings or brushed on pork steaks.

Put a nonreactive saucepan—stainless steel, enamelware, or ceramic nonstick—over medium-low heat, heat the MCT oil, and add the garlic. Sauté until lightly golden, about 3 to 5 minutes. Add everything else and stir, working in the tahini. Cook, stirring often, for about 5 minutes. Store in a tightly lidded jar in the refrigerator.

⅓ cup (33g) grated Parmesan cheese

⅓ cup (30g) cheddar cheese powder

¼ cup (15g) nutritional yeast flakes

4 teaspoons (20g) salt

2 teaspoons onion powder

2 teaspoons hot paprika

1 teaspoon garlic powder

½ teaspoon cayenne

YIELD: 1⅛ cups (110g), **18 serving** – Per serving: 40 calories; 2g fat (40.6% calories from fat); 4g protein; 3g carbohydrate; 1g dietary fiber; 2g net carbohydrate.

NACHO CHEESE POWDER

I created this so I could make Nacho Cheese Pork Rinds (page 30), a purpose it serves admirably. But it's also great for making Nacho Mac and Cheese (page 125), or nacho cheese sauce for pouring over shirataki or vegetables.

Simply assemble everything in your food processor with the S-blade in place and run until you have a fine, even powder. Store in a snap-top container in the fridge.

¾ cup (175ml) unsweetened canned coconut milk

3 tablespoons (45ml) lemon juice

2 tablespoons (8g) nutritional yeast flakes

1 clove of garlic

½ teaspoon salt

½ teaspoon ground turmeric

¼ teaspoon dry mustard

¼ teaspoon pepper

¼ teaspoon guar or xanthan, or to taste

⅛ teaspoon ground nutmeg

1 tablespoon (15ml) melted coconut oil

YIELD: 1 cup (235ml), **4 servings** – Per serving: 128 calories; 12g fat (74.3% calories from fat); 4g protein; 5g carbohydrate; 2g dietary fiber; 3g net carbohydrate.

VEGAN ALMOST BUT NOT QUITE ENTIRELY UNLIKE CHEESE SAUCE

Why was I trying to make vegan cheese sauce? Because I realized this book was getting pretty dairy heavy, and I know some keto folks avoid it. So, I adapted a recipe I found online, which called for things like arrowroot starch, and came up with this. As the title says, it is almost, but not quite, entirely unlike cheese sauce (shout-out to Douglas Adams fans), but is very tasty in its own right, especially over broccoli.

Put everything but the coconut oil in your blender and run it until you have a uniform sauce—you'll want to scrape down the sides once or twice.

Pour into a saucepan over medium-low heat. Bring to a simmer. Whisk in the coconut oil and let the whole thing simmer for 5 minutes or so.

2 tablespoons (28g) butter

2 cloves of garlic, crushed

¾ cup (175ml) heavy cream

¾ cup (175ml) half-and-half

1 ounce (28g) cream cheese

1 cup (100g) grated Parmesan cheese

2 tablespoons (8g) minced parsley

YIELD: 2½ cups (570ml), 5 servings – Per serving: 306 calories; 29g fat (83.5% calories from fat); 9g protein; 4g carbohydrate; trace dietary fiber; 4g net carbohydrate.

ALFREDO SAUCE

Rich and creamy, this sauce is everybody's favorite! Serve over shirataki, Zoodles (page 111), chicken, shrimp … anything, really!

In a heavy saucepan over low heat, melt the butter. Add the garlic and sauté for 4 to 5 minutes without browning it.

Add the cream and half-and-half and whisk them in. The butter will separate out a bit; do not panic. Let the whole thing come to a simmer.

Whisk in the cream cheese, stirring until it's melted. Then, add the Parmesan, about ¼ cup (25g) at a time. Keep whisking as the sauce smooths out and thickens a bit.

Whisk in the parsley, and you're done.

---

3 tablespoons (42g) butter

2 cloves of garlic, crushed

1 ounce (28g) cream cheese

½ cup (120ml) half-and-half

1 tablespoon (15ml) dry white wine

½ cup (50g) grated Parmesan cheese

Guar or xanthan

2 ounces (55g) crumbled Gorgonzola cheese

2 tablespoons (8g) minced fresh parsley

YIELD: 4 servings – Per serving: 242 calories; 22g fat (80.5% calories from fat); 9g protein; 3g carbohydrate; 1g dietary fiber; 2g net carbohydrate.

GORGONZOLA ALFREDO

Serve this with tofu shirataki fettuccini, over chicken or fish, with a steak … heck, eat it off your fingers. How can you go wrong?

Put a heavy-bottomed saucepan over low heat. Melt the butter and start the garlic gently stewing in it. You do not want the garlic to brown, so keep the temperature very low.

After a few minutes, add the cream cheese and stir until it melts. Now, add the half-and-half, wine, and Parmesan. Keep cooking and stirring until the whole thing is hot through. Use your guar or xanthan shaker to thicken it up to a little thicker than heavy cream.

Now, stir in the Gorgonzola and stir until it's half melted. Stir in the parsley and serve.

1½ cups (355ml) heavy cream

2 tablespoons (28g) butter

4 ounces (115g) cream cheese, cut into small cubes

Salt and pepper to taste

YIELD: 6 servings – Per serving: 305 calories; 32g fat (93.8% calories from fat); 3g protein; 2g carbohydrate; 0g dietary fiber; 2g net carbohydrate.

WHITE SAUCE

This is the keto version of béchamel, the classic white sauce. If you need it thicker than this, you can add a sprinkle of guar or xanthan.

Simply combine everything in a heavy-bottomed saucepan over low heat. Whisk as it heats until the cream cheese has melted in entirely.

1 cup (235ml) heavy cream

1 tablespoon (10g) minced shallot

1 egg yolk

2 tablespoons (15g) shredded Gruyère cheese

2 tablespoons (10g) shredded Parmesan cheese

1 dash of hot sauce

¼ teaspoon salt

YIELD: 1¼ cups (285ml), **5 servings** – Per serving: 197 calories; 20g fat (90.3% calories from fat); 3g protein; 2g carbohydrate; trace dietary fiber; 2g net carbohydrate.

½ cup (112g) butter

4 shallots, finely minced

1 cup (235ml) dry white wine

1 teaspoon ground fennel seed

YIELD: 4 servings – Per serving: 252 calories; 23g fat (94.5% calories from fat); 1g protein; 2g carbohydrate; trace dietary fiber; 2g net carbohydrate.

2 tablespoons (28g) butter, melted

½ cup (120ml) extra-virgin olive oil

2 tablespoons (28ml) sherry vinegar

2 tablespoons (28ml) balsamic vinegar

Salt and pepper

YIELD:1 cup (235ml), **8 servings** – Per serving: 146 calories; 16g fat (98.7% calories from fat); trace protein; trace carbohydrate, 0g dietary fiber; trace net carbohydrate.

SAUCE MORNAY

This de-carbed version of a classic sauce is beyond luscious. It's great on asparagus, broccoli, eggs, fish, chicken, shirataki noodles, fingers—you name it.

In a double boiler over hot but not boiling water, start the cream warming and add the shallot.

When the cream is just below simmering, whisk ¼ cup (60ml) of it into the egg yolk. Then, whisk the cream and yolk mixture back into the cream. *Do not try to simply whisk the yolk into the main pot of cream.*

Whisk in both cheeses and keep whisking as the sauce thickens, which will happen quite quickly. Stir in the hot sauce and salt, and your sauce is done. Try to refrain from simply eating it all out of the pot.

WHITE WINE SAUCE

I first created this for steamed mussels, but try it with scallops, shrimp, or even a simple fish fillet.

In a saucepan over medium-low heat, melt the butter. Throw in the shallots and sauté until they're starting to soften.

Add the wine and ground fennel seed and bring to just below a simmer. Let the whole thing cook for 6 to 7 minutes until it's reduced a little.

Serve with any kind of fish or seafood.

BUTTER VINAIGRETTE

This is perfect with fish and seafood! Try it with artichokes, broccoli, or asparagus, too.

Put the butter in a small saucepan over medium heat, melt it, and let it cook until the foam subsides and it's brown and smells nutty.

Put the olive oil and vinegars in your blender. Turn it on. Slowly pour in the butter. Season with salt and pepper to taste.

1 tablespoon (3g) instant coffee

1 teaspoon water

36 drops of liquid stevia, English toffee

½ cup (112g) butter, softened

YIELD: 8 servings – Per serving: 102 calories; 11g fat (99.5% calories from fat); trace protein; trace carbohydrate; 0g dietary fiber; trace net carbohydrate.

COFFEE BUTTER

I first used this on the Coffee Waffles, page 54, and it was fantastic. It would jazz up plain waffles or pancakes, too, or make a really intense cup of buttered coffee. I used unsalted butter and wound up adding about ⅛ teaspoon salt. You can do this, or just use salted butter.

Dissolve the instant coffee in the water and liquid stevia, making a paste. In a small food processor or in a bowl with a mixer, process or beat the butter until fluffy. Add the coffee mixture and beat it in well.

NOTE: I used my small food processor for this, but it might be too little volume for a full-size processor. You could use an electric mixer, instead.

½ cup (112g) butter, at room temperature

2 teaspoons lemon juice

1 tablespoon (4g) minced parsley

YIELD: 8 servings – Per serving: 102 calories; 11g fat (98.9% calories from fat); trace protein; trace carbohydrate; trace dietary fiber; negligible net carbohydrate.

NOTE: I used my small food processor for this, but it might be too little volume for a full-size processor. You could use an electric mixer, instead.

MAITRE D'HOTEL BUTTER

This is a classic and one of the secrets of top-notch steakhouses. Throw this on a good grilled rib eye or sirloin, and what more could you want? Maybe a glass of dry red?

Put the butter in your food processor and run until it's creamy. Add the lemon juice and run until it's evenly blended in. Add the parsley and pulse just until it's mixed in; you don't want to pulverize it.

Melt a good dollop of this on each steak as it comes off the heat.

If you make this ahead of time, you can scrape it out onto a piece of plastic wrap or wax paper, form it into a tidy roll, and stash it in the fridge. Then, you can slice pretty pats of it to melt on your steaks. It's not only tasty, but impressive, should you have anyone you'd like to impress.

½ cup (112g) butter

2 teaspoons lemon juice or vinegar

Salt and pepper

YIELD: 8 servings – Per serving: 102 calories; 11g fat (99.1% calories from fat); trace protein; trace carbohydrate; trace dietary fiber; 0g net carbohydrate.

BEURRE NOIR

This ultra-simple sauce is actually classical French cooking. It's a good way to up the fat content—and flavor!—of fish, but try it on fried eggs, too.

In a skillet or saucepan over medium-low heat, melt the butter and cook it until it browns. Stir in the lemon juice, season with salt and pepper to taste, and you're done.

NOTE: It helps to use a light-colored pan, so you can see the butter change color. I have nonstick skillets with copper-colored linings; they're perfect for this. Stainless steel would work well, too.

CHIPOTLE BUTTER

Melt this over steaks, burgers, or fish—it's smoky, fiery, and good!

½ cup (112g) butter

2 chipotle chiles canned in adobo, plus 1 tablespoon (15ml) adobo sauce

1 clove of garlic, crushed

2 tablespoons (20g) chopped onion

1 tablespoon (1g) chopped cilantro

YIELD: 8 servings – Per serving: 104 calories; 12g fat (96.8% calories from fat); trace protein; trace carbohydrate; trace dietary fiber; negligible net carbohydrate.

Run everything through the food processor until the chipotle and onion are pulverized. That's it!

MAPLE BUTTER

A great alternative to sugar-free pancake syrup—with all the maple flavor and none of the carbohydrates. It's great for roasting vegetables, too.

½ cup (112g) butter, softened

⅛ teaspoon maple flavoring

20 drops or to taste of liquid stevia, English toffee

YIELD: 8 servings – Per serving: 102 calories; 11g fat (99.5% calories from fat); trace protein; trace carbohydrate; 0g dietary fiber; trace net carbohydrate.

Just run everything through the food processor until it's combined.

VELOUTÉ

Velouté is one of the "mother sauces" of classic French cuisine. Traditional velouté is thickened with a roux—flour cooked in butter—before adding the stock. That's obviously not going to work for us! So try this. Our tester Wendy asked, "Where has this sauce been all my keto life?" Traditionally, it's made with chicken stock and served with poultry, but you can make it with seafood or fish stock instead and serve it with seafood. Wendy also says that for her purposes, a little extra salt was needed—she used homemade stock—and ¼ teaspoon xanthan, divided into two additions, was perfect.

1 cup (235ml) chicken stock

½ cup (120ml) heavy cream

1 ounce (28g) cream cheese, cut into small cubes

¼ teaspoon salt

1 pinch of pepper

Guar or xanthan

YIELD: 1½ cups (355ml), 6 servings – Per serving: 89 calories; 9g fat (92.0% calories from fat); 1g protein; 1g carbohydrate; trace dietary fiber; 1g net carbohydrate.

Combine everything except the guar or xanthan in a saucepan over medium-low heat. Bring to a simmer, whisking to melt in the cream cheese. Let it simmer for a minute or two and then thicken to the texture of heavy cream with your guar or xanthan shaker.

3 tablespoons (42g) butter, divided

1 shallot, minced

1 tablespoon (10g) diced onion

1 clove of garlic, crushed

1 cup (235ml) beef stock

1/3 cup (80ml) dry red wine

8 peppercorns

1 whole clove

1 bay leaf

1/4 teaspoon fresh thyme leaves

8 ounces (225g) sliced mushrooms

1 tablespoon (15ml) Worcestershire sauce

Guar or xanthan

Salt and pepper

**YIELD: 3 cups (700ml),
8 servings** – Per serving:
61 calories; 5g fat (73.0%
calories from fat); 1g protein;
3g carbohydrate; 1g dietary fiber;
2g net carbohydrate.

1/4 cup (35g) almonds

2 teaspoons butter

1 teaspoon beef bouillon granules

1 1/2 teaspoons lemon juice

1 recipe Velouté (page 251) made with beef stock instead of chicken stock

2 tablespoons (13g) chopped green olives

**YIELD: 1 3/4 cups (410ml),
7 servings** – Per serving:
120 calories; 12g fat (87.0%
calories from fat); 2g protein;
2g carbohydrate; 1g dietary fiber;
1g net carbohydrate.

MUSHROOM BORDELAISE

This is about as classic as sauces get. If you've popped for a really good beef rib roast, serve it with this and watch your guests' eyes grow wide. Our tester, Valerie, raves, "This was really delicious. I put it in a jar and let it cool. I was going to keep it in the fridge and use it for something later. I ended up eating it by itself as my lunch. The balance of flavor between the spices, wine, and broth was just right."

In a small saucepan over medium-low heat, melt 1 tablespoon (14g) of the butter. Add the shallot and onion and sauté until softened and starting to brown, about 5 to 7 minutes. Add the garlic and sauté for another minute or two.

Add the beef stock, wine, peppercorns, clove, bay leaf, and thyme. Turn the heat up to medium. Bring to a simmer and turn the heat down to hold it there. Let cook for 7 to 8 minutes.

While that's happening, melt the remaining 2 tablespoons (28g) of butter in a large saucepan over medium heat. Add the mushrooms and sauté, breaking them up further with your spatula, until they've softened, changed color, and exuded their liquid. Conveniently, this should take roughly as long as the stock/wine mixture needs to simmer.

When the mushrooms are sautéed and the stock/wine mixture has simmered, put a strainer over the saucepan with the mushrooms in it and strain the liquid into it. Stir in the Worcestershire. Thicken to the texture of heavy cream with your guar or xanthan shaker and season with salt and pepper to taste.

OLIVE AND ALMOND SAUCE

Our tester Rebecca, who rates this a 10, says it would be great on a burger or as a make-ahead for roast beef. She even suggested using it for a variation on Salisbury steak.

In a skillet over medium-low heat, sauté the almonds in the butter until golden.

Whisk the beef bouillon concentrate and lemon juice into the velouté. Stir in the almonds and all their butter and the olives. Done!

1½ cups (345g) sour cream

3 tablespoons (45ml) lime juice

⅔ cup (160ml) Mexican-style hot sauce (such as Cholula or Melinda's)

1 clove of garlic, crushed

Salt to taste

YIELD: 1½ cups (355ml), **12 servings** – Per serving: 64 calories; 6g fat (82.6% calories from fat); 1g protein; 2g carbohydrate; trace dietary fiber; 2g net carbohydrate.

CREMA CALIENTE

I came up with this for the Border Town Chuck (page 167), but That Nice Boy I Married—after licking the remains off his plate—insisted it needed its own entry. So here it is. It's super-simple.

Just stir everything together!

¼ cup (40g) finely diced onion

1 tablespoon (14g) coconut oil or fat of choice

2 red or purple plums, good and ripe

1 tablespoon (15ml) sherry

¼ teaspoon ground rosemary

1 clove of garlic, crushed

¼ cup (60ml) water

YIELD: 1 cup (235ml), **4 servings** – Per serving: 58 calories; 4g fat (57.0% calories from fat); trace protein; 6g carbohydrate; 1g dietary fiber; 5g net carbohydrate.

PLUM SAUCE

This sauce is really great with pork or chicken! Your plums need to be really ripe for this. Don't bother with second-rate plums.

In a heavy saucepan over medium-low heat, start the onion sautéing in the oil.

In the meanwhile, halve your plums, remove the stones, and then dice the flesh. Don't peel them! The peel adds a lot of flavor.

When the onions have softened, add the plums to the pan and sauté until they're starting to soften, too. Now, add the sherry, rosemary, and garlic and keep stirring for a couple of minutes. Your plums should be mostly dissolving into a sauce by now, with some bits of flesh and skin for texture.

Now, stir in the water, turn the heat down to the lowest setting, and let it cook for another 5 minutes. Use immediately or keep in a tightly lidded container in the fridge for a few days.

2 ounces (55g) anchovy fillets in olive oil

¼ cup (60ml) extra-virgin olive oil

1 teaspoon lemon juice

¼ cup (10g) fresh basil

5 cloves of garlic, peeled

YIELD: 6 servings – Per serving: 104 calories; 10g fat (86% calories from fat); 3g protein; 1g carbohydrate; trace dietary fiber; 1g net carbohydrate.

ANCHOVY DIP/SAUCE

That Nice Boy I Married is kinky for anchovies. I came up with this sauce for him.

Throw everything in your food processor and run it until the garlic is pulverized. Use as a dip for vegetables or as a sauce over meat, fish, or eggs.

2 tablespoons (30g) Virtue or Natural Mate sweetener

2 tablespoons (24g) garlic salt

2 tablespoons (20g) granulated garlic

2 tablespoons (14g) paprika

2 teaspoons chili powder

½ teaspoon ground ginger

½ teaspoon onion powder

½ teaspoon ground coriander

½ teaspoon cayenne

YIELD: ½ cup (85g), 6 servings – Per serving: 24 calories; trace fat (15.4% calories from fat); 1g protein; 5g carbohydrate; 2g dietary fiber; 3g net carbohydrate.

BEEF RUB

I came up with this for beef ribs, but try mixing it into ground beef before making burgers. Or sprinkle it on a rib eye before grilling!

Measure it all into a bowl and stir it up. That's it! Store it in an old spice shaker for easy application.

1½ tablespoons (23g) Virtue or Natural Mate sweetener or ¼ cup (60g) Truvia

1 tablespoon (12g) seasoned salt

1 tablespoon (10g) granulated garlic

1 tablespoon (12g) celery salt

1 tablespoon (7g) onion powder

1 tablespoon (7g) sweet smoked paprika

1 tablespoon (7g) hot smoked paprika

1 tablespoon (8g) chili powder

2 teaspoons pepper

1 teaspoon lemon pepper

1 teaspoon ground sage

1 teaspoon dry mustard

½ teaspoon dried thyme

½ teaspoon cayenne

YIELD: ¾ cup (80g), 12 servings – Per serving: 14 calories; trace fat (23.3% calories from fat); 1g protein; 3g carbohydrate; 1g dietary fiber; 2g net carbohydrate.

CLASSIC BARBECUE RUB

Great on chicken or pork, this classic rub is a snap to mix up. Keep a shaker of it around the kitchen because you'll find yourself reaching for it often.

Stir everything together. If your onion powder has clumped—an unfortunate habit of onion powder—you might run everything through the food processor. Store in an old spice shaker.

NOTE: To make a mopping sauce from this rub, simply combine 2 to 3 tablespoons (13 to 20g) of rub with ½ cup (120ml) of broth or very-low-carb beer and ¼ cup (60ml) of oil or melted bacon grease. Use this to baste the meat you have sprinkled with the rub as it cooks.

3 tablespoons (45g) salt

1 tablespoon (7g) hot smoked paprika

2 teaspoons onion powder

2 teaspoons garlic powder

2 teaspoons curry powder

1 teaspoon black pepper

YIELD: ⅓ cup (60g), 18 servings – Per serving: 4 calories; trace fat (trace% calories from fat); trace protein; 1g carbohydrate; trace dietary fiber, 1g net carbohydrate.

CHICKEN SEASONING REDUX

Years and years ago, I picked up something simply called "Chicken Seasoning" for a buck at Big Lots. I loved it, but you know how it is with Big Lots—they never had it again. I set about cloning it, and I did pretty well. Over the years, I've bumped up the paprika, changing to the hot smoked stuff. I've also reduced the salt. This is my favorite seasoning for simple roasted chicken. It's also fabulous on roasted nuts.

Just stir everything together and store in an old spice shaker. Sprinkle over chicken before roasting or use as a table seasoning.

---

1 tablespoon (15g) salt

2 teaspoons granulated garlic

2 teaspoons dried basil

2 teaspoons dried oregano

1 teaspoon ground cinnamon

1 teaspoon pepper

1 teaspoon dried ground rosemary

1 teaspoon dried dill

1 teaspoon dried marjoram

1 teaspoon dried thyme

1 teaspoon dried parsley

½ teaspoon ground nutmeg

YIELD: 5 tablespoons (20g), 8 servings – Per serving: 8 calories; trace fat (15.5% calories from fat); trace protein; 2g carbohydrate; 1g dietary fiber; 1g net carbohydrate.

GREEK SEASONING

If you can't find Greek seasoning in your grocery store, or if the brand they carry has additives you prefer to avoid, such as sugar, cornstarch, or the like, whip up a batch of your own. It's so quick and easy, not to mention versatile.

Stir it all together and store it in an old spice shaker. Done!

¼ cup (30g) chili powder

1½ teaspoons garlic powder

4 teaspoons (7g) dried onion flakes

1 teaspoon red pepper flakes or to taste

1½ teaspoons dried oregano

2 teaspoons paprika

2 tablespoons (14g) ground cumin

1 tablespoon (15g) salt

YIELD: ⅝ cup (80g),
16 servings – Per serving:
12 calories; 1g fat (32.2% calories from fat); trace protein; 2g carbohydrate; 1g dietary fiber; 1g net carbohydrate.

¼ cup (60g) salt or (48g) Vege-Sal

¼ cup (28g) hot smoked paprika

¼ cup (28g) ground cumin

2 tablespoons (12g) ground coriander

2 teaspoons pepper

2 teaspoons sweet paprika

2 teaspoons granulated garlic

YIELD: 1 cup (145g),
16 servings – Per serving:
15 calories; 1g fat (32.9% calories from fat); 1g protein; 3g carbohydrate; 1g dietary fiber; 2g net carbohydrate.

TACO SEASONING

Commercial taco seasoning often contains added sugars or starches. This is pure flavor! Mix it up, keep it in a snap-top container or zip-top bag, and you're always ready to stir up taco meat! This is enough for 4 pounds (1.8kg) of ground beef—or, for that matter, diced chicken.

Just measure everything and stir it all together. Store in an airtight container. For making taco meat, 2 gently rounded tablespoons (16g) is the right amount for 1 pound (455g) of ground beef.

SPANISH-OID RUB

I adapted this from a very authentic recipe that called for you to roast and grind your own spices. This is a lot simpler and still awfully good. Try it on any form of pork, from ribs to a slow-cooked shoulder—chicken, too.

Just measure everything into a bowl and stir. Store in a clean old spice shaker, tightly lidded.

SIMPLE PAN GRAVY

Many people seem to think that making gravy is a difficult, arcane skill, but I was doing it when I had to stand on a step stool to reach the stove top. You can do it, too!

I can't give exact measurements because it will depend on the size of your roast, how many drippings you have, and how many people you're serving. So, this is more a technique than a recipe.

When your roast—whether it's beef, pork, lamb, chicken, or whatever—is done, pull the pan out of the oven. Remove the roast to a platter and put it in a warm place while you make the gravy.

Next, skim the excess fat off your drippings. The easiest way to do this is to let the drippings cool slightly, then pour them into a zip-top bag, seal it, and hold it by one corner. Dangle it for a minute or two until the drippings separate into the dark layer at the bottom and the fat layer is at the top. Hold the bag over the roasting pan, snip a little bit off that bottom corner of the bag and let all the dark stuff run back into the pan. Then, as you get to the grease, pinch the corner to stop the flow. You can now either toss the fat or keep it it to cook with.

Let's get back to the roasting pan! Add some broth or stock to the pan; for a 5-pound (2.3kg) leg of lamb, for example, I used about 2½ cups (570ml). You'll want to use beef broth for a beef roast and chicken broth for poultry or pork. For lamb, I've been known to use either one or even a 50/50 mixture of the two. Place the pan over low heat and stir the broth around, scraping up all the nice browned bits in the bottom of the pan. This is where your real flavor is coming from.

Taste this mixture. Does it have a good, meaty flavor? If it's a little frail-flavored, let it simmer for 5 to 10 minutes to reduce it a bit.

Now, you need to thicken your gravy. Grab your guar or xanthan shaker. Start whisking the broth and lightly sprinkle the guar or xanthan over the liquid. Go slowly—fiber thickeners get gummy if you overdo it. It's far easier to add a little more than it is to fix gummy gravy. When your gravy is a little thinner than heavy cream, quit adding thickener!

GIBLET GRAVY

This is a painless way to get a few organ meats into the family. It basically goes like the Simple Pan Gravy (page 257), with one addition.

Before you ever put your turkey or chicken in to roast, tend to that little bag of giblets. Put the neck, heart, and gizzard in a saucepan and cover them with water. Bring to a simmer and let them cook until the gizzard is tender—it's likely to be at least an hour. Add water as needed. *Do not add the liver at this point.* Overcooked liver is dreadful.

Once your giblets are simmering, you'll get your bird in to roast, of course.

When the gizzard is easily pierced with a fork, add the liver to the pan, turn off the heat, and cover the pan. Let the residual heat poach the liver. After about 10 minutes, uncover the pan again and let the giblets cool.

Fish the cooled giblets out of the broth. Don't pour that broth down the drain —you're going to be using it in the gravy. Put the giblets on your cutting board.

Trim the cartilage off the gizzard and finely dice the rest. Pick as much meat as you can off the neck and mince it, too. The heart and liver can be diced without any further trimming.

When you make your gravy according to the Simple Pan Gravy technique, use the giblet broth, with additional broth as needed. When the gravy is thickened, stir in the diced giblets.

Because giblet gravy is, of course, from poultry, I should add: I like a touch of poultry seasoning in the gravy and a teeny smidge—maybe ¼ teaspoon—of coconut aminos or soy sauce. I also add just a suspicion of garlic, by peeling a clove, cutting it in half, impaling one of the halves on a fork, and stirring the gravy with it for a minute or so before removing. Season with salt and pepper to taste, of course.

AMAZING BBQ RUB REDUX

1½ tablespoons (10g) celery seed

¼ cup (60g) Natural Mate or Virtue sweetener

3 tablespoons (45g) salt or (36g) Vege-Sal

2 tablespoons (14g) onion powder

1 tablespoon (10g) granulated garlic

1 tablespoon (8g) chili powder

1 tablespoon (7g) hot smoked paprika or sweet, as you prefer

1 tablespoon (6g) pepper

½ teaspoon cayenne

¼ teaspoon ground cloves

YIELD: ⅞ cup (150g), **14 servings** – Per serving: 13 calories; trace fat (22.5% calories from fat); 1g protein; 2g carbohydrate; 1g dietary fiber; 1g net carbohydrate.

The original version of this rub appeared in *The Low-Carb Barbecue Book* and was always my favorite. I thought I'd do a version with today's sweeteners. You can use celery salt in this if you prefer—it's certainly easier—but grinding celery seeds gives a great flavor. If you prefer the celery salt, use 3 tablespoons (36g), plus an extra tablespoon (15g) or so of salt or (12g) Vege-Sal. Either way, this gives your ribs such a great flavor that sugary barbecue sauce is unneeded.

Grind the celery seed—I use a mortar and pestle, but a coffee grinder (dedicated to the purpose) makes a great spice grinder. Put it in a bowl. Add everything else, stir it together, and store in an old spice shaker.

COCOYO (COCONUT YOGURT)

1 can (14 ounces, or 390ml) of coconut milk

The contents of a probiotic capsule or yogurt starter

YIELD: 14 ounces (390ml), 3 **servings** – Per serving: 239 calories; 26g fat (91.1% calories from fat); 2g protein; 3g carbohydrate; 0g dietary fiber; 3g net carbohydrate.

This isn't a sauce or seasoning, but I didn't know where else to put it. This is for those of you who are dairy-free. You can culture coconut milk or coconut cream to make cocoyo (coconut yogurt) and coconut sour cream. You can use this in place of yogurt or sour cream in any of these recipes. You may well be able to buy coconut milk yogurt at your local health food store, which is easier, but not everyone has a good local health food store. For the probiotic capsule, I use one with ten different strains that I buy from Puritan's Pride.

Put your coconut milk in a snap-top container or jar and stir in the contents of the probiotic capsule or an envelope of yogurt starter. Put in a warm place—I use an old electric hot pad set on low for this purpose. I tuck it down in a bowl to hold it up around the container. Let it sit overnight and then refrigerate. Use just as you would plain yogurt.

Sometimes, cocoyo separates. You can stir it up, or you can pour off the liquid and use the remainder for sour cream.

You can also deliberately make sour cream by refrigerating your can of coconut milk overnight and then puncturing the bottom, draining off the liquid, and only culturing the thick coconut cream that will be left.

I should warn you: the first time I made cocoyo the results looked sort of gray and unappealing. I was discouraged. But I stuck it in the fridge, and by the next day, it looked fine and worked great in my recipes.

CHAPTER 15

Beverages

Beverages are among the greatest health issues we face. I am old enough to remember Coke machines that held 6-ounce (170ml) bottles, and into my adult years, the 12-ounce (340ml) can was standard. Now the 20-ounce (560ml) bottle, an increase of more than 200 percent, is standard. Similarly, in my youth, a 4-ounce (120ml) serving of orange juice—the quantity that provided the minimum daily requirement of vitamin C—was so much the standard that every household had "juice glasses" that held that quantity. If we were thirsty playing in the backyard, we didn't run inside for "juice boxes," we drank water from the hose —perhaps not optimal sanitation, but blessedly devoid of sugar.

Somewhere along the line, Americans decided that everything they drink should taste like candy. Black coffee has given way to frappuccinos. "Water enhancers"—sweet and fruity concentrates in dropper bottles—let us carry the cure to the dreaded plain water in our pockets. Fountain drinks have gotten big enough to high-dive into. "Hard soda" and whiskey sweetened with honey are edging out beer and Scotch on the rocks. (I have ranted in another book about the "-tini" craze. A martini consists of gin or vodka, dry vermouth, and either an olive or a twist of lemon. There is no such thing as a "caramel martini" or a "chocolate martini," even if you do serve it in a V-shaped glass.)

Enough.

If you were to make one and only one change in your diet, dropping every sugar-containing beverage—yes, that includes juice—would likely be the most beneficial.

1½ cups (150g) dried hibiscus

½ cup (50g) rose hips

Liquid stevia, various flavors

Chilled sparkling water, plain or flavored

YIELD: 2 quarts (1.9L), 16 servings – Per serving: 2 calories; trace fat (1.6% calories from fat); trace protein; 1g carbohydrate; trace dietary fiber; 1g net carbohydrate.

ANTIOXIDANT FIZZ

This brilliantly red beverage is not only delicious, but it's also loaded with antioxidants. Hibiscus has been used to lower blood pressure in traditional herbal medicine and is being studied for anti-inflammatory activity and other health benefits—even antiviral activity. Rose hips are, of course, one of the best-known herbal sources of vitamin C. All this, with the refreshing taste of a fizzy fruit punch—it's hard to beat.

Put your hibiscus and rose hips in a 2-quart (1.9L) pitcher that can withstand heat—I use plastic, and it holds up fine. Fill with boiling water. Let it cool and then strain, pressing the herbs to get out as much of the infusion as you can. Discard the herbs, put the strained tea back in the pitcher, and then fill the pitcher the rest of the way with water and chill.

What you have just made is a concentrate. The fun part is coming up with ways to use it! My favorite is this:

I put ½ cup (120ml) of the hibiscus/rose hip concentrate in a tall glass and add 12 drops of lemon drop–flavored stevia extract. I add ice and then fill with chilled raspberry sparkling water.

But just think of the variations! Try lemon-lime sparkling water or cranberry-lime! How about trying orange stevia extract? Or using plain liquid stevia and blackberry-citrus sparkling water? The combinations are endless.

Also, people like differing strengths—as I say, I like ½ cup (120ml) of the concentrate, the rest sparkling water, but some like a little more or a little less. Play with it! Any way you mix it, you get a refreshing, fruity, fizzy drink with virtually no carbohydrates or calories, but a ton of health benefits.

1½ cups (150g) hibiscus flowers

⅓ cup (35g) lemon balm

⅓ cup (35g) passion flower

2 tablespoons (12g) dried orange peel

3 tablespoons (28g) stevia herb, or to taste

YIELD: 8 servings – Per serving: 1 calorie; trace fat (1.4% calories from fat); trace protein; trace carbohydrate; trace dietary fiber; 0g net carbohydrate.

RUBY RELAXER

This delicious, fruit-punch-like herb tea has become my go-to beverage on evenings when I don't care to drink alcohol. The lemon balm and passion flower are both mildly sedative, while the hibiscus, with its brilliant color, adds antioxidants and matchless flavor.

Put all the flowers, orange peel, and stevia herb in a 2-quart (1.9L) pitcher and pour boiling water over them to fill. Let the tea stand and brew until cool.

Strain the tea, pressing all you can out of the herbs, and then pour a little more water through the herbs to rinse all the good stuff out of them. Put the tea back in the pitcher and add water to fill. (Remember, some of the space in the pitcher during brewing will have been taken up by the herbs.) Chill the tea.

This makes a concentrate. I like to mix it about 50/50 with cold water or cold sparkling water, but dilute to taste.

8 tea bags

2 quarts (1.9L) boiling water

YIELD: 8 servings – Per serving: 5 calories; 0g fat (0.0% calories from fat); trace protein; 1g carbohydrate; trace dietary fiber; 1g net carbohydrate.

ICED TEA

You know, tea—brewed, chilled, and poured over ice. I cannot for the life of me figure out why iced tea has not caught on worldwide. It's so perfectly refreshing. I like my iced tea plain, but if you like it sweetened, consider stevia or monk fruit drops or liquid sucralose. If you go for lemon in your iced tea, remember it has about 1 gram of carbohydrate per tablespoon (15g), so one wedge won't make much of a dent, but several might. Iced tea with lemon would be the perfect place for lemon drop stevia!

Tie the strings of your tea bags together with a simple overhand knot, to facilitate removal. Put them in a heat-tolerate pitcher.

Pour the boiling water over the tea bags and let them steep for 10 minutes or so. Carefully, fish them out with a tongs, let your tea cool, and then chill.

I don't have to remind you to pour it over ice, do I?

If you like sweet tea (ugh!), liquid sucralose, stevia, or monk fruit should do the trick.

8 tea bags, regular, decaf, or a mixture, as you prefer

¼ teaspoon liquid stevia, plain or lemon drop (or to taste)

1 pound (455g) strawberries

Boiling water

YIELD: 2 quarts (1.9L), 8 servings – Per serving: 21 calories; trace fat (6.8% calories from fat); 1g protein; 5g carbohydrate; 1g dietary fiber; 4g net carbohydrate.

STRAWBERRY ICED TEA

Our tester Rebecca says that unless you can get really ripe, seasonal strawberries, you might want to go with frozen. They'll probably be more flavorful than off-season fresh strawberries. Thaw them first, or they'll cool the tea too quickly. At this writing, SweetLeaf brand, one of my favorite brands of flavored stevia drops, is making a mixed berry flavor. It would be a great choice here.

Because you strain out the strawberries, the actual carb and fiber count will be a bit lower.

Put the tea bags, liquid stevia, and strawberries in a 2-quart (1.9L) pitcher. Fill with boiling water. Let it steep until it's cool.

Remove the strawberries and strain. Squeeze out the tea bags to get all the flavor. Add water to fill the space that used to be taken up by strawberries. Chill and serve over ice.

⅔ cup (160ml) lemon juice

½ teaspoon liquid stevia, lemon drop

2 quarts (1.9L) water

YIELD: 8 servings – Per serving: 5 calories; 0g fat (0.0% calories from fat); trace protein; 2g carbohydrate; trace dietary fiber; 2g net carbohydrate.

LEMONADE

Okay, this is way outside our macros, deriving most of its calories from carbohydrate. But it's 5 calories total! By the way, you can combine this 50/50 with the Iced Tea above for Arnold Palmers, or with the Strawberry Iced Tea above for Strawberry Arnold Palmers.

In a 2-quart (1.9L) pitcher, combine the lemon juice and liquid stevia. Add the water, stir, and chill. Serve over ice!

3 quarts (2.8L) brewed coffee

3 cups (700ml) heavy cream

½ cup (120ml) sugar-free coffee flavoring syrup, chocolate

½ cup (120ml) sugar-free coffee flavoring syrup, caramel

YIELD: 15 servings – Per serving: 168 calories; 18g fat (92.4% calories from fat); 1g protein; 2g carbohydrate; 0g dietary fiber; 2g net carbohydrate.

CARAMEL MOCHA LATTE

Want to make friends with the whole office? Show up with this one day. Or serve it at a brunch or open house or even church coffee hour. It's so simple! If you'd rather, you can use ½ teaspoon each chocolate and English toffee liquid stevia in place of the coffee syrups.

Just combine everything in your slow cooker and keep it on low to serve.

1 cup (235ml) brewed coffee, chilled

½ cup (120ml) unsweetened canned coconut milk

¼ teaspoon liquid stevia, chocolate

1 tablespoon (14g) whey protein powder, chocolate

YIELD: 1 serving – Per serving: 282 calories; 25g fat (75.1% calories from fat); 13g protein; 5g carbohydrate; trace dietary fiber; 5g net carbohydrate.

MORNING MOCHA

Somewhere between iced coffee and chocolate milk, this beverage combines protein, highly ketogenic fat, and caffeine in one get-out-the-door package.

Make it the night before, pour it into a car cup, and chill for a super-streamlined morning.

¾ cup (175ml) hot, strong brewed coffee

¼ cup (60ml) unsweetened canned coconut milk

12 drops of liquid stevia, English toffee

YIELD: 1 serving – Per serving: 114 calories; 12g fat (88.5% calories from fat); 1g protein; 2g carbohydrate; 0g dietary fiber; 2g net carbohydrate.

COCO-CARAMEL COFFEE

You know that coffee "creamer" is among the most evil substances posing as food in your grocery store, right? This is so much better and so much better for you. Also, it's a snap to do.

Just put everything in your blender, run it for 15 seconds or so, pour, and drink. You can easily double or triple this if you've got more than one coffee drinker on hand.

1 cup (235ml) heavy cream, chilled

¼ teaspoon liquid stevia, English toffee

12 drops of maple extract

½ cup (120ml) brewed espresso

8 teaspoons (40g) Walden Farms or Hershey's sugar-free chocolate syrup

24 drops of liquid stevia, dark chocolate

4 pinches of ground cinnamon

YIELD: 4 servings – Per serving: 416 calories; 44g fat (93.5% calories from fat); 2g protein; 4g carbohydrate; trace dietary fiber; 4g net carbohydrate.

MOCHA WITH MAPLE WHIPPED CREAM

Here's a recipe that would serve both as after-dinner coffee and dessert. Thanks to my invaluable tester, Rebecca, for tweaking this! She says it should be at Starbucks. Starbucks, are you listening? I'm only asking for a dime royalty per cup sold.

In a bowl with a handheld mixer, whip the cream with the English toffee stevia and maple extract until it mounds, but don't continue until it's stiff. Cover and refrigerate.

When it's time to construct your mocha, have the espresso hot and ready. Using 2 demitasse cups, drizzle the chocolate syrup down the insides. Add an espresso shot to each cup, then 6 drops of dark chocolate stevia to each.

Sprinkle a pinch of cinnamon over each cup. Divide the maple whipped cream among them.

1½ teaspoons instant coffee granules

1 cup (235ml) unsweetened pourable coconut milk, chilled

6 drops of liquid stevia (or to taste), your choice of flavor

2 ice cubes

Dash of ground nutmeg

YIELD: 1 serving – Per serving: 51 calories; 4g fat (70% calories from fat); trace protein; 2g carbohydrate; 0g dietary fiber; 2g net carbohydrate.

EASY ICED CAPPUCCINO

Here's another quick-and-easy coffee drink for a hot morning. It's so much cheaper and quicker than stopping on the way to work! Chocolate, vanilla, hazelnut, or English toffee liquid stevia would all be good in this.

Put everything but the nutmeg in your blender and run it until it's smooth. Pour into a car cup, sprinkle the nutmeg on top, and dash.

---

1 cup (235ml) unsweetened pourable coconut milk, chilled

2½ teaspoons (3g) instant coffee granules

32 drops of liquid stevia, vanilla

3 tablespoons (43g) whey protein powder, vanilla

½ teaspoon vanilla extract

3 ice cubes

YIELD: 1 serving – Per serving: 173 calories; 3g fat (14.5% calories from fat); 32g protein; 4g carbohydrate; 1g dietary fiber; 3g net carbohydrate.

WAKE UP AND GO!

This is coffee and breakfast in one. If you assemble everything but the ice cubes in your blender the night before—sticking the blender container in the fridge overnight—in the morning, you can just put it on the base, add the ice, run the blender, and you're out the door. I used vanilla stevia here to go with the vanilla protein powder, but you can change this up with other flavors. You can also substitute sugar-free coffee flavoring syrup for the stevia if you prefer—about 2 tablespoons (28ml) should do it.

Put everything in your blender and run it until it's smooth.

1½ cups (355ml) hot brewed coffee

2 tablespoons (28g) unsalted butter

2 tablespoons (28ml) MCT oil

24 drops of liquid stevia, English toffee

1 pinch of ground cinnamon

1 pinch of ground cloves

YIELD: 2 servings – Per serving: 226 calories; 25g fat (98.1% calories from fat); trace protein; 1g carbohydrate; trace dietary fiber; 1g net carbohydrate.

MEXICAN POWER COFFEE

I'll admit that the English toffee stevia standing in for Mexican piloncillo sugar is inauthentic. On the other hand, it's sugar free. And this tastes great and is highly ketogenic. Again, if you'd rather, use sugar-free caramel coffee flavoring syrup in place of the stevia.

Put everything in your blender and run until the butter is melted and the whole thing is creamy and frothy. Pour into 2 mugs, and you're done!

    If you find that blending has cooled your coffee a bit, feel free to zap it for 30 seconds or so in the microwave.

---

1 cup (235ml) hot brewed coffee

1½ tablespoons (21g) unsalted grass-fed butter

1½ tablespoons (21g) coconut oil

¼ teaspoon liquid stevia, chocolate

2 teaspoons cocoa powder

2 tablespoons (29g) whey protein powder, chocolate

YIELD: 1 serving – Per serving: 452 calories; 40g fat (76.3% calories from fat); 23g protein; 5g carbohydrate; 2g dietary fiber; 3g net carbohydrate.

POWER PACK MOCHA

A ringer from *The Low-Carb Diabetes Solution Cookbook*, this is another version of coffee-and-breakfast in one. You know those ads about "that 2:00 feeling?" Yeah, no. That's not happening.

Just assemble everything in your blender and run until the butter and coconut oil are worked in and the whole thing is frothy. Pour into a car cup and run!

½ cup (120ml) hot brewed coffee

1 tablespoon (15ml) Cognac

1 tablespoon (4g) whipped cream

YIELD: 1 serving – Per serving: 60 calories; 3g fat (87.1% calories from fat); trace protein; 1g carbohydrate; 0g dietary fiber; 1g net carbohydrate.

CAFE CHANTILLY

This is a nice alternative to Irish coffee as an after-dinner drink. You can use unsweetened whipped cream or choose to lightly sweeten it. The instructions are for one cup, but if you can't figure out how to make more, you need more than coffee—and probably don't need Cognac.

I trust this is self-explanatory—pour the coffee, add the Cognac, float the whipped cream on top.

1 quart (946ml) good and strong brewed coffee, cooled

1 cup (235ml) unsweetened pourable coconut milk

1 cup (235ml) unsweetened canned coconut milk

¼ teaspoon liquid stevia, English toffee

¼ teaspoon liquid stevia, vanilla

⅛ teaspoon vanilla extract

YIELD: 6 servings – Per serving: 77 calories; 8g fat (87.5% calories from fat); 1g protein; 2g carbohydrate; 0g dietary fiber; 2g net carbohydrate.

ICED CARAMEL COFFEE

Do you know how much sugar coffee shop iced coffees contain? Yikes! This will satisfy the yen without spiking your blood sugar. Top with whipped cream, if you like. This makes a lot, so you can stash it in your fridge and pour as a coffee fix is needed.

Run everything through your blender and then serve over crushed ice.

⅔ cup (160ml) brewed espresso, cooled

1 can (14 ounces, or 390ml) of unsweetened coconut milk

2 tablespoons (24g) powdered erythritol

20 drops of liquid stevia extract, your choice of flavor

1 cup (227g) ice cubes

YIELD: 2 servings – Per serving: 340 calories; 36g fat (89.9% calories from fat); 3g protein; 6g carbohydrate; 0g dietary fiber; 6g net carbohydrate.

COCOCCINO

My darling friend Virginia raves, "WINNER!!! You know how much I LOVE coffee and this was the bomb." She adds, "I split it into two servings. Drank one over half the ice, so nice… Took the other serving, put it in my little blender with a cup plus some of ice and made a frappuccino. Too yummy for words. Thank you, Dana." For the liquid stevia, vanilla, chocolate, hazelnut, or English toffee would all work.

Put everything but the ice in your blender and turn it on. Drop in the ice cubes, one at a time, and run until the ice is pulverized. Pour and drink.

¼ cup (60ml) unsweetened canned coconut milk

5 drops of liquid stevia (or to taste), French vanilla

¾ cup (175ml) hot brewed coffee

YIELD: 1 serving – Per serving: 114 calories; 12g fat (88.5% calories from fat); 1g protein; 2g carbohydrate; 0g dietary fiber; 2g net carbohydrate.

ERIC'S COCONUT COFFEE

My husband Eric has made tremendous changes in his diet over the years. But he's not willing to give up coffee, and I suspect there are a lot of people who'd agree. He's always had his coffee with cream, but found this version excellent.

Eric tried this with chocolate liquid stevia, too, and thought it was great. You could use hazelnut or English toffee liquid stevia, as well. And how about a dusting of cinnamon?

It's self-explanatory, really—put the coconut milk in a mug (you can warm it first if you like, but Eric didn't) and add the liquid stevia. Pour in the coffee, stir, and enjoy!

¾ cup (175ml) hot brewed coffee

¼ cup (60ml) heavy cream or unsweetened coconut milk

14 drops of liquid stevia, dark chocolate

3 drops of peppermint extract

YIELD: 1 serving – Per serving: 209 calories; 22g fat (93.0% calories from fat); 1g protein; 2g carbohydrate; 0g dietary fiber; 2g net carbohydrate.

PEPPERMINT MOCHA

Watching television one Sunday morning, I saw an ad for "holiday creamers." Creamer is revolting stuff, a true chemical garbage-storm. But the flavors sounded easy to reproduce. Have this while you decorate the Christmas tree!

Just stir together or run through the blender. It's easy to double, of course.

½ cup (120ml) strong brewed coffee, chilled

¼ cup (60ml) unsweetened canned coconut milk

¼ cup (60ml) unsweetened pourable coconut milk

1 egg

2 teaspoons powdered erythritol

1 teaspoon vanilla extract

9 drops of liquid stevia, your choice of flavor

1 pinch of salt

⅛ teaspoon ground nutmeg, or to taste

YIELD: 2 servings – Per serving: 204 calories; 17g fat (78% calories from fat); 7g protein; 4g carbohydrate; 0g dietary fiber; 4g net carbohydrate.

COCONUT COFFEE EGGNOG

Here's another recipe that serves as wake-up beverage and breakfast in one. If you prefer, you can make this with heavy cream or, for that matter, with all canned coconut milk—for richer results. Many thanks to our tester, Shayne, for tweaking this recipe for me. Have I mentioned my testers are insanely great?

You can also use pasteurized eggs if raw ones scare you. It will still be creamy, nutritious, and filling.

Just assemble everything in your blender and run until it's creamy and frothy. Pour and drink.

---

1 can (14 ounces, or 390ml) of unsweetened coconut milk

1 can (14 ounces, or 390ml) of unsweetened pourable coconut milk

¼ cup (20g) unsweetened cocoa

¼ teaspoon liquid stevia, vanilla

1 pinch of salt

YIELD: 3 servings – Per serving: 312 calories; 31g fat (85% calories from fat); 4g protein; 8g carbohydrate; 2g dietary fiber; 6g net carbohydrate.

COCO-COCOA

Who doesn't love a cup of cocoa on a chilly morning? Here's one that fits our macros and is even dairy-free! Even better, if you don't drink it all at once, you can stash it in the fridge and warm it in the microwave for a quick cup. Or even drink it cold, as chocolate milk!

You'll notice from the ingredients list that this is a can of coconut milk and a can of the pourable coconut milk—use the pourable milk to rinse out the other can. Put the milks in a heavy-bottomed saucepan over medium-low heat, along with everything else, and whisk until all the cocoa is worked in. Bring to a simmer and serve.

1 cup (235ml) unsweetened pourable coconut milk

½ cup (120ml) DaVinci sugar-free pineapple syrup

½ cup (113g) ice

¼ cup (60ml) unsweetened canned coconut milk

¼ cup (60ml) lime juice

3 tablespoons (45ml) white rum

2 tablespoons (28ml) dark rum

YIELD: 2 servings – Per serving: 164 calories; 8g fat (85% calories from fat); 1g protein; 3g carbohydrate; trace dietary fiber; 3g net carbohydrate.

¼ cup (60ml) tequila

2 tablespoons (28ml) lime juice

12 drops of liquid stevia, lemon drop or plain

Ice to fill

Cranberry lime sparkling water, chilled

YIELD: 1 serving – Per serving: 137 calories; trace fat (2.3% calories from fat); trace protein; 3g carbohydrate; trace dietary fiber; 3g net carbohydrate.

JESS'S PIÑA COLADA

My friend Jess asked me to de-carb piña coladas. The only problem was that I don't like them. So, I wrote up a recipe, farmed out the testing to her, and this is what emerged. Indeed, this was my first attempt, and Jess said, "Wow! This is pretty darn good! I was afraid it would be too pineapple-y and not coconutty enough, but I wouldn't change a thing." So, go buy yourself some teeny umbrellas.

You can order the pineapple syrup from www.davincigourmet.com or from Amazon—or, I suspect, any number of other websites.

This is a cocktail to plan in advance because it calls for freezing things: Put the pourable coconut milk and the pineapple syrup both in ice cube trays, measuring first, of course. Stick 'em in the freezer.

When you've got coconut milk and pineapple syrup ice cubes, plus some regular ice, of course, you're ready to mix. Put the canned coconut milk, lime juice, white rum, and dark rum in your blender. Pop the coconut and pineapple cubes from their trays. Grab your regular ice, too. Now, turn on the blender to maximum speed and add those cubes, one at a time, letting each grind up pretty well before adding more.

When it's slushy, pour and drink! Tiny umbrella is optional.

PINK FLAMINGO

Long about 1991, Dexter Bullard, an up-and-coming young theatrical director in Chicago, was also tending bar to make ends meet. He challenged my statement that I didn't like cocktails by mixing me a Pink Flamingo, a margarita made with half margarita mix, half cranberry juice cocktail. He was right—I liked it. It's too sugary for me now, though (indeed, it was back then—despite finding it yummy, I never ordered another), but this highball, based on the same flavors, is seriously tasty and remarkably refreshing. It's great for hot summer days when you want a little adult refreshment, but also need to stay hydrated.

In a tall glass, combine the tequila, lime juice, and liquid stevia. Fill the glass with ice, then the chilled cranberry lime sparkling water.

¼ cup (60ml) tequila

2 tablespoons (28ml) lime juice

12 drops of liquid stevia, plain

Ice to fill

Grapefruit sparkling water, chilled

YIELD: 1 serving – Per serving: 137 calories; trace fat (2.3% calories from fat); trace protein; 3g carbohydrate; trace dietary fiber; 3g net carbohydrate.

PALOMA

When you're me, you read menus for ideas. I saw a drink called a Paloma, made with tequila, lime juice, and grapefruit juice. Again, sparkling water came to the rescue—La Croix makes grapefruit sparkling water. Be careful—there's another one out there, I forget the brand name, that includes some grapefruit juice, hence more carbohydrates. You could make this with Fresca instead; I'm just not a soda fan.

In a tall glass, combine the tequila, lime juice, and liquid stevia. Fill the glass with ice, then the chilled grapefruit sparkling water.

¼ cup (60ml) tequila

2 tablespoons (28ml) lime juice

12 drops of liquid stevia, Valencia orange

Ice to fill

Orange or lime sparkling water, chilled

YIELD: 1 serving – Per serving: 137 calories; trace fat (2.3% calories from fat); trace protein; 3g carbohydrate; trace dietary fiber; 3g net carbohydrate.

MARGARITA FIZZ

Who doesn't love margaritas? Sadly, they're sugary. Even if you make them with the classic recipe, not a mix, there's that orange liqueur. But I am a tequila girl and had to come up with something for us. Use orange sparkling water if you like a more orange-y note to your margaritas and lime sparkling water if you like 'em heavier on the lime.

In a tall glass, combine the tequila, lime juice, and liquid stevia. Fill the glass with ice, then the chilled orange or lime sparkling water.

¼ cup (60ml) white rum

2 tablespoons (28ml) lime juice

18 drops of liquid stevia, plain (or liquid monk fruit or sucralose to equal 1 tablespoon [13g] sugar)

YIELD: 1 serving – Per serving: 137 calories; trace fat (2.3% calories from fat); trace protein; 3g carbohydrate; trace dietary fiber; 3g net carbohydrate.

DAIQUIRI

Before there were super-sweet varieties like the strawberry daiquiri, there was just rum, lime juice, and a little sweetener, shaken over ice. It's a classic!

Combine everything in a cocktail shaker. Add ice, shake well, and strain into a chilled glass.

¼ cup (60ml) DaVinci sugar-free pineapple syrup, frozen into 2 cubes

¼ cup (60ml) lime juice

¼ cup (60ml) tequila

12 drops of liquid stevia, Valencia orange

About ¾ cup (170g) ice

YIELD: 1 serving – Per serving: 146 calories; trace fat (2.3% calories from fat); trace protein; 5g carbohydrate; trace dietary fiber; 5g net carbohydrate.

1 bottle (750ml) dry red wine, such as Tempranillo or Rioja

½ cup (120ml) lemon juice

¼ cup (60ml) lime juice

¼ teaspoon liquid stevia, lemon drop

¼ teaspoon liquid stevia, Valencia orange

6 drops of orange extract

YIELD: 5 servings – Per serving: 117 calories; trace fat (0.4% calories from fat); trace protein; 6g carbohydrate; trace dietary fiber; 6g net carbohydrate.

PINEAPPLE MARGARITA

Yes, a pineapple margarita—you're welcome. You'll need to start ahead by freezing the pineapple syrup in ice cube trays. It's so worth it!

Put the pineapple syrup cubes, lime juice, tequila, and liquid stevia in your blender, put on the lid, and turn 'er on. Take the cap out and add one ice cube at a time, letting each grind up before adding another, until your drink is nice and slushy.

You can pour this into a salt-rimmed glass if you're feeling fancy. Or you can just drink it as is. It will be fantastic either way.

SANGRIA-ISH

Okay, I admit it: it has been so long since I had regular, sugary sangria that I can't tell you quite how this compares. But, it's fruity and refreshing without all the sugar of regular sangria.

Just mix it all together in a pitcher. Chill and serve over ice.

5 fluid ounces (150ml) heavy cream

3 fluid ounces (92ml) Mockahlua 2017 (below)

3 fluid ounces (90ml) vodka

2 fluid ounces (60ml) Irish cream sugar free syrup

1 fluid ounce (30ml) Irish whiskey

Ice

Sugar free chocolate syrup, such as Walden Farms or Hershey's (optional)

YIELD: 4 servings – Per serving: 219 calories; 14g fat (94.1% calories from fat); 1g protein; 1g carbohydrate; 0g dietary fiber; 1g net carbohydrate.

MUDSLIDE

I asked my Facebook fan page what one last recipe I should put in this book, and someone suggested sugar-free mudslides. These are super-yummy with a deceptively innocuous taste. Drink slowly. The measurements for this are all in "ounces" because I used a shot glass to measure everything. 2 fluid ounces = ¼ cup. 1 fluid ounce = 2 tablespoons.

Put the cream, Mockahlua, vodka, Irish cream syrup, and Irish whiskey in your blender. Add ice—I used about 2 cups (470g)—and run until the whole thing is slushy.

If you want to be fancy, or just love chocolate, pour a little sugar-free chocolate syrup around the mouth of each glass and let it run down the inside before pouring the mudslides.

2½ cups (570ml) water

3 tablespoons (9g) instant coffee granules

1 teaspoon vanilla extract

Liquid sweetener to equal 3 cups (600g) sugar (I used 1 tablespoon (15ml) Natural Mate liquid monk fruit.)

1 bottle (750ml) vodka

YIELD: 1½ quarts (1.4L), 32 servings – Per serving: 52 calories; 0g fat (0.0% calories from fat); trace protein; trace carbohydrate; 0g dietary fiber; trace net carbohydrate.

MOCKAHLUA 2017

The version in *500 Low-Carb Recipes* used Splenda and so included those maltodextrin carbohydrates. With a liquid sweetener—sucralose, monk fruit, or stevia—we can eliminate them.

You'll need a clean 2-quart (1.9L) bottle with a cork—I used an old wine bottle. Mix together the water, instant coffee granules, vanilla, and sweetener. Use a funnel to pour this into your bottle.

Pour in the vodka. Cork it and shake. That's it!

CHAPTER 16

Desserts

As always, I am torn regarding desserts. On the one hand, I feel that ideally we all need to get over feeling we need something sweet on a regular basis. On the other hand, for many the thought of never, ever again eating a dessert will convince them that a ketogenic diet is simply undoable, and that would be a shame.

So, I offer these recipes in the bright, good hope that you will use them—and very much enjoy them!—occasionally, rather than as staples of your ketogenic diet. I assure you, they are all worthy to be served to the broader, non-low-carbing public. No one is going to taste them and snip, "Oh. Diet food." Nope. You may have to wrestle them to get a serving for yourself.

About sweeteners: the Sweetener Wars are the bane of my professional existence. No matter what sweetener I use, someone will object. Many object to any artificial sweetener, while others hate the taste of stevia (though in my experience stevia products vary quite a bit), or prefer monk fruit, or whatever. I give up. I've used the sweeteners I wanted to use, and there's a section on page 16 about how to substitute if you wish.

4 eggs, at room temperature

1 pinch of cream of tartar

½ cup (120g) Swerve or (96g) erythritol

¼ teaspoon liquid stevia, vanilla

½ cup (115ml) melted butter

1 teaspoon vanilla extract

3 tablespoons (18g) almond meal

3 tablespoons (43g) vanilla whey protein powder

6 tablespoons (30g) cocoa powder

2 cups (475ml) half-and-half, lukewarm

YIELD: 9 servings – Per serving: 229 calories; 20g fat (74.1% calories from fat); 10g protein; 6g carbohydrate; 1g dietary fiber; 5g net carbohydrate.

FUDGY CHOCOLATE WHATCHAMACALLIT

Is it a brownie? Is it a cake? Who knows? It's just yummy.

Preheat the oven to 325°F (170°C, or gas mark 3). Grease an 8 × 8-inch (20 × 20cm) baking pan or coat with nonstick cooking spray.

First, separate your eggs, putting the whites in a deep, narrow mixing bowl. Because egg whites will stubbornly refuse to whip if you get even the tiniest speck of yolk in them, do yourself a favor: separate one egg at a time, letting the white flow into a custard cup and dumping the yolk into a larger mixing bowl. Then, dump your yolk-free white into the deep, narrow bowl and repeat until all 4 whites are in the one mixing bowl and the yolks in the other. If one yolk breaks, save that one for an omelet and grab a fresh custard cup to keep the rest of the whites yolk free. It sounds fussy, I know, but it saves endless trouble and cursing in the long run.

Add a small pinch of cream of tartar to the whites and use an electric mixer to whip at highest speed until stiff peaks form. Set aside.

Grab the yolks in the other bowl. Add the Swerve and liquid stevia. At a medium speed, use your mixer—no need to clean off the whites—to beat the yolks and sweeteners for 2 to 3 minutes until light. Now, add the melted butter a little at a time, beating the whole time. Beat in the vanilla extract, too.

A spoonful at a time, beat in the almond meal, vanilla whey protein, and cocoa powder. Scrape down the sides often and keep beating until it's all well incorporated.

Little by little, start beating in the half-and-half. When it is all in, turn off the mixer. The mixture will be very thin and runny. Do not panic.

Add about one-third of the whipped egg whites to the batter and using a rubber scraper, fold them in gently. Repeat with the next third, then the last third.

Pour into the prepared baking pan and bake for 50 minutes or until a bamboo skewer inserted into the center comes out clean. Cool and chill before cutting. Serve with whipped cream!

1½ cups (150g) walnuts

4 large eggs, at room temperature

Scant ¼ teaspoon salt

½ cup (96g) erythritol

1 recipe Coffee Whipped Cream (page 275)

Sugar-free chocolate syrup (such as Walden Farms or Hershey's), for serving (optional)

YIELD: 8 servings – Per serving: 278 calories; 26g fat (82.0% calories from fat); 9g protein; 4g carbohydrate; 1g dietary fiber; 3g net carbohydrate.

WALNUT TORTE WITH COFFEE WHIPPED CREAM

Behold your new holiday dessert! This is luscious, not to mention impressive. This recipe is all about the technique—do not skimp on the beating. It's the air you mix in that makes the torte rise.

Preheat the oven to 350°F (180°C, or gas mark 4). Cut a circle of baking parchment to cover the bottom of a 9-inch (23cm) springform pan. Do not grease the sides!

Put the walnuts in your food processor and pulse until they are finely chopped, stopping before they become nut butter.

Separate the eggs, putting the whites in a deep, narrow bowl and the yolks in a regular mixing bowl. Since the tiniest speck of yolk will keep whites from whipping, do yourself a favor and separate each white into a custard cup before adding the white to its proper bowl. If a yolk breaks, save that egg for scramble eggs later, grab a clean custard cup and another egg, and proceed.

Okay, you have your whites in one bowl and your yolks in another. Use your electric mixer on high to whip the egg whites until they are stiff but not dry. Do this before you beat the yolks, or you'll have to scrupulously wash your beaters.

Now, beat the yolks with the salt until light and fluffy, about 4 minutes. Keep beating as you add the erythritol a couple of spoonfuls at a time. When all the erythritol is in, turn the mixer to low and beat in the ground walnuts in 3 additions.

Use a rubber scraper to fold the whipped egg whites into the batter in 3 additions, incorporating gently but well. Scrape the batter into the prepared pan.

Bake for 40 to 45 minutes or until a bamboo skewer inserted into the center comes out clean. Remove from oven and let it cool for 5 minutes.

Use a thin-bladed knife and run it around the edge to loosen the cake from the pan. The cake will fall a bit as it cools—panic not, that's where the Coffee Whipped Cream is going. Fill the torte with the whipped cream just before serving. If you're not eating your torte all at once, it's better to simply top each slice with whipped cream and store the leftover torte and whipped cream separately.

If you'd like to gild the lily, you can drizzle a little Walden Farms or Hershey's sugar-free chocolate syrup over each slice, as well.

1 cup (235ml) heavy cream, chilled

1 teaspoon Instant coffee granules, regular or decaf

18 drops of liquid stevia

YIELD: 8 servings – Per serving: 103 calories; 11g fat (94.1% calories from fat); 1g protein; 1g carbohydrate; 0g dietary fiber, 1g net carbohydrate.

COFFEE WHIPPED CREAM

I first used this on the Walnut Torte (page 274), but quickly realized it had potential to make many sweet friends, including a cup of coffee. Coffee whipped cream on your coffee—how great would that be? The liquid stevia is the wild card, here. You can use plain, vanilla, chocolate, hazelnut, or English toffee stevia, all to great effect. Play with it! And keep in mind the flavor of the dessert it will be topping.

Put the cream in a deep, heavy bowl and add the instant coffee and the liquid stevia. Use an electric mixer or a whisk to whip just until stiff. Don't overwhip! You'll wind up with coffee-flavored butter.

---

2 cups (475ml) heavy cream

⅓ cup (64g) powdered erythritol

¼ teaspoon liquid stevia, lemon drop

6 tablespoons (90ml) lemon juice

2 teaspoons lemon zest

YIELD: 6 servings – Per serving: 278 calories, 29g fat (92.5% calories from fat); 2g protein; 4g carbohydrate; trace dietary fiber; 4g net carbohydrate.

LEMON POSSET

The superb cooking magazine *Cook's Illustrated* recently published a recipe for lemon posset. The question was, could it be made without sugar? The answer is a resounding "Yes!" Creamy and cool, with a rich lemon flavor, this is an ideal dessert.

In a saucepan over medium heat, combine the cream, erythritol, and liquid stevia. Bring to a boil, turn the heat down to keep it just boiling, and let cook for 5 minutes. Whisk in the lemon juice and lemon zest.

Divide into 6 small portions—it's darned rich!—and refrigerate for 4 to 5 hours. It will set up as it chills.

---

2 cups (475ml) heavy cream

⅓ cup (64g) powdered erythritol

¼ teaspoon liquid stevia, plain or lemon drop for a lemon-lime flavor

⅓ cup (80ml) lime juice

2 teaspoons lime zest

YIELD: 6 servings – Per serving: 277 calories; 29g fat (92.8% calories from fat); 2g protein; 3g carbohydrate; trace dietary fiber; 3g net carbohydrate.

LIME POSSET

Having found Lemon Posset (above) a smashing success, Lime Posset was imperative. Angele, our tester, rates this a 10, both for flavor and for ease. If you love Key lime pie, you've got to try this.

In a saucepan over medium heat, combine the cream, erythritol, and liquid stevia. Bring to a boil, turn the heat down to keep it just boiling, and let cook for 5 minutes. Whisk in the lime juice and zest.

Divide into 6 small portions—it's darned rich!—and refrigerate for 4 to 5 hours. It will set up as it chills.

1½ tablespoons (11g) unflavored gelatin

½ cup (96g) powdered erythritol

½ teaspoon liquid stevia, plain or Valencia orange

¾ cup (175ml) boiling water

1½ pounds (680g) cream cheese, softened

1 cup (230g) sour cream

¼ cup (60ml) lime juice

2 teaspoons grated lime zest

½ teaspoon orange extract

¼ cup (60ml) tequila

1 recipe Sweet-and-Salty Almond Crust (below)

Paper-thin slices of lime or strips of lime zest, for garnish

YIELD: 12 servings –
Per serving: 422 calories; 37g fat (79.2% calories from fat); 13g protein; 9g carbohydrate; 2g dietary fiber; 7g net carbohydrate.

1½ cups (218g) almonds

⅓ cup (76g) vanilla whey protein powder

¼ cup (48g) powdered erythritol

¼ cup (55g) butter, melted

1 tablespoon (15g) kosher salt

YIELD: 12 servings –
Per serving: 163 calories; 14g fat (70.8% calories from fat); 8g protein; 4g carbohydrate; 2g dietary fiber; 2g net carbohydrate.

MARGARITA NO-BAKE CHEESECAKE

I originally came up with this for *The Low-Carb Barbecue Book* after seeing Emeril Lagasse make a margarita cheesecake on television. I've updated this to use erythritol and stevia instead of Splenda, but you could use liquid sucralose if you prefer. Please note that because this is a no-bake cheesecake, it does contain the alcohol found in ¼ cup (60ml) of tequila. It's not for children nor for those avoiding alcohol. You can leave the tequila out, but then it's just a Lime Orange Cheesecake.

Combine the gelatin, erythritol, and liquid stevia in a saucepan and pour the boiling water over them. Stir over low heat until the gelatin is completely dissolved. Turn off the heat.

Put the softened cream cheese in a mixing bowl and beat with an electric mixer until very soft and creamy. (If you have a stand mixer, you can start the cheese beating before you dissolve the gelatin and just leave the mixer mixing on its own.) When the cheese is very smooth and creamy, add the sour cream and beat that in well, scraping down the sides of the bowl as needed. Next, beat in the lime juice, lime zest, orange extract, and tequila.

Go back to your saucepan of gelatin. It should still be liquid! If it's not, you'll need to heat it again, gently. Beat the gelatin mixture into the cheese mixture and make sure everything is very well combined. Pour into the Sweet-and-Salty Almond Crust (below) and chill for at least 4 or 5 hours, and overnight is better.

Run a knife around the cake, between the cake and the rim of your springform pan, before removing the rim. Slice with a thin-bladed knife. Dipping the knife in hot water before each slice is a good idea, although not essential.

Garnish with paper-thin slices of lime, strips of lime zest, or both.

SWEET-AND-SALTY ALMOND CRUST

Emeril Lagasse made his crust with crushed pretzels, to get that salty note so characteristic of margaritas. We're not going to use pretzels, of course, so I came up with this crust instead. I like kosher salt for this because the larger grains make a real contribution.

Preheat the oven to 325°F (170°C, or gas mark 3). Coat a 9-inch (23cm) springform pan with nonstick cooking spray.

Put your almonds in your food processor with the S-blade in place. Run the food processor until the almonds are ground. Add the vanilla whey protein powder and Splenda and pulse to mix. You may need to open the processor and run a knife around the bottom edge of the bowl to get everything into the path of the blade.

Now, turn the processor on and pour in the butter while it's running. Let everything blend—and once again, you may need to do the knife-around-the-bottom-edge-of-the-processor trick. When the butter is evenly distributed, turn off the processor. Add the kosher salt and pulse the processor just enough to distribute the salt throughout the mixture.

Press firmly into the prepared pan, making sure you cover the seam around the bottom, but don't expect to be able to build it all the way up the sides. Bake for about 10 minutes or until lightly golden and cool before filling.

MOCHACHINO CHEESECAKE

Says tester Christina, "I served this to company and it was raved over. We have a neighbor who gets a $30 flourless chocolate cake at a French bakery in Dallas. This really does put that cake to shame."

1 recipe Crisp Chocolate Crust (below)

1 pound (455g) cream cheese, softened

1 egg

¼ cup (60ml) heavy cream

⅔ cup (53g) cocoa powder

¼ cup (48g) powdered erythritol

1 tablespoon (3g) instant coffee granules, regular or decaf

¼ teaspoon liquid stevia, chocolate

YIELD: 12 servings –
Per serving: 330 calories; 31g fat (78.2% calories from fat); 10g protein; 9g carbohydrate; 4g dietary fiber; 5g net carbohydrate.

Preheat the oven to 325°F (170°C, or gas mark 3).

Make your crust first, making it in an 8-inch (20cm) springform pan you've sprayed with nonstick cooking spray instead of a pie plate. Bake for 12 minutes and let cool before filling.

Using your electric mixer, beat together the cream cheese, egg, and cream until quite smooth; you'll need to scrape down the sides of the bowl several times. Now beat in the cocoa powder, erythritol, instant coffee, and liquid stevia. When it's all well blended and very smooth, pour into the crust.

Put a pan of water on the floor of the oven and then put the springform pan on the rack above it. Bake for 50 to 60 minutes or until set almost to the center—the very center can still be a little wobbly when the pan is jiggled.

Remove from the oven, cool, and then chill before serving. A little whipped cream is nice on top of this, but hardly essential.

CRISP CHOCOLATE CRUST

This version of the recipe calls for your crust to be made in a pie plate, but it also serves beautifully as a cheesecake crust when pressed into a springform pan. And really, what cheesecake wouldn't benefit from a chocolate crust?

1½ cups (218g) almonds

¼ cup (48g) erythritol

2 squares bitter chocolate, melted

3 tablespoons (45ml) melted butter

2 tablespoons (20g) vanilla whey protein powder

YIELD: 12 servings –
Per serving: 164 calories; 15g fat (75.3% calories from fat); 6g protein; 5g carbohydrate; 3g dietary fiber; 2g net carbohydrate.

Preheat the oven to 325°F (170°C, or gas mark 3). Coat a 10-inch (25cm) pie plate with nonstick cooking spray.

Using the S-blade in your food processor, grind the almonds until they're the texture of cornmeal. Add the erythritol and pulse to combine. Pour in the melted chocolate and melted butter and run the processor until evenly distributed—you may need to stop the processor and run the tip of a knife blade around the outer edge to get everything to combine properly. Then, add the vanilla whey protein and pulse again to combine.

Turn out into the prepared pan. Press firmly and evenly into place. Bake for 8 minutes. Let cool before filling.

CRUST

2 cups (200g) pecan halves

¼ cup (48g) erythritol

1½ teaspoons ground ginger

⅛ teaspoon salt

¼ cup (55g) butter, chilled

1 tablespoon (15ml) water

12 drops of liquid stevia, English toffee

FILLING

1 cup (245g) canned pumpkin

½ cup (120ml) heavy cream

2 teaspoons vanilla extract

1 teaspoon ground cinnamon

½ teaspoon liquid stevia, English toffee

½ teaspoon ground ginger

¼ teaspoon ground nutmeg

¼ teaspoon salt

1½ pounds (680g) cream cheese, softened

½ cup (96g) powdered erythritol

1 teaspoon molasses

4 eggs

Dulce de Leche Whipped Cream (page 279), for serving

YIELD: 12 servings – Per serving: 420 calories; 41g fat (85.3% calories from fat); 8g protein; 8g carbohydrate; 2g dietary fiber; 6g net carbohydrate.

PUMPKIN CHEESECAKE WITH GINGER-PECAN CRUST

When asked, "On a scale of 1 to 10, with 1 being, 'Oh dear God, you expect me to eat this?' and 10 being 'Wow, I'd be happy to pay big bucks for this in a restaurant!' where do you rate this recipe?" Rebecca replied, "15!! (Everybody LOVED it!) … everybody exclaimed about the crust's flavor and how the cheesecake part was the PERFECT texture." Those 12 servings are pretty generous. If you're serving this after Thanksgiving dinner—quite an idea, huh?—you can probably get 16 servings out of it because people will presumably be pretty full already.

To make the crust, preheat the oven to 350°F (180°C, or gas mark 4), positioning the rack in the middle. Coat a 9-inch (23cm) springform pan thoroughly with nonstick cooking spray.

Put the pecan halves, erythritol, ground ginger, and salt in your food processor and run until the pecans are ground to a meal. Cut the butter into 4 tablespoons (14g), add, and pulse until it's cut in. Mix the water and liquid stevia in a cup. With the processor running, drizzle the mixture in. When a dough forms, turn off the processor.

Turn the dough out into the prepared pan and press it firmly and evenly across the bottom, making sure to cover the seam at the bottom edge.

Bake the crust for 12 to 14 minutes. Let it cool while you make your filling.

To make the filling, in a medium-size mixing bowl, whisk together the pumpkin, heavy cream, vanilla, cinnamon, liquid stevia, ginger, nutmeg, and salt.

In large mixing bowl, use your electric mixer to beat the cream cheese until quite creamy, about 2 to 3 minutes. Scrape down the sides of the bowl often. Beat in the erythritol and molasses, blending very well.

Add the pumpkin mixture and mix until well blended. Then, beat in the eggs, one at a time, still scraping down the sides of the bowl often to make sure everything is evenly blended.

Tear off a big piece of heavy-duty aluminum foil—about 20 inches (50cm) long. Wrap the outside of your springform pan with it—you'll be putting it in a water bath, and you don't want water leaking in through the seams!

Scrape the batter into the foil-wrapped pan. Place it in a larger roasting pan and pour hot water around the springform to about 1 inch (2.5cm) deep. Place the whole shebang in the oven.

Bake for 60 to 70 minutes or until mostly set but still a little jiggly in the center.

Carefully, lift the springform from the water bath and place it on a wire rack to cool. Grab a thin-bladed paring knife. Run it around the edge of the cake, loosening it from the sides. This should prevent cracking as it cools.

When cool, chill well. Serve with Dulce de Leche Whipped Cream.

2 tablespoons (28ml) sugar-free coffee flavoring syrup, caramel (Monin O'Free brand)

1 cup (235ml) heavy cream

YIELD: 12 servings – Per serving: 68 calories; 7g fat (94.5% calories from fat); trace protein; 1g carbohydrate; 0g dietary fiber; 1g net carbohydrate.

DULCE DE LECHE WHIPPED CREAM

This is a must for the Pumpkin Cheesecake with Ginger-Pecan Crust, but consider it for other desserts—or in your coffee. Or maybe just a bowl of Dulce de Leche Whipped Cream. Why not?

I've specified Monin O'Free syrup because it's made with erythritol, giving it cooking properties that some other sugar-free syrups lack. If you object to the artificial sweeteners in the syrup, you could use English toffee–flavored liquid stevia instead. I'd use about 30 drops. If you use stevia, you can simply add it to chilled heavy cream and whip.

Put your caramel syrup in a small saucepan and cook over low heat until reduced to 1 tablespoon (15ml). Mix with the heavy cream and then chill the combination for several hours.

Whip as you would regular whipped cream!

2 cups (475ml) heavy cream

6 eggs

⅓ cup (64g) erythritol

½ teaspoon liquid stevia, vanilla

1 teaspoon vanilla extract

1 pinch of salt

1 pinch of ground nutmeg

6 tablespoons (90ml) sugar-free caramel coffee flavoring syrup

---

YIELD: 6 servings – Per serving: 341 calories; 34g fat (88.3% calories from fat); 7g protein; 3g carbohydrate; trace dietary fiber; 3g net carbohydrate.

FLAN

I cribbed this from *200 Low-Carb, High-Fat Recipes* because it's easy, nutritious, seriously keto, and our tester, Rebecca, gave it a 10. She also says the servings are very generous, and you could likely serve eight. I think this would make a great summer breakfast!

Preheat the oven to 350°F (180°C, or gas mark 4). Grease a 10-inch (25cm) pie plate (or a 9½-inch [23.5cm] deep pie plate).

Put the cream, eggs, erythritol, liquid stevia, vanilla, salt, and nutmeg in your blender and run until all well combined.

Put a shallow baking pan on the oven rack. Place the prepared pie plate in it. Pour water into the outer pan up to within about ½ inch (1.3cm) of the rim of the pie plate. Now, pour the custard mixture into the pie plate. Bake for about 50 to 60 minutes or until just set.

Carefully, remove the pie plate from the water bath to let it cool for 30 minutes before chilling.

You can run a knife around the edge and invert the flan onto a plate and then top with the caramel syrup to serve, but it's easier to just cut wedges like a pie or spoon it out. Still, top it with the syrup to serve!

KETO BROWNIES

2 ounces (55g) bitter chocolate

1 cup (225g) butter

½ cup (96g) erythritol

½ teaspoon liquid stevia, chocolate, vanilla, or English toffee

2 eggs

½ cup (114g) vanilla whey protein powder

1 pinch of salt

YIELD: 12 servings – Per serving: 208 calories; 19g fat (79.8% calories from fat); 9g protein; 2g carbohydrate; 1g dietary fiber; 1g net carbohydrate.

I'm pretty sure these are the lowest-carb brownies I've ever come up with. Be aware—our testers say that the texture improves remarkably as these cool, so do not expect to eat them straight out of the oven. They also note not to overbake—you'll see butter floating on the surface, but that's okay. Take them out on time. Also, one tester wanted them sweeter; how sweet you like them will likely depend on how long you've been avoiding sugar. Feel free to add a couple more tablespoons (24g) of erythritol and/or a bit more liquid stevia.

Preheat the oven to 350°F (180°C, or gas mark 4). Coat an 8 × 8-inch (20 × 20cm) baking dish with cooking spray.

In the top of a double boiler over boiling water or in a saucepan over a heat diffuser set over very low heat, melt the chocolate and the butter together. Stir until they're well combined. Scrape this into a mixing bowl.

Add the erythritol, stir well, and then stir in the liquid stevia. Next, beat in the eggs, one at a time. Stir in the vanilla whey protein powder and salt.

Pour into the prepared baking pan. Bake for 15 to 20 minutes. Do not overbake! Let cool in the pan and then cut into 12 bars. Store in a tightly covered container in the refrigerator.

½ cup (114g) vanilla whey protein powder

¼ cup (60g) Natural Mate sweetener

¼ cup (24g) almond meal

½ cup (40g) cocoa powder

1 tablespoon (3g) instant coffee granules, regular or decaf

½ teaspoon salt

½ cup (112g) butter

2 eggs

¼ cup (60ml) water

½ teaspoon liquid stevia, dark chocolate

6 ounces (170g) Lily's sugar-free chocolate chips

YIELD: 25 small brownies – Per brownie: 92 calories; 7g fat (61.3% calories from fat); 5g protein; 4g carbohydrate; 2g dietary fiber; 2g net carbohydrate.

ESPRESSO CHOCOLATE CHIP BROWNIES

Super-dark and dense, these are somewhere between a brownie and a truffle. Oh, they're so good!

Preheat the oven to 350°F (180°C, or gas mark 4). Coat an 8 × 8-inch (20 × 20cm) pan with nonstick cooking spray.

Put the vanilla whey protein, Natural Mate, almond meal, cocoa powder, instant coffee, and salt in your food processor and pulse to combine. Add the butter and pulse until it's cut in and well combined with the dry ingredients.

With the motor running, add the eggs, one at a time, through the feed tube, letting the first be incorporated before adding the second and stopping to scrape down the sides of the bowl if needed.

Mix the water with the liquid stevia in a cup. With the motor running, pour this mixture through the feed tube, again, scraping down the sides if needed.

Add the chocolate chips and pulse until just mixed in—you don't want to pulverize them!

Spread the batter evenly in your prepared pan. Bake for 20 minutes or until a toothpick inserted into the center comes out clean. Don't overbake!

Let cool in the pan before cutting into 25 squares.

NOTE: You can use any sugar-free semisweet chocolate that's sweetened with stevia, inulin, and/or erythritol (ChocoPerfection is one such brand). To make chocolate chips out of bars, break them up, put them in your food processor, and pulse until you have bits about the right size. They'll be uneven, and you'll get some chocolate dust, but they'll taste just fine.

½ cup (112g) butter, at room temperature

½ cup (96g) erythritol

1 teaspoon dark molasses (optional)

½ teaspoon liquid stevia, English toffee

1 egg

1 cup (260g) natural peanut butter

½ teaspoon salt

½ teaspoon baking soda

½ teaspoon vanilla extract

1 cup (96g) almond meal

½ cup (114g) vanilla whey protein powder

1 teaspoon guar or xanthan gum

YIELD: 5 dozen cookies –
Per cookie: 56 calories; 4g fat (64.5% calories from fat); 3g protein; 2g carbohydrate; trace dietary fiber; 2g net carbohydrate.

PEANUT BUTTER COOKIES

Rich and crumbly, these are adapted from a recipe in *The Joy of Cooking* my mother made every year for Christmas. I think Mom would approve.

You may omit the molasses if you like, in the interests of having no sugar whatsoever. It's there to lend a brown sugar flavor and does not increase the per-cookie carb count by even 1 gram.

Preheat the oven to 375°F (190°C, or gas mark 5). Line cookie sheets with baking parchment or coat with nonstick cooking spray.

In a mixing bowl with an electric mixer, beat the butter with the erythritol, molasses (if using), and liquid stevia until light and fluffy. Beat in the egg, then the peanut butter, salt, baking soda, and vanilla.

In a small bowl, combine the almond meal, vanilla whey protein, and guar or xathan, stirring until they're combined.

Turn the mixer back on and beat in the almond meal mixture, about one-third at a time, until it's all blended in.

Use clean hands to roll dough into 1-inch (2.5cm) balls and arrange on the prepared cookie sheets. Use a fork to press them down, making crisscross patterns on top.

Bake for 10 to 12 minutes until set. Cool on wire racks before storing in a cookie tin or snap-top container.

1½ cups (150g) pecans

5 tablespoons (75g) Virtue or Natural Mate, divided

4 tablespoons (55g) butter, at room temperature

1 pinch of salt

12 ounces (340g) cream cheese, at room temperature

2 eggs

1 teaspoon vanilla extract

¼ teaspoon liquid stevia, vanilla

1 teaspoon ground cinnamon

YIELD: 16 bars – Per bar: 177 calories; 18g fat (87.3% calories from fat); 3g protein; 3g carbohydrate; 1g dietary fiber; 2g net carbohydrate.

CINNAMON CHEESECAKE BARS

Cheesecake in a cookie! How can you beat that? I cut this into 16 cookie-size bars, but you can make them bigger if you like.

Preheat the oven to 350°F (180°C, or gas mark 4). Coat an 8 × 8-inch (20 × 20cm) pan with nonstick cooking spray.

Combine the pecans, 2 tablespoons (30g) of the Virtue, butter, and salt in your food processor and pulse until you have a soft dough.

Turn the dough out into the prepared pan and press firmly and evenly into place. Bake for 15 to 18 minutes until just turning golden. Remove from the oven and turn the heat down to 325°F (170°C, or gas mark 3).

Put the cream cheese, eggs, vanilla, and liquid stevia in the food processor and run until smooth, scraping down the sides once or twice. Spread this evenly over the pecan crust. Bake for 15 minutes.

While it's baking, stir together the remaining 3 tablespoons (45g) of Virtue or Natural Mate and the cinnamon.

When the 15 minutes are up, sprinkle the cinnamon-Virtue mixture evenly over the whole thing. Bake for another 5 minutes. Let cool before cutting into 16 bars and store in the fridge.

1 cup (175g) Lily's sugar-free chocolate chips

¾ cup (195g) natural peanut butter (the kind with just peanuts in it)

2 tablespoons (28g) coconut oil

5 ounces (140g) pork rinds

YIELD: 24 bars – Per bar: 113 calories; 8g fat (66.7% calories from fat); 6g protein; 4g carbohydrate; 1g dietary fiber; 3g net carbohydrate.

COCOA-PEANUT PORKIES

The first time I tried this, I thought, "Dana, you have gone right 'round the bend, making pork rind cookies." Hah. They're fantastic. I have gotten more glowing feedback on this recipe than on almost any other. Try them—really.

I first created this recipe using CarbSmart chocolate chips. Sadly, they are no longer with us. I now use Lily's stevia-sweetened chocolate chips, which taste good, but melt a bit differently. I've altered the recipe to accommodate them.

You can use another brand of sugar-free semisweet chocolate, if you like, but be aware that many, if not most, are sweetened with maltitol. Two issues: one, you absorb roughly half of maltitol, which means that, unlike erythritol, you can't completely discount it from your carb count. Two, maltitol can cause gut issues ranging from mild embarrassment to serious dashing for the restroom, depending on how sensitive you are and how much of it you eat. Read labels!

We adore these as they are, but if your kids, just being weaned off of sugar, think they're not quite sweet enough, there's an easy fix: add a glycerine-based liquid stevia extract to taste when you're stirring up the chocolate—peanut butter mixture. NOW dark chocolate flavor would be good; so would English toffee flavor. Go easy—think drops, not spoonfuls.

Line a 9 × 13-inch (23 × 33cm) pan with nonstick foil (this is optional, but sure makes cleanup a breeze). Or coat with nonstick spray if you prefer.

Originally, I microwaved the chocolate and peanut butter for these no-bake cookie bars, but my experiences microwaving Lily's chips have been … disappointing. So, put your chocolate chips, peanut butter, and coconut oil in a saucepan over the very lowest heat possible. If you have a heat diffuser, use it. You could also use a double boiler. The point is not to scorch your chocolate.

In the meanwhile, smash your pork rinds. I just poke a hole in the bag to let the air out and bash 'em with my fists. You want bits somewhere between pea- and hazelnut-size. Dump your broken-up pork rinds into your biggest mixing bowl.

When the chocolate—peanut mixture is all melted, stir it together well and then scrape it into the bowl with the pork rinds. Use your scraper to stir thoroughly, coating every inch of the pork rinds with the mixture.

Dump your mixture into the prepared pan and use a scraper to spread or press them out into an even layer. Chill thoroughly and then cut into 24 bars. Store in the fridge.

2 cups (475ml) heavy cream

1 cup (235ml) unsweetened pourable coconut milk

2 ounces (55g) bitter chocolate

1 teaspoon liquid stevia, chocolate

1 teaspoon chocolate extract

4 egg yolks

1 tablespoon (15ml) vodka

1 tablespoon (15ml) vegetable glycerine

YIELD: 6 servings – Per serving: 379 calories; 39g fat (89.2% calories from fat); 4g protein; 6g carbohydrate; 1g dietary fiber; 5g net carbohydrate.

CHOCOLATE ICE CREAM

This has a dark chocolate flavor, which I prefer. If you want it sweeter, who am I to argue? For that matter, you could use vanilla stevia instead of chocolate to give a mellower flavor. If you're going to eat this all up immediately, you can skip the vodka and glycerine—they're there to keep the ice cream from freezing rock-hard if you store it in the freezer. I buy the chocolate extract locally, but if you can't find it, you can get it online.

In a large saucepan, combine the heavy cream and coconut milk. Place over medium-low heat and bring to just below a simmer.

Break the chocolate into pieces and add to the hot cream, whisking it in as it melts. Add the liquid stevia and chocolate extract.

In a mixing bowl, whisk the egg yolks until well mixed.

When the chocolate has blended completely with the cream—use a rubber scraper to make sure there's no uncombined chocolate lurking at the bottom of the saucepan—scoop a ladleful of the hot cream and pour it into the yolks, whisking all the time. When it's blended in, repeat with a second ladleful of cream and then a third. Now, you can pour the whole thing into the cream mixture remaining in the saucepan.

Keep cooking and whisking the custard mixture until it will coat a spoon and a finger drawn through it leaves a clean line, about 5 minutes.

Let the custard cool and then transfer to a snap-top container and chill overnight.

The next day, whisk in the vodka and glycerine, blending well.

Freeze according to the instructions that came with your ice cream maker.

1 pound (455g) frozen strawberries, unsweetened

2 cups (475ml) heavy cream

¼ teaspoon liquid stevia (I'd use lemon drop.)

½ tablespoon lemon juice

1 tablespoon (15ml) vodka

1 tablespoon (15ml) vegetable glycerine

YIELD: 6 servings – Per serving: 309 calories; 29g fat (84.7% calories from fat); 2g protein; 10g carbohydrate; 2g dietary fiber; 8g net carbohydrate.

INSTANT STRAWBERRY ICE CREAM

This takes a pretty good food processor, but oh, gosh, is it good. I made this with heavy cream, but if you're dairy-free, you can use canned coconut milk. It works fine. You can also use another kind of frozen berries—how about blueberries?

Just put everything in your food processor and run it until the strawberries are ground up. This may require prying a strawberry off the blade a few times! The strawberries freeze the coconut milk, and you get really-truly ice cream with an insanely great strawberry flavor.

If you're going to eat this all up right away, you can skip the vodka and vegetable glycerine—they're in there to help keep the ice cream from turning rock-hard in the freezer.

13 ounces (365ml) unsweetened canned coconut milk

2 cups (475ml) unsweetened pourable coconut milk

12 whole star anise

2 teaspoons vanilla extract

4 egg yolks

⅓ cup (64g) powdered erythritol

½ teaspoon liquid stevia, vanilla

1 tablespoon (15ml) vegetable glycerine

1 tablespoon (15ml) vodka

YIELD: 6 servings – Per serving: 213 calories; 18g fat (73.2% calories from fat); 5g protein; 9g carbohydrate; 2g dietary fiber; 7g net carbohydrate.

COCONUT–STAR ANISE ICE CREAM

I saw this suggested as a Vietnamese ice cream flavor. I thought I'd try it with coconut milk instead of half-and-half—and without the sugar, of course. You'll need to start a day early! The anise flavor is delicate; if you'd like it stronger, our tester Rebecca suggests adding ¼ teaspoon anise extract.

The glycerine and vodka are to keep the ice cream scoopable; otherwise, sugar-free ice cream gets rock-hard in the freezer. You can buy vegetable glycerine at any pharmacy. I assume you know where to buy vodka. Thanks to my friend Soren Schreiber-Katz for the technique!

I know the carb count seems high, but Mastercook is counting 3 grams of carbohydrate for each star anise—36 total grams! But you strain those out and toss them. You can, of course, skip the anise and just make vanilla ice cream.

In a large saucepan over low heat, combine the coconut milks and star anise. Bring it up to just barely simmering and let it cook for 30 minutes. Stir in the vanilla.

While that's happening, in a large bowl, whisk the egg yolks with the erythritol and liquid stevia.

Strain the coconut milk and discard the star anise. Whisk the hot coconut milk into the egg yolks ½ cup (120ml) at a time, whisking constantly, so as not to wind up with very odd scrambled eggs.

When all the coconut milk is mixed with the egg yolks, return the mixture to the saucepan over the lowest possible heat—if you have a heat diffuser, use it! (You could do this in a double boiler, if you don't mind the extra pan.) Continue stirring over the heat until you have a custard that coats the back of a wooden spoon, about 4 to 5 minutes.

Pour the custard into a heatproof container with a lid. Let it cool and then refrigerate overnight.

The next day, whisk in the glycerine and vodka and freeze according to the instructions that came along with your ice cream maker. Store any leftover ice cream in a snap-top container in the freezer.

13 ounces (365ml) unsweetened canned coconut milk

1 cup (235ml) unsweetened pourable coconut milk

4 egg yolks

1 teaspoon vanilla extract

2 tablespoons (28ml) Monin O'Free caramel coffee flavoring syrup

1 teaspoon liquid stevia, English toffee

¼ teaspoon butter flavoring

¼ teaspoon salt

⅓ cup (37g) chopped pecans

1 tablespoon (15ml) vegetable glycerine

1 tablespoon (15ml) vodka

YIELD: 6 servings – Per serving: 222 calories; 21g fat (85.9% calories from fat); 4g protein; 4g carbohydrate; 1g dietary fiber; 3g net carbohydrate.

BUTTER PECAN COCONUT ICE CREAM

Here's an ice cream for all of you who shun dairy—keep in mind, you need to make the custard the day before so it has time to chill. The Monin O'Free syrup is specified because it contains erythritol, which contributes to the texture. You can skip the butter flavoring if you like —your ice cream will be more caramelly than buttery, but still yummy. Thanks to my friend Soren Schreiber-Katz for the suggestion of vodka and glycerine to keep the ice cream from becoming utterly rock-like in the freezer.

In a large saucepan over medium-low heat, combined the canned and pourable coconut milks and bring to a simmer.

In the meanwhile, in a large bowl, whisk the egg yolks with the vanilla, caramel syrup, liquid stevia, butter flavoring, and salt.

When the coconut milk is simmering, use a ladle to transfer ½ cup (120ml) into the yolk mixture, whisking all the while. When it's whisked in, transfer another ladleful of coconut milk into the yolk mixture, again whisking all the while.

Now, pour the yolk mixture into the saucepan with the remaining coconut milk, whisking it in, and keep whisking over medium-low heat until the custard is thick enough to coat a spoon and leave a clean line when you run your finger through it, about 5 minutes.

Transfer the custard to a heatproof container and chill overnight.

Toast the chopped pecans—I gave mine 5 minutes in a 350°F (180°C, or gas mark 4) oven.

Pull the custard out of the refrigerator and whisk in the glycerine and vodka.

Freeze the custard according to the instructions that come with your ice cream maker. When it's half-frozen, add the pecans so they get worked in.

Need I instruct you to store any leftovers in the freezer?

¾ cup (101g) hazelnuts

¾ cup (171g) vanilla whey protein powder

½ cup (96g) erythritol

3 tablespoons (15g) cocoa powder

1 teaspoon baking soda

½ teaspoon guar or xanthan

½ teaspoon salt

1 cup (235ml) water

½ teaspoon liquid stevia, chocolate

1 tablespoon (15ml) white vinegar

1 teaspoon vanilla extract

5 tablespoons (75ml) MCT oil

YIELD: 9 servings – Per serving: 220 calories; 16g fat (63.8% calories from fat); 16g protein; 5g carbohydrate; 2g dietary fiber; 3g net carbohydrate.

COCKEYED CAKE DECARBED

This is my version of a snack cake that appeared in Peg Bracken's *I Hate to Cook Book* in 1960. Peg is my professional idol—and the cake is mighty tasty, too. The erythritol creates a crystallized layer at the bottom of the cake. At first, I thought that was a flaw, but decided I really liked it—it's candy-like. You can use almond meal instead of hazelnuts, but you'll add a gram or two of carb to every serving. It's cheaper and easier, though—your decision. You can up the fat content with a dollop of whipped cream.

Preheat the oven to 350°F (180°C, or gas mark 4). Coat a 9 × 9-inch (23 × 23cm) pan with nonstick cooking spray.

Run the hazelnuts through your food processor until you have a fine meal, stopping short of nut butter. Turn the nut meal out into a mixing bowl.

Add the vanilla whey protein, erythritol, cocoa powder, baking soda, guar or xanthan, and salt to the hazelnut meal. Stir everything until it's evenly distributed. If your baking soda has lumps—mine did—crush 'em. Dump the mixture into the prepared baking pan.

Stir together the water and liquid stevia in a cup.

Make 3 holes or grooves in the dry ingredients. Into one pour the vinegar, into another the vanilla, and into the third the MCT oil.

Pour the water-stevia mixture over it all and use a spoon to stir until there are no lumps of dry stuff left.

Bake for 30 minutes until a toothpick inserted into the center comes out clean. Let cool thoroughly before cutting into 9 squares.

Cover with foil or plastic wrap and store in the refrigerator or transfer to a snap-top container and freeze—a single square doesn't take long to thaw.

NOODLE KUGEL

2 packages (8 ounces, or 225g each) of tofu shirataki, fettuccini

1 cup (115g) full-fat cottage cheese

½ cup (120g) cream cheese, softened

¼ cup (48g) powdered erythritol

¼ teaspoon liquid stevia, vanilla

2 eggs

½ cup (115g) sour cream

1 teaspoon vanilla extract

½ teaspoon ground cinnamon

⅛ teaspoon ground nutmeg

½ teaspoon lemon zest

2 tablespoons (28g) butter

½ cup (55g) slivered almonds

YIELD: 6 servings – Per serving: 274 calories; 24g fat (77.3% calories from fat); 11g protein; 5g carbohydrate; 1g dietary fiber; 4g net carbohydrate.

For the uninitiated, a kugel is one of a whole class of dishes in Jewish cookery, both sweet and savory. I wanted to know whether noodle kugel, a traditional dessert, would work with shirataki. My tester Wendy said she'd been looking for just such a recipe. With extra sweetener and cinnamon sprinkled on top, this dish was pronounced perfect.

Preheat the oven to 350°F (180°C, or gas mark 4). Coat an 8 × 8-inch (20 × 20cm) baking dish with nonstick cooking spray.

Drain, rinse, and microwave the shirataki according to the directions on page 23.

In a medium-size mixing bowl, using your electric mixer on medium speed, beat together the cottage cheese, cream cheese, erythritol, and liquid stevia.

Beat in the eggs, one at a time. Then, turn the mixer speed to medium-low and use it to blend in the sour cream, vanilla, cinnamon, nutmeg, and lemon zest.

Give your shirataki a final draining and then fold into the cheese mixture. Spoon the mixture into your prepared baking dish and spread it so it's level. Place it in the oven and set the timer for 20 minutes.

In a small skillet over medium-low heat, melt the butter and then stir the almonds in it until they're just getting a little golden.

When the timer beeps, sprinkle the toasted almonds over the kugel and put it in to bake for another 10 to 15 minutes or until set.

Serve hot! You can mix up a little cinnamon and powdered erythritol to sprinkle over each serving if you like.

COCONUT RUM BALLS

½ cup (130g) almond butter

3 ounces (85g) cream cheese, softened

½ teaspoon liquid stevia, chocolate or English toffee

¼ cup (60ml) dark rum

1 tablespoon (5g) cocoa powder

½ cup (40g) unsweetened shredded coconut

YIELD: 24 servings – Per serving: 56 calories; 5g fat (78.0% calories from fat); 1g protein; 1g carbohydrate; 1g dietary fiber; 0g net carbohydrate.

The original version of this recipe called for dipping them in "dipping chocolate," but that recipe called for maltitol-based sugar-free imitation honey. I was not able to work out a new version—it tasted fine, but the texture was off. So, I offer them to you like this and suggest that if you want to glorify them a bit, you could roll them in cocoa powder or dip them in Waldon Farms or Hershey's sugar-free chocolate syrup as you eat them.

Line a cookie sheet or jelly-roll pan with baking parchment or foil.

In a bowl, beat the almond butter and cream cheese together until blended. Mix the liquid stevia with the rum and add, along with the cocoa powder, beating them in thoroughly. Then, beat in the coconut.

Form into 24 balls, placing them on the prepared pan. Refrigerate until ready to serve.

1½ teaspoons unsweetened gelatin powder

2 tablespoons (28ml) cold water

3 tablespoons (45ml) boiling water

1 cup (235ml) strong brewed coffee, regular or decaf

¼ cup (48g) erythritol

¼ teaspoon liquid stevia (I used chocolate, but vanilla or toffee would be good here, too.)

1 tiny pinch of salt

1 can (13½ ounces, or 385ml) of unsweetened coconut milk, chilled

---

YIELD: 4 servings – Per serving: 191 calories; 20g fat (89.2% calories from fat); 3g protein; 3g carbohydrate; 0g dietary fiber; 3g net carbohydrate.

8 ounces (225g) fresh strawberries

1 recipe Whipped Cream (page 289)

YIELD: 6 servings – Per serving: 147 calories; 15g fat (87.8% calories from fat); 1g protein; 4g carbohydrate; 1g dietary fiber; 3g net carbohydrate.

COFFEE MOUSSE

Creamy, rich, smooth, and fluffy, this dessert is suitable for company. It also makes a great summer breakfast, especially for you Bulletproof Coffee™ fans. If you're willing to take the trouble, a little cocoa powder or espresso-grind coffee dusted on top looks pretty and tastes good.

Put the gelatin in a small dish and add the cold water. Let it sit for a few minutes until all the water has absorbed and the gelatin has swelled up. Now, add the boiling water and stir until the gelatin dissolves.

In a medium-size mixing bowl, combine the gelatin with the coffee, erythritol, liquid stevia, and salt. Whisk until the erythritol is dissolved and everything is well combined. Put the bowl in the refrigerator—you want to chill it until it's the texture of egg white.

When the gelatin mixture has thickened, you're ready to continue. Put your coconut milk into a small, deep mixing bowl and whip it on high speed until it's fluffy and thickened. Don't expect it to turn out like whipped cream; it won't get that stiff. But do whip it for a good 4 to 5 minutes on high.

Grab your bowl of gelatin and use the same beaters to whip it until it, too, is fluffy and thickening.

Now, with the mixer running, add the coconut milk to the gelatin mixture. Whip them together. Spoon the mixture into 4 pretty dessert dishes and chill for at least several hours, and overnight is great.

STRAWBERRIES AND WHIPPED CREAM

I know of no simpler nor prettier nor more agreeable company dessert than this. If you wish, you can add a little dish of Walden Farms or Hershey's sugar-free chocolate syrup for dipping, as well.

Wash the berries, but leave the hulls on. Arrange them on your chip-and-dip platter, with the whipped cream in the dip bowl. Bear it forth to acclaim.

1 cup (235ml) heavy cream, chilled

¼ teaspoon liquid stevia, vanilla

YIELD: 12 servings – Per serving: 68 calories; 7g fat (94.5% calories from fat); trace protein; 1g carbohydrate; 0g dietary fiber; 1g net carbohydrate.

NOTE: You can sub liquid monk fruit or sucralose, but add a capful of vanilla extract. And of course, you can make yours sweeter or less sweet than this.

WHIPPED CREAM

Some of you are thinking "Duh!" But I've had one friend tell me she'd tried to whip cream and it hadn't worked. Turned out she'd tried to do it in her food processor. And a young man of my acquaintance expressed amazement that it was possible to make whipped cream at home. He thought it only came in tubs or aerosol cans at the grocery store. So here it is.

There are only a few vital points: the cream must be labeled either "heavy cream" or "heavy whipping cream"—the two are near enough that it makes no difference. It must be well chilled. You must use either a whisk, an old-fashioned eggbeater (should you happen to have one kicking around somewhere), or—best—an electric mixer. Your bowl should be deep and narrow if possible, and chilling it and the beaters in the freezer for 10 to 15 minutes before whipping is a great idea.

Put your chilly cream and liquid stevia in that nice, cold, deep, narrow bowl and start beating it with your chosen implement. It will start to fluff up. Depending on what you wish to use it for, you can quit when it mounds nicely—this is good for putting on coffee drinks—or keep going until it's pretty stiff and makes a soft peak when you pull the mixer out.

Once it reaches that stage, quit beating immediately! If you overbeat your cream, you will wind up with butter. Using an electric mixer the whole thing shouldn't take more than a couple of minutes and only a little bit longer with a whisk or an eggbeater.

This will hold okay in the fridge for an hour or so, so you can make it before supper if you like.

---

1 cup (235ml) heavy cream, chilled

¼ teaspoon maple flavoring

¼ teaspoon liquid stevia, English toffee

YIELD: 8 servings – Per serving: 103 calories; 11g fat (94.5% calories from fat); 1g protein; 1g carbohydrate; 0g dietary fiber; 1g net carbohydrate.

MAPLE WHIPPED CREAM

Rebecca, my ace tester, tried the Mocha with Maple Whipped Cream on page 264 and insisted the whipped cream get its own listing. She thinks you should put it on pumpkin desserts.

This is pretty straightforward: Put all the ingredients in a deep, narrow bowl and use your electric mixer to whip it just about stiff. As always, don't overwhip or you'll get maple butter. Which might be nice, but there's a perfectly good recipe for Maple Butter on page 251. Oh, and popping your bowl and your beaters into the freezer for 10 minutes before you do this doesn't hurt a bit.

2 cups (475ml) heavy cream

1 cup (175g) Lily's sugar-free chocolate chips

2 egg yolks

2 tablespoons (28ml) dark rum

YIELD: 6 servings – Per serving: 402 calories; 38g fat (84.7% calories from fat); 4g protein; 11g carbohydrate; 4g dietary fiber; 7g net carbohydrate.

POT DE CHOCOLAT

I have published a number of variations of this super-easy, super-chocolaty, showstopping company dessert—which I first discovered in Peg Bracken's *I Hate To Cook Book*—over the years. This time, I wanted to know whether it worked with all heavy cream (instead of half-and-half) and with Lily's sugar-free chocolate chips. It does—it comes out like little bowls of ganache. I'm pretty sure the cream is hot enough to kill any germs from the raw egg, but if you're worried, pasteurize the eggs first (see page 21).

As for that carb count, the Lily's label—which is where I got the numbers for the Mastercook database—includes the erythritol in them. You'll digest considerably fewer grams. And look at that fat percentage!

If you're dairy-free, this works fine with canned coconut milk in place of the cream.

If you don't want to use rum, you can replace it with 1 tablespoon (15ml) of rum flavoring or another flavoring of your choice—how about peppermint extract?

Put the cream in a heavy-bottomed saucepan over low heat and bring just to a simmer.

In the meanwhile, combine the chocolate chips, egg yolks, and rum in your blender.

When the cream is hot, start pouring it into the blender, turning on the blender when it's about half in. Run the blender until the chocolate is all melted.

Pour it into 6 little dishes, because it's super-rich. I have some teeny Chinese teacups that serve the purpose nicely.

Chill for several hours, preferably overnight.

1 recipe Crisp Chocolate Crust
(page 277)

8 ounces (225g) cream cheese,
at room temperature

1 teaspoon liquid stevia,
English toffee

1 cup (260g) creamy natural
peanut butter

1 tablespoon (14g) butter,
melted

1 teaspoon vanilla extract

1 cup (235ml) heavy cream

Walden Farms or Hershey's
sugar-free chocolate syrup,
for serving

YIELD: 12 servings –
Per serving: 433 calories; 40g fat
(79.4% calories from fat);
12g protein; 11g carbohydrate;
4g dietary fiber; 7g net
carbohydrate.

PEANUT BUTTER SILK PIE

This is high carb enough to be a special-occasion-only dessert, but wow!
If you'd like, you can just make the filling and serve it in dessert dishes.

Make your Crisp Chocolate Crust first, pressing it into a 9-inch (23cm) pie plate.

Using an electric mixer, beat the cream cheese, liquid stevia, peanut butter, butter, and vanilla together until creamy.

In a separate bowl, whip the heavy cream until stiff peaks form.

Turn the mixer to its lowest setting and beat the whipped cream into the peanut butter–cream cheese mixture in 3 additions. Spread the peanut butter filling in the Crisp Chocolate Crust.

Serve with sugar-free chocolate syrup.

1¼ cups (169g) hazelnuts

½ cup (114g) vanilla whey
protein powder

¼ cup (60g) Virtue or Natural
Mate sweetener

1½ teaspoons ground
cinnamon

1 teaspoon baking soda

½ teaspoon salt

¼ teaspoon ground nutmeg

⅓ cup (77g) full-fat Greek
yogurt

2 tablespoons (28ml)
unsweetened pourable
coconut milk

2 eggs

½ cup (120ml) MCT oil

1 cup (120g) shredded zucchini

YIELD: 8 servings – Per serving:
345 calories; 30g fat (76.1%
calories from fat); 16g protein;
6g carbohydrate; 2g dietary fiber;
4g net carbohydrates.

ZUCCHINI CAKE

My friend, Dr. William Davis, of Wheat Belly fame, sent me samples of
a new sweetener called Virtue, made of erythritol and monk fruit. This
is the first recipe I tried it in, and it was great! You can make this with
almond meal if you prefer—it's easier because you can buy it preground,
and it's certainly cheaper—but it will add a few grams of carbohydrate.
Whipped cream or a schmear of whipped cream cheese would be good
on this, but hardly essential.

Preheat your oven to 325°F (170°C, or gas mark 3). Coat a 9-inch (23cm) Bundt
pan thoroughly with nonstick cooking spray.

Put the hazelnuts in your food processor and run until they have the texture of
cornmeal. Transfer to a mixing bowl.

Use 2 tablespoons (14g) of the hazelnut meal to "flour" your Bundt cake pan.

Add the vanilla whey protein, Virtue, cinnamon, baking soda, salt, and nutmeg to
your food processor. Pulse until everything is well combined. Dump the mixture into
the mixing bowl with the ground hazelnuts.

In a separate bowl, combine your yogurt, coconut milk, eggs, and MCT oil. Whisk
these together well.

Pour the liquid ingredients into the dry ingredients and whisk until you're sure you
have no lumps or pockets of dry stuff left. Stir in the zucchini. Pour the batter into
the prepared pan.

Bake for 70 minutes until a tester inserted near the center comes out clean. Let
cool in the pan and then turn out onto a wire rack to cool completely.

ACKNOWLEDGMENTS

All of my books have required help from others to one degree or another. But this one simply would not have happened without a tremendous degree of help from a great number of people.

First of all, my recipe testers: Rebecca Jaxon, Julie McIntosh, Wendy McCullough, Amanda Page, Jess Bledsoe, Tere Ervin, Angele St. Hilaire, Alan Blues, Virginia Hudson, Sheryl Bramnik, Christina Prentice Robertson, Lee Kelly, Judy Purrington, Valerie Howells, and Shayne Sherbert. They worked their butts off for this book, not only testing recipes, but offering essential feedback, and even occasional recipe ideas of their own. They have done a heck of a job, and their work made this book possible.

Melissa Kirkwood, my good friend, took on some of the overwhelming task of proofreading, cleaning up the manuscript, and running metric conversions. Again, without her help, this book would not be here.

And, always and forever, Eric Schmitz, aka That Nice Boy I Married. He, too, proofread, cleaned up software artifacts in the manuscript, and spent hours and hours running metric conversions. He also made countless grocery and health food store runs on his way home, and ate endless leftovers. I have no idea what I would do without him.

ABOUT THE AUTHOR

n retrospect, Dana Carpender's career seems inevitable: She's been cooking since she had to stand on a step stool to reach the stove. She was also a dangerously sugar-addicted child, eventually stealing from her parents to support her habit, and was in Weight Watchers by age eleven. At nineteen, Dana read her first book on nutrition, and she recognized herself in a list of symptoms of reactive hypoglycemia. She ditched sugar and white flour and was dazzled by the near instantaneous improvement in her physical and mental health. A lifetime nutrition buff was born.

Unfortunately, in the late 1980s and early 1990s, Dana got sucked into the low-fat/high-carb mania, and whole-grain-and-beaned her way up to a size 20, with nasty energy swings, constant hunger, and borderline high blood pressure. In 1995, she read a nutrition book from the 1950s that stated that obesity had nothing to do with how much one ate, but was rather a carbohydrate intolerance disease. She thought, "What the heck, might as well give it a try." Three days later, her clothes were loose, her hunger was gone, and her energy level was through the roof. She never looked back, and she has now been low-carb for twenty-two years and counting—more than one-third of her life.

Realizing that this change was permanent, and being a cook at heart, Dana set about creating as varied and satisfying a cuisine as she could with a minimal carb load. And being an enthusiastic, gregarious sort, she started sharing her experience. By 1997, she was writing about it. The upshot is more than 2,500 recipes published and more than a million books sold and she still has ideas left to try! Dana lives in Bloomington, Indiana, with her husband, three dogs, and a cat, all of whom are well and healthily fed.

INDEX

500 KETOGENIC RECIPES

500 KETOGENIC RECIPES

500 KETOGENIC RECIPES

INDEX